T0100208

.NET MAUI in Action

.NET MAUI
in Action

MATT GOLDMAN
FOREWORD BY KYM PHILLPOTTS

MANNING
SHELTER ISLAND

For online information and ordering of this and other Manning books, please visit
www.manning.com. The publisher offers discounts on this book when ordered in quantity.
For more information, please contact

 Special Sales Department
 Manning Publications Co.
 20 Baldwin Road
 PO Box 761
 Shelter Island, NY 11964
 Email: orders@manning.com

 Manning Publications Co.
 20 Baldwin Road
 PO Box 761
 Shelter Island, NY 11964

Development editor: Connor O'Brien
Technical editor: Gerald Versluis
Review editor: Aleks Dragosavljević
Production editor: Andy Marinkovich
Copy editor: Alisa Larson
Proofreader: Jason Everett
Technical proofreader: Allan Makura
Typesetter: Dennis Dalinnik
Cover designer: Marija Tudor

ISBN: 9781633439405
Printed in the United States of America

brief contents

contents

foreword

In today's highly competitive market, cross-platform app development has become a fundamental component for businesses of all industries to stay ahead of the game. Companies are now digital first, and leveraging cross-platform app development to create customized applications that can run seamlessly on multiple platforms is an essential practice.

As a .NET developer, you may already be familiar with Xamarin.Forms, which allows you to build mobile apps for Android and iOS using C# and the .NET framework. Now with the introduction of .NET Multi-platform App UI (MAUI), the evolution of Xamarin.Forms, there has never been a better time to expand your skills and start building cross-platform apps.

As an instructor at Xamarin University, I spent several years helping developers worldwide learn cross-platform development. One of the biggest challenges faced by students, particularly beginners, was navigating the extensive background knowledge and tools necessary for building apps across various platforms. That's why this book by Matt Goldman is so important. It provides a highly accessible guide to getting started with cross-platform development, regardless of your experience level or iOS/Android development background. The book emphasizes making this technology more approachable to .NET developers, enabling them to use their existing skills and apply them to cross-platform app development.

It goes without saying that a single book cannot transform you from a novice to an expert. However, this book emphasizes empowering developers to be self-sufficient and continue their .NET MAUI learning journey beyond the book's contents. The book achieves this by emphasizing best practices and offering practical tips, which equip readers with the skills and knowledge necessary to improve as cross-platform developers.

This book stands apart by boldly exploring critical enterprise application development principles like authentication, security, services, and full-stack architecture patterns that are suitable for .NET MAUI. Moreover, the book does not neglect topics such as MVVM architecture patterns, advanced UI concepts, and Github Actions to deploy apps to stores, which makes it an ideal resource for anyone seeking an on-ramp to these subjects.

My compliments to Matt for producing an outstanding book on .NET MAUI cross-platform app development. The book's structure is well-organized and easily digestible, and it is filled with useful examples that readers can effortlessly follow. Whether you are an experienced .NET developer or a novice starting out, this book is a valuable reference for anyone who wants to be successful with .NET MAUI development.

—KYM PHILLPOTTS, Senior Technical Program Manager, Microsoft

preface

As a teenager making games on my Amiga in the 1990s, I was captivated by the shareware games in the Public Domain catalog and the idea that people could make money from something I did for fun. Better yet were the breakaway indie hits that turned a hobby into a full-time career, the most famous being the turn-based artillery game Worms.

Today, apart from rare indie success stories, most apps and games are made by huge games studios or development companies. But, for a brief time at the start of the consumer smartphone revolution, when small apps made by indie solo devs filled the first iteration of the App Store, it looked like the era of solo devs had returned.

A level playing field where indie developers could make it big got me interested in smartphone development. And when Xamarin came along, it seemed like an efficient way to build apps for mobile platforms using my existing .NET skills.

Unlike many I admire, I didn't come to cross-platform .NET development as an iOS or Android (or both) expert wanting to use the .NET abstractions in Xamarin. Rather, I was a .NET developer who wanted to build iOS and Android apps. Unfortunately, I underestimated the learning curve, and it took me a lot of time and frustration to get comfortable with Xamarin, including realizing that it was a .NET tool for iOS and Android developers rather than an iOS and Android tool for .NET developers.

One of the goals of .NET MAUI, and this book, is to change that. *.NET MAUI in Action* is written specifically for .NET developers with no previous mobile or desktop experience who want to build cross-platform mobile and desktop apps. While I still champion the dream of the solo dev, it's primarily written for enterprise app development and specifically the discipline and methodology of an enterprise software development team, which will serve you well as a solo dev, too.

As a .NET developer, you're already a nascent .NET MAUI developer, as I hope you'll have fun discovering with this book. I can't wait to see what you build!

acknowledgments

It feels like this book has been dominating my life for as long as I can remember. There's been a huge amount of effort that's gone into it from several people, and while I can't possibly thank them all here, I'm going to at least try.

First, I'd like to thank Connor, my editor. Your input and guidance along the way were invaluable, as were your support and encouragement. You also patiently listened during some of my rants, which I sincerely appreciate!

I'd also like to thank Gerald Versluis, the book's technical editor. Gerald is a Senior Software Engineer at Microsoft working on .NET MAUI in addition to a variety of projects, ranging from frontend to backend and anything in between that involves Azure, ASP.NET, and other .NET technologies. Gerald, thank you for your technical input over the last year; it's given me a lot of confidence having you check the accuracy of everything. And with that, I'd also like to thank the rest of the .NET MAUI team for the incredible work they continually put into this product.

Next, I'd like to say thank you to the team at Manning for making this book a reality and for the awesome work that's gone into everything around this book, from start to finish. In no particular order, thank you, Brian, Charlotte, Stjepan, and Aira. And my sincere thanks (and humble apologies) to anyone else I've neglected to name.

I also want to thank my colleagues at SSW for their support, input, and encouragement while I've been writing this book. I'd name everyone here if I could, but given the limited space, I'll just say a special thanks to Adam for your ongoing support, to Luke for your technical assistance, and to Camilla and the SSW TV team for all your help promoting this book as well as .NET MAUI.

I also need to thank Stephanie, my mum, for your invaluable assistance with editing and vocabulary.

To all the reviewers: Aleksander Rokic, Allan Makura, Ashley Eatly, Carsten Jørgensen, Chriss Jack Barnard, Dan Sheikh, Darrin Bishop, David M. Williams, David Paccoud, Emanuele Origgi, Grant Cooley, Henrique Fleury Cusinato, Jason Hales, Jeelani Shaik, Jeffrey Shergalis, Joe Cuevas, Joel Kotarski, John Gibbs, Juan Luis, Karthikeyarajan Rajendran Lakshminarayanan as, Mario De Ghetto, Mario Solomou, George Onofrei, Paul Brown, Randall Kenner, Renato Gentile, Richard Young, Rohit sharma, Samuel Bosch, Santosh Shanbhag, Timo Salomäki, Timo Steigerwald, Werner Nindl, and Wes Shaddix, your suggestions helped make this a better book.

Finally, and most importantly, I want to thank Megan. Thank you for putting up with me all this time while I've focused almost exclusively on the book. Thank you for keeping our home running, and thanks also for your help with the book itself when I asked. Your name belongs on the cover almost as much as mine does; in a way, we're both the authors. But in another, more accurate way, I'm the author.

about this book

In New South Wales where I live, riding a motorcycle requires taking a two-day pre-learner course, after which you're allowed to ride a relatively small one with L plates. They don't actually teach you to ride a motorcycle; instead, they teach you enough to learn safely on your own. Even after you graduate to a full license, there's always more to learn.

This book is a little like a pre-learner course for .NET MAUI. It's too big of a topic for everything to be included in a volume of this size, but it gives you all you need to know to go out into the world and confidently hone your skills as a .NET MAUI developer. By the end of the book, you'll not only be able to comfortably build apps with .NET MAUI but also know how to teach yourself what isn't covered here when you're ready to go further.

Who should read this book?

.NET MAUI in Action is written for .NET developers who want to explore this new technology to build mobile and desktop apps. You won't need any previous experience, although some experience building UI apps of any kind, even web, will be beneficial for some of the more abstract concepts.

If you've previously worked with Xamarin.Forms, you'll immediately appreciate how much easier .NET MAUI is, and this book will walk you through all the differences in one concise, procedural volume (rather than having to wade through piece-meal docs or blog posts).

xvii

While you don't need to know anything about mobile or desktop development, the book focuses on using existing C# and .NET skills, so you should be comfortable building software in C# already. By the end of the book, you'll be comfortable building mobile and desktop apps too.

How this book is organized: A roadmap

The book has three sections that cover 12 chapters.

Part 1 introduces .NET MAUI and walks you through building some simple apps:

- Chapter 1 explains what .NET MAUI is, where it came from, and introduces the technology and some of the concepts you'll use to build apps.
- Chapter 2 walks you through building your first .NET MAUI app and explains the tools used to build them.
- Chapter 3 is where we roll up our sleeves and start making real apps. We start using mobile- and desktop-specific functionality that makes the technology distinct from other areas of .NET development. Data binding, one of the core concepts in .NET MAUI, is also introduced.

Part 2 is all about the UI, the part of .NET MAUI that makes it what it is:

- Chapter 4 introduces the cross-platform controls we use in .NET MAUI apps. We explore some of the terminology around UI development and look at ways to present information to, and get input from, our users.
- Chapter 5 covers one of the most important topics in UI development: layout. We look at the different ways .NET MAUI supports creating any design.
- Chapter 6 expands upon the work in chapter 5 by explaining some of .NET MAUI's more advanced layout techniques and shows you how to replicate a well-known mobile app in .NET MAUI.
- Chapter 7 is about pages and navigation. Pages are the building blocks of an app, and equally important is how to get your user between those pages.

Part 3 is about advanced app development. It covers enterprise architecture patterns, targeting multiple platforms, mobile development patterns and antipatterns, and professional deployment and distribution.

- Chapter 8 shows how to develop a .NET MAUI app as part of a full-stack enterprise solution.
- Chapter 9 introduces the MVVM pattern, the de-facto standard for building apps with .NET MAUI.
- Chapter 10 covers multiplatform layouts. It shows how to tailor your app to different platforms and different idioms (mobile, desktop, and tablet).
- Chapter 11 is about breaking out of the box and creating controls beyond what .NET MAUI provides. This chapter covers componentization as well as customizing the way .NET MAUI implements controls on each platform.

- Chapter 12 is the final piece of the puzzle and shows you how to add professional finishing touches to your app. It rounds out the book by showing you how to deploy your app to the stores using GitHub Actions, although the workflows used should translate to whichever CI/CD platform you use.

If you are new to .NET MAUI, I recommend reading through the book from start to finish. If you're comfortable skipping the basics, part 2 can serve as a reference, but part 3 should be read in order as each chapter builds on the previous.

About the code

This book contains many examples of source code both in numbered listings and in line with normal text. In both cases, source code is formatted in a fixed-width font `like this` to separate it from ordinary text. Sometimes code is also in **bold** to highlight code that has changed from previous steps in the chapter, such as when a new feature adds to an existing line of code.

    In many cases, the original source code has been reformatted; we've added line breaks and reworked indentation to accommodate the available page space in the book. In some cases, even this was not enough, and listings include line-continuation markers (➡). Additionally, comments in the source code have often been removed from the listings when the code is described in the text. Code annotations accompany many of the listings, highlighting important concepts.

    You can get executable snippets of code from the liveBook (online) version of this book at https://livebook.manning.com/book/.net-maui-in-action. The complete code for the examples in the book is available for download from the Manning website at www.manning.com.

    Apart from chapter 1, every chapter in this book has code samples available online from Manning. Some chapters have a `Resources` folder, where you can find things like images and other assets referred to in the text. In most cases, the code represents the completed code at the end of the chapter. For later chapters, there are two folders: one called `chapter-start` and another called `chapter-complete`. `Chapter-complete` shows the code you will have written by the end of the chapter, and `chapter-start` contains the code to start from (and will be identical to the `chapter-complete` folder for the previous chapter).

> **NOTE** All the screenshots in the book show the code running in light mode (except for the themes in chapter 10). If you are running in dark mode, you'll see slightly different results. This won't be because you've done anything wrong, and you can switch to light mode to double-check.

liveBook discussion forum

Purchase of *.NET MAUI in Action* includes free access to liveBook, Manning's online reading platform. Using liveBook's exclusive discussion features, you can attach comments to the book globally or to specific sections or paragraphs. It's a snap to make notes for yourself, ask and answer technical questions, and receive help from the author and other users. To access the forum, go to https://livebook.manning.com/book/.net-maui-in-action/discussion. You can also learn more about Manning's forums and the rules of conduct at https://livebook.manning.com/discussion.

Manning's commitment to our readers is to provide a venue where a meaningful dialogue between individual readers and between readers and the author can take place. It is not a commitment to any specific amount of participation on the part of the author, whose contribution to the forum remains voluntary (and unpaid). We suggest you try asking the author some challenging questions lest his interest stray! The forum and the archives of previous discussions will be accessible from the publisher's website for as long as the book is in print.

Other online resources

Not only is .NET MAUI under continual development, but it's open source, and the team is active on GitHub. The GitHub repo should be your first port of call for any problems or questions you may have. You can find it here: https://github.com/dotnet/maui/. If you encounter any problems, either with code samples in the book or with your own code, a great place to start is the `Issues` tab in the official repo; you'll likely find the problem has already been reported and that work is underway, and you'll often find a workaround that people have shared.

> **NOTE** Any known problems at the time of writing may not be accommodated in the text, but if a workaround is known, it is included in the code samples. You should check these, too, when encountering any problems.

The .NET MAUI team is also active in many online communities, and the communities themselves are also a great source of support. One awesome active .NET MAUI community is Twitter, which you can find here: https://twitter.com/hashtag/dotnetmaui?src=hashtag_click. Another is Reddit, and you can find the .NET MAUI sub-reddit here: https://www.reddit.com/r/dotnetMAUI/.

For a one-stop shop to find all the best online .NET MAUI resources, Javier Suarez aggregates everything he can find into a GitHub repo called Awesome .NET MAUI. You can find it here: https://github.com/jsuarezruiz/awesome-dotnet-maui. It's open source, and Javier accepts community contributions.

Finally, you can find me in many online communities, but the best place to start is probably GitHub, as my profile includes links to all my other accounts. You can find it here: https://github.com/matt-goldman.

about the author

MATT GOLDMAN is a solution architect at SSW. He has built a number of consumer and enterprise apps for a range of national and multinational customers, as well as for the Australian government. Matt is a regular speaker at user groups and conferences and maintains open-source libraries for use in .NET MAUI apps.

about the cover illustration

The figure on the cover of *.NET MAUI in Action,* titled "Spahis," is taken from a book by Louis Curmer published in 1841. Each illustration is finely drawn and colored by hand. Spahis were light-cavalry regiments of the French army who were primarily recruited from the Arab and Berber populations of Algeria, Tunisia, and Morocco.

In those days, it was easy to identify where people lived and what their trade or station in life was just by their dress. Manning celebrates the inventiveness and initiative of the computer business with book covers based on the rich diversity of regional culture centuries ago, brought back to life by pictures from collections such as this one.

Part 1

Introducing .NET MAUI

Software development is rare among professional occupations in that we get to create something tangible. It's satisfying to see the fruits of our efforts, but building mobile and desktop apps, in my opinion, takes that tangibility to a new level.

In this part, we'll get to know .NET MAUI, and we'll experience that tangibility firsthand as we literally hold our first app in our hands. We'll discover the fundamentals of building mobile and desktop apps with this new technology and explore the anatomy of a .NET MAUI app and start to gain an appreciation for the process of using it to build products.

Introducing .NET MAUI 1

This chapter covers

- What .NET MAUI is
- How MAUI fits into .NET
- Why you would use .NET MAUI to build desktop and mobile apps
- Writing cross-platform UIs

.NET MAUI is here, and if you're reading this book, you already know a thing or two about it. But how does it work, and how did we get here? In this chapter, we look at the architecture of .NET MAUI and get an overview of how it works. We also see how to use it to build cross-platform mobile and desktop apps. To begin, let's look at the history of cross-platform development and see how .NET MAUI is the fulfilment of a dream at Microsoft over 20 years in the making.

1.1 How did we get here?

The dream of write once, run anywhere (WORA) cross-platform software began in earnest in 1996 with the release of the first version of Java by Sun Microsystems. Before Java, software developers could only write their code against APIs provided by the operating system. Java was different—not only was it a new programming language, but it was also a runtime with its own set of APIs, allowing developers to ignore the target platform or operating system. Sun provided a runtime for nearly every available operating system (called the Java Virtual Machine, or JVM), which meant developers didn't have to worry about whether they were building a Windows application, a Unix application, a Linux application, or a Mac application. They were building a *Java* application.

Microsoft started its own journey toward a cross-platform runtime shortly afterward, releasing the first public version of the .NET Framework in 2000. It wasn't cross-platform, but the development paradigm was similar—developers no longer had to write code against Windows APIs; they used the .NET Base Class Library (BCL) to write code using the .NET APIs. Like the JVM, the .NET Framework was a runtime installed independently of the operating system, so developers didn't have to worry about what version of Windows their users had installed; they just needed to ensure that users had the right version of the .NET Framework, as summarized in figure 1.1.

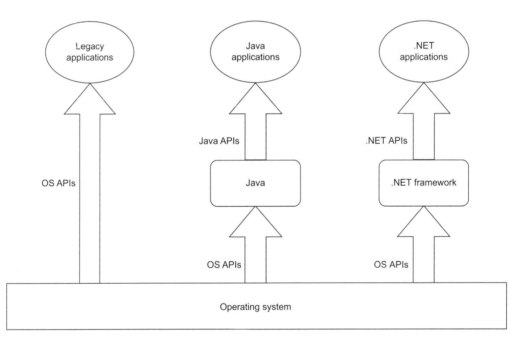

Figure 1.1   Legacy applications are built directly on top of operating system APIs. Java and .NET provide their own APIs for developers to use and runtimes that hide the platform APIs.

But this approach still had one problem: the .NET Framework was Windows-only. Developers writing .NET applications couldn't target macOS or Linux, both of which were gaining momentum. This didn't change (at least, from Microsoft's perspective) until 2016, with the release of .NET Core. .NET Core diverged from .NET Framework in a few ways, most critically by stripping out key Windows dependencies and abstractions for Windows APIs. Unlike .NET Framework, which had to be installed and would only work on Windows, .NET Core is a truly portable runtime that can be shipped alongside the code it executes and runs on Windows, Mac, and Linux.

While this was a huge step closer to the WORA dream, UI applications were still missing from the picture. .NET Core applications are command-line-only (this includes web servers and other services). .NET Framework provided platforms for developing UI applications for Windows, initially with Windows Forms and later with the Windows Presentation Foundation (WPF). While these were ported to .NET Core (and later versions), they are still Windows-only.

Outside of Microsoft, the journey toward cross-platform UI applications in .NET took on a life of its own. Within a year of the release of the first version of the .NET Framework, the .NET specification became an open standard. Open standards drive the modern web and enable the development of competing or complementary runtimes. For example, because HTML, JavaScript, and CSS are open standards, anyone can build a web browser, and developers and users can choose which technologies to use. While the journey to .NET being fully open was by no means a straight line or without bumps, opening the .NET standard enabled Miguel de Icaza (who was working at Novell at the time) to release an open source .NET compiler for Linux called *Mono*.

By the end of the 2000s, the iOS and Android operating systems and, more importantly, their application distribution platforms (the iOS App Store and Google Play store, respectively), had become well established, and any discussion around cross-platform UI applications became dominated by mobile. iOS and Android use different languages and paradigms for app development, and while it's possible to learn both, most developers prefer not to write and maintain multiple versions of their software if they don't have to.

Mono was ported to iOS in MonoTouch and to Android in MonoDroid. These eventually evolved into Xamarin, which provided not only a .NET compiler for iOS and Android but also a complete abstraction of the iOS and Android APIs in .NET. Using Xamarin, you still had to learn the iOS and Android APIs, but you wrote your code in a .NET language like C# instead of a vendor-provided language (like Objective-C or Swift for iOS or Kotlin for Android). Using Xamarin, you could also share your non-UI code between the two platforms, so any business logic or code for communicating with a backend could be written once and used in a Xamarin.iOS project and a Xamarin.Android project.

In 2014, Xamarin introduced Xamarin.Forms, which provided an API for writing cross-platform UI code using an extensible application markup language (XAML)— the markup language originally introduced in WPF. This allowed developers to share both business logic and UI across iOS, Android, and the Universal Windows Platform (UWP) (and, at the time, Windows Phone). Like the other abstractions, the UI code you write in XAML is an abstraction; when you compile your app for iOS, your XAML code is interpreted into iOS's native UI, and when you compile for Android, the XAML is compiled to native Android UI code.

Xamarin was acquired by Microsoft in 2016 and has been under active development there ever since. Xamarin.Forms is now a stable and mature product used to build many successful enterprise and consumer applications. But the current version, Xamarin.Forms 5, will be the last. Coming in its place is .NET MAUI, which Microsoft describes as the next evolution of Xamarin.Forms. While .NET MAUI shares a lot of its DNA with Xamarin and Xamarin.Forms, it is an entirely new platform built from the ground up to usher in a new era of truly cross-platform WORA applications written in .NET. It's an exciting time to be a .NET developer.

1.2   What is .NET MAUI?

The .NET Multiplatform App UI (MAUI) is a new framework from Microsoft for building cross-platform UI applications that target Windows, macOS, iOS, and Android. With .NET MAUI, you can build a rich, interactive, native UI application that runs on any of these platforms. With a single code base, you can build an application that supports all the platforms and share 100% of the code between them. In short, you write an application in a .NET language, and it runs without any changes on any of the target platforms. All your logic can be written in a .NET language, and your UI can be defined in either XAML or your .NET language of choice.

> ### .NET MAUI development languages
> You can write .NET MAUI apps in C# and use either XAML or C# to define your UI. It's technically possible to use other languages, but they are not officially supported. In this book, we use C# to write our logic and XAML to define our UI (although there are some exceptions), as these are the most common approaches.

Figure 1.2 shows the architecture of a .NET MAUI application. Let's examine the layers and steps to see how a .NET MAUI application comes together.

At the bottom is the target operating system (Android, iOS, macOS, or Windows). The next layer up shows the .NET runtime that will execute the .NET MAUI app on each target OS. For Android, iOS, and macOS, this runtime is Mono; for Windows, it is WinRT.

The next layer up is the first abstraction: the .NET BCL. It provides access to all the common language features we expect—such as lists and generics—that don't form part of .NET's primitives. From .NET 5 onward, .NET (without Core or Framework) has become the new standard, also replacing the .NET Standard. From a developer perspective, .NET versions 5 and onward have become target frameworks, with (for example) `net7.0` replacing `netcoreapp` or `netstandard`. When writing a .NET MAUI app, you have access to the BCL across all platforms.

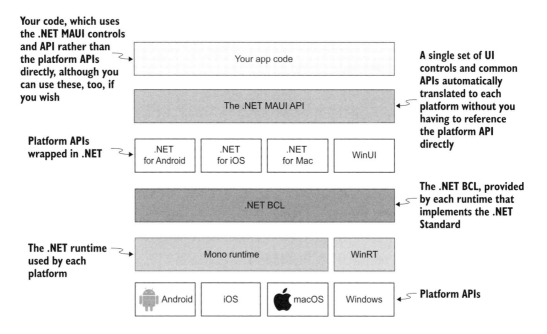

Figure 1.2 **.NET MAUI is built bottom-up. Each platform provides APIs, and there is a .NET runtime for each platform (WinRT on Windows, Mono on everything else) built on these APIs. Each layer provides APIs used to build the APIs in the layer above. Meanwhile, your code is written top-down: you write a .NET MAUI app, and the architecture encapsulates it for lower layers.**

The next layer, which sits on top of the BCL, provides access to abstractions for platform-specific APIs. .NET for Android and .NET for iOS are the next iterations of Xamarin.Android and Xamarin.iOS, respectively. These are bindings to the platform APIs, using the same types and namespaces used by Objective-C, Swift, Java, or Kotlin developers. .NET for Mac is new but operates the same way, and the WinUI API is used for Windows. This includes everything available in each platform's API, from simple layouts and controls like buttons and text entry fields to more sophisticated APIs like ARKit on iOS and ARCore on Android, for developing augmented reality (AR) applications.

The last abstraction is .NET MAUI. This is a unified API that provides UI elements common to all supported platforms. It includes views (like layouts, buttons, text, and entry fields), navigation APIs, and many more. You can also access common hardware features such as Bluetooth, location services, and device storage.

While we looked at the layers bottom-up, the philosophy of building a .NET MAUI app is very much considered top-down:

1 Build a cross-platform application by writing .NET MAUI code (rather than, say, iOS or Android code).

2   If you want to, you can write platform- or OS-specific code in your application, but you don't have to.

3   .NET MAUI compiles your code for the target platform. Understanding how .NET MAUI builds your application for various platforms is not necessary to build a .NET MAUI application, although having a good understanding of these platforms is beneficial: you'll be better able to troubleshoot OS- or platform-specific errors, and you'll open up the entire spectrum of platform APIs, not just those exposed in top-level .NET MAUI wrappers. We'll cover some platform-specific aspects of .NET MAUI development as we go.

.NET MAUI is much more than just the next version of Xamarin.Forms. Whereas Xamarin was a software development kit (SDK) that you installed independently of .NET, MAUI is a *workload*, meaning it is a part of .NET, just like ASP.NET or console app development. This approach provides a few benefits, which we cover later; most importantly, it demonstrates Microsoft's commitment to the future of .NET MAUI and its inclusion as a core part of .NET.

1.3   Cross-platform vs. "native" apps

When you decide to build an application, either as an independent developer or as part of an enterprise development team, you must ask a few questions and make some decisions:

- Will you build an installable, native binary executable application? Or will you build a web app?
- If you build a web app, will you use a single-page application (SPA) framework (such as Angular or Blazor), or will you use a traditional server-generated page framework (like ASP.NET Core or PHP)?
- If you build an installable app, will you build one for each platform where you want your users to run it, or will you build a single app that runs on every platform?

These are just some of the questions and decisions you need to resolve. Your decision process might look something like figure 1.3.

To help with this decision, it's important to understand something (and potentially dispel a myth): apps built with .NET MAUI *are* native apps. That is to say, any app you write with .NET MAUI compiles to a native binary executable for each target platform. The same is true on iOS as if it were written in Swift and on Android as if it were written in Kotlin (although .NET code is still just-in-time [JIT] compiled by default, you can enable ahead-of-time [AOT]).

With that in mind, perhaps a bigger decision than whether to use a cross-platform framework such as .NET MAUI or vendor-provided languages is whether to build a binary application as opposed to a web app (although with .NET MAUI Blazor, you get the best of both worlds, as we'll see in section 1.4). That decision is up to you

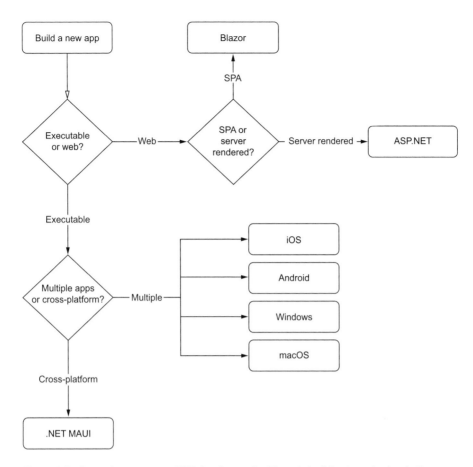

Figure 1.3 Assuming you are a .NET developer, the biggest decision to make is whether you want to build a web app or an installable/executable app. If you choose to build an executable, .NET MAUI is a no-brainer.

and/or your team and depends on many factors. Both approaches have pros and cons; and while web app development has advantages for many situations, there are compelling reasons to choose a binary application instead:

- *Multithreading*—Applications running in a web browser can only use one thread at a time. Depending on your performance requirements, this may not be a problem.
- *Encryption*—Web applications use encryption to communicate with backend services, but you can't securely store data offline in a web browser.
- *Access to device hardware features*—Many hardware features are available to browsers now, such as camera and location services and even Bluetooth. Other features, such as telephony or (SMS) messaging, are difficult or impossible to access

from a browser app. But providing access to them consistently and reliably is much easier using an installed binary application.

- *Access to platform APIs*—You may want to access certain platform features such as ARKit on iOS or ARCore on Android, which will influence your decision to choose an installed binary application rather than a web app.

This is by no means an exhaustive list. Several factors may influence your decision to choose one approach rather than the other. However, all other things being equal, perhaps the most compelling reason to build an installable app rather than a web app is branding. Having an app store presence is considered critical for most businesses that wish to reach a broad sector of the market, and store presence provides a level of trust to your users that, rightly or wrongly, may not be there with a web app alone. My clients often reveal the desire to have a presence in the App Store and Google Play store as a motivating factor when I ask them why they want a mobile app.

Nevertheless, the reasons listed earlier can be compelling. Multithreading can be important for performance-intensive applications. Browser-based apps can simulate multithreading, but in a binary app running on hardware with a multicore CPU, those threads can actually run simultaneously, meaning background processes don't lock up the UI.

Being able to encrypt data at rest as well as in motion can be an important consideration if security is a chief concern or feature of your app, and this requirement rules out building a browser-based app. Additional platform features, such as biometric identification, add an extra layer of security (as well as convenience) to binary apps.

Verinote, an app built in Xamarin.Forms and currently being upgraded to .NET MAUI, takes advantage of these security features (see figure 1.4). Designed for law enforcement (or any regulated industry), Verinote lets users in the field capture notes with photographs, audio recordings, and sketches and syncs the notes back to a cloud service. It needs to work offline as well as online, so if no connection is available, data is cached locally until the cloud service can be reached. Due to the highly sensitive nature of the information users of this app work with, security is a paramount concern. Verinote encrypts cached data (as well as all data in motion) and uses platform-provided biometric authentication to secure access to the app. Because of these dependencies on security features provided by native platform APIs, Verinote could not have been built as a web app (Verinote also has a web app component, but it does not, and cannot, store any data offline).

Device features and platform APIs unlock almost limitless possibilities for mobile and desktop developers. I mentioned ARKit and ARCore earlier (the iOS and Android augmented reality [AR] libraries, respectively), which you can use to build rich, compelling experiences and products for users. Some examples include the proliferation of AR measuring apps and awesome new retail experiences like Ikea's mobile app. My toddler is particularly fond of the My Very Hungry Caterpillar app, which puts the

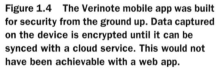

Figure 1.4   The Verinote mobile app was built for security from the ground up. Data captured on the device is encrypted until it can be synced with a cloud service. This would not have been achievable with a web app.

caterpillar from Eric Carle's *Very Hungry Caterpillar* into your space and lets you feed and interact with it (see figure 1.5). These kinds of apps are a little beyond the scope of this book but are nevertheless very achievable with .NET MAUI.

If you've decided to build a binary, installable application, the next decision is whether to build multiple versions of the app—one for each platform—or to build your product using a single cross-platform code base. This decision may seem like a no-brainer, and in most cases it probably is. There may be some niche scenarios where your requirements are specifically for only one platform or you want to build different versions for different platforms (although you can still do this with .NET MAUI), but most of the time it makes sense to use a cross-platform framework and build a single app that can be deployed to multiple target platforms.

Figure 1.5 **The Very Hungry Caterpillar enjoying a snack on my keyboard. Making augmented reality apps like this for mobile devices is simplified through the use of APIs provided by Apple and Google. Building a similar experience in a web browser would be extremely difficult, if not impossible.**

A cross-platform developer today has the luxury of choice in this respect. A popular approach is to build a web app and wrap it in an installable binary. Options include Ionic for Angular apps or Electron for anything web-based. This is an attractive option for some people, but while it can give you full access to native platform APIs, it has some limitations. Chief among these is that you are still using a web view to render and run your code, which carries with it all the performance and threading limitations of a web app.

The alternative approach is to use a single code base that can be built as a native app for each target platform. This is the approach used by .NET MAUI, as well as some other options such as React Native and Flutter, and it provides several advantages. These include multithreading and other performance benefits as well as full access to all native platform APIs—in the case of .NET MAUI, guaranteed on the day of release. With web-app wrappers, you are often dependent on plugins to provide this functionality, and there are no guarantees that the features you need access to are available.

The key distinction between .NET MAUI and other frameworks in this category is that the UI you build in .NET MAUI is an abstraction of the platform's native UI. This means when an application built in .NET MAUI runs on iOS, it looks like an iOS application; when it runs on Windows, it looks like a Windows application; and the same for the other supported platforms, as shown in figure 1.6.

Of course, you can customize your UI to not use the native look and feel and instead use a fully custom UI that looks the same no matter where you run it. Many people prefer this approach, and it takes no more effort in .NET MAUI than in other cross-platform frameworks. However, building an application that looks *consistent* but

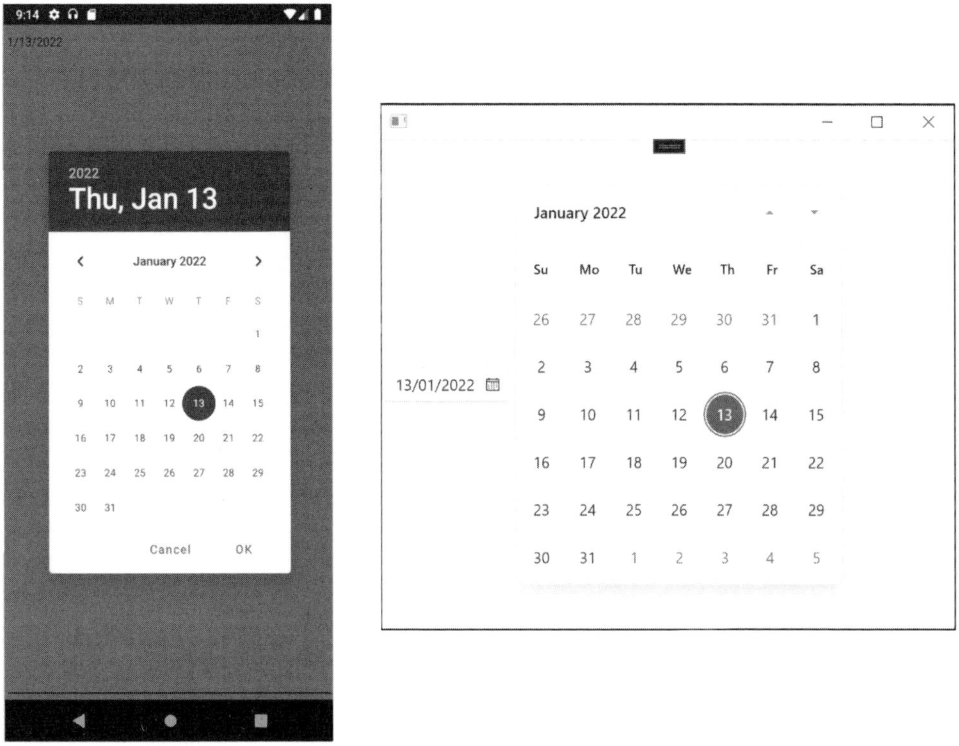

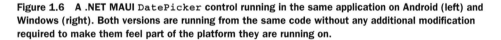

Figure 1.6   A .NET MAUI `DatePicker` control running in the same application on Android (left) and Windows (right). Both versions are running from the same code without any additional modification required to make them feel part of the platform they are running on.

not *identical* on each platform while also remaining consistent with the platform requires no extra effort at all. Achieving this with React Native or Flutter would require multiple implementations of the same control—one for each platform.

This "consistent but not identical" approach is the preferred way of building applications for many vendors. Let's look at Microsoft Word as an example (see figure 1.7).

On macOS, MS Word *looks* like a macOS application. On Windows, it *looks* like a Windows application. But both are consistent, and the branding, navigation, and UX are as familiar and comfortable to a user of one platform as they are to a user of another.

The truth is, all the available options are good. They are well established and mature and have their share of supporters and detractors. Some provide a better approach to particular aspects of cross-platform software development, while others provide a better approach in different areas. Choosing one framework over another will likely depend on which is most squarely in your comfort zone; the key factors are generally the primary backer of the framework and the primary development language. If you love Microsoft and are an experienced C# developer, .NET MAUI is your

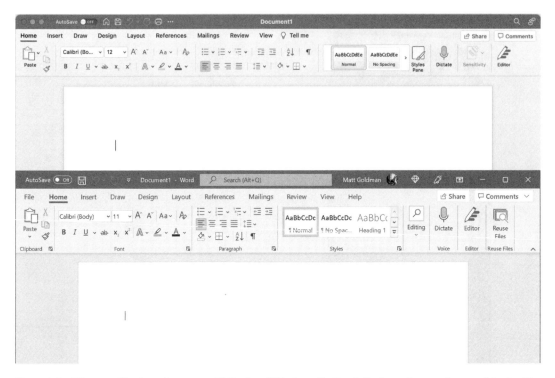

Figure 1.7   Microsoft Word running on macOS (top) and Windows (bottom). Each version remains consistent with its platform while retaining the product's brand and UX.

obvious choice. If you're a Google fan and are comfortable with Dart, you'll probably choose Flutter.

We're lucky to have so many options. With the advent of NodeJS, a JavaScript developer who was previously confined to web UI development can now build a full-stack application in their favorite language. You may not think it's the best fit, but there are advantages to be gained from consistency across the stack. More importantly, the developer has a choice.

As .NET developers, we have this choice, too. As I said earlier, it's a great time to be a .NET developer. You can write server and cloud applications in ASP.NET Core, web apps with Blazor, and native desktop and mobile apps with .NET MAUI. And better yet, you can share code between all of them.

1.4   *.NET MAUI and the .NET ecosystem*

Writing a cross-platform application in .NET MAUI is a great option for .NET developers. You can use your favorite language and developer tools and continue to use the skills and experience you have built up as a .NET developer. You have access to all the same resources you use in other .NET projects, including your existing support networks, packages, and patterns (although there are some new patterns to learn for mobile development). As .NET MAUI apps are .NET projects, many, if not all, of your favorite NuGet packages are available to use in your .NET MAUI apps (whether these packages are suitable for mobile development is another matter—some are not), as are many specifically tailored to mobile and cross-platform UI development.

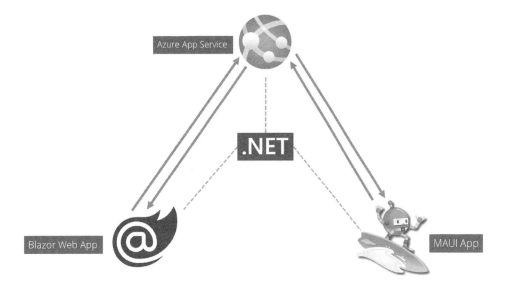

Figure 1.8   You can build full-stack cloud, web, and desktop/mobile applications with all the components sharing a single code base.

If you are building a full-stack solution, you get the benefit of being able to share code between the different layers (see figure 1.8). This may not always be applicable, as different layers usually have very different responsibilities, but it's an excellent option. For example, if you are building a chat app with an ASP.NET Core web API with SignalR running in Azure, a Blazor web UI, and a .NET MAUI mobile and desktop UI, you can share the logic and connectivity that links the UI to the web API across your Blazor and .NET MAUI apps and (in some cases) use the same NuGet packages in both your client and server applications. If you make changes to your API, you can update the client code once and have the change automatically reflected across all your client UI applications.

   As mentioned in section 1.2, because .NET MAUI is a core part of .NET and a workload rather than an SDK, you can use all your familiar development tools. If it works with .NET, it works with .NET MAUI. This includes Visual Studio (Mac or Windows), Visual Studio Code and the .NET CLI (although Visual Studio will provide a first-class experience), any build or DevOps tools, NuGet packages, and anything else you can think of. The various components that make up your .NET developer experience—and the .NET ecosystem as a whole—are at your disposal as a .NET MAUI developer.

.NET MAUI isn't an add-on; it *is* .NET. That means if it works with .NET, it works with .NET MAUI—which counts for your skills as much as any other tool.

1.5   .NET MAUI development paradigms

XAML is the de facto choice for building applications in .NET MAUI. As mentioned in section 1.1, Microsoft created XAML for WPF, but it has since been used for Silverlight (in fact, Silverlight was specifically a XAML renderer plugin for web browsers), Windows Phone, UWP, Xamarin.Forms, and now .NET MAUI.

XAML is a good choice for most people. It's an XML-based markup language for defining a UI, the same as HTML, or the plain XML used for building Android UIs, so it is usually comfortable and quick to learn for people coming from Angular, plain HTML, or Android—especially those with XAML experience (WPF or Xamarin.Forms). The different "flavors" of XAML can sometimes trip people up—there are subtle differences between WPF, Xamarin.Forms, and .NET MAUI XAML—but these differences are easy to learn, and the excellently overhauled XAML IntelliSense that you get with Visual Studio 2022 makes it even easier.

Complementary to XAML is the Model-View-ViewModel (MVVM) pattern (see figure 1.9). With MVVM, your XAML-defined UI is called the View. The View consists of anything the app needs to display things onscreen according to your design, including UI controls and any code required to change *how* they are displayed. The ViewModel represents the state of your View and contains logic for interacting with the Model. The ViewModel responds to events in the View, passes data to the Model, and changes the state of the View when the Model provides information that requires the View state to change. The Model, consisting of objects and services that represent the problem your app solves, contains business logic. The MVVM pattern is covered in more depth in chapter 9.

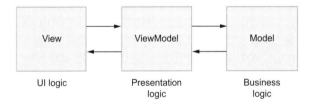

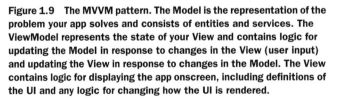

Figure 1.9   The MVVM pattern. The Model is the representation of the problem your app solves and consists of entities and services. The ViewModel represents the state of your View and contains logic for updating the Model in response to changes in the View (user input) and updating the View in response to changes in the Model. The View contains logic for displaying the app onscreen, including definitions of the UI and any logic for changing how the UI is rendered.

But XAML isn't your only choice. You can also declare your UI in code rather than in markup. This means declaring an instance of the class representing the UI control or view you want to display onscreen and specifying its properties. Some people prefer this approach, but personally, I prefer to define my UI in XAML—probably because the code approach evokes memories of drawing buttons onscreen by specifying the coordinates to draw a white line for the top and left borders and a black line for the bottom and right borders (and then inverting them when the user clicked on the button). I didn't have access to a UI library back then and had to draw all my controls by hand.

In addition to declaring your UI in code, you can use the Model-View-Update (MVU) paradigm instead of MVVM (see figure 1.10). (At the time of writing, MVU support is experimental in .NET MAUI.) MVU, also known as the Elm Architecture, differs from MVVM in two key ways: the Model is immutable, and data flows in only one direction. This means you can't change the Model in response to UI changes (user input), because doing so would violate both rules. Instead, changes in the View flow to an Update, which generates a new Model. The View then changes in response to the new Model.

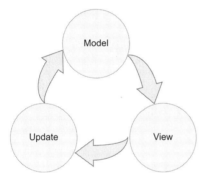

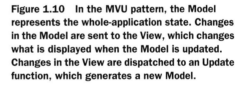

Figure 1.10 In the MVU pattern, the Model represents the whole-application state. Changes in the Model are sent to the View, which changes what is displayed when the Model is updated. Changes in the View are dispatched to an Update function, which generates a new Model.

MVU will be familiar to people coming from a native iOS development (Objective-C or Swift) background or React developers (the React virtual DOM is a version of the MVU pattern). In .NET MAUI, you need to bring in a library to support this pattern (Comet for C# and Fabulous for F#). Xamarin.Forms had tighter coupling between the Xamarin.Forms API and the underlying platforms, so providing these kinds of patterns was more difficult. In .NET MAUI, abstractions provide a clean separation between the layers of the model (shown in figure 1.2), allowing different implementations to be brought in at any layer. This makes these MVU libraries "first-class citizens" in the .NET MAUI ecosystem, and Microsoft fully endorses them.

MVU is not covered in this book because we have limited space and the focus is on the core way of doing things. But if you are interested in MVU, there are plenty of resources online and a thriving community of .NET MVU enthusiasts.

.NET MAUI also gives you another option: building your UI using Blazor. Blazor is an SPA framework created by Microsoft that lets you build applications that run client-side in web browsers using .NET rather than JavaScript or TypeScript. To learn more

about Blazor, check out *Blazor in Action* by Chris Sainty (Manning 2022, www.manning
.com/books/blazor-in-action).

This approach may seem similar to the web app wrapping solutions mentioned in
section 1.3, and in many ways it is. It lets you write a web app in a SPA framework
(Blazor) and use a wrapper (.NET MAUI) to bundle that web app into an installable
binary executable targeted at multiple platforms.

.NET MAUI Blazor uses a web view to render the UI, just like Electron, Ionic, or
Cordova. The key difference is that the C# code you write in a .NET MAUI Blazor app
is run as .NET managed code, just like in a XAML MAUI app, rather than being run
by the scripting engine in the web view, which is what you get with a web wrapper like
Cordova, Ionic, or Electron. Additionally, with a .NET MAUI Blazor app, you get
access to all the platform APIs that are exposed via .NET abstractions (as shown in figure 1.2).

With .NET MAUI, you can build a full-stack application using .NET at every layer.
You can use ASP.NET Core for your API, Blazor for your web app, and .NET MAUI for
your mobile and desktop clients. If you choose to use .NET MAUI Blazor, you can
even place your views in a Razor class library to share Blazor-compatible UIs across different web, mobile, and desktop projects.

.NET MAUI with Blazor may be a good option in a lot of cases. However, this book
focuses on .NET MAUI development with XAML and the MVVM pattern because the
purpose is to teach you .NET MAUI, not Blazor; and as mentioned earlier, XAML with
MVVM is the de facto choice for .NET MAUI apps. Even if you go on to learn other
approaches, to fully understand .NET MAUI, you should learn this approach first.

Summary

- .NET MAUI is a cross-platform, write once, run anywhere (WORA) UI application platform. You can build just one .NET MAUI app, and it will run on multiple platforms without further modification.
- You can write native apps with .NET MAUI. .NET MAUI apps are native apps.
- You can build apps in .NET MAUI with functional, performance, and security
  advantages over web apps.
- You can use the entire .NET ecosystem to build .NET MAUI apps. This includes
  all your favorite NuGet packages and your existing skills as a .NET developer.
- You can write .NET MAUI app UIs in XAML, C#, F#, or Blazor (we use XAML
  in this book).

Building
a .NET MAUI app

2

This chapter covers

- An introduction to Visual Studio for macOS and Windows and the .NET CLI
- Creating a cross-platform mobile and desktop app with .NET MAUI
- Running a .NET MAUI app and seeing changes in real time with Hot Reload

I work with .NET developers all day, every day. Most are full-stack developers and work with a web UI framework like Angular or React. But I often hear them say things like "I don't know mobile development" or "I don't know native desktop development." This is a misconception and couldn't be further from the truth.

Any .NET developer can build mobile or desktop UI apps with .NET MAUI. There's a small learning curve to get to grips with some of the UI- and markup-specific syntax and the design patterns—and that's what this book is for. Anyone with experience with a web UI framework (especially Angular) should feel very comfortable working in .NET MAUI, although prior experience is not necessary for this book. In this chapter, we see just how easy it is for .NET developers to get started building mobile and desktop UI apps with .NET MAUI.

2.1   Saying "Aloha, World!" with .NET MAUI

In this section, we build our first .NET MAUI App: Aloha, World! We look at the tools and templates available to developers for building .NET MAUI apps and talk about some of the pros and cons of each approach.

Which approach you choose is up to you and depends on your comfort, experience, and workflow. Regardless of the approach you prefer, I recommend walking through using both Visual Studio (for either Windows or macOS, depending on what you have available) and the command line so you at least gain familiarity with both approaches.

> ### Which option should I choose?
>
> It's up to you to decide whether to use Visual Studio or the .NET CLI. Whether you choose Visual Studio for Mac or Visual Studio for Windows will depend on what hardware and operating system you have available.
>
> Visual Studio, on both macOS and Windows, includes sophisticated development features that you don't get with the CLI. For example, the XAML Live Preview in Visual Studio can give you real-time feedback on design changes (see section 2.4 for more information). Visual Studio also has powerful IntelliSense, and now IntelliCode—code-completion features that can be indispensable when writing .NET MAUI apps—not to mention mature testing and debugging features.
>
> Another advantage of using Visual Studio is that it's easy to choose your target platform; you simply use a drop-down built into the Run button. Using the .NET CLI is a little more complicated; and, perhaps more importantly, the .NET CLI doesn't support targeting Windows (you can still build and run .NET MAUI apps on Windows using a command prompt, but you have to use MSBuild rather than the .NET CLI).
>
> Visual Studio is a great option for .NET developers and, except where I'm explicitly demonstrating the .NET CLI, is used in the examples and screenshots throughout this book (although all the samples also work fine with the .NET CLI). But Visual Studio is not without its detractors. For many people, Visual Studio is *too* powerful, and some prefer a lightweight alternative. This is where the .NET CLI comes in.
>
> The primary benefit of any GUI is discoverability; it's much easier to click around in Visual Studio than to delve into the documentation of the .NET CLI to figure out how to do this or that. But while a CLI may have a steeper learning curve, there's no question that an adept CLI user can see significant productivity and efficiency gains over their GUI-using counterpart.
>
> Entering the following commands takes a second or two:
>
> ```
> mkdir AlohaWorld
> cd AlohaWorld
> dotnet new blankmaui
> ```
>
> It takes the .NET CLI about 0.4 seconds to build a new .NET MAUI app from the template; the equivalent in Visual Studio can take significantly longer. In addition to the

efficiency gains, using the .NET CLI may seem more familiar to developers coming from other frameworks. The Angular CLI, for example, has commands with many analogs in the .NET CLI.

If you choose to use the .NET CLI, you will still need to use software to edit your code. Visual Studio Code, a text editor with developer-focused features such as syntax highlighting, is a popular choice for many developers and has a rich community-supported extension ecosystem. But you can use anything you like—essentially, a .NET MAUI app is a collection of text files (until you execute `dotnet build` to compile them), so any software capable of editing text files will work. But using a developer-centric text editor like Visual Studio Code will vastly simplify your development experience.

Personally, I like to use a combination of Visual Studio and the .NET CLI. I find the .NET CLI much quicker for some tasks and Visual Studio indispensable for others (such as debugging). Most of my .NET MAUI development takes place in Visual Studio, but you should find the most comfortable mode of working for you. Whichever you choose, it's worth at least learning the fundamentals of all the tools at your disposal.

Ensure that you have the .NET MAUI workload installed via the Visual Studio installer or the .NET CLI. **We're also using a blank .NET MAUI project template that you need to install separately.** If you are unsure whether you are ready to proceed, **see appendix A to get set up with all the right tools.** Once you're ready, dive in to create your first .NET MAUI app.

> **NOTE** .NET MAUI technically supports .NET 6 onward. However, .NET 7 is the minimum version used for this book. Be sure you select .NET 7 when prompted in wizards (and select .NET 8 when it ships).

2.1.1 Visual Studio 2022

Visual Studio is the primary first-party tool provided by Microsoft for developing apps with .NET MAUI. The latest version, 2022, is the minimum required version for .NET MAUI and has built-in support for a lot of features that make developing .NET MAUI apps more efficient. We'll see some of these features, like XAML Live Preview and .NET Hot Reload (covered later in this chapter), as we progress through the book.

Visual Studio is available for Windows and macOS, with different editions ranging from the free Community edition to the top-tier Enterprise edition. .NET MAUI works with all of them. Everything covered in this book can be done with the Community edition, although if you already have a Visual Studio subscription, you can use it for .NET MAUI. For more information, see appendix A.

MAC

To get started, open Visual Studio 2022 and click New. The next screen asks you to choose a template. Scroll down the list on the left to the Multiplatform section. Here, **click App** to bring up the .NET MAUI templates. **Choose Blank .NET MAUI Template** from the list (see figure 2.1), and **click the Continue button**.

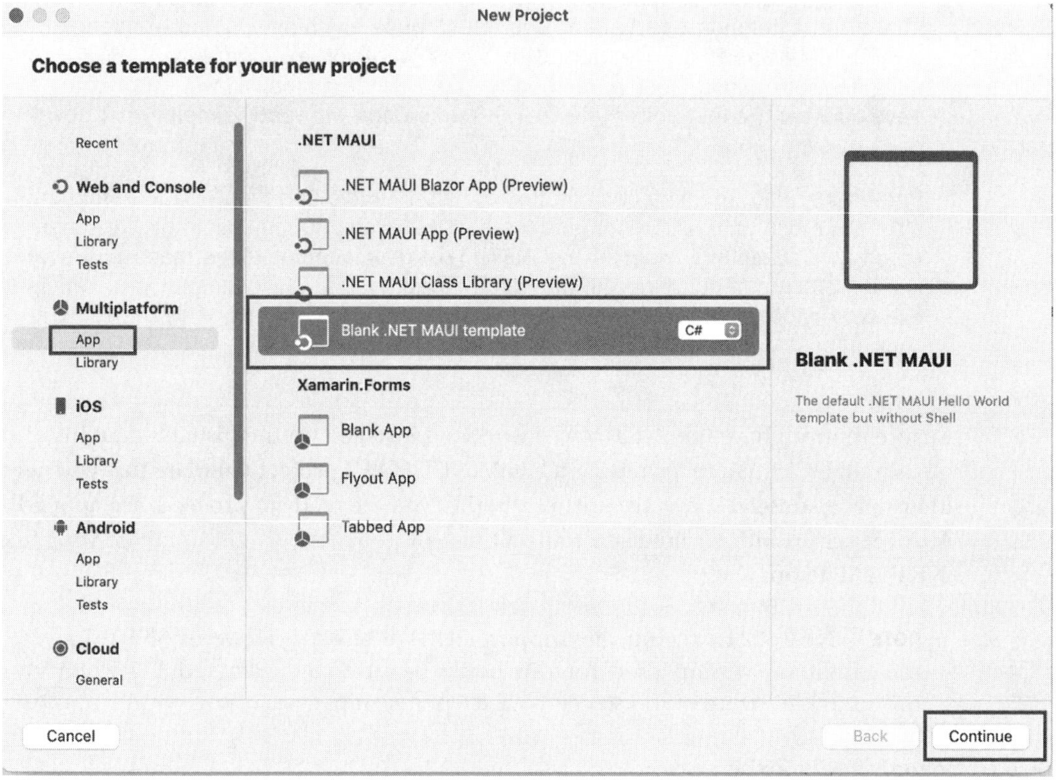

Figure 2.1   Find App in the Multiplatform section on the left. This shows the available .NET MAUI templates; choose Blank .NET MAUI Template to generate a new blank app.

Enter `AlohaWorld` **as the project name**. By default, the solution name is set to the same name as the project name. Leave it as is for now; it makes sense for these to be different when building complex, multiproject solutions, which we're not doing here. Visual Studio will suggest a default location to save the app; feel free to select a location of your choice. You're also given options for version control; we're not using version control for this app, but if you're a Git user and want to use it for this app, feel free to leave it selected.

Visual Studio will take a short time to create the new solution based on the .NET MAUI app template. When it's complete, you should see a collection of files and folders in Solution Explorer, as shown in figure 2.2.

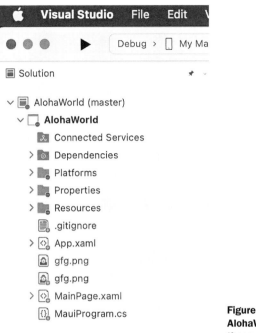

Figure 2.2   The files in the newly created AlohaWorld .NET MAUI app. We talk about these files in section 2.3.

We look at these files in section 2.3 and see how .NET MAUI starts and launches an app. Your .NET MAUI app has been created from the template and is ready for you to work on.

WINDOWS

To get started, open Visual Studio and click Create a New Project. Visual Studio shows you a list of available project templates, with the most recently used templates on the left and all project templates on the right. **Select Blank .NET MAUI Template** from the list. If you can't see it, you can use the filtering features (use the drop-down boxes to filter by language, platform, or project type), although I often find that they don't limit the results much. To make it easier, you can enter the search term maui in the search box to filter the available templates (see figure 2.3). With Blank .NET MAUI Template selected, **click Next.**

Choose a folder to save your project into (or use the default location), and **enter** AlohaWorld as the project name. **Then click Create.** Visual Studio will take a short time to create the new solution based on the .NET MAUI app template. When it's complete, you should see a collection of files and folders in Solution Explorer, as shown in figure 2.4.

We look at these files in section 2.3 and see how .NET MAUI starts and launches an app. For now, your.NET MAUI app has been created from the template and is ready for you to work on.

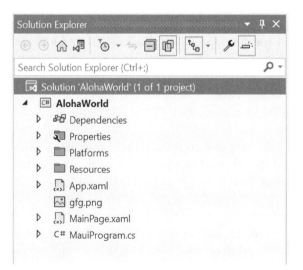

Figure 2.3   You can filter project templates in Visual Studio using the language, platform, and project type dropdowns, but the free text filter is the quickest way to find what you're looking for. In this example, we've entered `maui` **as a search term and narrowed the list of project templates to .NET MAUI projects.**

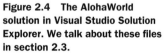

Figure 2.4   The AlohaWorld solution in Visual Studio Solution Explorer. We talk about these files in section 2.3.

2.1.2   .NET CLI overview

The .NET CLI is a comfortable and familiar tool for most .NET developers. Some people prefer to remain strictly in the GUI, and that's fine. The .NET CLI is easy to use, though—the only thing you really need to learn is how to use the interactive help. The commands are deliberately discoverable, and once you learn them, they can make your development experience much more efficient.

As .NET MAUI is a .NET workload rather than an external package, the project templates work the same way as all other .NET templates and accept the same inputs and switches. These are covered in the Microsoft documentation and are also discoverable via online help, which can be accessed by adding `--help` after any `dotnet` command.

Let's start by looking at the available templates. **Open your command prompt of choice, and enter** `dotnet new list`. You should see a list of templates available to the .NET CLI tool—conveniently, the .NET MAUI templates are at the top. Table 2.1 briefly explains these templates and their use cases.

Table 2.1   A summary of the .NET MAUI templates

Template name	Short name	Description
.NET MAUI App	`maui`	The main template used to create new .NET MAUI apps.
.NET MAUI Blazor App	`maui-blazor`	Used to create a new .NET MAUI app that uses Blazor to define its UI.
.NET MAUI Class Library	`mauilib`	Creates a new class library for sharing code between different .NET MAUI projects.
.NET MAUI ContentPage (C#)	`maui-page-csharp`	Creates a new .NET MAUI application page (see section 1.3) with the UI defined declaratively in C#.
.NET MAUI ContentPage	`maui-page-xaml`	Creates a new .NET MAUI application page with the UI defined in XAML markup (and a corresponding C# code-behind file).
.NET MAUI ContentView (C#)	`maui-view-csharp`	Creates a new .NET MAUI content view (a reusable UI component that can be used in .NET MAUI application pages) with the UI defined declaratively in C#.
.NET MAUI ContentView	`maui-view-xaml`	Creates a new .NET MAUI content view with the UI defined in XAML markup (and a corresponding C# code-behind file).
.NET MAUI ResourceDictionary (XAML)	`maui-dict-xaml`	Creates a new .NET MAUI resource dictionary in XAML. This allows you to define and name colors, styles, and templates that can be referenced by name for reuse throughout your app.

Table 2.1   A summary of the .NET MAUI templates *(continued)*

Template name	Short name	Description
Blank .NET MAUI template	`blankmaui`	An additional template that I provide. It is the same as the default template (`maui`), except the default template uses Shell (which we won't talk about until chapter 5). This template does not use Shell, so it should be easier to work with for the first few chapters.

The .NET CLI has some conventions that make it easy to use. For example, if you use the `dotnet new` command with a template of your choice without specifying any other parameters, the .NET CLI creates a new solution based on your selected template, using all the default options and using the name of the containing folder as the solution name.

Overriding default values

To override the default behavior, you can specify additional command-line parameters to the .NET CLI. For example, you can specify a different output directory or solution name (or both) using the available command-line switches. If we wanted to call our application HelloWorld instead of AlohaWorld and build it in a directory called Code at the root of our hard drive, we could do so with the following command:

```
dotnet new blankmaui -n HelloWorld -o C:\code\HelloWorld
```

For more information about all the available command-line switches, use the online help (`dotnet new --help`) or consult the documentation.

We're going to take advantage of this simplicity to create a brand-new .NET MAUI app.

2.1.3   .NET CLI in action

Create a folder called AlohaWorld. You can use your operating system's file browser (Explorer on Windows or Finder on macOS) or the command line. Then, using your command-line terminal of choice, navigate into that folder.

In the new folder you created, **enter the command**

```
dotnet new blankmaui
```

and **press Enter**. If the command executes successfully, you'll see a message saying

```
The template "Blank .NET MAUI template" was created successfully.
```

You can now examine the folder's contents to see the files created by this template. Use your operating system's file browser or the command line to show the contents of the folder (in figure 2.5, we use the command line). This creates a new .NET MAUI app which is now ready to work on.

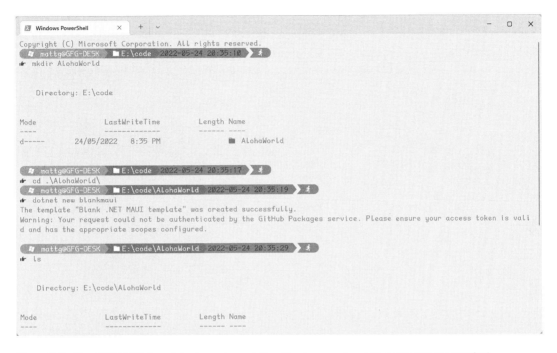

Figure 2.5   The .NET MAUI template generates solution files to use, shown here listed in the terminal.

2.2   *Running and debugging your app*

Now that we've created our first .NET MAUI app, let's see it in action! The following sections guide you through the steps of running your brand-new .NET MAUI app, depending on your chosen development approach.

> ### Single project solutions
> If you are coming from Xamarin.Forms, you'll notice some differences. In Xamarin.Forms, we had a project for each platform (e.g., MyApp for the shared logic and UI, MyApp.Android for Android, and MyApp.iOS for iOS) and set the project for the target platform we wanted to run our app on as the startup project. In .NET MAUI, we have a single project solution and use multitargeting to choose where to run it. We can add class libraries or other projects if we wish, but this is not necessary for targeting different platforms.

2.2.1   *Visual Studio for Windows*

The following steps guide you through building and running your .NET MAUI app. You see how to choose Windows as your target platform and run AlohaWorld as a Windows app. You can also run the app on Android or iOS from Visual Studio for Windows—for steps to do this, see appendix A.

Use the drop-down on the Run button in the toolbar. From the menu, **choose the Framework submenu**, and **choose Net7.0-windows[your windows build version]** as the target (see figure 2.6).

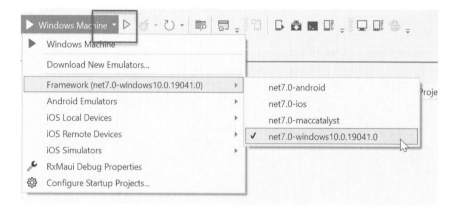

Figure 2.6   Use the drop-down to select a target platform.

Windows Developer Mode

Note that you must enable Developer Mode on Windows if you have not already done so. Developer Mode lets you run unsigned apps on Windows. By default, executables that are not signed by a trusted authority are blocked from running. When you develop apps in .NET MAUI, they are unsigned, so Developer Mode is required; but you should consider disabling it while you're not actively using it, to help to keep your system secure.

You can do this in the built-in Settings app. Press the Windows key, and start typing `settings`. The app will appear in your search results, and you can press Enter to open it.

Enable Developer Mode in Windows to run unsigned .NET MAUI apps.

You can now **run your app on Windows by clicking the Run button** on the toolbar. You could also choose to run the app on Android; we cover targeting different platforms in chapter 10.

The app should run, as shown in figure 2.7. The next section goes through what you see onscreen; for now, click the Click Me button and see what happens. Have fun with your first .NET MAUI app!

2.2.2 *Visual Studio for Mac*

Visual Studio 2022 for Mac makes it easy to run and debug .NET MAUI apps on macOS or iOS. Near the top-left corner of the screen is a Run button (see figure 2.8); to the right of it is the profile (Release or Debug) and then the target (by default, My Mac).

Clicking My Mac drops down a list of all the target devices you can run your .NET MAUI app on. This includes the Mac you are running Visual Studio on and any currently supported iOS device simulators. For more about setting up an iOS device for .NET MAUI development, see http://mng.bz/V19x.

Figure 2.7   **The AlohaWorld app running on Windows. Click the Click Me button to see changes.**

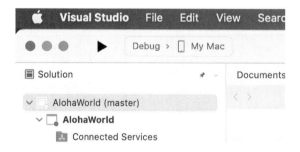

Figure 2.8   The Run button in Visual Studio 2022 for Mac, with the profile and target next to it

Leave My Mac selected, and click the Run button. Your app runs, as shown in figure 2.9. The next section goes through what you see onscreen; for now, click the Click Me button and see what happens.

2.2.3   *.NET CLI*

Using your terminal console of choice, **navigate to your solution folder and enter the** Run **command corresponding to your target platform**. The target platform is the platform on which you want to run your .NET MAUI app, not the platform you have developed it on. Use the reference guide in table 2.2 to choose the right target platform.

The Run command is

```
dotnet build -t:Run -f:net7.0-[target platform]
```

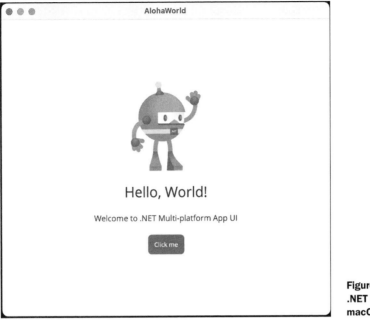

Figure 2.9   The AlohaWorld .NET MAUI app running on macOS

Table 2.2   .NET MAUI target platforms

Operating system	Target platform	Notes
macOS	Mac Catalyst	Mac Catalyst is a bridge that lets you run apps built for iOS on macOS. .NET MAUI uses Mac Catalyst to run apps on macOS. You can only target macOS when developing on macOS.
iOS	iOS	You can target iOS when developing on either macOS or Windows (although a macOS computer is required to publish .NET MAUI apps to the App Store).
Android	Android	You can target Android when developing on either macOS or Windows.

NOTE   While Windows is a target platform for .NET MAUI, it's missing from table 2.2 because you can't build .NET MAUI apps for Windows with the .NET CLI. It's best to stick to Visual Studio, although you can use MSBuild if you want to use a command terminal.

To run your app on iOS, you would use the command

```
dotnet build -t:Run -f:net7.0-ios
```

Let's look at the components of this command to see how it works and what it does (figure 2.10).

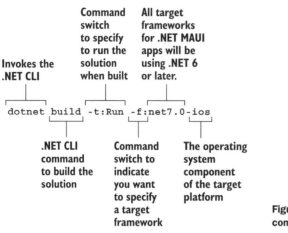

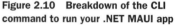

Figure 2.10   Breakdown of the CLI command to run your .NET MAUI app

The first thing to notice is the `dotnet` command. This is the name of the executable you want your operating system to run; in this case the .NET CLI. The second part, `build`, is the command we want the .NET CLI to execute. This tells the .NET CLI to build our project or solution, and the .NET CLI expects a .csproj or .sln file in the current directory (we can use additional parameters to specify a different project if we wish).

The next part, `-t:Run`, tells the .NET CLI that want it to run the solution after the build has completed. Finally, the `-f:` switch tells the .NET CLI that we are going to pass a framework parameter that we want it to use as the target platform. In the example in figure 2.10, we have passed in iOS. All frameworks use `net7.0-` as the prefix, as .NET MAUI requires .NET 6 at minimum (other options will be available for this prefix when newer versions of .NET are released).

Now that we understand how to use the `dotnet build` command to run our .NET MAUI app, **run the command to build and run the app on your target platform**. Congratulations—you have built and run your first .NET MAUI app! Click the Click Me button to see the changes to the counter.

2.3   Anatomy of a .NET MAUI app

Now that the app is running, let's look at how .NET MAUI runs the code and how it differs from a normal C# program. In a C# program, .NET usually looks for the *entry point*, which is a static method called `Main` that returns either `int` or `void` and has either no parameters or a single parameter of type `string[]` called `args` (see figure 2.11).

In a .NET MAUI app, .NET expects a method that returns an object of type `MauiApp`; this is in the `MauiProgram.cs` file created by the template. The file contains a static method called `CreateMauiApp` that uses the generic hostbuilder pattern common

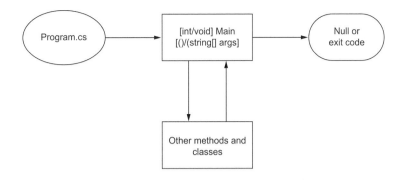

Figure 2.11   A regular C# program starts with the `Main` method in Program.cs and executes code until it exits, returning either `null` or an exit code.

across .NET with a return type of `MauiApp` (figure 2.12). A simplified version of this flow is shown in figure 2.13.

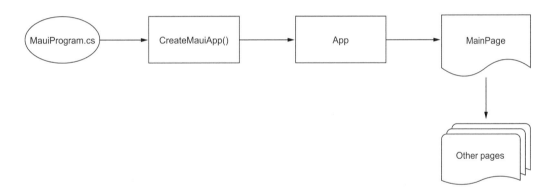

Figure 2.12   A .NET MAUI app starts with the `CreateMauiApp` method in MauiProgram.cs and launches an instance of the `App` class, which displays a `Page` assigned to the `MainPage` property of the `App` class.

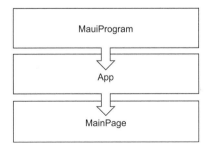

Figure 2.13   In a .NET MAUI app, `MauiProgram` is the entry point, which launches `App`, which displays `MainPage`.

The `CreateMauiApp` method (listing 2.1) has a return type of `MauiApp`, which is what runs our application. This static method builds this for us using a version of the .NET host builder, which ASP.NET Core or Blazor developers will recognize.

An extension method called `UseMauiApp` is called on the hostbuilder and passed App as a type parameter. The `UseMauiApp` extension method expects a type that implements the `IApplication` interface, and the `App` class inherits the `Application` class, which implements this interface.

Listing 2.1   MauiProgram.cs

```
namespace AlohaWorld;

public static class MauiProgram
{
    public static MauiApp CreateMauiApp()
    {
        var builder = MauiApp.CreateBuilder();
        builder
            .UseMauiApp<App>()
            .ConfigureFonts(fonts =>
            {
                fonts.AddFont("OpenSans-Regular.ttf",  "OpenSansRegular");
                fonts.AddFont("OpenSans-Semibold.ttf", "OpenSansSemibold");
            });
        return builder.Build();
    }
}
```

The CreateMauiApp method is a static method with a return type of MauiApp.

In a .NET MAUI app, we use the .NET hostbuilder pattern.

The .UseMauiApp extension method expects a type parameter with a type that implements the IApplication interface.

The hostbuilder executes the Build() method and returns the result.

The `App` class (listing 2.2) has a member called `MainPage`; in the constructor of the App class, we assign a value to this member of type `ContentPage` (which inherits the `Page` base class). .NET MAUI then displays that page to the user when the app has finished loading.

The type that we are instantiating is also called `MainPage`, but this is the name of the class, whereas in the `App` class, `MainPage` is a member of type `Page`. `Page` is a type in .NET MAUI that is used to define pages in an application. A page is a full-screen view, and a view is something that appears onscreen. We talk more about pages and views in chapter 4.

The important point is that to start our app, we need an object of type `Page` (it doesn't have to be called `MainPage`—it can be called anything you like, although it is called `MainPage` in all the templates) that we set as the value of the `MainPage` member in our `App` class. .NET MAUI loads the app and displays this page to the user.

Listing 2.2   App.xaml.cs

```
namespace AlohaWorld;

public partial class App : Application
{
    public App()
```

The App class inherits the Application class.

```
        {
            InitializeComponent();

            MainPage = new MainPage();
        }
    }
}
```

The Application base class provides a property of type Page called MainPage. In the App class, we assign a ContentPage called MainPage to this property, and .NET MAUI displays this page on load.

This is all you need to know to get up and running with .NET MAUI—but there is more to the story. On Windows, the process just described is accurate; but on macOS, iOS, and Android, the operating system SDKs expect specific entry points to start an app, and .NET MAUI gives you instances of these that you can customize if you need to. These are the `AppDelegate` class for macOS and iOS and the `MainActivity` class for Android. You can see these in figure 2.14.

These files are contained in a folder called `Platforms` and a subfolder named according to the relevant OS. .NET MAUI provides these to the OS as the entry point and loads the `MauiProgram` behind the scenes, as shown in figure 2.15.

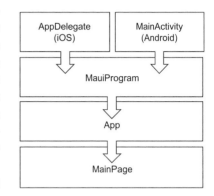

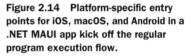

Figure 2.14   Platform-specific entry points for iOS, macOS, and Android in a .NET MAUI app kick off the regular program execution flow.

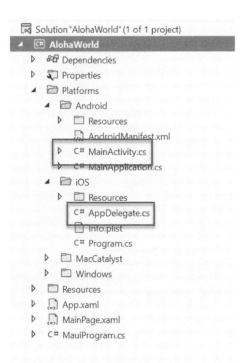

Figure 2.15   `MainActivity` is the entry point for Android apps, and `AppDelegate` is the entry point for macOS and iOS apps, shown here in Solution Explorer in Visual Studio.

As you progress on your .NET MAUI journey, you will find there are times when you need to gain a deeper understanding of these files and how they work, and we dip into them throughout the book. It's important to be aware of them; but for now, and for the most part, you won't need to touch them when building .NET MAUI apps.

.NET MAUI goes from launch to getting an object of type ContentPage and assigning it to the MainPage property of the App class, to displaying that page. Let's look at how MainPage.xaml, the ContentPage we assign to MainPage in the App class, is structured.

The following snippet shows the views (layouts and controls) of the MainPage.xaml file without any of their properties (the full code is in listing 2.3), commented with numbers corresponding to figure 2.16:

```
<ContentPage>
    <ScrollView>                     <!-- 1 -->
        <VerticalStackLayout>        <!-- 2 -->
            <Image />                <!-- 3 -->
            <Label />                <!-- 4 -->
            <Label />                <!-- 5 -->
            <Button />               <!-- 6 -->
        </VerticalStackLayout>
    </ScrollView>
</ContentPage>
```

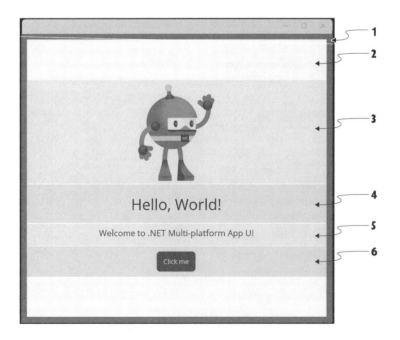

Figure 2.16   The layouts and views used in the .NET MAU app: 1. ScrollView, 2. VerticalStackLayout, 3. Image, 4. Label, 5. Label, 6. Button. The size may differ depending on your screen.

Within the content page, the first child element is a `ScrollView`. A `ScrollView` is a UI container that lets the user scroll to see content that is too big to fit onscreen:

```
<ContentPage>
    <ScrollView>           <!-- 1 -->
        ...
```

Inside the `ScrollView` is a `VerticalStackLayout`. This layout component lets you arrange views sequentially and vertically (the first one appears at the top, the next one is underneath it, and so on):

```
...
        <VerticalStackLayout>          <!-- 2 -->
...
```

Inside the `VerticalStackLayout` are an image, two labels, and a button:

```
...
        <VerticalStackLayout>      <!-- 2 -->
            <Image .../>           <!-- 3 -->
            <Label .../>           <!-- 4 -->
            <Label .../>           <!-- 5 -->
            <Button .../>           <!-- 6 -->
        </VerticalStackLayout>
...
```

Listing 2.3 shows the full code of the `MainPage.xaml` file. The first thing to note is that it is an XML file. XAML (which stands for eXtensible Application Markup Language) is just XML with some custom element names that we use for building .NET MAUI UIs. We consume those element names is by importing the relevant namespaces. This is done on lines 1 and 2 in the code:

```
<ContentPage xmlns="http://schemas.microsoft.com/dotnet/2021/maui"
             xmlns:x="http://schemas.microsoft.com/winfx/2009/xaml"
             x:Class="AlohaWorld.MainPage"
...
```

Line 1 brings in the `http://schemas.microsoft.com/dotnet/2021/maui` schema as the default namespace. This includes most of the tag names we will use. Line 2 brings in the `http://schemas.microsoft.com/winfx/2009/xaml` schema and assigns it to the x namespace. This includes tags for metadata about our UI, rather than the UI itself.

The first example is on line 3, where we use the `Class` tag from the x namespace to associate the XAML markup file with a C# class. You can see the corresponding code-behind class file associated with the XAML markup file in Solution Explorer if you are using Visual Studio.

All views are classes

All views in .NET MAUI apps are C# classes. This includes `ContentPage` views (complete application pages) as well as controls (items displayed on a page). When you use a XAML file, you are using XAML markup to tell the view how to display the UI, but the view itself is still a class.

Everything you can do in XAML, you can do in C#, so you could build your app without using XAML. Doing so isn't covered in this book, but if you like that approach, you can read about it in the .NET MAUI documentation.

You can have a .NET MAUI view that is a C# file without a XAML file, but you can't have a XAML view without C#.

Lines 1–4 contain the XML declaration and define the `ContentPage` tag, which is the enclosing tag for the rest of the XAML file. We've already looked at lines 2–4 and seen that they are namespace and class declarations.

Listing 2.3   MainPage.xaml

The ContentPage tag encloses all other UI elements. Also sets the
default namespace (xmlns) to the standard .NET MAUI schema.

```
<?xml version="1.0" encoding="utf-8" ?>
<ContentPage xmlns="http://schemas.microsoft.com/dotnet/2021/maui"
             xmlns:x="http://schemas.microsoft.com/winfx/2009/xaml"
             x:Class="AlohaWorld.MainPage">
    <ScrollView>
        <VerticalStackLayout Spacing="25" Padding="30,0"
            VerticalOptions="Center">
            <Image
                Source="dotnet_bot.png"
                SemanticProperties.Description="Cute dot net bot waving hi
to you!"
                HeightRequest="200"
                HorizontalOptions="Center" />
            <Label
                Text="Hello, World!"
```

Associates the XAML file with the class it corresponds to

Sets the x namespace to the XAML metadata schema

Labels that declare their Text properties

An Image that declares a Source property that tells .NET MAUI where to get the image to display. This can be a URL or an embedded resource (more in section 2.4).

The VerticalStackLayout tag with properties for padding (space between the VerticalStackLayout boundary and elements it contains) and spacing (the space between rows)

A ScrollView control contains the VerticalStackLayout that defines the rest of the layout. By enclosing the VerticalStackLayout in a ScrollView, we can scroll any content that doesn't fit onscreen.

Semantic properties used by assistive technologies to provide descriptive information about onscreen elements

```
            SemanticProperties.HeadingLevel="Level1"
            FontSize="32"
            HorizontalOptions="Center" />

        <Label
            Text="Welcome to .NET Multi-platform App UI"
            SemanticProperties.HeadingLevel="Level2"
            SemanticProperties.Description="Welcome to dot net Multi
platform App U I"
            FontSize="18"
            HorizontalOptions="Center" />

        <Button
            x:Name="CounterBtn"
            Text="Click me"
            SemanticProperties.Hint="Counts the number of times you click"
            Clicked="OnCounterClicked"
            HorizontalOptions="Center" />

      </VerticalStackLayout>
    </ScrollView>

</ContentPage>
```

A Button that defines its Text property (the text shown on the button) and the event handler delegated to by the button's Clicked event. The Button has a Name declaration (from the x: namespace defined earlier). Naming elements lets us access them from in code or with binding references in XAML (more in chapter 3).

We discuss pages and layouts more in chapters 4–6. Now that we understand how a .NET MAUI app is laid out, let's make some small changes to the code and watch them update in the app in real time.

Accessibility in .NET MAUI apps

Accessibility (*a11y*, as it's often shortened) is a critical consideration when building apps in .NET MAUI. We often rely on visual cues to provide us with meta-information about things onscreen and the things themselves. For example, heading size can indicate importance or hierarchy. A visually impaired user may not have access to these cues.

It's important to make the UI as visually accessible as possible. The Web Content Accessibility Guidelines (WCAG) 2.1 standard provides substantial guidance for making apps that look great and are highly accessible.

Assistive technologies such as screen readers can help visually impaired users, sometimes replacing visual use of the screen altogether. For these users, it's important to provide metadata that screen readers can interpret to replace visual cues. Semantic properties in .NET MAUI allow us to do this. In listing 2.3, semantic properties are used to declare to a screen reader the heading level of a `Label`. This enables a screen reader to not just read the content of the `Label` to the user but also let the user know where in the hierarchy the `Label` sits, something a non-visually impaired user can discern visually.

A11y is a huge topic and one that is important to learn. While this book doesn't focus on it primarily, I will draw your attention to it whenever a relevant topic comes up.

2.4   *Seeing real-time changes with Hot Reload*

So far, we've been calling the app AlohaWorld, but it says "Hello, World!" Let's change that. The following steps show how to make a couple of small changes to the app while it is running and see them reflected in real time (without having to restart the app). As you progress as a .NET MAUI developer, this capability will become a critical part of your inner development loop. This trick is called *Hot Reload,* and it is currently only supported in Visual Studio and Visual Studio for Mac. The .NET CLI does not support Hot Reload for .NET MAUI apps.

Figure 2.17   Dotnet Bot— the official .NET mascot

One of the changes we are going to make is to the Dotnet Bot that we see onscreen (figure 2.17). Dotnet Bot is the official mascot of .NET, and there's a cool website where you can make your own version for use in any of your projects. **Head over to https://mod-dotnet-bot.net and click the Get Started button. Build your own version of the Dotnet Bot, and click the Share button to download it**. Once you've downloaded the file, **rename it if necessary** to make sure it complies with .NET MAUI file-naming requirements (the filename must contain only lowercase letters and underscores).

2.4.1   *Visual Studio for Windows*

Open your app in Visual Studio if it's not open already. Choose your target platform, and run the app. You should see something like figure 2.10. Switch back to Visual Studio, and follow these steps:

1   Open the file `MainPage.xaml`.
2   Find the `Text` property of the `Label` element that is assigned the value `'Hello, World!'`. Change this value to `'Aloha, World!'`.
3   Switch back to your running app. You should see your label updated to show the "Aloha, World!" message.
4   In Solution Explorer, right-click the `Resources` folder, and choose Add Existing Item from the context menu.
5   Use the file browser to select the custom Dotnet Bot you downloaded earlier.
6   Once your custom Dotnet Bot is imported, right-click the image in the `Resources` folder and select Properties.
7   In the Properties window, ensure that the Build Action is set to `MauiImage`.
8   Back in the `MainPage.xaml` file, note that the `Source` property of the `Image` element is set to `dotnet_bot` on line 13. Change this to the filename (including the extension) of the file you imported in steps 4 and 5.
9   Save the changes to the `MainPage.xaml` file.

To the right of the Run button on the toolbar is a button with a red flame on it (see figure 2.18). This is the Hot Reload button. **Click it**, and Visual Studio will show you a warning, letting you know that it can't apply your changes with Hot Reload and you'll have to let it rebuild. **Go ahead and rebuild, and then switch to the running app** to see your changes reflected, as shown in figure 2.19.

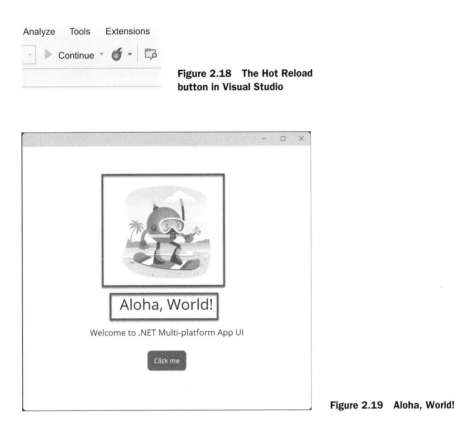

Figure 2.18   The Hot Reload button in Visual Studio

Figure 2.19   Aloha, World!

You may have noticed that the Hot Reload button is also a drop-down. Expanding it shows another cool option in Visual Studio: Hot Reload on File Save. As it suggests, enabling this automatically applies Hot Reload (for supported changes) when you save a file. This is the equivalent of running `dotnet watch run` for a .NET (non-MAUI) app with the .NET CLI.

Why does Hot Reload need to rebuild sometimes?

Hot Reload is an awesome feature of .NET. It lets us make changes to code while an app is running, without having to stop debugging and rebuild the app. But as you just saw, it's not without limitations.

(continued)
When we build an application with .NET, it gets compiled to Common Language Runtime (CLR) code. This includes a kind of directory of all our classes and their public members (methods and properties) and resources. This directory can't be altered at runtime, so while we can change the code inside a method, we can't add or remove classes, methods, or resources (such as images) without a rebuild.

Congratulations on making your first code changes to a .NET MAUI app. We examine these changes in more detail throughout the book; for now, feel free to experiment and change other values in the XAML file. You'll quickly see how powerful it is to be able to change XAML layouts or code in a running app without having to stop and rebuild every time.

2.4.2   Visual Studio for Mac

Open your app in Visual Studio for Mac if it's not already, and run the app on your Mac. You should see something similar to figure 2.10. Switch back to Visual Studio, and follow these steps:

1 Open the file `MainPage.xaml`.
2 Find the `Text` property of the `Label` element assigned the value `'Hello, World!'`. Change it to `'Aloha, World!'`.
3 Switch back to the running app. The label should be updated to show the "Aloha, World!" message (see figure 2.20).
4 Back in Visual Studio, in Solution Explorer, right-click the `Resources` folder, and from the context menu, choose Add > Existing files.
5 Use the file browser to select the custom Dotnet Bot that you downloaded earlier.
6 Select your file, and from the Add File to Folder dialog, choose the option to copy the file to the directory.
7 Once your custom Dotnet Bot is imported, expand the `Resources` folder if you haven't already, right-click the image you added, and select Properties.
8 In the Properties window, ensure that the Build section is expanded; then, in the Build Action drop-down, select `MauiImage`.
9 Back in the `MainPage.xaml` file, note that the `Source` property of the `Image` element is set to `dotnet_bot` on line 13. Change this to the filename (including the extension) of the file you imported in steps 4, 5, and 6.
10 Save the changes to the `MainPage.xaml` file.
11 Switch back to the running app. The Dotnet Bot that was there is missing.
12 Stop the app, and start it again. This time you should see your custom Dotnet Bot.

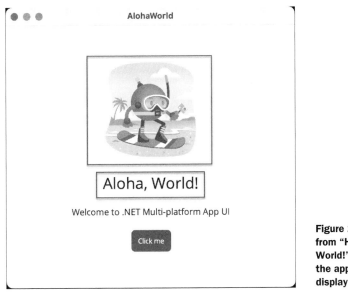

Aloha, World!

Welcome to .NET Multi-platform App UI

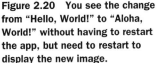

Figure 2.20 You see the change from "Hello, World!" to "Aloha, World!" without having to restart the app, but need to restart to display the new image.

Hot Reload will apply changes automatically while your app is running, but as you saw, changing an image didn't work. See the sidebar "Why does Hot Reload need to rebuild sometimes?" for why this is so—the same is true for macOS and Windows.

Congratulations on making your first code changes to a .NET MAUI app. We go through these changes in more detail throughout the book; for now, feel free to experiment and change other values in the XAML file. You'll quickly see how powerful it is to be able to change XAML layouts or code in a running app without having to stop and rebuild every time.

Summary

- You can create a .NET MAUI app from a template provided by .NET using the .NET CLI, Visual Studio for Mac, or Visual Studio for Windows.
- You can build and run a .NET MAUI app on any of the target platforms (iOS, Android, macOS, or Windows). You can also do this from the CLI, Visual Studio for Mac, or Visual Studio for Windows.
- To choose the platform you want to run your .NET MAUI app on, use the drop-down selector in the Run button.
- You can make changes to your app while it's running. .NET Hot Reload applies those changes in real time without you needing to restart the app.
- You can build the UI in your .NET MAUI app using either XAML or C#. XAML is the most popular approach.
- You can use the familiar hostbuilder pattern in .NET MAUI apps.

Making .NET MAUI apps interactive

3

This chapter covers

- Defining app permissions in metadata files
- Using location, messaging, and other common operating system and device features
- Saving and encrypting data to users' devices
- Connecting UI properties with data binding
- Using collections and templates to display lists of data

In chapter 2, we built and ran our first .NET MAUI app and made some small changes, but our app didn't really do anything. You may have spotted the Click Me button, which, when clicked, increases a number displayed onscreen. In this chapter, we look at how this works and see that we can get and set values on UI elements from code.

Increasing a counter isn't the most exciting thing in the world, and it's something you can easily do with a web app. So, in this chapter, we start to explore device capabilities that make it fun to build mobile and desktop applications with .NET MAUI.

In this chapter, we see how *data binding* is used to bind values and commands from our UI to our code, and we see how the class corresponding to our view can easily manipulate our view. We go through a couple of examples that demonstrate this while also learning how to persist data locally on our device and access common device and OS features through the .NET MAUI APIs.

3.1 Using OS and device features

One of the reasons people choose to build a mobile or desktop app rather than a web app is for ease of access to device and OS features. Some of these features can be accessed via web apps and some can't, but in .NET MAUI, accessing common device and OS features is simple. Figure 3.1 shows how location and sharing, the two features we will use in this chapter, are easily accessed in .NET MAUI across any supported platform.

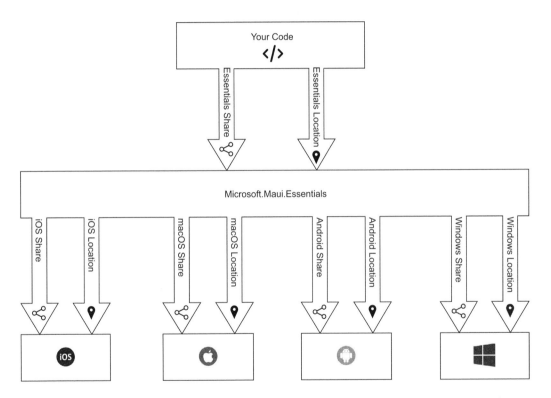

Figure 3.1 .NET MAUI provides abstractions of common features (location and sharing in this example), so you can access them on all platforms using a single codebase in your app.

.NET MAUI gives you access to common features found across all supported platforms. You can see an exhaustive list of capabilities provided in the Microsoft documentation, and we use many of these throughout this book. In this section, we focus on two common device features: geolocation and sharing. To see these features in action, we're going to build an app called FindMe! that gets the user's location and lets them share it, as shown in figure 3.2.

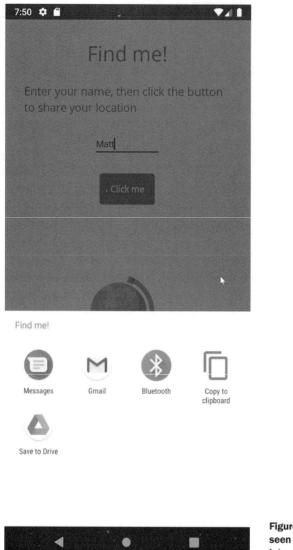

Find me!

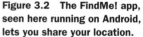

Figure 3.2 The FindMe! app, seen here running on Android, lets you share your location.

The user will enter their name and click a button, which will show them multiple options for sharing their location with a friend.

iOS, Windows, macOS, and Android all have a geolocation API that can be used to get information about your user's location. On a desktop, your location is approximated using several data points, including your IP address and Wi-Fi information; on a mobile device, this information is combined with GPS data to provide a more precise location. With .NET MAUI, you don't need to know how these work—just that you can access them via a common abstraction (figure 3.3).

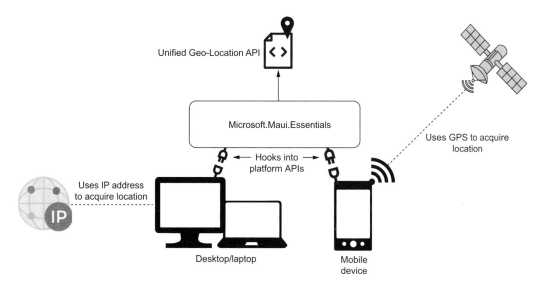

Figure 3.3 .NET MAUI provides a geolocation API you can call in your code. This API is an abstraction of each platform's individual API for accessing the user's location, and this in turn is an abstraction of different techniques for physically locating your user.

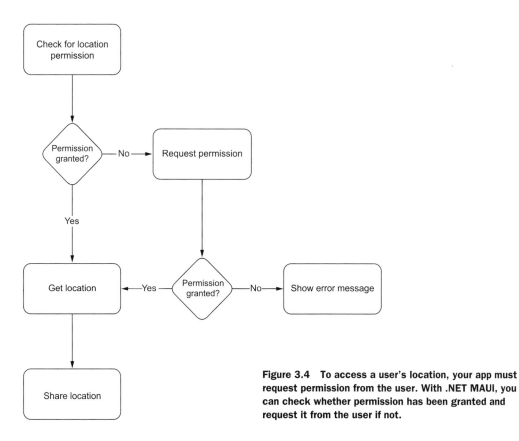

Figure 3.4 To access a user's location, your app must request permission from the user. With .NET MAUI, you can check whether permission has been granted and request it from the user if not.

On all platforms, users must explicitly provide consent for your app to access their location. And on iOS and Android, your app must declare what permissions it will request from your users as part of its descriptive metadata. .NET MAUI provides methods to both request consent and verify that your user has consented to access their location while using the app (figure 3.4). Declaring required permissions is done in the app's metadata rather than in code and therefore must be done in a specific way for each platform.

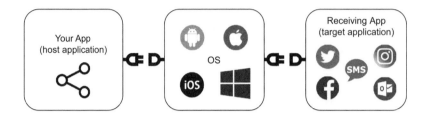

Figure 3.5   All supported OSs provide a sharing API. When an app calls that API, the user is presented with a list of apps that have registered as target applications and can choose to share the content being provided by the host application with the target application.

The other feature we use in this chapter is sharing. All four supported OSs provide a sharing API that, when activated, prompts your user to select a target application. This application may include email, SMS, or any app that has registered a sharing capability with the OS (social media apps, for example, nearly always expose a share capability to the OS). Having a sharing API in the OS that lets the user choose where they want to share means you don't have to cater to every sharing mechanism in every app on every OS; in .NET MAUI, you can use a common abstraction that gives you access to sharing on every target platform (figure 3.5).

> **NOTE**   Registering your app as a sharing target is not covered here—.NET MAUI doesn't provide a unified API for registering a sharing target, so you would need to write OS-specific code for each platform where you wanted to do this (albeit abstracted into .NET). While we do cover the basics of platform-specific code throughout the book, with a bit more depth in chapter 11, the core focus of this book is on shared functionality that doesn't require OS-specific code. For now, you'll be able to share *from* your app but not share *to* your app.

Let's get started with building the FindMe! app. **Create a new .NET MAUI project called FindMe** using the `blankmaui` template. Before we start writing any UI or logic code, we need to declare what permissions we will request from the user. As our app is going to access the user's location, we need to declare that this is a permission that we will request from the user.

Each platform has a specific metadata file that declares information about the app needed by the OS and distribution platforms (e.g., the iOS App Store and the

Microsoft Store); depending on the target platform, this information includes either a declaration of any permissions required by the app or a declaration of which capabilities (such as network access, location, etc.) are used by the app, from which the required permissions are inferred. Table 3.1 and figure 3.6 shows the name and location of these metadata files for each platform.

Table 3.1   Names and locations of the app metadata files for each platform

Platform	File name	Location
Android	AndroidManifest.xml	[Your app]/Platforms/Android/
iOS	Info.plist	[Your app]/Platforms/iOS/
macOS	Info.plist	[Your app]/Platforms/macOS/
Windows	package.appxmanifest	[Your app]/Platforms/Windows/

Platform	iOS	macOS	Windows	Android
Metadata File	Info.plist	Info.plist	App.manifest	Androidmanifest.xml

Figure 3.6   The metadata files for .NET MAUI apps on each platform

You should easily spot a pattern here: all these files are in a folder in `Platforms` named for each platform. This folder also contains other platform-specific files, which we'll look at in more detail later.

The app metadata files are all XML, so you can easily modify them in any text editor. However, depending on whether you are using an IDE—and if so, which one—you may have access to a graphical tool that exposes visual editors for well-known values in these files. You are welcome to experiment, but the easiest way to make these changes is in the XML directly, and it is advisable to get comfortable with doing it this way.

TIP If using Visual Studio, you can right-click these manifest files, choose Open With, and then select XML (Text) Editor from the dialog that pops up.

Where can I learn about platform-specific metadata files?

The .NET MAUI documentation includes some information about the platform-specific metadata files, which is a good place to start. As you progress as a .NET MAUI developer, you will likely encounter scenarios where you want to dig down into platform specifics, not just for these metadata files. Throughout the book, we dip our toes into platform specifics here and there, which will get you started with the basics.

> **(continued)**
>
> We look at this topic in a bit more depth in chapter 8, but it is important to know how to find information yourself about platform-specific APIs and implementation details and how to translate them to .NET MAUI scenarios. These are not explicitly covered here; the goal of the book is to be comprehensive rather than exhaustive and to make you self-sufficient. The Other Online Resources section at the start of the book is a good place to start.

3.1.1   *Android metadata*

Let's start with Android. **Open FindMe > Platforms > Android > AndroidManifest.xml.** Inside the `<manifest>...</manifest>` tags are three child elements: `uses-sdk`, `application`, and `uses-permission`. The first declares what minimum Android API version is required to run your app (for example, if you want to use Android features that were only introduced in a specific version—there is also a minimum version requirement to submit apps to the Google Play store) and the target version.

The second element contains metadata about how your app is presented and handled by the Android OS. Here you declare where our app icon can be found (for both standard and round icons), whether you support right-to-left (for languages like Arabic or Hebrew), and whether your app should be included in a device backup (you may want to exclude it if, for example, your app contains sensitive data).

The third element is of most interest to us in this case. It declares that the app will request the user's permission to access their device network state information, declaring it using the Android API-specific namespace.

We're going to add some code. First, let's declare the permissions we are going to ask the user for. The following listing shows the permissions we want to declare, with the added permissions in bold.

Listing 3.1   Permissions to add to AndroidManifest.xml

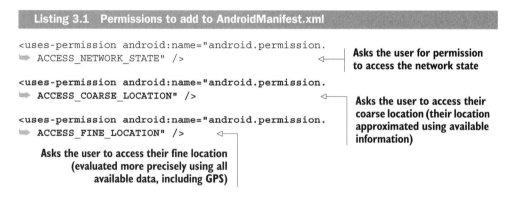

```
<uses-permission android:name="android.permission.
   ACCESS_NETWORK_STATE" />
```
Asks the user for permission to access the network state

```
<uses-permission android:name="android.permission.
   ACCESS_COARSE_LOCATION" />
```
Asks the user to access their coarse location (their location approximated using available information)

```
<uses-permission android:name="android.permission.
   ACCESS_FINE_LOCATION" />
```
Asks the user to access their fine location (evaluated more precisely using all available data, including GPS)

In addition to declaring the permissions we will ask for, we need to declare the Android API features we will use. We'll also specify that while the app will use these features, they will not be required to install the app. Add the following features after the permissions.

Listing 3.2   Features to add to AndroidManifest.xml

Uses the location (approximated with Wi-Fi, IP address, etc.)
feature but doesn't block the app if it's not available

```
<uses-feature android:name="android.hardware.location"
   android:required="false" />
<uses-feature android:name="android.hardware.location.
   Gps" android:required="false" />
```

Uses GPS to improve
location accuracy, but
doesn't block the app
if it's not available

Once you have added these, your `AndroidManifest.xml` file should look like listing 3.3.

Listing 3.3   AndroidManifest.xml full code

```
<?xml version="1.0" encoding="utf-8"?>
<manifest xmlns:android="http://schemas.android.com/apk/res/android">
    <uses-sdk android:minSdkVersion="21" android:targetSdkVersion="31" />
    <application android:allowBackup="true" android:icon="@mipmap/appicon"
    android:roundIcon="@mipmap/appicon_round" android:supportsRtl="true">
    </application>
    <uses-permission android:name="android.permission.ACCESS_NETWORK_STATE" />
    <uses-permission android:name="android.permission.ACCESS_COARSE_LOCATION" />
    <uses-permission android:name="android.permission.ACCESS_FINE_LOCATION" />
    <uses-feature android:name="android.hardware.location" android:required
    ="false" />
    <uses-feature android:name="android.hardware.location.gps" android:
    required="false" />

</manifest>
```

Those are all the changes we need to make to the Android manifest, so you can **save and close that file**. Let's move on to iOS.

3.1.2   iOS metadata

Open the iOS version of the `Info.plist` file. Plist is short for *property list* (the term used by Apple in place of *manifest*), and the list of properties is enclosed in a dictionary of key-value pairs called `<dict>...</dict>`. The process of declaring that we need the user's location on iOS is slightly different—rather than declaring both the permission and the feature, for iOS we declare the reason we need a permission. Once we've done this, the requirements for both the feature and the permission are implicit. Add the key-value pair from listing 3.4 to the end of the dictionary in the `Info.plist` file.

Listing 3.4   Key-value pair to add to the iOS `Info.plist` file

```
<key>NSLocationWhenInUseUsageDescription</key>
<string>We need your location in order to share it.</string>
```

The key for this item in the dictionary, using the
recognized key that describes why we need the
user's location when the app is in use

The value in the dictionary for this
key, specified as a string with the
reason we have provided

Close and save the file, and then **make the same change to the Mac Catalyst** version of the `Info.plist` file.

Why is the Mac platform called Mac Catalyst?

A significant portion of Apple's revenue comes from app sales, most of which happen at the iOS App Store. In an effort to increase the variety and volume of apps available on the Mac App Store, Apple introduced the Catalyst program, which enables iOS developers to package their apps for the Mac. Starting in 2021, all apps submitted to the iOS App Store are also marked for release on the Mac App Store by default—developers must opt their app out of this option. But many developers appreciate the convenience.

.NET MAUI takes advantage of the Mac Catalyst program and uses the Catalyst platform to package apps for the Mac. The outcome for developers and users is the same as if the app had been written specifically for the Mac, but under the hood, it means .NET MAUI can provide an abstraction of the UI SDK used in iOS (`UIKit`) rather than having to also provide an abstraction of the macOS UI SDK as well (`AppKit`). The situation may change in the future, and Apple may unify these SDKs; but in the meantime, Catalyst provides a convenient way for .NET MAUI to package your app for the Mac.

3.1.3   Windows metadata

The last platform we need to specify permissions for is Windows. **In the Windows platform folder, open `Package.appxmanifest`.** Package.appxmanifest is another XML file (the same as the other platforms). Toward the bottom of the file, you'll see a `Capabilities` node. Inside this node, under any existing capabilities, **add the following line**:

```
<DeviceCapability Name="location" />
```

That's all we need to do to tell Windows apps we will ask for the user's permission. Our platform setup is complete, so let's move on to something a little more interesting. We'll make some small changes to the UI and then write the code that gets the user's location and calls the sharing API.

3.2   The FindMe! UI

Open the `MainPage.xaml` file. It contains the UI definition for the page, and we need to make a few small changes to adapt this UI to suit our FindMe app. First, let's change the title displayed on our page. The second element in the `VerticalStackLayout` is a `Label` with its `Text` property set to "Hello, world!". **Change this text to "Find me!"** The next `Label` is a kind of subtitle (although it is semantically set to the same title level) with text that reads "Welcome to the dot net Multi Platform App UI." **Change this text to "Enter your name, then click the button to share your location."** Note that the text is also entered into a property called `SemanticProperties.Description`; change the value here as well to match what you entered in the `Text` property.

Semantic properties

Semantic properties are descriptive values used by assistive technologies such as screen readers to help people use your app. For example, someone who is visually impaired may not be able to easily distinguish color, so typical conventions, such as a red label to indicate an error or a green tick to indicate success, would not work for some users. Color and, in particular, contrast can be used to enhance the readability of your app, but you can't rely on any single technique.

Accessibility (or a11y, as it's often shortened) is a big topic that you will need to invest some time in. Microsoft provides a variety of resources in this area (we talked briefly about these in chapter 2), including documentation and videos, and much of it is specific to .NET MAUI. A great place to start is the Accessibility page in the Fundamentals section of the official .NET MAUI documentation. Becoming familiar with this is essential.

The next UI element is a `Button`. Before it, add a `Label` control with the following snippet:

The element type is Entry rather than label. An Entry is a single-line user input field.

Instead of the Text property that we set on the Label, we set a Placeholder value (Entries have a Text property too, but we use it later in this chapter). The value of this property is displayed when the user has not yet entered a value of their own.

```
<Entry
    Placeholder="Enter your name"
    SemanticProperties.Hint="Enter your name to be used when sharing location"
    HorizontalOptions="Center"
    x:Name="UsernameEntry"/>
```

We give this UI element a name so we can refer to it in our C# code. There is no Microsoft style guide for XAML naming conventions, but you should establish one of your own.

.NET MAUI naming conventions

Microsoft provides some coding convention guidelines for each of its .NET languages, and some XAML syntax conventions are available for the Universal Windows Platform (UWP) but not for .NET MAUI (or even Xamarin.Forms). With that said, some best practices have become the de facto standards across the industry. You should become familiar with these, but ultimately you and/or your team will need to define the best approach for your product.

In this book, we use PascalCase for all public properties and underscored _camelCase for private fields. For XAML properties, we use PascalCase with the convention of [*property or action*][*ElementType*]: for example, `LoginButton` or `UsernameEntry`.

Following these conventions makes it easier for anyone reviewing your code—including you—to understand what a property is for and what it does.

Change the value of the `Clicked` property on the `Button` element. It currently refers to a method in the code-behind file called `OnCounterClicked`; **change this to**

`OnFindMeClicked`. This method doesn't exist yet, but we will create it shortly. You also need to update the semantic hint; **change the `SemanticProperties.Hint` value** to "Presents apps available to share your name and location via."

Finally, for a bit of flair, let's replace the Dotnet Bot with an image more fitting to our scenario. In chapter 2, we looked at customizing this bot; you can use a custom bot or any image you choose (that you have the right to use, of course!). For example, you may want to use something that resembles the commonly used location pin icon or a globe (as used in the screenshots in this example—if you want to use this actual image, you can find it in the chapter's resources folder). **Add your image to the Resources/Images folder**, the same way we did in chapter 2, and **update the `Source` property on the `Image` element** in the UI grid to the filename of your new image.

With the UI changes complete, we need to build the logic. When the user clicks on the find me button, we'll call an event handler. This event handler will check that the appropriate permissions have been granted, and will then call a method to share the user's location. This method will get the user's name from the UI, and then get their location from the location API. Finally, it will use the share API to share the user's location. This process is shown in figure 3.7.

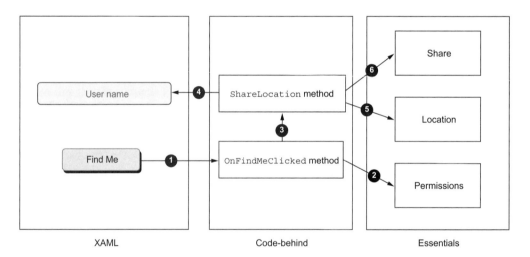

Figure 3.7 When the user clicks the Find Me button, an event is raised, and the `OnFindMeClicked` event handler in the code-behind is triggered (1). This uses the .NET MAUI permissions APIs to verify that the user has granted the app permission to access the location (2). It then calls the `ShareLocation` method (3), which gets the user's name from the `UsernameEntry` field in the UI (4) and the location from the Location API (5) and shares the user's name and location using the Share API (6).

Let's start making the changes to the code-behind file. Open `MainPage.xaml.cs`. When we share our location, we will send someone a link to open our location in Bing Maps. Bing provides a URL format that supports opening a location with latitude and longitude coordinates, so let's add a field to hold the base URL. Add this at the top of the MainPage class:

```
string _baseUrl = "https://bing.com/maps/default.aspx?cp=";
```

We also need a variable to hold the user's name that they provide in the Entry we added to the XAML. Add this property after the _baseURL field:

```
public string UserName { get; set; }
```

Now let's add a method that does the actual work of getting the user's name and sharing their location. Add the following method to the end of the MainPage class.

Listing 3.5 ShareLocation method

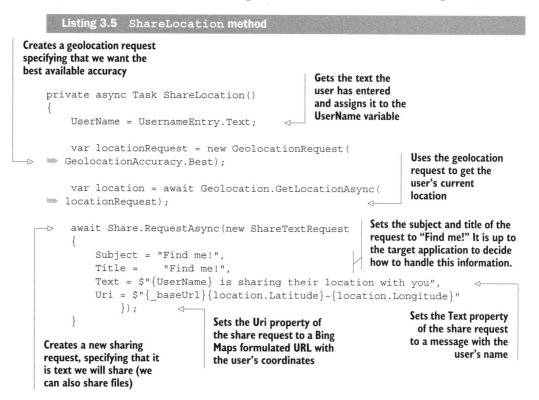

Creates a geolocation request specifying that we want the best available accuracy

Gets the text the user has entered and assigns it to the UserName variable

```
private async Task ShareLocation()
{
    UserName = UsernameEntry.Text;

    var locationRequest = new GeolocationRequest(
        GeolocationAccuracy.Best);

    var location = await Geolocation.GetLocationAsync(
        locationRequest);

    await Share.RequestAsync(new ShareTextRequest
    {
        Subject = "Find me!",
        Title =   "Find me!",
        Text = $"{UserName} is sharing their location with you",
        Uri = $"{_baseUrl}{location.Latitude}~{location.Longitude}"
    });
}
```

Uses the geolocation request to get the user's current location

Sets the subject and title of the request to "Find me!" It is up to the target application to decide how to handle this information.

Sets the Text property of the share request to a message with the user's name

Creates a new sharing request, specifying that it is text we will share (we can also share files)

Sets the Uri property of the share request to a Bing Maps formulated URL with the user's coordinates

Now that we've created the method to share the user's location, we need a way to call it. We've already told the UI to call a method called OnFindMeClicked in the XAML, so let's add it and use it to call the ShareLocation method. We can get rid of the OnCounterClicked method, as we are not using it anymore, and replace it with the OnFindMeClicked method shown in the next listing. You can also delete the count field.

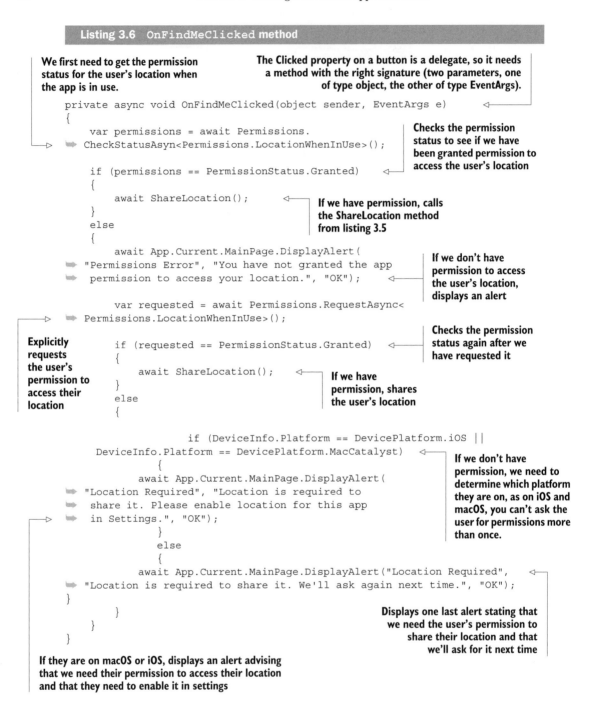

Listing 3.6   OnFindMeClicked method

We first need to get the permission status for the user's location when the app is in use.

The Clicked property on a button is a delegate, so it needs a method with the right signature (two parameters, one of type object, the other of type EventArgs).

```
private async void OnFindMeClicked(object sender, EventArgs e)
{
    var permissions = await Permissions.
    CheckStatusAsyn<Permissions.LocationWhenInUse>();

    if (permissions == PermissionStatus.Granted)
    {
        await ShareLocation();
    }
    else
    {
        await App.Current.MainPage.DisplayAlert(
        "Permissions Error", "You have not granted the app
        permission to access your location.", "OK");

        var requested = await Permissions.RequestAsync<
        Permissions.LocationWhenInUse>();

        if (requested == PermissionStatus.Granted)
        {
            await ShareLocation();
        }
        else
        {

            if (DeviceInfo.Platform == DevicePlatform.iOS ||
            DeviceInfo.Platform == DevicePlatform.MacCatalyst)
            {
                await App.Current.MainPage.DisplayAlert(
                "Location Required", "Location is required to
                share it. Please enable location for this app
                in Settings.", "OK");
            }
            else
            {
                await App.Current.MainPage.DisplayAlert("Location Required",
                "Location is required to share it. We'll ask again next time.", "OK");
            }
        }
    }
}
```

Checks the permission status to see if we have been granted permission to access the user's location

If we have permission, calls the ShareLocation method from listing 3.5

If we don't have permission to access the user's location, displays an alert

Explicitly requests the user's permission to access their location

Checks the permission status again after we have requested it

If we have permission, shares the user's location

If we don't have permission, we need to determine which platform they are on, as on iOS and macOS, you can't ask the user for permissions more than once.

Displays one last alert stating that we need the user's permission to share their location and that we'll ask for it next time

If they are on macOS or iOS, displays an alert advising that we need their permission to access their location and that they need to enable it in settings

We have now finished writing all the code we need for the FindMe app (figure 3.8). Congratulations! Run your app, and have fun sharing your location.

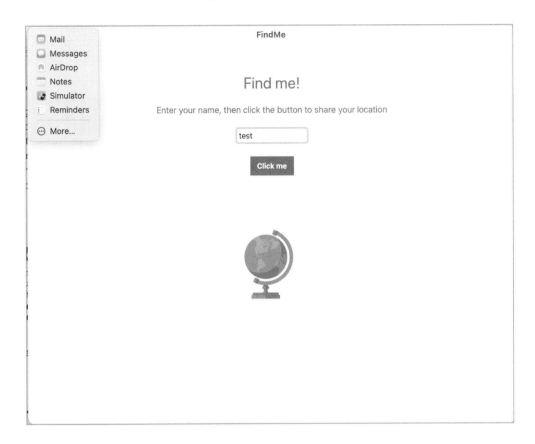

Figure 3.8   The finished FindMe app running on macOS

3.3   Persisting data on your user's device

At the start of the last section, we talked about how to access device and OS features not available to web apps. While this is true, the example we used—accessing a user's location—is something you can do in a web app (although sharing is not currently consistently supported by web browsers). In this section, we explore storing data. You can also do this in a web app, but there are limitations you don't have in .NET MAUI.

Table 3.2 shows that the major distinguishing features of a .NET MAUI app compared to a web app (specifically, a single-page application) is secure storage. Web apps are constrained by the permissions and APIs available to web browsers and cannot store encrypted data in a way that is both secure and reversible. If a web app wants to access encrypted data, it must store the key in the browser's cache, which is susceptible to a number of attacks. Platform executable apps, on the other hand, have full access to all the APIs provided by the OS or platform and are only constrained by the permissions granted to them by the user.

Table 3.2   Comparison of data storage options in web apps and .NET MAUI apps

Storage feature	Web app	.NET MAUI app
Files	A user can open and save files. Filesystem access is inconsistent between browsers and OSs, so access to specific files cannot be guaranteed. The app cannot open a file without the user.	A user can open and save files. Abstractions are provided to common locations, meaning a developer can expect a consistent result across platforms. The app can open a file without a user, so data necessary for the app's operation can be loaded in the background.
Preferences	Can be stored in the browser cache but needs to be serialized to a structured text format like JSON. Can also use the Web Storage API.	A common abstraction is provided to the app configuration location on each platform. Data is stored in key-value pairs.
Encryption	Web apps cannot store encrypted data securely. There are ways to encrypt data in a web app, but if you want your app to also be able to read that data, the app needs to store the key, which would be exposed.	A common abstraction is provided that lets you store data in an encrypted location, with a key that is managed by the OS.
Structured data	Web apps can use the IndexedDB API, an object-oriented database API available in modern web browsers.	The .NET ecosystem makes countless options available, including Entity Framework (EF) Core. Any database engine available in the .NET Standard can be used in a .NET MAUI app.

.NET MAUI provides a feature for this called `SecureStorage`. `SecureStorage` uses key-value pairs, just like `Preferences`; but unlike `Preferences`, a cryptographic key is obtained from the OS to encrypt the value of the stored data. The differences between the two APIs are shown in figure 3.9.

`SecureStorage` uses an abstraction of each platform's underlying encrypted data management API. On macOS and iOS, for example, `SecureStorage` uses the `KeyChain`, while on Android, it uses `Keystore`. The cryptographic key is managed by the OS and is only available to the app, and in most cases it is backed by a hardware encryption chip.

Encryption with .NET MAUI apps

Hardware-based encryption is guaranteed on iOS and macOS, as all macOS and iOS devices ship with a built-in encryption chip. On Android, especially if the device is a tablet or phone, hardware encryption is highly likely but not guaranteed. Most modern Windows laptops have a Trusted Platform Module (TPM) chip that provides hardware encryption, while relatively few desktops do. Windows 11's TPM requirement will likely shift this balance in the future.

This is useful information but not strictly necessary for building apps with .NET MAUI. .NET MAUI provides `SecureStorage` as an abstraction, so whether hardware- or software-based encryption is used, the API you use in your code is the same.

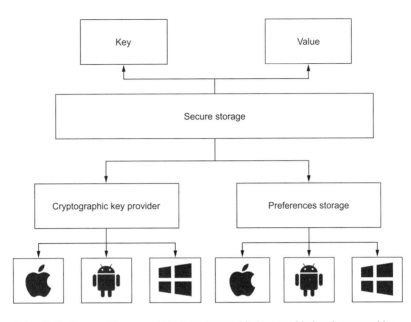

Figure 3.9 `SecureStorage` **uses a cryptographic key provided and managed by the OSes to encrypt the value of an entry stored using the Preferences API.**

While encryption is the clear standout differentiator between web apps and native apps like those built with .NET MAUI, structured data storage is also more versatile in .NET MAUI apps. The `IndexedDB` provided in modern web browsers is powerful, but it is still a collection of key-value pairs, albeit an indexed collection that provides fast search and retrieval. The range of database options available in .NET MAUI apps is significantly broader and more varied, offering object-relational mappers (ORMs), relational databases, and plenty of NoSQL options.

In the remainder of this section, we build MauiTodo, a simple to-do app for creating a list of tasks. We'll use a database to store our to-do items so they are persisted between uses; and because we want to include confidential to-do items, we will encrypt the database and store our to-do items securely. Figure 3.10 shows the high-level architectural design for the MauiTodo app.

In MauiTodo, the app we build in this section, we use *SQLite*, a popular open source database engine. You could use the EF Core SQLite provider, but we use a package called SQLite-net, an implementation of SQLite specifically designed for mobile apps. We'll also add *SQLCipher* to encrypt the contents of our database. SQLCipher will handle the encryption and decryption of the data for us, but we'll use the `SecureStorage` API to let the OS manage the database encryption key.

Start by creating a new .NET MAUI project called MauiTodo using the `blankmaui` template. Next we'll define the data model. We want a class to represent our to-do items, so **add a folder called `Models`, and add to it a new class file called `TodoItem.cs`.** Update your class to look like listing 3.7.

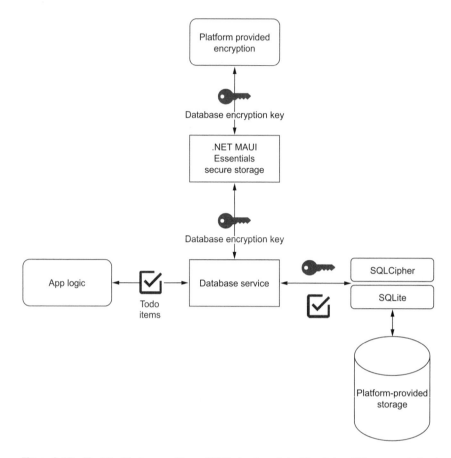

Figure 3.10   The MauiTodo app will use SQLite to store data. The data will be encrypted using SQLCipher. The database encryption key will be a GUID, which itself will be encrypted and stored by the OS and accessed with the .NET MAUI SecureStorage API.

Listing 3.7   TodoItem class

```
using System;

namespace MauiTodo.Models
{
    public class TodoItem
    {
        public int Id { get; set; }

        public string Title { get; set; }

        public DateTime Due { get; set; }

        public bool Done { get; set; } = false;
    }
}
```

We don't need to go through this in detail—you can see that it's a plain-old CLR object (POCO) with some properties that represent a typical to-do item. Now that we've got the model, we want to add the database functionality to store and retrieve our to-do items. As mentioned previously, we'll use SQLite, so **add the `sqlite-net-pcl` and `sqlite-net-sqlcipher` NuGet packages**.

Consuming NuGet packages

One of the things that makes .NET MAUI an awesome tool for .NET developers is having access to the .NET ecosystem. A significant component is the plethora of libraries available as NuGet packages.

Any NuGet package you are familiar with and like using in your code is available for you to use in your .NET MAUI apps, provided it doesn't have a dependency on a specific platform. One example might be the Windows Compatibility Pack and, more broadly, some packages popular with Xamarin.Forms developers that have a Xamarin.Forms dependency. These won't work with your .NET MAUI apps.

If you are coming from Xamarin.Forms, a major advantage of .NET MAUI is the single-project solution. To consume a NuGet package, you need to import it only once, rather than once for your shared project and once for each platform.

On Android, we require an additional NuGet package called `SQLitePCLRaw.provider.dynamic_cdecl`; however, this package will cause unintended side effects on other platforms. We can add the package just for Android using an `MSBuild` condition in our `.csproj` file. **Add the following code to `MauiTodo.csproj`**, just after the `ItemGroup` with the existing package references.

Listing 3.8 Android-specific package references

```
<ItemGroup Condition="$([MSBuild]::GetTargetPlatformIdentifier(
    '$(TargetFramework)')) == 'android'">
  <PackageReference Include="SQLitePCLRaw.provider.dynamic_cdecl"
   Version="2.1.4" />
</ItemGroup>
```

As this is the only time we will use this, we don't need to explore the specifics of how it works. However, you can see that the approach is already applied in the `.csproj` file by the template. If you're curious, you can look up the specifics of `MSBuild` conditions in the documentation at http://mng.bz/x4Z6.

Now that the packages are installed, we need to update the `TodoItem` class to indicate to SQLite that the `Id` property is the primary key and should be auto-incremented by the database. Add the `PrimaryKey` and `AutoIncrement` attributes from the `SQLite` namespace to the `Id` property:

```
[PrimaryKey, AutoIncrement]
public int Id { get; set; }
```

Create a folder called `Data`, and in this folder, **create a new class file, `Database.cs`.** In this class, we're going to add methods for adding, retrieving, and deleting to-do items from a SQLite database with a data file in a special location for storing user data. The location is different on each platform, but we'll use an abstraction in .NET MAUI to set the path automatically. We'll also initialize the database with an encryption key, which will be a GUID, and we'll encrypt and securely store the GUID with `SecureStorage`.

SQLite needs a connection string to connect to a database. In our case, this will include the path to the data file we are working with directly and will also define how `DateTime` values will be stored. As we are using SQLCipher, we will also provide the key used to encrypt and decrypt the database. SQLite-net includes helper methods that generate this connection string for us based on values we provide, and SQLCipher has additional extension methods covering the encryption key, shown in figure 3.11.

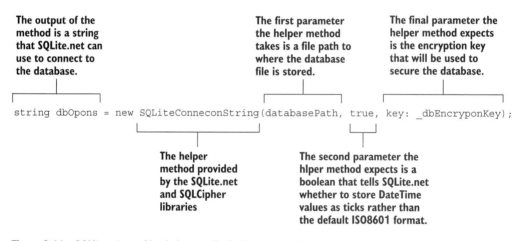

Figure 3.11 SQLite-net provides helper methods for constructing connection strings. SQLCipher provides additional extensions that enable the construction of connection strings that include encryption keys.

SQLite includes a lightweight ORM that allows us to interact with the database using POCOs rather than having to write SQL statements every time we want to write data to or retrieve data from the database. We can also use those POCOs as our table definitions (figure 3.12).

We've defined a model in our to-do app using a C# type that represents our to-do items, and we'll let SQLite generate tables for us using this definition. We want to be confident that our table has been created in the database before we start reading from or writing to it.

While we need our table before we can start using it, we don't need to block our app from continuing to run while the table is being set up. Fortunately, the method provided by SQLite-net for creating the table is asynchronous, but as we can't have async constructors, we'll wrap the call that creates the table in its own async method.

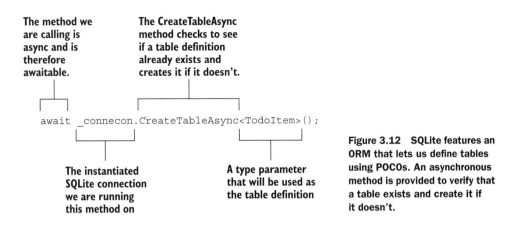

Figure 3.12 SQLite features an ORM that lets us define tables using POCOs. An asynchronous method is provided to verify that a table exists and create it if it doesn't.

We can then call this method from our constructor using a discard (_), which will run the method in a thread without blocking the UI.

Async/await in .NET MAUI apps

As a UI developer, it's important to ensure that long-running (or possibly failing) operations don't lock up the app. This is a poor user experience, and you will lose users. As a .NET developer, you may already be familiar with async/await and asynchronous programming.

In either case, it's well worth spending some time learning how these patterns are best applied in UI development. Throughout the book, we'll see more examples, and I'll call out specific patterns, tips, or traps as we encounter them. If you want to learn more, plenty of excellent resources are available online (especially from Brandon Minnick and Brian Lagunas). You can find these by searching for their names along with *async* or *await* as keywords. Another excellent resource is SSW Rules, a free resource provided by my employer, which you can also find easily by searching.

Once our table is created, we can continue to use POCOs and the ORM to interact with it. Adding items is as simple as calling `_connection.InsertAsync(item)`; the ORM is smart enough to infer the table we want to insert `item` into based on its type. Querying a table for entries is simple, too, using a language integrated query (LINQ) and a lambda expression (see the sidebar "LINQ and lambda expressions"). The full code for the `Database.cs` file is in the following listing.

Listing 3.9 Database class

```
using MauiTodo.Models;
using SQLite;

namespace MauiTodo.Data
{
    public class Database
```

Queries SecureStorage for a value with a key of "dbKey". In this case, "key" refers to the identifier of this securely stored item (as in key-value pair), and not the cryptographic key used to secure it. As the SecureStorage API is async only, we need to call .Result because we can't wait for the call in the class constructor.

```
    {
        private readonly SQLiteAsyncConnection _connection;

        public Database()
        {
            var dataDir = FileSystem.AppDataDirectory;
            var databasePath = Path.Combine(dataDir, "MauiTodo.db");

            string _dbEncryptionKey = SecureStorage.
GetAsync("dbKey").Result;

            if (string.IsNullOrEmpty(_dbEncryptionKey))
            {
                Guid g = new Guid();
                _dbEncryptionKey = g.ToString();
                SecureStorage.SetAsync("dbKey", _dbEncryptionKey);
            }

            var dbOptions = new SQLiteConnectionString(
databasePath, true, key: _dbEncryptionKey);

            _connection = new SQLiteAsyncConnection(dbOptions);

            _ = Initialise();
        }

        private async Task Initialise()
        {
            await _connection.CreateTableAsync<TodoItem>();
        }

        public async Task<List<TodoItem>> GetTodos()
        {
            return await _connection.Table<TodoItem>().ToListAsync();
        }
```

The Filesystem.AppData-Directory helper returns the application data path for the platform the app is running on.

Creates a new GUID if the database encryption key is empty

As no encryption key was returned from SecureStorage, sets the value to the new GUID

Sets a read-only field to hold the async database connection

Using the ORM, we can use a type parameter to request a table with a design matching the specified type. We await the result and cast it to a List.

SQLite-net includes a lightweight ORM, so we can initialize a table based on a model. The CreateTableAsync method takes a type parameter that serves as the model for the table and then creates a table based on that model if one does not exist already.

Uses a helper method from SQLite-net to create a connection string for the database datafile. This helper method takes a path, a Boolean that determines whether DateTime values are stored as ticks, and an encryption key used to encrypt and decrypt the database.

"Throw away" call to an async method. We need to return a constructed class with an initialized connection, but we don't need to wait for the database engine to initialize the tables.

```
public async Task<TodoItem> GetTodo(int id)
{
    var query = _connection.Table<TodoItem>().
Where(t => t.Id == id);

    return await query.FirstOrDefaultAsync();
}

public async Task<int> AddTodo(TodoItem item)
{
    return await _connection.InsertAsync(item);
}

public async Task<int> DeleteTodo(TodoItem item)
{
    return await _connection.DeleteAsync(item);
}

public async Task<int> UpdateTodo(TodoItem item)
{
    return await _connection.UpdateAsync(item);
}
    }
}
```

Uses a LINQ lambda expression to create a query definition, using a type to represent a table design

Awaits the query's result, casts it to the specified type, and returns this awaitable call

The ORM has an InsertAsync method that is smart enough to determine which table to insert the provided parameter into based on the type of the provided parameter

We have a database in our app that can securely store our secret to-do items and provides methods to store and retrieve to-do items. The next step is to build a UI to display and enter to-do items and code to connect that UI to the database.

LINQ and lambda expressions

As .NET MAUI apps are .NET apps, we can use everything in the C# toolbox. You're likely already familiar with LINQ, especially if you work with EF Core, but if not, it's worth investing some time to learn about it (you can start with the Microsoft documentation), as it's useful in several scenarios. These scenarios are not just related to databases; LINQ also works with collections, and collections are at the heart of nearly all apps.

Lambda expressions let you declare an anonymous function. This means you can tell your code to go execute some other code and return the result without having to declare that other code as a method. Lambda expressions are incredibly powerful when used with LINQ but are also useful for a range of scenarios. I also encourage you to read the Microsoft documentation on lambda expressions if they are not something you are familiar with.

As you can see, any .NET skills are transferrable to .NET MAUI apps. If you're a .NET developer, you're a .NET MAUI developer!

In the `MainPage.xaml` file, we will make some changes to the UI. We'll update the page title and add a text entry where the user can specify the title for new to-do items and a date picker for the due date. We need a button to confirm adding new to-do items, and finally, we want a way to display a list of the to-do items stored in the database.

We will add these ourselves rather than modifying the existing controls. **In the XAML, delete the `ScrollView` and everything inside it**. This should leave you with the `<ContentPage...>`...`</ContentPage>` tags. The `ScrollView` that we removed is a layout, and we're going to replace it with a different kind of layout called a `Grid`. We'll learn more about layouts in chapter 4; for now, **add an opening and closing `Grid` tag with the following properties and child elements.**

Listing 3.10   UI for the MauiTodo app

```
<Grid RowDefinitions="1*, 1*, 1*, 1*, 8*"          ⟵  Adds a grid layout
      MaximumWidthRequest="400"                          with five rows
      Padding="20">

        <Label Grid.Row="0"                    ⟵  Adds a label with
               Text="Maui Todo"                     the page title
               SemanticProperties.HeadingLevel="Level1"
               SemanticProperties.Description="Maui Todo"
               HorizontalTextAlignment="Center"
               FontSize="Title"/>
                                               Adds an entry where the
        <Entry Grid.Row="1"              ⟵    user can enter the title of
               HorizontalOptions="Center"      a new to-do item
               Placeholder="Enter a title"
               SemanticProperties.Hint="Title of the new todo item"
               WidthRequest="300"
               x:Name="TodoTitleEntry" />
                                               Adds a date picker. A date picker shows
                                               the native platform's standard control
        <DatePicker Grid.Row="2"          ⟵   for choosing a date and returns the
               WidthRequest="300"              selected value as a DateTime type.
               HorizontalOptions="Center"
               SemanticProperties.Hint="Date the todo item is due"
               x:Name="DueDatepicker" />

        <Button Grid.Row="3"
                Text="Add"
                SemanticProperties.Hint="Adds the todo item to the database"
                WidthRequest="100"
                HeightRequest="50"           Adds a ScrollView inside the grid on the
                HorizontalOptions="Center"   fifth row (row 4). We want a ScrollView
                Clicked="Button_Clicked"/>   because we will fill it with the to-do
                                             items that the user adds, which may
        <ScrollView Grid.Row="4">      ⟵    extend beyond the page.
            <Label HorizontalTextAlignment="Center"
                   SemanticProperties.Description="The list of todo items
 in the database"
                   x:Name="TodosLabel" />    ⟵  Adds a label that
        </ScrollView>                            will show the list
                                                 of to-do items the
    </Grid>                                      user has added
```

Adds a button that the user can click to add a new to-do item

We've now defined a simple UI for entering and listing the user's to-do items. All the controls in this UI are familiar except the new DatePicker. A DatePicker allows the user to choose a date with a graphical selector rather than entering it into a text field.

Let's add code to the code-behind to wire up some functionality:

- We'll add properties and fields that hold an instance of the database, the values of to-dos in the database, and any values the user wants to add to a new to-do item.
- We'll update the class constructor and add a method to initialize our page on load.
- We'll add a method to respond to button clicks and add a new to-do to the database.

Update your code-behind file (`MainPage.xaml.cs`) as shown next.

Listing 3.11   Code for the MauiTodo main page

```
using MauiTodo.Data;
using MauiTodo.Models;

namespace MauiTodo;

public partial class MainPage : ContentPage
{
    string _todoListData = string.Empty;          // Contains the values of
                                                   // the to-do items that
                                                   // we want to display
                                                   // onscreen

    readonly Database _database;                   // Stores an
                                                   // instance of our
                                                   // database class
    public MainPage()
    {
        InitializeComponent();
        _database = new Database();                // In the constructor, we create an
                                                   // instance of the database class and
        _ = Initialize();                          // assign it to the _database field.
    }
        // Uses the discard variable to call our Initialize method

    private async Task Initialize()
    {
        var todos = await _database.GetTodos();    // Gets the list of to-do
                                                   // items in the database

        foreach (var todo in todos)
        {
            _todoListData += $"{todo.Title} - {todo.
Due:f}{Environment.NewLine}";                      // Adds the title and date of
        }                                          // each to-do item (using the
                                                   // :f syntax to format it to a
        TodosLabel.Text = _todoListData;           // culture-formatted string)
    }                                              // and a new line to the
        // Assigns the value of the _todoListData  // _todoListData field
        // field to the text property of the
        // TodosLabel in the UI
```

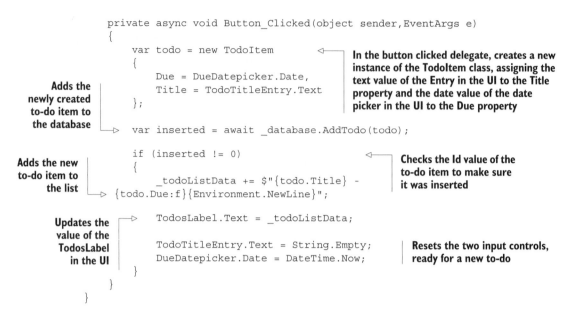

```
private async void Button_Clicked(object sender, EventArgs e)
{
    var todo = new TodoItem
    {
        Due = DueDatepicker.Date,
        Title = TodoTitleEntry.Text
    };

    var inserted = await _database.AddTodo(todo);

    if (inserted != 0)
    {
        _todoListData += $"{todo.Title} -
{todo.Due:f}{Environment.NewLine}";

        TodosLabel.Text = _todoListData;

        TodoTitleEntry.Text = String.Empty;
        DueDatepicker.Date = DateTime.Now;
    }
}
}
```

In the button clicked delegate, creates a new instance of the TodoItem class, assigning the text value of the Entry in the UI to the Title property and the date value of the date picker in the UI to the Due property

Adds the newly created to-do item to the database

Adds the new to-do item to the list

Checks the Id value of the to-do item to make sure it was inserted

Updates the value of the TodosLabel in the UI

Resets the two input controls, ready for a new to-do

This completes our MauiTodo app for now. Run the app, and you should see something that looks like figure 3.13. You can add multiple to-do items, give them all different due dates, and see them appear in the list at the bottom of the screen.

Figure 3.13   MauiToDo running on Windows. When you click the Add button, an event handler gets the values from the `Entry` and `DatePicker` and uses them to create a new to-do item with those values for the title and due date, respectively. It then adds them to the list of to-do items on the screen.

3.4 *Data binding: Connecting the UI to the code*

So far, we've been using our code-behind to get values from and assign values to properties of the UI element. By including the `http://schemas.microsoft.com/winfx/2009/xaml` schema in our XAML file, we can use `x:...` to assign names to our UI elements (such as `x:Name="TodoTitleEntry"`) and reference those UI elements by their assigned name in code. This lets us use `TodoTitleEntry.Text` to read the value of the text property of the UI element called `TodoTitleEntry`.

XAML is a markup language, but the UI elements we use in XAML are still classes. When we add an `<Entry... />` to our view, at runtime, our view (also as a class) instantiates an object of type `Entry`. If you examine the properties of the `Entry` class, you will see that it has a property called `Text` of type `string`, where we get the value the user entered.

On its own, the ability to access properties of XAML elements in code is powerful and gives us a neat way of getting and setting values from the UI. But a better way is to use *data binding*. Data binding lets us bind a property to another property, meaning that when one changes, so does the other (figure 3.14).

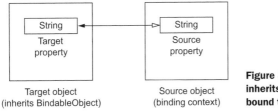

Figure 3.14   **A property on a class that inherits from `BindableObject` can be bound to a property of the same type.**

Data binding connects a source property and a target property (figure 3.15). The target property must belong to an object that inherits the `BindableObject` base class (all the built-in UI controls in .NET MAUI inherit `BindableObject`). The target property is bound to the source, so the target is where the binding is set. The source property can belong to an object of any type but must match the target property type. If the target and source properties are not the same type, a value converter can be used—we'll learn more about value converters later, in chapter 8.

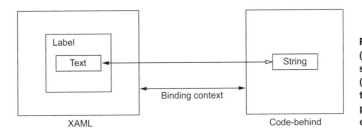

Figure 3.15   **Each view (target object) can have a single binding context (source object). Properties of the target view are bound to properties of the same type on the source object.**

Each view can have a single *binding context*, which is the source object. Once the binding is set, properties on that view (target) can be bound to the source's properties by referencing the property name. Individual properties of the control can still be bound arbitrarily to any property of any other object, but this requires explicit referencing, and setting the binding context for a control means any of the control properties can bind to any of the source properties by just using the property name.

Controls vs. views

Sometimes it may seem like the terms *view* and *control* are used interchangeably. In some circumstances, they can be; but for the sake of disambiguation, remember that views come in three categories—pages, layouts, and controls:

- *Page*—A special kind of view that (usually) fills the whole screen and can be navigated. A `Page` contains one child layout, which can in turn contain multiple other layouts.
- *Layout*—A view used to arrange items onscreen. Examples of layouts we've seen are `ScrollView` (technically a control, but it behaves like a layout) and `Grid`.
- *Control*—A view that explicitly either displays something onscreen or receives user input. A `Label` is a control, as is an `Entry`.

The binding context is inherited and cascades from parent to child components in a view. Binding contexts can be explicitly defined for any view, but if you don't explicitly define a binding context for a control in a `ContentPage`, the binding context will be the same as that of the `ContentPage`. For example, if you add a layout or collection to a `ContentPage`, the layout inherits the `ContentPage`'s binding context, as will any of its child controls. If you explicitly set the binding context of the layout or collection, child controls inherit that, instead.

In figure 3.16, the binding context for a page has been set to the page's code-behind. The `Title` and `Button` inherit this binding context and bind to properties on the `ContentPage` code-behind. The binding context for the `VerticalStackLayout` has been set to an object property in the code-behind. The `Subtitle` and `Button` inside this layout inherit this binding context and bind to properties on the `Object`. Understanding binding contexts is important, so we'll look at them in more detail later in this section.

Views can also be bound to other views. For example, both `Label` and `Entry` have a property called `Text` of type `string`, so these properties can be bound (figure 3.17). By binding these two properties, you can have one automatically update the other.

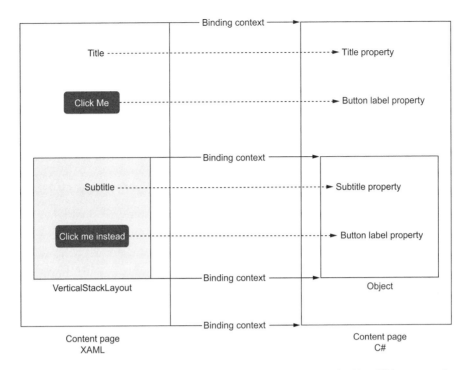

Figure 3.16 The binding context can be set at any level and is inherited by child components from that point down.

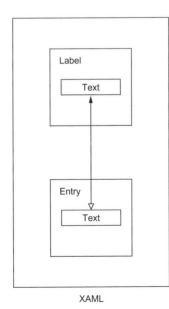

Figure 3.17 Properties of views can be bound to properties of other views.

3.4.1   *View-to-view bindings*

View-to-view bindings can be set in XAML and enable you to bind properties in a view without any intervention in the code-behind. **Create a new .NET MAUI project called Bindings**, and in `MainPage.xaml`, delete the `ScrollView` and its contents. Add the following code to replace the `ScrollView` (place it within the `ContentPage` containing tags).

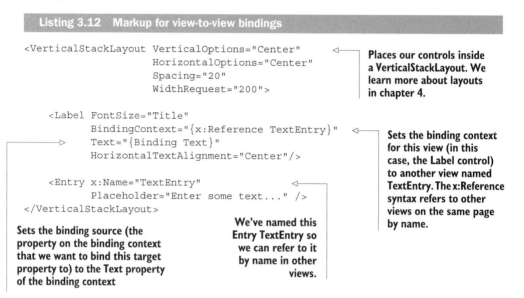

```
Listing 3.12   Markup for view-to-view bindings
```

```
<VerticalStackLayout VerticalOptions="Center"          ◁─────  Places our controls inside
                     HorizontalOptions="Center"                a VerticalStackLayout. We
                     Spacing="20"                              learn more about layouts
                     WidthRequest="200">                       in chapter 4.

    <Label FontSize="Title"
           BindingContext="{x:Reference TextEntry}"    ◁───   Sets the binding context
    ┌────▷ Text="{Binding Text}"                              for this view (in this
    │      HorizontalTextAlignment="Center"/>                 case, the Label control)
    │                                                         to another view named
    │  <Entry x:Name="TextEntry"             ◁─────────────   TextEntry. The x:Reference
    │         Placeholder="Enter some text..." />             syntax refers to other
    │ </VerticalStackLayout>                                  views on the same page
    │                                                         by name.
    │
  Sets the binding source (the         We've named this
  property on the binding context      Entry TextEntry so
  that we want to bind this target     we can refer to it
  property to) to the Text property    by name in other
  of the binding context              views.
```

Before running this project, **delete the `count` field and the `OnCounterClicked` method from the code-behind.** Then run your project and start typing some text in the `Entry`. You should see something like figure 3.18 (depending which platform you are running on).

The quick br

The quick br

Figure 3.18   The `Text` property of a `Label` bound to the `Text` property of an `Entry`. When the value of `Text` on the `Entry` changes, the `Label` changes automatically.

Note how as you type, the text of the label changes. In previous examples, we've used the code-behind to get properties from UI controls and then set properties on other controls. With data binding, we point one property at the other, and the rest is taken care of for us.

View-to-view binding is useful when you have properties of the same type on two interrelated views. In this example, we update a `Label` with the text entered in an `Entry`. Similar behavior that you may have seen in a real-world app is updating numbers on a mock-up of a credit card as a user enters them. Another useful real-world example you may be familiar with is changing the zoom level on an image or map in response to a slider. Let's go ahead and add this functionality to our Bindings app.

In the app's `MainPage.xaml` file, add the two controls from the next listing under the `Entry` in the `VerticalStackLayout`.

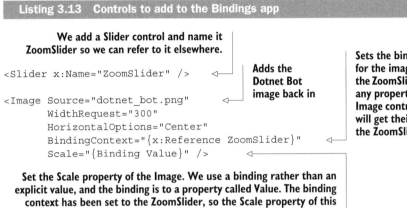

Listing 3.13 Controls to add to the Bindings app

We add a Slider control and name it ZoomSlider so we can refer to it elsewhere.

```
<Slider x:Name="ZoomSlider" />

<Image Source="dotnet_bot.png"
       WidthRequest="300"
       HorizontalOptions="Center"
       BindingContext="{x:Reference ZoomSlider}"
       Scale="{Binding Value}" />
```

Adds the Dotnet Bot image back in

Sets the binding context for the image control to the ZoomSlider. This means any properties on the Image control that we bind will get their values from the ZoomSlider object.

Set the Scale property of the Image. We use a binding rather than an explicit value, and the binding is to a property called Value. The binding context has been set to the ZoomSlider, so the Scale property of this Image is bound to ZoomSlider.Value.

Run the Bindings app, and you should see something similar to figure 3.19.

Figure 3.19 The Bindings app with the `Scale` property of an `Image` bound to the `Value` property of a `Slider`

Try moving the `Slider` back and forth—you should see the scale of the image respond in real time. We've used data binding to bind the `Scale` property of the `Image` to the `Value` property of the `Slider`. When `Value` changes on the `Slider`, `Scale` changes on the `Image`.

We could have done this without data binding, but the process would have been much more convoluted. We would have to create a method to be called by the `Value-Changed` event of the `Slider` and, with each change in value, set the `Scale` property of the `Image`.

3.4.2 *Collections and bindings in code*

Data binding is an incredibly powerful feature of .NET MAUI, and it does much more than just remove boilerplate code. It opens a range of possibilities that we wouldn't have without it.

One of the most powerful uses of data binding is setting a binding source for a `CollectionView`, which is a property called `ItemsSource`. A `CollectionView` displays a collection of items, such as a `List<T>`, onscreen. Collections or lists are the core of many apps, and with .NET MAUI, you can use data binding to define how you want each individual item in the collection to be displayed.

The most powerful feature of `CollectionView` is the use of a `DataTemplate`. A `DataTemplate` is the definition of how to display things onscreen. In our current example, we are using a `Label` that can only be used to display text. With a `Data-Template`, you can define any layout you can imagine and bind aspects of that layout to properties on your binding context.

While a `DataTemplate` defines how to display an item onscreen, an `ItemTemplate` is the specific `DataTemplate` in use for the `CollectionView`. `ItemTemplate` is a property of a `CollectionView`, and a `DataTemplate` is assigned to it. `DataTemplates` can be defined inline (as we will do in the following example) but can also be independent, reusable views. We see how to do this later in the book.

Rather than inherit the entire collection that the `CollectionView` is bound to, the binding context for an `ItemTemplate` is the item itself. This means for a collection of objects with a string property called `Name`, you can set the binding for the `Text` property of a `Label` in the `ItemTemplate` to `Name`, and it will display the desired value.

Looking back at our MauiTodo app, we can significantly improve how we display our to-do items. At the moment, we have a `Label` that displays the title of every to-do item in our database, separated with a newline character. This is primitive and fairly limited; for example, we cannot display the due date or format different items based on their properties (overdue, completed, etc.).

We'll update our app to use a `CollectionView`. This will let us define a specific layout for presenting each item in the to-do list, and we'll bind the `CollectionView` in code to an `ObservableCollection` of `TodoItems`. An `ObservableCollection` is a generic collection like a `List`, except it is automatically wired up through the XAML engine to provide a notification when items are added or removed without us having to do any extra steps in the code. This will automatically update the CollectionView in the UI if we add or remove to-do items.

Let's start with the UI. **In the MainPage.xaml file, delete the ScrollView on row 4 of the Grid and its contents, and replace it with this CollectionView.**

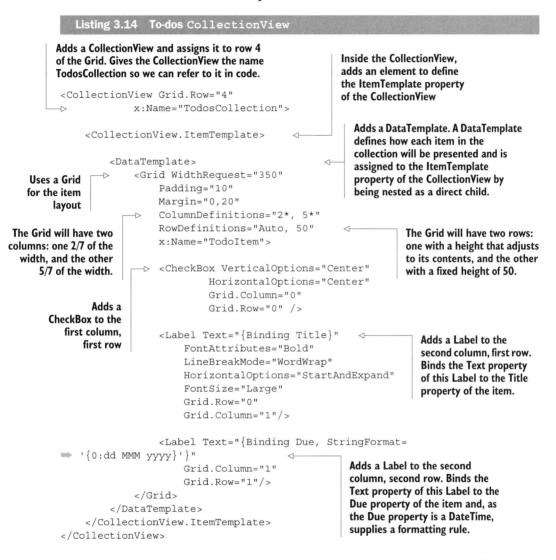

Listing 3.14   To-dos CollectionView

Adds a CollectionView and assigns it to row 4 of the Grid. Gives the CollectionView the name TodosCollection so we can refer to it in code.

Inside the CollectionView, adds an element to define the ItemTemplate property of the CollectionView

```
<CollectionView Grid.Row="4"
                x:Name="TodosCollection">

    <CollectionView.ItemTemplate>

        <DataTemplate>
            <Grid WidthRequest="350"
                Padding="10"
                Margin="0,20"
                ColumnDefinitions="2*, 5*"
                RowDefinitions="Auto, 50"
                x:Name="TodoItem">

                <CheckBox VerticalOptions="Center"
                        HorizontalOptions="Center"
                        Grid.Column="0"
                        Grid.Row="0" />

                <Label Text="{Binding Title}"
                    FontAttributes="Bold"
                    LineBreakMode="WordWrap"
                    HorizontalOptions="StartAndExpand"
                    FontSize="Large"
                    Grid.Row="0"
                    Grid.Column="1"/>

                <Label Text="{Binding Due, StringFormat=
'{0:dd MMM yyyy}'}"
                    Grid.Column="1"
                    Grid.Row="1"/>
            </Grid>
        </DataTemplate>
    </CollectionView.ItemTemplate>
</CollectionView>
```

Adds a DataTemplate. A DataTemplate defines how each item in the collection will be presented and is assigned to the ItemTemplate property of the CollectionView by being nested as a direct child.

Uses a Grid for the item layout

The Grid will have two columns: one 2/7 of the width, and the other 5/7 of the width.

The Grid will have two rows: one with a height that adjusts to its contents, and the other with a fixed height of 50.

Adds a CheckBox to the first column, first row

Adds a Label to the second column, first row. Binds the Text property of this Label to the Title property of the item.

Adds a Label to the second column, second row. Binds the Text property of this Label to the Due property of the item and, as the Due property is a DateTime, supplies a formatting rule.

As you can see, we've added a CollectionView and provided a definition of how each item in the collection should be displayed, but we haven't bound it to a collection. We'll do this now in the code. **Open the MainPage.xaml.cs file**, and at the very top of the class (before the private member definitions), **add an ObservableCollection of TodoItems**:

```
public ObservableCollection<TodoItem> Todos { get; set; } = new();
```

ObservableCollection is in the System.Collections.ObjectModel namespace, so **add the required using statement at the top of the file**. Then, in the constructor, **set the ItemsSource property** of the CollectionView to the ObservableCollection:

```
TodosCollection.ItemsSource = Todos;
```

Now we need to get rid of the code we're not using anymore. Delete the private _todoListData string and every line that references it: the assignment to it in the foreach loop in the Initialise method, assigning the value to the Label in the Initialise method, adding to it in the Button_Clicked method, and assigning it to the Label in the Button_Clicked method.

Next we'll add some logic back in to handle initializing the collection and updating it when a user adds a new to-do item. Let's start with initializing. In the foreach loop in the Initialise method, **add the to-do item in the loop to the Observable-Collection**:

```
Todos.Add(todo);
```

Finally, **add the same logic in the Button_Clicked method in the if statement**, where previously we added the item to the string:

```
Todos.Add(todo);
```

Those are all the changes we need for now. To recap, we have added a Collection-View to the UI and defined a data template that specifies how items in the Collection-View should be displayed. We've added an ObservableCollection—a special type of collection that sends notifications when its content changes—to the code-behind and bound it as the source of the items the CollectionView will display. And we've added some code to add to-do items to the CollectionView when the page initializes and when a user adds a new to-do item.

Run the app and add some to-do items. You should see something like figure 3.20.

3.4.3   *ItemsSource bindings in XAML*

Using code to set binding contexts is powerful, but given that data binding is what gives XAML its superpowers, we should also look at how to set the ItemsSource for our CollectionView in XAML. We can set the binding context for any view directly in XAML, as we saw in section 3.4.2 when we set the binding context of one control to the properties of another. Let's refactor the MauiTodo app to do all the binding in the XAML.

Open the MainPage.xaml.cs code-behind file, and in the constructor, **remove the line we added in the previous section to set the items source**:

```
TodosCollection.ItemsSource = Todos;
```

Instead, we'll set up this binding in the XAML. **Open the MainPage.xaml file**, and in the <ContentPage...> opening tag, **add a name (so that it can be referenced) and a**

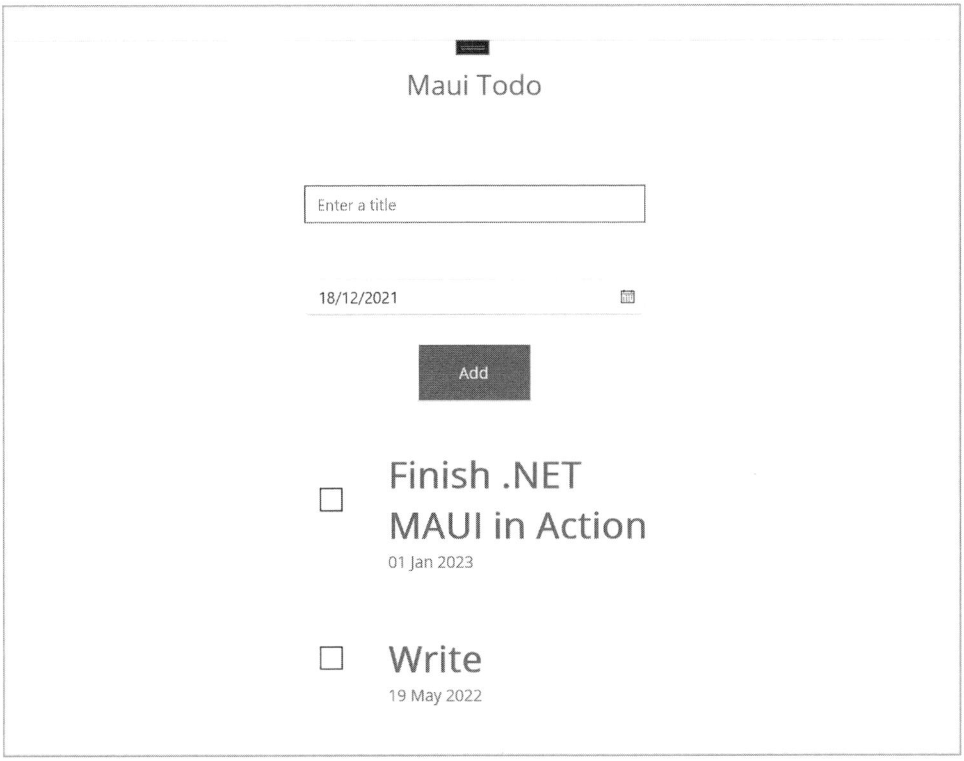

Figure 3.20 MauiTodo with a `CollectionView` running on Windows

binding context. Then, in the `CollectionView`, **bind the `ItemsSource` property to the Todos `ObservableCollection`** in the binding context. The following listing shows the new opening `ContentPage` tag and the new opening `CollectionView` tag, with the added lines in bold.

Listing 3.15 MainPage.xaml `ContentPage` tag changes

```
<ContentPage xmlns="http://schemas.microsoft.com/dotnet/2021/maui"
             xmlns:x="http://schemas.microsoft.com/winfx/2009/xaml"
             x:Class="MauiTodo.MainPage"
             BackgroundColor="{DynamicResource SecondaryColor}"
             x:Name="PageTodo"
             BindingContext="{x:Reference PageTodo}">

    ...

<CollectionView Grid.Row="4"
                ItemsSource="{Binding Todos}"
                x:Name="TodosCollection">
```

Uses the Name attribute from the XAML namespace (aliased to x) to specify a name for the page

Sets the binding context for the page. Use the name you created for the page as a reference, setting the binding context for the page to itself.

Binds the ItemsSource property of the CollectionView to the Todos property of the binding context

Run the app again. It should run without any problems, and you should see the same result (similar to figure 3.19). While there is no visible change to the UI, the improvement to the code is significant. Previously, we had the binding for the `ItemsSource` property of the `CollectionView` set in code and all other bindings set in XAML. Now the XAML is responsible for setting all the bindings. This will become even more important when we learn about the MVVM pattern in chapter 9 and see how this approach can help us to maintain a clean separation of concerns in our code.

Summary

- You can access common cross-platform device and OS features using the .NET MAUI APIs. They give you access to things like location, sharing, storage, and much more.

- You must request permission from the user before accessing any privacy-sensitive features, such as location, and you can request these permissions at runtime. In the app metadata, defined in a file specific to each platform, you declare which permissions you will request and, for Android, what features you will use.

- As part of .NET, MAUI gives you access to the entire NuGet ecosystem. This means you can use your existing .NET skills and use the packages you are already familiar with to build .NET MAUI apps.

- You can store data locally for use offline, which elevates your .NET MAUI app beyond a web page. You can persist key-value pairs with `Preferences` API, and can also save encrypted key-value pairs with the `SecureStorage` API.

- You can save more complex data than key-value pairs, including images, videos, or sound recordings, using the file system. When you pair this with NuGet, you can use a database like SQLite to store and retrieve complex data structures and work completely offline.

- You can use code to retrieve values from and set values to elements in the UI. But with data binding, you simply connect properties between UI elements and other UI elements or between UI elements and code. Once bound, changes in the source property are automatically reflected in the target.

- You represent lists of complex models onscreen using a `CollectionView`. A `CollectionView` has a property called `ItemsSource` that can be bound to a `List` of items using data binding. `CollectionView` also has a property called `ItemTemplate`, and you assign it a `DataTemplate` that defines how each item in the collection should be displayed.

Part 2

Views, layouts, and controls

In this part, we'll dive into the building blocks of .NET MAUI apps. We'll see how apps are constructed of pages, layouts, and controls.

Pages are the building blocks of an app. We'll see the different ways that .NET MAUI lets you display them to your users, as well as the ways that users can navigate between the different parts of the app.

Controls are at the heart of what .NET MAUI is—an abstraction of controls provided by the target platforms. We'll see how we can do things like display images, text, and collections of data and how to get input from the user.

One of the most important aspects of any UI is layout, and in this part, we'll see how we can use the layouts that .NET MAUI provides to arrange our controls to build any UI, including a familiar one you may already know.

Controls

This chapter covers

- What is meant by the broad term *view*
- Built-in cross-platform controls that are abstracted for use in .NET MAUI apps
- Displaying collections or lists of data using templated views
- Using common modifiers to change the appearance of views
- Adding views and updating their functionality

Controls are views that either directly render something onscreen (like an Image or a Label) or take input from a user (like a CheckBox or DatePicker). Roughly 30 controls ship with .NET MAUI out of the box, covering all the common use cases for UI applications. We've already used several of them in our apps and seen how they work, such as Image, Label, and Entry.

In addition, the .NET MAUI Community Toolkit and free and commercial UI kits provide a range of additional controls and stylized or customizable versions of the built-in controls. And, of course, you can build your own controls, as we see in chapter 11.

You can find a link to the .NET MAUI documentation in the "Other Online Resources" section at the start of the book; it provides comprehensive coverage for these controls, including their properties, events, and commands. I'm not going to repeat the documentation here; instead, I've broken the controls down into categories (grouped roughly the same as in the docs) and will provide a summary of each control, explaining its use case, primary data type, and corresponding property name. Throughout the book, and as we've already seen, you'll learn how to use these controls in situ rather than by rote.

The documentation is an excellent source for the minutiae of each control's individual properties, and if you're using Visual Studio, IntelliSense is also an invaluable tool. Simply dropping a control onto your page or layout using XAML or C# immediately opens all the control's properties for you to explore.

While I won't cover all the details of every control here, some properties are common across all controls. Additionally, there are supplementary controls that I call *control modifiers* that can be applied to any control. This chapter goes through the shared properties and control modifiers you're likely to find most useful in your .NET MAUI apps.

4.1   *What do we mean by "views"?*

Views in a UI are the things displayed onscreen. Unlike other parts of an app (a service, for example), views are what your users see and interact with.

In a .NET MAUI app, there are three types of view: *controls*, *layouts*, and *pages*. In the hierarchy of a .NET MAUI app, a page is something the app itself can display, as shown in figure 4.1.

A .NET MAUI app doesn't know how to directly render a layout or a control, but it does know how to display a page on the screen. A page in turn knows how to render a layout, and layouts know how to render controls, as shown in figure 4.2.

Important note on terms

In the official .NET MAUI documentation, *control* is used as an umbrella term for everything you see onscreen, including pages, layouts, and interactive and display elements like buttons and images, while *view* is used to describe those elements.

To make the concept easier to understand, I have switched these around here and used the industry's commonly used definitions: *view* for the umbrella term and *controls* for the interactive and display elements (the definition of *pages* remains the same).

It's important to know the official terms, especially when referring to the documentation, and I normally use them in this book. However, I made an exception here as I feel the concepts are easier to understand using the standard terms, especially when we discuss the MVVM pattern later in the book.

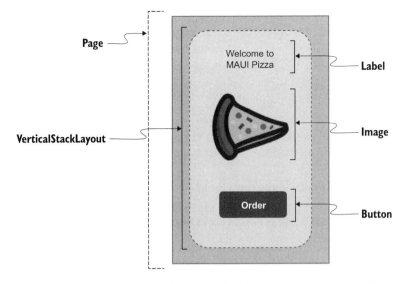

Figure 4.1   Everything onscreen in a UI app is a view and must be contained within a page (which, being onscreen, is also a view). A page takes up the full screen or window and can be navigated to or instantiated. In .NET MAUI, a page can only contain one child: in this case, a `VerticalStackLayout`**, which displays its child items vertically. Layouts can contain an arbitrary number of child items, which can be controls, like** `Button`**s or** `Label`**s, or other layouts, like** `Grid`**s or** `HorizontalStackLayout`**s.**

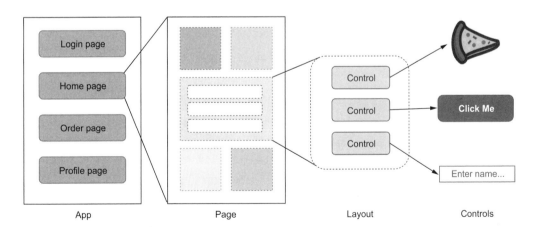

Figure 4.2   An app knows how to render pages, and pages know how to display a single layout. Layouts define how to arrange controls or other layouts on the screen. In this example, an app renders a home page with a `Grid` **layout as a child. The** `Grid` **layout here has five child items, including a** `VerticalStack-Layout` **in the middle. The** `VerticalStackLayout` **has three controls as child items: an** `Image`**, a** `Button`**, and an** `Entry`**.**

In this chapter, we look specifically at controls. We look at layouts and pages in the coming chapters.

4.2   *Cross-platform controls*

Out of the box, .NET MAUI provides a collection of controls that cover a broad spectrum of use cases for mobile and desktop apps. These controls are abstractions of their native platform implementations, as discussed in chapter 1, meaning that when you want to accept text input from a user, you use an `Entry` that looks like an iOS control on iOS, a Windows control on Windows, etc., without having to implement the same control once for each platform.

We discussed this simple "consistent, but not identical" approach in chapter 1. You can, of course, make these controls look identical on each platform, as we discuss in chapter 11. This section provides a brief overview of these controls and their use cases.

You have seen how to use some of these controls in the apps we've already built, and we will use others in future apps. In general, they are very simple to consume in your apps, and you can find full coverage for all of them in the .NET MAUI documentation.

4.2.1   *Displaying information*

The controls discussed in this section are used for presenting information to your user. That means these controls do not accept user input. We've already used the `Label` control; table 4.1 summarizes its usage as well as the other controls in this category.

Table 4.1   Summary of the .NET MAUI controls for displaying information to the user

Control	Primary data type	Primary data type name	Use case
Label	String	Text	Displays text onscreen. We've used `Label`s in every app we've looked at so far; it's almost impossible to build an app without them!
ProgressBar	Double	Progress	Displays a value expressed as a fraction. Usually used to indicate progress: e.g., how much of a file has downloaded.
ActivityIndicator	Bool	IsRunning	Shows that something is happening. Different from a `ProgressBar` in that it just shows that an activity is happening rather than indicating the completion status of that activity.

4.2.2   *Accepting input*

.NET MAUI provides several controls that allow you to accept input from your user. Each of these has a property that represents the user's selected value. These properties are all bindable, so you can either use data binding or read the property's value from the control directly in your code-behind. Table 4.2 lists these controls along with their value properties and use cases.

Table 4.2 Controls provided by .NET MAUI for accepting input

Control	Value property	Primary data type name	Use case
Entry	Text	String	Allows a user to enter text
Editor	Text	String	Allows a user to enter text across multiple lines
CheckBox	IsChecked	Bool	Provides a yes/no, true/false, or on/off option
DatePicker	Date	DateTime	Allows a user to select a date
Slider	Value	Double	Allows a user to select a value between a minimum and maximum (by default, between 0 and 1)
Stepper	Value	Double	Increases or decreases a number by a specified amount (1 by default)
TimePicker	Time	TimeSpan	Allows the user to select a time
RadioButton	IsChecked	Bool	Allows the user to select one option from a group of displayed options by checking a box
Picker	SelectedItem	Object	Allows the user to select one option from a group of listed options by picking it from a list

Note that just like the other controls in this chapter, these have many more properties than are listed here, some of which we'll cover as we progress through the book. It's also easy to discover these properties through IntelliSense as you're coding—I encourage you to do that with all controls, especially these. Most are self-evident, but full coverage is available in the .NET MAUI documentation.

4.2.3 *Accepting commands*

.NET MAUI offers a collection of controls that allow you to accept commands from your user. These controls differ from controls that accept input (see the previous section) in that these strictly tell your app that the user wants to do something, as opposed to the user providing a value.

Each of these controls has a bindable property of type ICommand that you can use to execute an action in response to the user interacting with the control. They also have event handlers you can use in your code-behind file without binding. Table 4.3 shows the various command inputs and their use cases.

Table 4.3 Controls in .NET MAUI that initiate an action or command

Control	ICommand property name[a]	Event handler	Use case
Button	Command	Clicked	A simple control the user can tap or click to initiate an action. Uses text to convey its intent.

Table 4.3   Controls in .NET MAUI that initiate an action or command *(continued)*

Control	`ICommand` property name[a]	Event handler	Use case
ImageButton	Command	Clicked	Same as `Button`, but uses an image to convey its intent instead of text.
SearchBar	SearchCommand	SearchButtonPressed, TextChanged (inherited from Input)	Presents a recognizable search box. It has text input and a magnifier icon. The `SearchCommand` `ICommand` and `SearchButton-Pressed` event handlers are both linked to the magnifier icon. Any of the commands or event handlers can be linked to code that searches or filters a list.

[a] The `ICommand` property of each control is bindable, or you can use the event handler instead.

Note that in the .NET MAUI documentation, two additional controls are grouped into this category. These are `RadioButton` and `SwipeView`, which I cover in control modifiers.

4.2.4   *Displaying graphics*

.NET MAUI provides three ways to present graphics: `Image`, `Shapes`, and `Graphics-View`. The `Image` control allows you to display a graphical image (like a JPEG, PNG, or SVG file) from various sources, and we've used this control in our apps already. The other two, `Shapes` and `GraphicsView`, allow you to draw directly on the screen programmatically. The controls for displaying graphics are listed in table 4.4.

Table 4.4   A summary of the controls available in .NET MAUI for displaying graphics

Control	Use case
Image	Displays images. The `Source` property can accept images from a file, a resource, a URL, or a `Stream` and is populated automatically using static constructors (meaning you only need to supply the `Source` property, and the type is inferred). We've used `Images` in a couple of our apps already, using the `Resource` image type, and we use a URL later in this chapter.
Shapes	Lets you draw simple geometric shapes onscreen or render complex images with an SVG-compatible `Path` control. It's useful for quickly placing a simple shape onto your page.
GraphicsView	Exposes a canvas that lets you draw simple or complex images onscreen using brushes and paths. `GraphicsView` is new to .NET MAUI and part of the `MAUI.Graphics` library.

4.3   Displaying lists and collections

.NET MAUI provides a few controls that are useful for displaying collections of data. We used one of these controls, `CollectionView`, in the MauiTodo app to display a collection of to-do items, using a `DataTemplate` to define how each to-do item should be presented.

The most efficient way to display a collection of data in your app is to define a template for each item in the collection and then let the app render out the collection based on your template (figure 4.3). A number of controls in .NET MAUI provide this functionality. While they have different use cases and the way they arrange items in the collection differs, they share some similarities, and three of them have common properties for declaring the collection of data and the template.

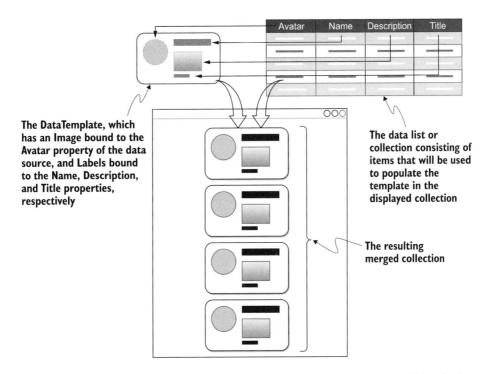

Figure 4.3   Templated views take a template and a collection of data and render each item in the collection according to the template.

The key properties of these controls are `ItemsSource` and `ItemTemplate`. `Items-Source` is a bindable property that can be bound to a collection of type `IEnumerable<T>` (or any inherited collection type). This makes it easy to set these bindings in XAML; and while you can't *directly* assign a collection to this property in code, you can use the `SetBinding` method, inherited from `BindableObject`, to set the binding in code. We use XAML bindings in this book, but you can refer to the documentation if this is an approach you want to follow.

`ItemTemplate`, as the name suggests, defines how each item in the collection is presented. The collection-based view uses the template you provide and renders each item in the collection according to the template. As we saw in MauiTodo, you assign a `DataTemplate` to the `ItemTemplate` property of a collection control.

In addition to statically defining a single-item template, you can use a data template selector to choose different templates at runtime based on the properties of each item in the collection. One of these controls, `TableView`, differs from the other three in this category in that it doesn't have an `ItemsSource` property. `TableView` doesn't use a template or a data source; instead, you add child views statically. The following sections summarize the collection views available in .NET MAU and their potential use cases.

4.3.1 *CollectionView*

As mentioned, we used `CollectionView` in MauiTodo, and we use it again in later examples. `CollectionView` is arguably the workhorse of .NET MAUI apps and likely something you will use a lot.

`CollectionView` supports multiple layout types. Figure 4.4 shows two of them: vertical list and horizontal list. `CollectionView` also supports vertical-grid and horizontal-grid

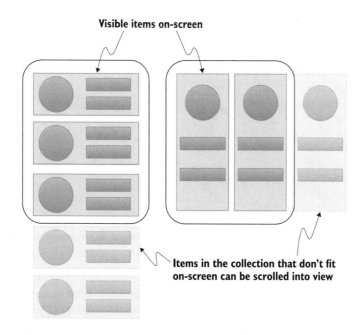

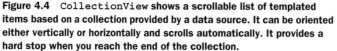

Figure 4.4 `CollectionView` shows a scrollable list of templated items based on a collection provided by a data source. It can be oriented either vertically or horizontally and scrolls automatically. It provides a hard stop when you reach the end of the collection.

layouts. A vertical list is the default, so you can use this layout by instantiating a `CollectionView` without specifying any layout parameters.

Like the other controls in this section (except `TableView`), `CollectionView` has a bindable `ItemsSource` property that provides the list of items for the `CollectionView` to render. The `CollectionView` has a `DataTemplate` that defines how each item should be presented.

There's lots more to learn about `CollectionView`, particularly with regard to controlling `ItemsLayout`, which we've only touched on briefly, and—more importantly—around item selection. `CollectionView` allows you to specify whether users can select one or multiple items in the collection and provides bindable properties called `SelectedItem` and `SelectedItems` to support each mode, respectively. We revisit both of these in MauiTodo in the coming chapters.

We use `CollectionView` throughout this book. I encourage you to experiment as much as possible, consulting the documentation where necessary.

4.3.2   ListView

`ListView` is conceptually similar to `CollectionView`, although it is focused on presenting items using one of a set of predefined templates (`TextCell`, `ImageCell`, `EntryCell`, and `SwitchCell`). Whereas with `CollectionView`, your `DataTemplate` can be an arbitrary layout of your own design, in `ListView`, your `DataTemplate` must reference one of these cell types. However, an additional cell type called `ViewCell` lets you define a custom layout for items.

Another difference between `ListView` and `CollectionView` is that `CollectionView` supports multiple selection (you can select more than one item in the collection), whereas `ListView` supports single selection only. Another difference is that `ListView` supports context actions, which `CollectionView` does not, although you can use the `SwipeView` modifier control (covered later in this chapter) to add this functionality to items in a `CollectionView`.

Anything you can achieve with `ListView`, you can also do with `CollectionView`, but `CollectionView` provides better flexibility. For example, you may want to display a collection of `SwitchCell`s with context actions and nothing else. In this case, it could be easier to use `ListView`, but I recommend using `CollectionView` instead. `CollectionView` was introduced as a more mature version of `ListView`, and while `ListView` is still available, `CollectionView` is what you should use in .NET MAUI.

4.3.3   CarouselView and IndicatorView

`CarouselView` is similar to `CollectionView`; in fact, it's an extension of `CollectionView` and is built on top of it. It binds to a collection of items and renders each item based on a template in a horizontally or vertically scrolling sequence. However, subtle differences between `CollectionView` and `CarouselView` naturally lend the controls to different scenarios.

CarouselView defaults to a horizontal orientation, which can help to focus on a single item at a time, whereas the focus of a CollectionView (or ListView) is to display the collection itself. However, the main distinguishing feature of CarouselView is that it can return to the beginning when you reach the end of the collection, displaying the items in a carousel rather than a one-dimensional list (hence the name). You've probably seen carousels like this on websites; think of a scrolling section that shows the same three or four cards in a looping sequence, as shown in figure 4.5.

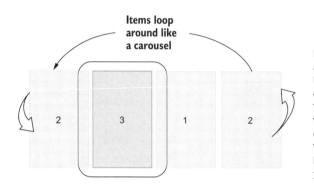

Items loop around like a carousel

Figure 4.5 CarouselView shows a scrollable list of templated items based on a collection provided by a data source. Unlike a Collection-View, it can be configured to return to the beginning when you reach the end (like a carousel). Carousel-View can be oriented vertically or horizontally. And unlike a carousel, you can scroll in both directions.

Unlike a CollectionView, CarouselView does not allow selection of items per se. However, it offers a bindable property called CurrentItem that can be used to determine the currently focused item from the collection.

Let's see a CarouselView in action. **Download the CellBoutique app from the chapter-start folder**. Note that the Models folder contains a class called Product with four properties:

- Title—The name of the product
- Description—A brief description of the product
- Price—The product's price
- Image—A URL pointing to an image of the product

If you look at the code in MainPage.xaml.cs, you'll see that we've overridden the OnAppearing method: in this method, we populate an ObservableCollection of type Product with a few items. Also note that in the constructor, the page's binding context has been set to itself so we can bind to properties of the page in the XAML.

In MainPage.xaml, we'll add a CarouselView and bind its ItemsSource property to this ObservableCollection, and we'll define a DataTemplate that will show all four properties. We'll also specify the ItemsLayout property so we can specify the spacing between individual items.

Add the code from the following listing to MainPage.xaml between the <Content...> ...</Content> tags. The added code is **bold**.

Listing 4.1   Updated `MainPage.xaml` from the CellBoutique app

Specifies a LinearItemsLayout, and sets the Orientation to Horizontal;
these are the defaults but need to be set when specifying ItemsLayout

Adds a margin of 10 to
provide spacing between
the CarouselView and the
edge of the page

Adds the CarouselView and binds its ItemsSource property
to the Products property of the binding context

```xml
<?xml version="1.0" encoding="utf-8" ?>
<ContentPage xmlns="http://schemas.microsoft.com/dotnet/2021/maui"
             xmlns:x="http://schemas.microsoft.com/winfx/2009/xaml"
             x:Class="CellBoutique.MainPage">

    <CarouselView ItemsSource="{Binding Products}"

                  Margin="10">

                <CarouselView.ItemsLayout>

        <LinearItemsLayout Orientation="Horizontal"

                                ItemSpacing="60"/>
        </CarouselView.ItemsLayout>
        <CarouselView.ItemTemplate>
            <DataTemplate>
                <VerticalStackLayout Spacing="20">
                    <Image Source="{Binding Image}"
                           WidthRequest="400"
                           HeightRequest="500"
                           Aspect="AspectFill"
                           HorizontalOptions="Center"/>
                    <HorizontalStackLayout Spacing="20">
                        <VerticalStackLayout WidthRequest="200"
                                             Spacing="10">
                            <Label Text="{Binding Title}"
                                FontAttributes="Bold" />
                            <Label Text="{Binding Description}"
                                LineBreakMode="WordWrap"/>
                        </VerticalStackLayout>
                        <Label FontAttributes="Bold"
                            HorizontalTextAlignment="End"
                            Text="{Binding Price, StringFormat='{0:c}'}"/>
                    </HorizontalStackLayout>
                </VerticalStackLayout>
            </DataTemplate>
        </CarouselView.ItemTemplate>
    </CarouselView>
</ContentPage>
```

Specifies the
CarouselView.ItemsLayout
property

Sets the ItemsSpacing
property of the
LinearItemsLayout to
60 to provide space
between items

Defines the
CarouselView's
ItemTemplate

Adds a layout and
some controls that
are bound to
properties of the
Product type

Go ahead and run the app, and you should see something like figure 4.6.

ImageSource in .NET MAUI

We've already seen how to display an image in a .NET MAUI app. There's one in the template, which we've replaced with our own .NET MAUI bot, and we've also imported an image to use in the FindMe! app. The Image control has a property called Source of type ImageSource. ImageSource has four methods that allow you to display an image from different sources: FromFile, FromUrl, FromResource, and FromStream.

Source is a bindable property, so you can either set the value directly, as we have done in previous examples, or use a binding, as we did in listing 4.1. When you use the Image control in XAML, .NET MAUI is smart enough to know what type of Image-Source you are using and displays the image accordingly. If you want to use your own product photos, feel free to import them into the CellBoutique app (if you recall from earlier examples, they go in the Resources/Images folder) and change the Image property on a couple of the Product entries. You'll see your local image displayed instead of one loaded from a URL without having to make any other code changes.

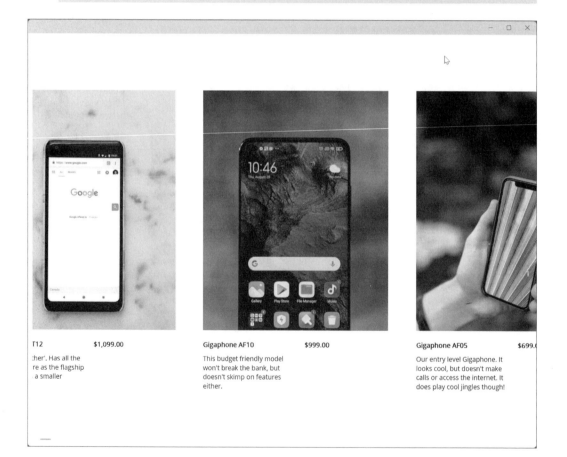

Figure 4.6   The CellBoutique app using CarouselView running on Windows. Items are displayed in a scrollable carousel, so the list repeats on a loop as you scroll through it. You can use a scroll wheel or the arrow keys to scroll through items on a desktop OS.

When using `CarouselView` on Windows (as in figure 4.6) or macOS, you can navigate through the carousel items using the mouse's scroll wheel or the arrow keys on your keyboard. If you have a touchpad that supports swipe gestures, that may work here too. When using `CarouselView` on Android (as in figure 4.7) or iOS, you can use a swipe gesture to navigate between items in the stack.

$1,199.00   Gigaphone XT12

The 'little brother'. Has
same hardware as the
‏‎   XT16 but with a smalle
X50   screen.

Figure 4.7   The CellBoutique app running
with `CarouselView` on Android. Items are
displayed in a scrollable carousel, so the list
repeats on a loop as you scroll through it.
You can use a swipe gesture to scroll
through items on a mobile OS.

4.3.4 *TableView*

Unlike the other controls in this section, the child items displayed by TableView are added directly rather than being rendered automatically from a source list or collection. TableView does not have an ItemsSource property.

Like ListView, with TableView, you must use specific types of cells to display content (figure 4.8). In TableView, these cells are as follows:

- TextCell—Displays two Labels: a primary and secondary
- ImageCell—Like a TextCell but adds an image
- SwitchCell—Displays text and a Switch
- EntryCell—Displays a Label and editable text
- ViewCell—Displays a custom layout

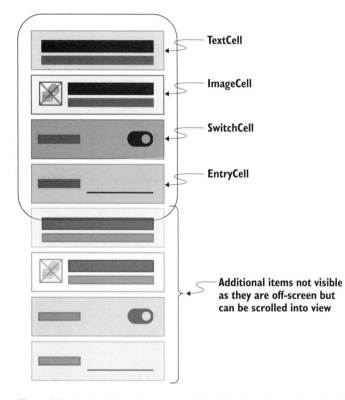

Figure 4.8 TableView shows a scrollable list of static, non-templated items. Each item in a TableView can be different and unrelated and is entered manually rather than items being displayed in a collection from a data source.

The documentation suggests four use cases for TableView: a menu, a form, presenting data, and settings. You will likely find that forms and settings are what you use TableView for.

The best use case for `TableView` is providing a settings page or screen consistent with the native OS settings app. While it's becoming more popular to create a unique app-themed or branded settings page (you can read about this approach in a Microsoft blog post by James Montemagno at http://mng.bz/AoGQ), an OS-consistent settings page is still the dominant choice (see, for example, the Messenger app by Meta or Outlook by Microsoft). `TableView` is best suited for these kinds of settings pages.

4.4   Common properties and control modifiers

There are few (if any) limits in terms of what modifications you can make to controls in .NET MAUI, but you can make some common modifications to any control (or layout, if it makes sense) using simple built-in tools. We look at these common modifiers here:

- Clipping
- Borders
- Shadows
- Gesture recognizers
- `SwipeView`
- `RefreshView`

In this section, we see how some of these controls can be used to enhance MauiTodo. We'll also look at the two most-used properties common to all views: `Height` and `Width`.

4.4.1   Height and Width

In a .NET MAUI app, all views have `Height` and `Width` properties. These properties are read-only and can be used to get the height or width of a view. This is useful if you are building a responsive layout or need to adjust the size or position of a visual element in response to another.

As they are read-only, you can't use `Height` and `Width` to set the height or width of a view, only to get it. Instead, we specify `HeightRequest` and `WidthRequest` (from the `VisualElement` base class that all controls and layouts inherit). These are values specified in device-independent units (DIUs).

> **Device-independent units**
>
> Working directly with pixels is impractical for modern UI development because every screen has a different resolution. And worse, even screens with the same resolution can be vastly different sizes. For example, it's not uncommon to find a mobile phone with a 1080p screen (or even 4K) with a diagonal screen size of 6 inches or less. This could be the same resolution as a 55-inch or even 85-inch TV screen.
>
> Back when I used to write games on my Amiga 1200, I didn't have this problem. Every screen my games ran on reliably had a resolution of 320 × 240, so I could comfortably use precise pixel coordinates to place a sprite onscreen and be confident that it would appear in the same position for everyone who ran it.

(continued)

We don't have that luxury anymore, but fortunately, the problem has been solved by the introduction of device-independent units (DIUs). They have slightly different names on different platforms (e.g., device-independent pixels, density-independent pixels, or points), but most platforms conform to the same sizing convention, roughly equivalent to 160 units per inch or 64 units per centimeter. This means if you give a size value of 2 for spacing in a grid, the space will be approximately 1/32 of a centimeter or 1/80 of an inch, regardless of the size or resolution of the display.

Note my use of the words *roughly* and *approximately*. The system is not perfect (see note on the pixel-perfect myth in chapter 5), but it is close enough in most cases to give you the desired UI effect.

Whenever you see a height, width, or thickness value in a .NET MAUI app, whether in this book or any code you look at, if the size is not proportional (specified with an asterisk [*]), the size is in DIUs.

When a layout calculation is triggered (e.g., when a page loads), a method called Get-SizeRequest calculates the layout bounds based on a combination of factors, including the requested height and width and any other constraints, such as the height and width of the parent element. HeightRequest and WidthRequest are good enough to give you the height and width you want; so as long as you understand that they will be constrained by other factors (like the size of the parent container), it's safe to think of them in terms of setting the height and width of a view. We've used HeightRequest and WidthRequest to specify the size of images in CellBoutique and several other places, and we look at them again in the next section.

4.4.2   *Clipping*

Sometimes you need to modify the shape of a view, and this is where the Clip property comes in. Clip is on the VisualElement base class, so it can be specified on any control or layout and is of type Geometry.

You can use three predefined "simple" geometries in .NET MAUI, assigning them to the Clip property of a view: EllipseGeometry, LineGeometry, and RectangleGeometry. The names are self-evident and allow you to specify an ellipse, a line, or a rectangle.

Let's add a Clip to the Image in the DataTemplate of our CellBoutique app to make each image an ellipse. We'll need to reduce the height and width of the image to allow the full ellipse to be visible. Then we'll specify the Clip property with Ellipse-Geometry, set the Center property to the x and y values that are half the width and height, and do the same for the RadiusX and RadiusY properties. The next listing shows the updated MainPage.xaml file in CellBoutique, with added or changed lines in **bold**.

Listing 4.2 Adding ellipse clipping to CellBoutique

```xml
<?xml version="1.0" encoding="utf-8" ?>
<ContentPage xmlns="http://schemas.microsoft.com/dotnet/2021/maui"
             xmlns:x="http://schemas.microsoft.com/winfx/2009/xaml"
             x:Class="CellBoutique.MainPage">

    <CarouselView ItemsSource="{Binding Products}"
                  Margin="10">
        <CarouselView.ItemsLayout>
            <LinearItemsLayout Orientation="Horizontal"
                               ItemSpacing="60"/>
        </CarouselView.ItemsLayout>
        <CarouselView.ItemTemplate>
            <DataTemplate>
                <VerticalStackLayout Spacing="20">
                    <Image Source="{Binding Image}"
                        WidthRequest="300"
                        HeightRequest="400"
                        Aspect="AspectFill"
                        HorizontalOptions="Center">
                        <Image.Clip>
                            <EllipseGeometry Center="150,200"
                                             RadiusX="150"
                                             RadiusY="200"/>
                        </Image.Clip>
                    </Image>
                    <HorizontalStackLayout Spacing="20">
                        <VerticalStackLayout WidthRequest="200"
                                             Spacing="10">
                            <Label Text="{Binding Title}"
                                FontAttributes="Bold" />
                            <Label Text="{Binding Description}"
                                LineBreakMode="WordWrap"/>
                        </VerticalStackLayout>
                        <Label FontAttributes="Bold"
                            HorizontalTextAlignment="End"
                            Text="{Binding Price, StringFormat='{0:c}'}"/>
                    </HorizontalStackLayout>
                </VerticalStackLayout>
            </DataTemplate>
        </CarouselView.ItemTemplate>
    </CarouselView>
</ContentPage>
```

Annotations:
- **Changes the self-closing Image tag to be an explicit <Image...>...</Image> declaration**
- **Specifies the image's Clip property**
- **Adds an EllipseGeometry with a Center at 150, 200 (half the width and height)**
- **Reduces the width of the image so the full ellipse can be shown in the carousel**
- **Reduces the height of the image so the full ellipse can be shown in the carousel**
- **Sets the RadiusX property to half the width**
- **Sets the RadiusY property to half the height**

Run CellBoutique now, and you should see a result similar to figure 4.9.

In .NET MAUI, you're not limited to these simple geometries. You can also use a *composite geometry*, where you combine more than one geometry to achieve the desired effect. To do this, rather than assign a geometry to the Clip property of a view, you can assign a GeometryGroup. Inside this group, you can specify as many geometries as you like.

Let's say the marketing manager of CellBoutique asks you to update the app for the Christmas period by displaying all the images in a snowman shape. We can use a

Figure 4.9   CellBoutique running on Android. The images have been clipped using `EllipseGeometry`.

composite geometry to achieve this by combining two ellipse geometries. The following listing shows this effect added to CellBoutique.

Listing 4.3   CellBoutique with a composite geometry clipping the images

```xml
<?xml version="1.0" encoding="utf-8" ?>
<ContentPage xmlns="http://schemas.microsoft.com/dotnet/2021/maui"
             xmlns:x="http://schemas.microsoft.com/winfx/2009/xaml"
             x:Class="CellBoutique.MainPage">
```

If you run CellBoutique now, you should see a result similar to figure 4.10.

In addition to simple and composite geometries, you can create any arbitrary shape using a `Path`. We won't cover `Path` geometries here, but you can consult the .NET MAUI documentation to learn more about this topic.

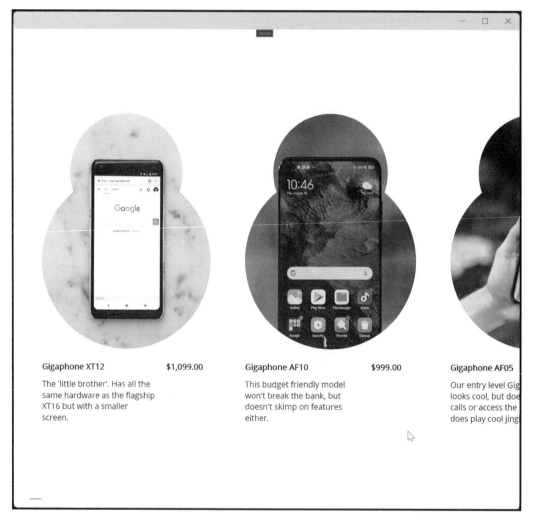

Figure 4.10 CellBoutique running on Windows. The images have been clipped with a composite geometry comprising two ellipses: a larger one at the bottom to create the "body" of a snowman shape and a smaller one at the top to create the "head."

4.4.3 Borders

One of the stated goals of .NET MAUI was "borders everywhere," and it delivers on this promise. Applying a border to any view in .NET MAUI is simple by wrapping that control in a border.

You can wrap any view in a `Border` to apply the border to it by specifying the `Stroke`, `StrokeThickness`, and `StrokeShape` properties. The `Stroke` property is a `Brush`, which means you can define a linear gradient, a radial gradient, or a single color, which you can specify using the `Colors` enum, a hex value, or a static or dynamic resource. StrokeThickness, as the name suggests, defines how thick the border will be in DIUs.

Brushes

You can use a Brush in a few places in .NET MAUI, including the Stroke property of a Border, but also for view backgrounds. There are three types of Brush: Solid-Color, LinearGradientBrush, and RadialGradientBrush. SolidColor is the default, which is why you can specify a single color using one of the available methods (enum, hex, or by referencing a resource); we use it in this section, but you can use a gradient for a Border too.

We learn more about LinearGradientBrush in chapter 7, where we use it to set a gradient for a page background.

StrokeShape defines the shape of the border around the view. You can use an Ellipse, Rectangle, or RoundRectangle (a rectangle with rounded corners) predefined border, but you're not limited to rectangles and ellipses. You can draw more complex shapes using the Path, Polygon, and Polyline implementations of the IShape interface (the type that StrokeShape expects), or even a simple line.

Let's add borders to MauiTodo. So far, we've relied on layout alone to visually distinguish the different to-do items in the CollectionView, but we'll use a Round-Rectangle border to add a card-like effect to the items. **Open MainPage.xaml, and wrap the Grid inside the DataTemplate in a Border tag. Set the Stroke property to Black and the StrokeThickness to 3.** As we'll be using a card style to display the to-do items, we can also reduce the spacing because we won't need as much room to separate individual items in the list (figure 4.11).

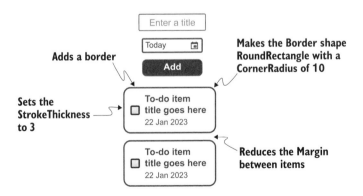

Figure 4.11 Adding borders to the to-do items in MauiTodo. The Border Shape is RoundRectangle with a CornerRadius of 10. The Border Stroke is the Primary color StaticResource, and the Stroke-Thickness is 3. Using borders also means we can reduce the space between items in the collection.

The next listing shows the updated `DataTemplate` in the `MainPage.xaml` file in Maui-Todo, with the main changes in **bold**. Update your code to match.

Listing 4.4   Borders in MauiTodo

Adds a Border to wrap around the Grid, and sets the Stroke to the Primary color StaticResource

```
<DataTemplate>
    <Border Stroke="{StaticResource Primary}"
```

Sets the StrokeThickness of the Border to 3

```
        StrokeThickness="3"
```

Moves the Padding property from the Grid to the Border and reduces it from 10 to 5

```
        Padding="5"
```

```
        Margin="0,10">
```

Moves the Margin property from the Grid to the Border and reduces the vertical margins from 20 to 10

Defines the Border's StrokeShape property

```
        <Border.StrokeShape>
```

```
            <RoundRectangle CornerRadius="10"/>
        </Border.StrokeShape>
```

Sets the StrokeShape to the RoundRectangle predefined shape with a CornerRadius of 10

```
        <Grid WidthRequest="325"
              ColumnDefinitions="1*, 5*"
              RowDefinitions="Auto, 25"
              x:Name="TodoItem">

            <CheckBox VerticalOptions="Center"
                      HorizontalOptions="Center"
                      Grid.Column="0"
                      Grid.Row="0" />

            <Label Text="{Binding Title}"
                   FontAttributes="Bold"
                   LineBreakMode="WordWrap"
                   HorizontalOptions="StartAndExpand"
                   FontSize="Medium"
                   Grid.Row="0"
                   Grid.Column="1"/>

            <Label Text="{Binding Due, StringFormat='{0:dd MMM yyyy}'}"
                   VerticalOptions="End"
                   Grid.Column="1"
                   Grid.Row="1"/>
        </Grid>
    </Border>
</DataTemplate>
```

Note that the four corners don't need to have the same radius. You can add four individual values separated by a space, corresponding to the top-left, top-right, bottom-right, and bottom-left corners, respectively.

There's also a nice shorthand way to define the `StrokeShape`. We can specify the property within the `Border` tag directly, as shown next.

Listing 4.5   Simplified `StrokeShape`

```
<Border Stroke="Black"
        StrokeThickness="3"
        StrokeShape="RoundRectangle 10"       <──┐   The Border.StrokeShape tag
        Padding="10">                              │   has been replaced with a
    <Grid>                                         │   shorthand inline property.
        ...
    </Grid>
</Border>
```

Run the MauiTodo app, and you should see it with the borders added. Figure 4.12 shows MauiTodo running on Windows with borders and reduced spacing.

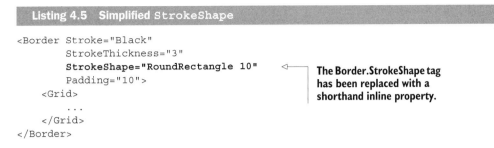

Figure 4.12   MauiTodo running on Windows.

4.4.4 *Shadows*

.NET MAUI makes it easy to add a shadow to any view. The Shadow property is on the VisualElement base class, which every control and layout inherits. Shadow requires four properties:

- Brush—Specifies the color of the shadow and can be set with the Colors enum.
- Opacity—Specifies how opaque the shadow will be and can be specified with a value between 0 and 1.
- Radius—Defines the radius of the shadow and can be specified with a number in DIUs.
- Offset—Specifies the offset of the shadow (conceptually, the position of the light source). The last value, Offset, is of type Point, so it requires a pair of values (also in DIUs) for the x and y coordinates.

As mentioned, you can add a Shadow to any view. In the MauiTodo app, we'll add a Shadow to the Border, as this is the outermost view of any card and thus the view we want to apply the Shadow to. This listing shows a Shadow added to the DataTemplate in the MauiTodo app, with the added Shadow in **bold**.

Listing 4.6 Border with a Shadow

```
<Border Stroke="{StaticResource Primary}"
        StrokeThickness="3"
        StrokeShape="RoundRectangle 10"
        Padding="10">
    <Border.Shadow>            ⊲──┤ Adds a tag to specify the Shadow
                                   property on the Border
        <Shadow Brush="Black"
                                   Sets the Offset of the
                Offset="20,20"  ⊲──┤ Shadow to 20,20

                                   Gives the Shadow
                Radius="40"     ⊲──┤ a Radius of 40

                Opacity="0.8" />  ⊲──┐ Sets the Opacity of
    </Border.Shadow>                  the Shadow to 0.8
    <Grid ...>
        ...
    </Grid>
</Border>
```

Adds a Shadow with a Black Brush ┌▷

If you run MauiTodo now, you should see a result similar to figure 4.13.

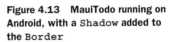

Figure 4.13   **MauiTodo running on Android, with a** `Shadow` **added to the** `Border`

4.4.5   *Gesture recognizers*

Capacitive touchscreens became ubiquitous following the launch of the first iPhone, and with them, touch gestures have become ubiquitous as a UI interaction paradigm. .NET MAUI supports the following five gesture recognizers:

- Tap
- Pan
- Swipe
- Pinch
- Drag and drop

Except for pinch, these gestures have analogous interactions that can be achieved using a mouse or equivalent cursor device. The View base class has a collection called GestureRecognizers, and as all controls and layouts inherit it, these gestures can be added to any view in .NET MAUI. We see some of these in action later in the book.

4.4.6   RefreshView

Pull-to-refresh is another ubiquitous UI paradigm that's become popular since the proliferation of capacitive touchscreens. You pull down from the top of the screen and then let go to update the content.

.NET MAUI makes it easy to implement this with RefreshView. RefreshView is a wrapper that can be placed around any other view to add the pull-to-refresh functionality, including scrolling views like ScrollView and the list and collection views we looked at earlier in the chapter. It lets you scroll to the top before invoking the refresh functionality, preventing it from interfering with scrolling views.

RefreshView has two bindable properties you can use: Command and IsRefreshing. The Command is the logic to be executed to refresh the view, and IsRefreshing is a Boolean you can set to false when the logic has been completed. When the user invokes the refresh, an ActivityIndicator (built into the RefreshView, rather than one you explicitly define yourself) is displayed until IsRefreshing is set to false.

4.4.7   SwipeView

I've said a few times that lists and collections are at the heart of most apps. Tapping (or clicking) items in a list or collection is an established interaction paradigm for selecting or interacting with that item. Another UI paradigm that has become ubiquitous is the use of a swipe to reveal additional functionality. For example, in the Outlook mobile app, you can swipe on an item in your mailbox to reveal configurable actions such as delete and archive.

In .NET MAUI, you can use SwipeView to add this functionality to any view. Like Border, SwipeView wraps other views, which is how you add the SwipeView functionality to them.

SwipeView has four collections of SwipeItems: LeftItems, RightItems, TopItems, and BottomItems. You can add SwipeItems to these collections, which are revealed depending on the direction in which a user swipes. A property called Mode with two options, Execute and Reveal, determines what happens when your user swipes on the SwipeView.

Let's add SwipeView to MauiTodo. We'll add a SwipeItem to the LeftItems collection to delete the to-do item and a SwipeItem to RightItems that marks the item as done (something we can't currently do with the checkbox and won't be able to until we get to the MVVM pattern in chapter 7).

Taking inspiration from fruit, we'll make the delete SwipeItem tomato red and the done SwipeItem lime green. We'll also add an icon for each of them (you can find the `check.svg` and `delete.svg` files in this chapter's resources folder). Here is the updated `DataTemplate` for `MauiTodo` with the `SwipeView` included.

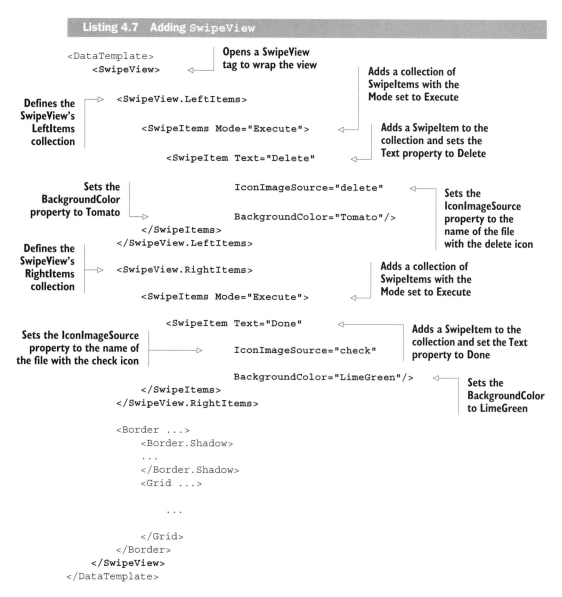

Listing 4.7   Adding `SwipeView`

```
<DataTemplate>
    <SwipeView>                          Opens a SwipeView
                                         tag to wrap the view

        <SwipeView.LeftItems>                    Adds a collection of
                                                 SwipeItems with the
                                                 Mode set to Execute
            <SwipeItems Mode="Execute">
                                                 Adds a SwipeItem to the
                                                 collection and sets the
                <SwipeItem Text="Delete"         Text property to Delete

                    IconImageSource="delete"          Sets the
                                                      IconImageSource
                    BackgroundColor="Tomato"/>        property to the
                                                      name of the file
            </SwipeItems>                             with the delete icon
        </SwipeView.LeftItems>
        <SwipeView.RightItems>               Adds a collection of
                                             SwipeItems with the
            <SwipeItems Mode="Execute">      Mode set to Execute

                <SwipeItem Text="Done"
                                             Adds a SwipeItem to the
                                             collection and set the Text
                    IconImageSource="check"  property to Done

                    BackgroundColor="LimeGreen"/>       Sets the
            </SwipeItems>                               BackgroundColor
        </SwipeView.RightItems>                         to LimeGreen

        <Border ...>
            <Border.Shadow>
            ...
            </Border.Shadow>
            <Grid ...>

                ...

            </Grid>
        </Border>
    </SwipeView>
</DataTemplate>
```

Defines the SwipeView's LeftItems collection

Sets the BackgroundColor property to Tomato

Defines the SwipeView's RightItems collection

Sets the IconImageSource property to the name of the file with the check icon

Run the MauiTodo app. Add some to-do items if you haven't already, and try swiping left and right on them. You should see something similar to figure 4.14.

Starting to swipe a card reveals the action that the swipe provides, and completing the swipe gesture (swiping the item completely to the left or the right) executes the action. The alternative `Mode` we can use is `Reveal`, which instead of executing, shows the available actions to the user; the user must then explicitly execute an action with a

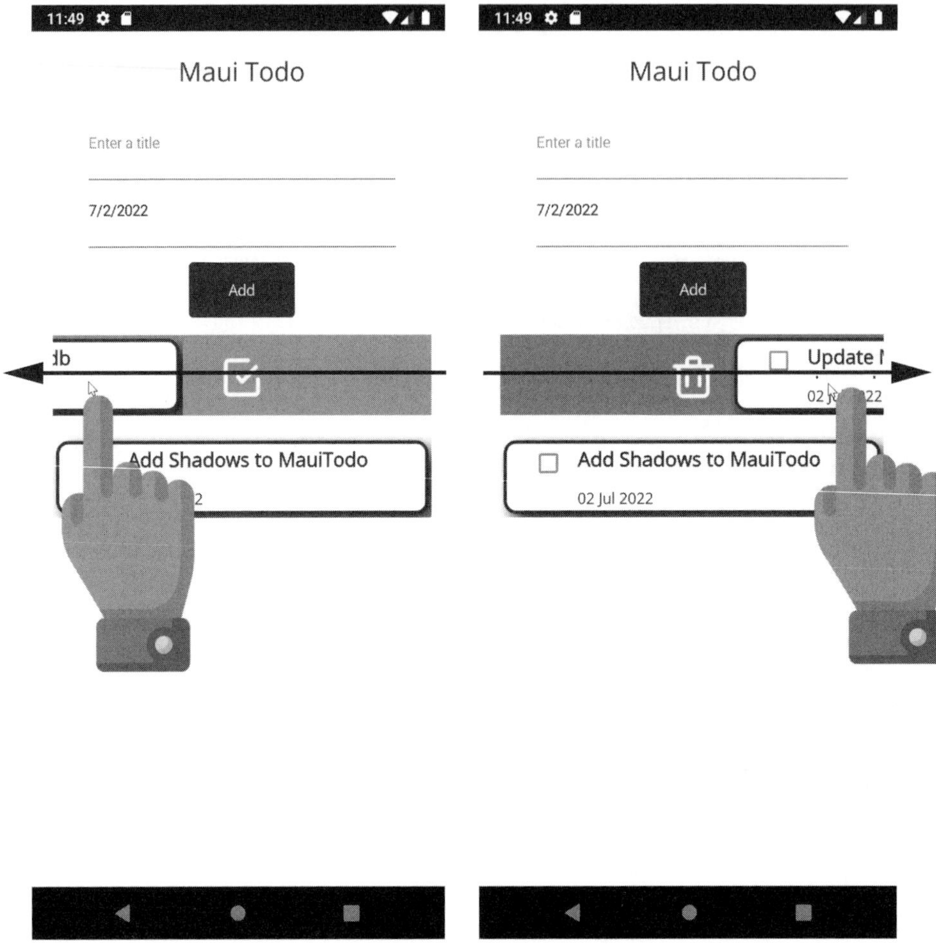

Figure 4.14 MauiTodo with `SwipeView` added. The `SwipeItemsMode` is set to `Execute`, so as the user starts to swipe, the action is revealed, and completing the swipe gesture executes the action.

tap or click. **Change the `SwipeItems` mode in MauiTodo from `Execute` to `Reveal`.** The result should be as shown in figure 4.15.

You can choose whether to use `Execute` or `Reveal`, depending on your needs. `Reveal` is a better option when you want to show multiple actions.

To execute the actions that your `SwipeView` adds, you can use an event handler called `Invoked` or the `Command` and `CommandParameter` bindable properties. Let's add an event handler to these swipe actions. Add the method from listing 4.8 to Main-Page.xaml.cs.

Figure 4.15   MauiTodo with `SwipeView` added. The `SwipeItems` mode is set to `Reveal`, so when a user swipes, additional actions are revealed. The user must tap or click an action to execute it.

Listing 4.8   `SwipeItem_Invoked` **method**

**Adds a method with the standard
event handler signature**

```
private async void SwipeItem_Invoked(object sender, EventArgs e)
    {
        var item = sender as SwipeItem;

        await App.Current.MainPage.
DisplayAlert(item.Text, $"You invoked the {item.Text} action.", "OK");
    }
```

**Casts the sender to a temporary
variable of type SwipeItem**

**Displays an alert acknowledging the
swipe action the user has made**

Next, let's wire up this event handler to the swipe items. The next listing shows the
`DataTemplate` with the `Invoked` event handler added to the swipe items; add the lines
in **bold**.

Listing 4.9 `DataTemplate` with the `Invoked` event handler

```
<DataTemplate>
    <SwipeView>
        <SwipeView.LeftItems>
            <SwipeItems Mode="Reveal">
                <SwipeItem Text="Delete"
                           IconImageSource="delete"
                           BackgroundColor="Tomato"
                           Invoked="SwipeItem_Invoked"/>
            </SwipeItems>
        </SwipeView.LeftItems>

        <SwipeView.RightItems>
            <SwipeItems Mode="Reveal">
                <SwipeItem Text="Done"
                           IconImageSource="check"
                           BackgroundColor="LimeGreen"
                           Invoked="SwipeItem_Invoked"/>
            </SwipeItems>
        </SwipeView.RightItems>
        <Border ...>
            <Border.Shadow>
                ...
            </Border.Shadow>
            <Grid ...>
                ...
            </Grid>
        </Border>
    </SwipeView>
</DataTemplate>
```

**Sets the Invoked
property of the
SwipeItem to the
SwipeItem_Invoked
event handler**

If you run the app now and execute the swipe items (by sliding the item to reveal the
action and then tapping the icon), you should see an alert. The result is shown in figure 4.16.

These alerts are placeholders for the functionality to mark a to-do item as done or
to delete one. We can't actually implement this functionality yet; later, in chapter 9, we
see why this is the case, how we can refactor MauiTodo to use the MVVM pattern, and
how doing so will help us solve this problem.

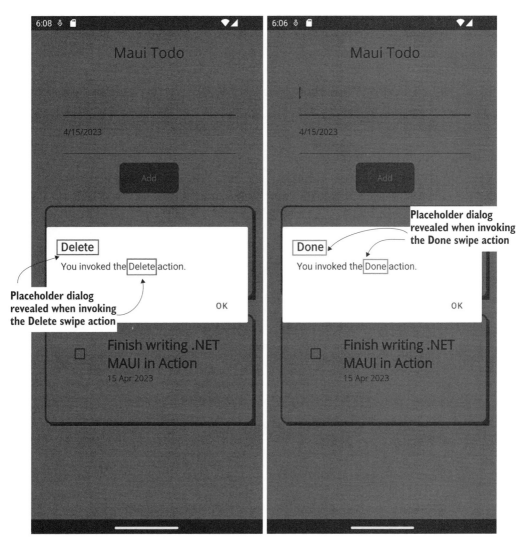

Figure 4.16 MauiTodo running on Android. Executing a swipe action by swiping one of the to-do items to the side and then tapping the icon that is revealed calls an event handler, which parses the sender (in this case, a SwipeItem) and displays an alert using the Text property of the sender.

Summary

- Views are the visual components of an app. They include pages, which are navigable sections of an app; layouts, which control how things are arranged onscreen; and controls, which show something to or get something from the user.
- You can use a number of built-in controls in .NET MAUI to display information to a user or accept input from them.

- .NET MAUI provides several controls that can bind to a data source and use a template to render each item in the data source to the screen.
- You can modify the appearance of any control or layout to include borders and shadows and clip the shape of a layout or control using a geometry.
- You can add recognizers for gestures, such as tap and swipe, to views in .NET MAUI to add well-known UX paradigms to your apps.

Layouts 5

This chapter covers

- The different types of built-in layouts you can use in .NET MAUI apps
- The importance of layouts and when to use which one
- How and when to use ScrollView
- How to combine layouts to create a UI

Layout is the most important aspect of a UI design. UI design consists fundamentally of three aspects: layout, typography, and color (of course, there are more, but at a high level, these are the key components of a design). You can create a great-looking UI in black and white with only one typeface, but fancy typography and pretty colors won't rescue a bad layout. From the experts:

> *Layout is the most critical piece of a website's design. It is quite literally the foundation for the rest of the pieces that will eventually be added to the website.*

> —*Design for Developers*, Stephanie Stimac, Manning 2022

Stimac uses the word "website" here, but she's really talking about UI. And that can be web, desktop, or mobile UI. As a .NET MAUI developer, you're in luck, as we have plenty of options for how we can lay out our UI. The layouts included in .NET MAUI are

- `Grid`
- `HorizontalStackLayout`
- `VerticalStackLayout`
- `FlexLayout`
- `BindableLayout`
- `AbsoluteLayout`

We'll look at the first three (`Grid`, `HorizontalStackLayout`, and `VerticalStackLayout`), with examples of varying complexity, and then look at how you can combine them to achieve any design. We'll look at the last three (`FlexLayout`, `BindableLayout`, and `AbsoluteLayout`) in the next chapter.

RelativeLayout: Where has it gone?

If you've previously used Xamarin.Forms, you may be familiar with another layout called `RelativeLayout`. While `RelativeLayout` is included in .NET MAUI for compatibility with Xamarin.Forms, you shouldn't use it in .NET MAUI apps because it can be expensive to calculate (meaning it takes more CPU cycles), resulting in slower apps.

You can achieve the same results as a `RelativeLayout` by using a `Grid`. If you're migrating from Xamarin.Forms, consider updating your layout to use a `Grid` instead. Of course, with `RelativeLayout` included for combability, you have the luxury of making this update after you upgrade. See appendix B for more details.

`ScrollView` is also included in this chapter, even though it's technically a control and not a layout. The reason is that you will usually use it as part of how you lay out your UI, rather than to show something to the user or get feedback from them. That, combined with the fact that it displays child controls, means it essentially behaves as a layout.

By the end of this chapter, you'll understand why `Grid` is the most important layout and why it will form the basis of any nontrivial UI.

5.1   *Grid*

`Grid` is the most powerful layout in .NET MAUI, and you will likely find that most of your UI layouts are implemented with a `Grid`. As the name suggests, `Grid` lets you arrange child elements in rows and columns. It's easy to picture a table when you hear "rows and columns," but this would be a limiting way to think about the `Grid` layout in .NET MAUI.

A `Grid` isn't used for displaying rows and columns; there are better options in .NET MAUI for displaying tabular data. Instead, a `Grid` uses rows and columns to arrange your views on the screen. If you're familiar with the popular design tool

Figma, the concept is the same as the layout grids that Figma, as well as most other design tools, uses.

In this section, we'll look first at a simple example of using Grid. We'll then see a more complex design and gain an appreciation for using Grid to build awesome layouts. At the end of the chapter, we'll see another practical, hands-on example that uses Grid as the chief layout for a page, in tandem with other layouts, to replicate the UI of a well-known app.

5.1.1 Grid basics

You might think that using a Grid means following squares like on the graph paper you used in school. This isn't how it works in .NET MAUI. To use a Grid in .NET MAUI, you decide how many rows and columns your view will be laid out in and the sizes of those rows and columns.

If you're familiar with the classic three-column layout in web design, you should already be familiar with the concept of a grid system. It simply means that you lay out your UI in rows and columns, rather than use a fixed-size grid to construct your UI.

Let's start with a simple example, one that logically lends itself to a simple grid pattern: a calculator. Let's start right from the very beginning, with a sketch of what a calculator app might look like (figure 5.1).

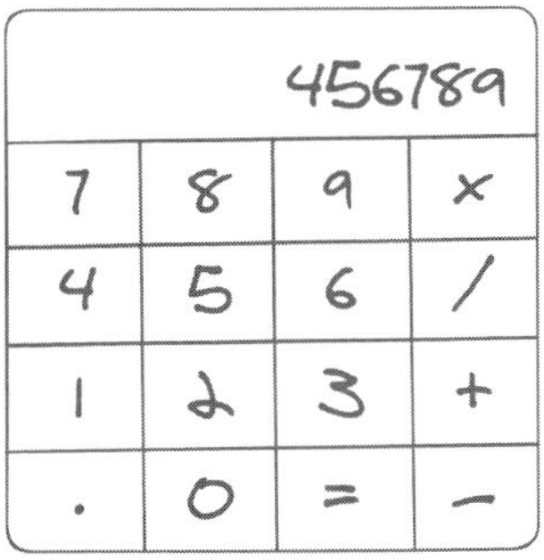

Figure 5.1 A quick sketch of the design for our calculator app. This design is comprised of five rows and four columns.

Figure 5.1 shows a simple sketch of our calculator app's UI. We can see a "screen" at the top to display the numbers the user is entering and the result of their calculation and then rows of buttons for entering numbers and selecting mathematical operators.

If we think of this design as a grid, we can easily say that it has five rows and four columns. Row and column numbers start at 0, so we would define the screen as being in row 0. The buttons would all be in rows 1 to 4 and columns 0 to 3. Let's build this calculator app in .NET MAUI.

5.1.2   *Building MauiCalc*

Create a new blank .NET MAUI app called MauiCalc. Open the `MainPage.xaml` file and delete everything between the `<ContentPage>`...`</ContentPage>` tags. We know that this layout is going to be a grid, so add a `Grid` to the page, as in the following listing.

> **Listing 5.1   The MauiCalc `MainPage` with the grid added**

```
<?xml version="1.0" encoding="utf-8" ?>
<ContentPage xmlns="http://schemas.microsoft.com/dotnet/2021/maui"
             xmlns:x="http://schemas.microsoft.com/winfx/2009/xaml"
             x:Class="MauiCalc.MainPage">

    <Grid>          ◁——┐  Adds a Grid tag
    </Grid>            │  to the page
</ContentPage>
```

Now that we've added the `Grid`, we need to add row and column definitions. Row definitions have a `Height` property, and column definitions have a `Width` property. There are two ways to define rows and columns in a `Grid`. The first is to add the definitions as XAML elements inside the `Grid`:

```
<Grid>
    <Grid.RowDefinitions>
        <RowDefinition Height="*" />
        <RowDefinition Height="*" />
    </Grid.RowDefinitions>
    <Grid.ColumnDefinitions>
        <ColumnDefinition Width="*" />
        <ColumnDefinition Width="*" />
    </Grid.ColumnDefinitions>
</Grid>
```

In this example, the `Grid` has two rows and two columns, and instead of specifying a width or height, we've used an asterisk (*), indicating that we want these to be proportionally sized. We'll talk about row and column sizing in the next section, but for now, know that proportionally sized means they will be equally distributed. There's a much simpler way, though, and that is to directly specify the row and column definitions as part of the `Grid` declaration:

```
<Grid RowDefinitions="*,*"
      ColumnDefinitions="*,*">
</Grid>
```

This gives us the same result—a `Grid` with two rows and two columns. But you can see that declaring the row and column definitions is much easier this way.

We can also specify row and column spacing using the RowSpacing and ColumnSpacing properties, respectively. By default, there will be no space between columns and rows in a Grid, but using these properties, we can specify that we want a gap between each row and column, specified in DIUs.

Let's add these row and column definitions to MauiCalc now. Listing 5.2 shows the MainPage.xaml code with the row and column definitions added. The added parts are in **bold**.

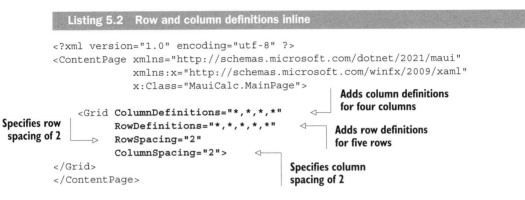

Listing 5.2   Row and column definitions inline

```xml
<?xml version="1.0" encoding="utf-8" ?>
<ContentPage xmlns="http://schemas.microsoft.com/dotnet/2021/maui"
             xmlns:x="http://schemas.microsoft.com/winfx/2009/xaml"
             x:Class="MauiCalc.MainPage">

    <Grid ColumnDefinitions="*,*,*,*"
          RowDefinitions="*,*,*,*,*"
          RowSpacing="2"
          ColumnSpacing="2">
    </Grid>
</ContentPage>
```

Specifies row spacing of 2

Adds column definitions for four columns

Adds row definitions for five rows

Specifies column spacing of 2

MauiCalc has a simple UI, and this Grid declaration is all we need to define its layout. Now we need to start adding some controls.

To place controls in a Grid, we can use attached properties called Grid.Row and Grid.Column. These can be used in any control or layout to position them where we want them in a Grid. Grid rows and columns start at 0, which for a row is at the topmost of the Grid and for a column is leftmost. So, if we want something in the upper left corner, we will place it in Grid.Row 0 and Grid.Column 0 (figure 5.2).

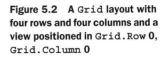

Figure 5.2   A Grid layout with four rows and four columns and a view positioned in Grid.Row 0, Grid.Column 0

If we have, say, a Grid with five rows and three columns and we want to place our view in the middle, we will place it in Grid.Row 2 and Grid.Column 1 (figure 5.3).

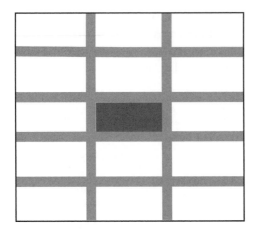

Figure 5.3   A Grid **layout with five rows and three columns, with a View positioned in** Grid.Row **2,** Grid.Column **1.**

You can use these attached properties to position any view at the desired location within a Grid:

```
<Button Grid.Row="2"
        Grid.Column="1"
        Text="Click me!" />
```

Let's add the buttons now to our calculator app. Figuring out which row and column each button needs to go into is simple enough, but to make it easier, let's look at the design again with grid numbers added (figure 5.4).

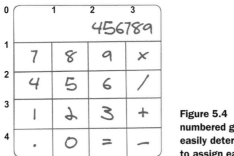

Figure 5.4   **The MauiCalc design with a numbered grid added. This grid helps us easily determine which row and column to assign each button to.**

Looking at figure 5.4, we can easily see that the Button for the number 1, for example, will be in row 3, column 0, and the Button for the number 9 will be in row 1, column 2. None of the buttons are in row 0, as we have reserved this for the screen. The following listing shows the updated MainPage.xaml class, with the added buttons shown in **bold**.

Listing 5.3   `MainPage` with the buttons added

```
<?xml version="1.0" encoding="utf-8" ?>
<ContentPage xmlns="http://schemas.microsoft.com/dotnet/2021/maui"
             xmlns:x="http://schemas.microsoft.com/winfx/2009/xaml"
             x:Class="MauiCalc.MainPage">


<Grid ColumnDefinitions="*,*,*,*"
      RowDefinitions="*,*,*,*,*"
      RowSpacing="2"
      ColumnSpacing="2">
```

Adds a Button to the Grid and positions it in row 1

```
    <!-- Row 1 -->
```

Positions the Button in column 0

```
    <Button Grid.Row="1"
```

Sets the CornerRadius of the Button to 0 (we want square corners)

```
            Grid.Column="0"
            CornerRadius="0"
```

Sets the Text property of the Button to 7 (this will be the top leftmost number button)

```
            Text="7"
            Clicked="Button_Clicked"/>
```

Sets the Clicked property of the Button to an event handler called Button_Clicked

```
    <Button Grid.Row="1"
            Grid.Column="1"
            CornerRadius="0"
            Text="8"
            Clicked="Button_Clicked"/>
```

Adds the next Button in row 1

```
    <Button Grid.Row="1"
            Grid.Column="2"
            CornerRadius="0"
            Text="9"
            Clicked="Button_Clicked"/>
```

Positions this Button in the second column; column 1

```
    <!-- Row 2 -->
```

Starts placing the Buttons on the next row, row 2

```
    <Button Grid.Row="2"
            Grid.Column="0"
            CornerRadius="0"
            Text="4"
            Clicked="Button_Clicked"/>

    <Button Grid.Row="2"
            Grid.Column="1"
            CornerRadius="0"
            Text="5"
            Clicked="Button_Clicked"/>

    <Button Grid.Row="2"
            Grid.Column="2"
            CornerRadius="0"
            Text="6"
            Clicked="Button_Clicked"/>

    <!-- Row 3 -->
```

```
<Button Grid.Row="3"                      Starts placing
        Grid.Column="0"                   Buttons on the
        CornerRadius="0"                  next row, row 3
        Text="1"
        Clicked="Button_Clicked"/>

<Button Grid.Row="3"
        Grid.Column="1"
        CornerRadius="0"
        Text="2"
        Clicked="Button_Clicked"/>

<Button Grid.Row="3"
        Grid.Column="2"
        CornerRadius="0"
        Text="3"
        Clicked="Button_Clicked"/>

<!-- Row 4 -->

<Button Grid.Row="4"                      Starts placing
        Grid.Column="0"                   Buttons on the
        CornerRadius="0"                  next row, row 4
        Text="."
        Clicked="Button_Clicked"/>

<Button Grid.Row="4"
        Grid.Column="1"
        CornerRadius="0"
        Text="0"
        Clicked="Button_Clicked"/>

<Button Grid.Row="4"
        Grid.Column="2"
        CornerRadius="0"
        Text="="
        Clicked="Button_Clicked"/>

<!-- Column 3 (Operator buttons) -->

<Button Grid.Row="1"                      Starts placing Buttons
        Grid.Column="3"                   in the rightmost
        CornerRadius="0"                  column, column 3
        Text="+"
        Clicked="Button_Clicked"/>

<Button Grid.Row="2"
        Grid.Column="3"
        CornerRadius="0"
        Text="-"
        Clicked="Button_Clicked"/>

<Button Grid.Row="3"
        Grid.Column="3"
        CornerRadius="0"
```

```
                        Text="X"
                        Clicked="Button_Clicked"/>

        <Button Grid.Row="4"
                Grid.Column="3"
                CornerRadius="0"
                Text="/"
                Clicked="Button_Clicked"/>
    </Grid>
</ContentPage>
```

That adds all the `Buttons` to our calculator app, and there are a couple of things you may have noticed. The first is that each `Button` has its `Clicked` event delegated to an event handler called `Button_Clicked`. We'll add a single method to handle all button clicks, as adding an event handler for each individual button would be unwieldy. We'll add this method shortly.

The second is that we have started placing `Buttons` on row 1, rather than row 0, which is the top row. This is because we have left the top row free to place the screen, which will show the numbers the user is entering and the result of any calculations.

We want the screen to take up the whole of the top row rather than just one column in the row, and to do this, we will use a property called `ColumnSpan`. `ColumnSpan` lets you declare that while your view originates in a particular column, it should span the specified number of columns. Our calculator app has four columns, and we want the screen to span across all of them. Therefore, we would declare that it be placed in `Grid.Column` 0 and have a `ColumnSpan` of 4.

You can use the same trick for rows as well as columns. If you want a view to occupy more than one vertical row, you can use the `RowSpan` property to specify how many rows the view should span across.

Let's add the screen to MauiCalc. The following listings shows the code to add to `MainPage.xaml`, with the added code shown in **bold**.

Listing 5.4   The LCD screen row

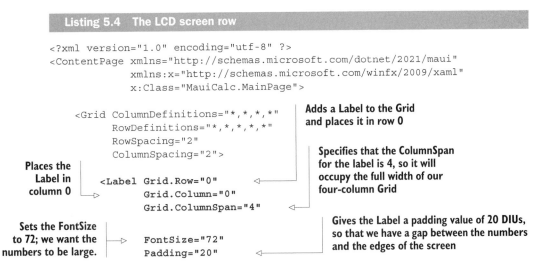

```
<?xml version="1.0" encoding="utf-8" ?>
<ContentPage xmlns="http://schemas.microsoft.com/dotnet/2021/maui"
             xmlns:x="http://schemas.microsoft.com/winfx/2009/xaml"
             x:Class="MauiCalc.MainPage">

    <Grid ColumnDefinitions="*,*,*,*"         Adds a Label to the Grid
          RowDefinitions="*,*,*,*,*"          and places it in row 0
          RowSpacing="2"
          ColumnSpacing="2">                  Specifies that the ColumnSpan
                                              for the label is 4, so it will
        <Label Grid.Row="0"                   occupy the full width of our
               Grid.Column="0"                four-column Grid
               Grid.ColumnSpan="4"

               FontSize="72"
               Padding="20"
```

Places the Label in column 0

Sets the FontSize to 72; we want the numbers to be large.

Gives the Label a padding value of 20 DIUs, so that we have a gap between the numbers and the edges of the screen

Sets the text color to black ⌐⟶

```
                TextColor="Black"
                HorizontalTextAlignment="End"        ⟵
```

Sets the HorizontalAlignment to end; the numbers on a calculator's display come in from the right-hand side.

```
                x:Name="LCD"/>            ⟵
```

```
      <!—Buttons omitted for brevity -->
```

Gives the Label a name so that we can set its text property in code

```
          </Grid>
      </ContentPage>
```

Now that we've added the LCD screen, this completes the layout for the calculator app. You can't run it just yet, as we are referencing an event handler that doesn't exist. We'll add an empty event handler for now just so that we can run the app and review the layout. The following listing shows the code to add to `MainPage.xaml.cs`.

Listing 5.5   The `Button_Clicked` method

```
private void Button_Clicked(object sender, EventArgs e)        ⟵
{
}
```
Adds a method called Button_Clicked with the standard event handler signature

Now that you've added the method, delete the existing `OnCounterClicked` method, and the app will compile and run. **Before you run the app, add some numbers to the `Text` property of the LCD label**. This will let you get a feel for what the app will look like. If you run it now, you should see something like figure 5.5.

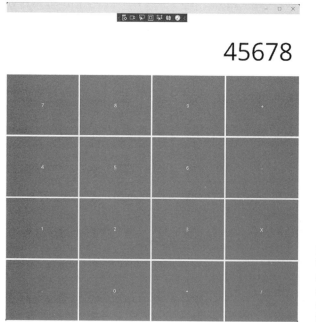

45678

Figure 5.5   MauiCalc running on Windows, with the buttons laid out in a grid, in rows 1 to 4 and columns 1 to 4, and a number display in row 0, spread across all four columns

Now that we've got our layout sorted, we can start thinking about the other two aspects of this UI: color and typography. We can make some small UI tweaks to give it a more calculator-like appearance. First, we'll give the screen a more LCD-like background color. We can also use an LCD-styled font to give the screen a more LCD-like appearance. Skeuomorphism may have fallen out of fashion, but it still works in some scenarios, and this is one of them.

First, **download the font from the chapter's resources folder**. The file is called `LCD.ttf`. Place it inside the MauiCalc project in the `Resources/Fonts` folder. We need to wire this up in `MauiProgram` so that we can use it in our code.

To register a font, we can add it to the `ConfigureFonts` extension method on `MauiAppBuilder`. The `IFontCollection` is already passed in to this lambda method, so to add a font, we simply call `fonts.AddFont` and pass it the filename of the font we want to register and an alias for the font for us to refer to in code.

Open `MauiProgram.cs` and update the font registrations to include our LCD font. The following listing shows you how to do this, with the added code shown in **bold**.

Listing 5.6 Adding a font registration to MauiProgram

```
namespace MauiCalc;

public static class MauiProgram
{
    public static MauiApp CreateMauiApp()
    {
        var builder = MauiApp.CreateBuilder();
        builder
            .UseMauiApp<App>()
            .ConfigureFonts(fonts =>
            {
                fonts.AddFont("OpenSans-Regular.ttf", "OpenSansRegular");
                fonts.AddFont("OpenSans-Semibold.ttf", "OpenSansSemibold");
                fonts.AddFont("LCD.ttf", "LCD");        ⟵─────────┐
            });                                         Adds a font registration
                                                        in MauiProgram, tells it to
        return builder.Build();                         register the LCD.ttf font, and
    }                                                   gives it an alias of LCD
}
```

Registering fonts

You define which files in your project are fonts by setting their `BuildAction` property to `MauiFont`. You can do so using the Properties panel in Visual Studio or by registering it in the `.csproj` file:

```
<MauiFont Include="[your font file]" />
```

If you look in the `MauiCalc.csproj` file now, you'll see an entry already matching this, but it has a wildcard for the whole `Resources/Fonts` folder. So, if you want to

---

(continued)

add a font to your .NET MAUI app, simply copy the font file to this folder, and it will be available for you to register by filename in the `MauiProgram` configuration builder.

If you've come from Xamarin.Forms, you'll note the striking difference in how easy this is, compared to the old way!

Now that we've got a cool LCD font in our calculator, we can add a background color for the screen. Rather than use one of the predefined colors, let's add the specific color we want to use. To do this, we'll add it to the `ResourceDictionary` in Resources/ `Styles.xaml`. We'll look at how this works in more detail in chapter 11, but for now, add the line in **bold** in the following listing to the `Styles.xaml` file.

Listing 5.7   The LCD color in `Styles.xaml`

```
<?xml version="1.0" encoding="UTF-8" ?>
<?xaml-comp compile="true" ?>
<ResourceDictionary
    xmlns="http://schemas.microsoft.com/dotnet/2021/maui"
    xmlns:x="http://schemas.microsoft.com/winfx/2009/xaml">

    <Color x:Key="LcdBackgroundColor">#D1E0BA</Color>        ◁

    <!--code omitted for brevity -->

</ResourceDictionary>
```

Adds a color with the hex value D1E0BA and gives it a key of LcdBackgroundColor so that we can refer to it by name

Let's also update the vertical text alignment of the LCD so that the numbers are shown just above the keypad. The following listing shows the changes in **bold**.

Listing 5.8   The LCD styling in `MainPage`

```
<?xml version="1.0" encoding="utf-8" ?>
<ContentPage ...>

    <Grid ...>

        <Label Grid.Row="0"
               Grid.Column="0"
               Grid.ColumnSpan="4"
               BackgroundColor="{StaticResource
    ⇨ LcdBackgroundColor}"                ◁

               FontFamily="LCD"            ◁
               FontSize="72"
               Padding="20"
               TextColor="Black"
               HorizontalTextAlignment="End"
               VerticalTextAlignment="End"
```

Sets the BackgroundColor of the Label control to the color we defined in Styles.xaml

Sets the FontFamily of the Label to the font we defined in MauiProgram.cs

```
          x:Name="LCD"
          Text="456789"/>          ◁────
```

The Text property is set to some numbers, so we can get a feel for what it will look like when running.

```
     <!—code omitted for brevity -->

  </Grid>
</ContentPage>
```

Run the MauiCalc app again now, and you should get something like figure 5.6.

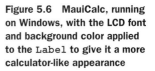

456789

Figure 5.6   MauiCalc, running on Windows, with the LCD font and background color applied to the Label to give it a more calculator-like appearance

We've now completed the UI for the MauiCalc app. Now, all that's left to do is make it actually perform some calculations! First, delete the Text property from the LCD Label control. Next, update your MainPage.xaml.cs file to match the following listing.

Listing 5.9   The full code for MainPage.xaml.cs

```
namespace MauiCalc;

public partial class MainPage : ContentPage
{
    public string CurrentInput { get; set; } =
➡ String.Empty;                           ◁───

    public string RunningTotal { get; set; } =
➡ String.Empty;                           ◁───
```

Declares a string variable to store the current number the user is entering

Declares a string variable to store the running total of the numbers the user is calculating

Declares a private string variable to
store the arithmetic operator the
user has selected

Declares an array of strings to
store the available arithmetic
operators to compare the
user's selection against

```
private string selectedOperator;

string[] operators = { "+", "-", "/", "X", "=" };

string[] numbers = { "0", "1", "2", "3", "4",
"5", "6", "7", "8", "9", "." };

bool resetOnNextInput = false;

public MainPage()
{
    InitializeComponent();
}

private void Button_Clicked(object sender, EventArgs e)
{
    var btn = sender as Button;

    var thisInput = btn.Text;

    if (numbers.Contains(thisInput))
    {
        if (resetOnNextInput)
        {
            CurrentInput = btn.Text;
            resetOnNextInput = false;
        }
        else
        {
            CurrentInput += btn.Text;
        }

        LCD.Text = CurrentInput;
    }
    else if (operators.Contains(thisInput))
    {
        var result = PerformCalculation();

        if (thisInput == "=")
        {
            CurrentInput = result.ToString();

            LCD.Text = CurrentInput;
```

Declares an array of strings to
store the available numbers
the user can select from

Declares a Boolean to determine
whether the screen will reset the
next time the user presses a Button

Assigns the
value of the
Button's Text
property to a
temporary
variable

Casts the sender in the
Button_Clicked event handler
to a Button type, so that we
can read its Text property

Checks to see
whether the
Button the
user has
pressed is a
number

Checks to see whether the display
should reset (e.g., if the user's last
press was equals or an arithmetic
operator)

If we're
resetting the
display, sets the
CurrentInput to
the number the
user has just
pressed

Ensures that the display won't
reset again if the user enters
another number

Sets the Text property of the
LCD Label to the CurrentInput

Checks to see whether
the Button the user has
pressed is an arithmetic
operator

If we're not
resetting the
display (e.g., if the
user is adding
digits to a number),
appends the
currently pressed
digit to the number

Calls the PerformCalculation
method and assigns the result
to a temporary variable

Sets the CurrentInput variable
to the result of the calculation

Checks to see whether the user
has pressed equals or another
arithmetic operator, so that we
know whether to reset the
running total after updating
the display

Updates the Text
property of the LCD
Label to show the
result value

As we are resetting
the running total
because the user has
pressed equals, sets
the running total
to empty

Sets the running total
to the result of the
calculation

Sets the CurrentInput
to empty

```
            RunningTotal = String.Empty;
            selectedOperator = String.Empty;

            resetOnNextInput = true;
        }
        else
        {
            RunningTotal = result.ToString();

            selectedOperator = thisInput;

            CurrentInput = String.Empty;

            LCD.Text = CurrentInput;
        }
    }
}
```

As we are resetting the
running total because
the user has pressed
equals, sets the selected
operator to empty

As we are resetting the
running total because
the user has pressed
equals, resets the display
on the next Button press

Sets the selected operator to
the arithmetic operator of the
Button the user has pressed so
it can be used to calculate the
running total

Sets the Text property of the LCD
Label to the CurrentInput

```
private double PerformCalculation()
{
    double currentVal;
    double.TryParse(CurrentInput, out currentVal);

    double runningVal;
    double.TryParse(RunningTotal, out runningVal);

    double result;

    switch (selectedOperator)
    {
        case "+":
            result = runningVal + currentVal;
            break;
        case "-":
            result = runningVal - currentVal;
            break;
        case "X":
            result = runningVal * currentVal;
            break;
        case "/":
            result = runningVal / currentVal;
            break;
        default:
            result = currentVal;
            break;

    }

    return result;
}
}
```

Casts CurrentInput,
which is a string, to a
double so we can
perform arithmetic
operations on it

Casts the RunningTotal,
which is a string, to a
double so we can
perform arithmetic
operations on it

Checks to see which
arithmetic operator the
user has selected so we
can perform the
appropriate operation

Returns the result
of the calculation

This gives us a fully working version of MauiCalc. Run it now and test it out by performing some calculations.

5.1.3   *Row and column sizing*

If you run the app on a phone (Android or iOS), you will notice that the layout of the Buttons doesn't work as nicely as on a desktop (where, in particular, you can resize the window to make them look nicer). The layout also suffers on a desktop if you resize the window to be taller and narrower rather than roughly square (figure 5.7).

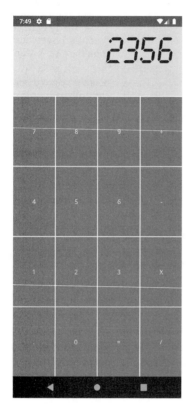

Figure 5.7   MauiCalc running on Android. Because the rows and columns are proportional, on a portrait orientation device the Buttons look unpleasantly elongated.

Solving this problem is a question of design rather than a technical problem. Ideally, we would design our app to adapt to different orientations and screen proportions. We'll look at how to do that in chapter 10, but in the meantime, let's look at an alternative layout, still using Grid, that might be more portrait friendly (figure 5.8).

We can achieve this layout using absolute rather than proportional sizing. So far, we've made all our rows and columns an equal share of the total available height or width, but we have two other ways of breaking these down.

The first is to still use proportional sizing but use a ratio rather than an equal share. This allows us to declare that we want any row or column to take up a specific proportion of the available height or width, rather than an equal share. We do this by prepending a number to the asterisk.

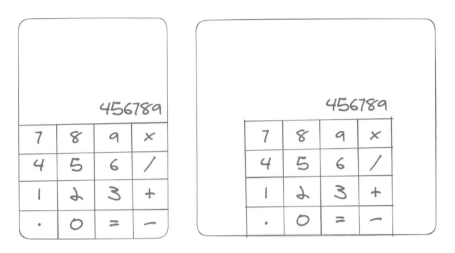

Figure 5.8 An updated design for MauiCalc that keeps the Buttons the same size irrespective of the size of the screen

For example, let's say we want the first column to take up half the screen, the second to take up a third, and the last column to take up one sixth of the space. For the rows, we want the first row to take up one twelfth of the screen, the middle row to take up three twelfths, and the last row to take up eight twelfths. This can be written using proportional sizing like so:

```
ColumDefinitions="3*, 2*, 1*"
RowDefinitions="1*, 3*, 8*"
```

It's important to remember that these are relative proportions, not DIUs. So the row definitions can also be written as

```
RowDefinitions="4*, 12*, 32*"
```

and you will get exactly the same result, as shown in figure 5.9.

We can use this logic with MauiCalc to get closer to the look that we want. We can make this look better on a phone by specifying that the screen should take up the top half of the available space and the Buttons should take the remaining space.

We know that we have five rows: one row is the screen, and four rows are Buttons. That means that the screen row needs to be four times as high as any of the Button rows and will therefore take up half the vertical space. We can achieve this by setting the height of the screen row to 4* and leaving all the Button rows as * (it's not necessary to write 1*). Listing 5.10 shows the updated Grid with its new row and column definitions.

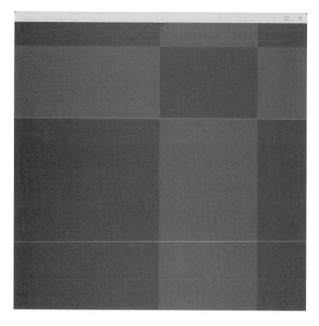

Figure 5.9   A `Grid` **with relatively proportioned rows and columns. The first column takes up half the screen, the second column takes up one third, and the last column takes up one sixth. The first row takes up one twelfth, the second takes up three twelfths, and the last row takes up eight twelfths.**

Listing 5.10   Updated `Grid` **with proportional screen and rows**

```
<Grid ColumnDefinitions="*,*,*,*"
      RowDefinitions="4*,*,*,*,*"

      RowSpacing="2"
      ColumnSpacing="2">
```

The height of the first row has been changed from * to 4*, and given that there are four other rows of height *, this makes it take up half the available height of the Grid.

If you run the updated MauiCalc app now on iOS or Android, you should see something like figure 5.10.

Figure 5.10 shows is a big improvement. It looks much better than the vertically stretched buttons we had before and opens up some space at the top of the screen where we can display more information, like the running total, memory (if we choose to add a memory button later on), or anything else we can think of. This new layout works well on desktop, too, as you can see in figure 5.11.

This looks OK, although we can already see that now we have the reverse problem—the `Buttons` are now stretched horizontally. And let's not forget that a window on a desktop OS can be resized, so this could end up looking like figure 5.12.

This layout still doesn't give us the sketched-out design from figure 5.8. To do that, we need to combine the proportional sizing we've been using so far with absolute sizing.

Absolute sizing is easy: instead of specifying a proportion, you specify a value in DIUs. With this approach, we can specify the height and width of each row and column, which means we can make every `Button` exactly square.

Let's update the row and column definitions. We'll make each column 100 DIUs wide and each `Button` row 100 DIUs tall. We can then set the screen row back to * to

Figure 5.10   The updated MauiCalc app
running on Android, with the screen now
taking up half the of the available height
of the Grid

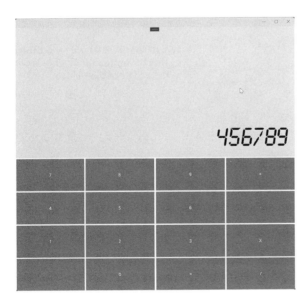

Figure 5.11   MauiCalc running on
Windows, with the rows proportioned
so that the screen takes up half the
available height

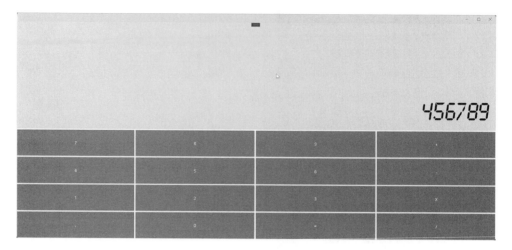

Figure 5.12 MauiCalc running on Windows, with the rows proportioned so that the screen takes up half the available height but with the window stretched horizontally

let it take up any remaining available height. Listing 5.11 shows the updated definitions. The changed lines are shown in **bold**.

Listing 5.11   MauiCalc with fixed height and width buttons

The columns have now all been specified as 100 DIUs wide.

```
<Grid ColumnDefinitions="100,100,100,100"
      RowDefinitions="*,100,100,100,100"

      HorizontalOptions="Center"

      RowSpacing="2"
      ColumnSpacing="2">
```

The rows for the Buttons have all been specified as 100 DIUs high, with the screen allowed to take the remaining available height.

Sets the horizontal options to Center, so that the buttons and screen appear in the middle of the window

If you run this now on a phone, it will look roughly the same as it did before. If you run it on desktop, you'll see we got the design we intended, but it still doesn't look great (figure 5.13).

Nevertheless, this layout matches our design goal, and improving the look is a design challenge rather than a technical one. The layout is now correct, and we have used Grid to achieve what we wanted to achieve.

You can make some other design choices to improve this design. For example, changing the background color and LCD font color and adding a corner radius to the Buttons can give you something like figure 5.14.

You can find the source code for this design in the FancyCalc folder in this chapter's chapter-complete folder, but it's not listed here as it's outside the scope of the Grid discussion. In fact, the changes here are changes to the controls; the layout remains unchanged.

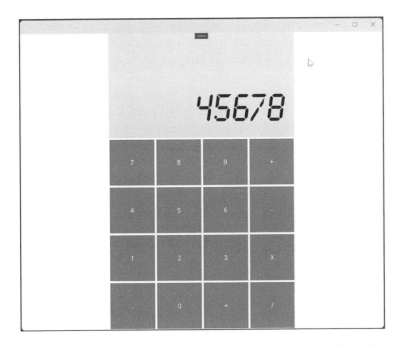

Figure 5.13   MauiCalc running on Windows with fixed height and width of the Buttons. It now matches the design we intended, providing a consistent look across desktop and mobile. But there is room for improvement.

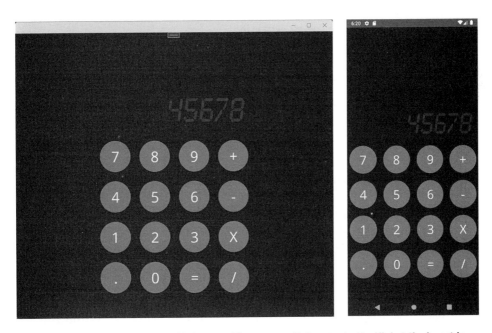

Figure 5.14   FancyCalc—the MauiCalc app with some small changes to the UI, but the layout is the same

Apart from the LCD text color, the differences between MauiCalc and FancyCalc are in the `Styles.xaml` file. We'll look at this file in more depth, and how to accommodate different platforms and screen sizes, in chapter 10.

5.2   ScrollView

`ScrollView` is a control that allows its child content to be scrolled. It's useful in cases where you have content of indeterminate length and need to provide a way to present more content to the user than can fit on the screen. Figure 5.15 shows an example.

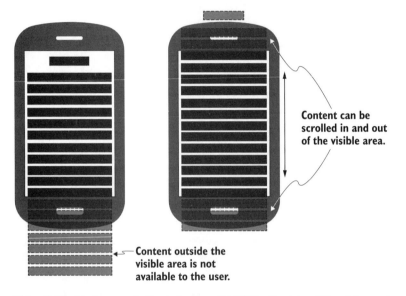

Content can be scrolled in and out of the visible area.

Content outside the visible area is not available to the user.

Figure 5.15   Large amount of text shown on the left in a `VerticalStackLayout`. The content is too long to fit on the screen, so the user is only able to read the first few lines. On the right, the same text is shown in a `ScrollView`, so the user can swipe up and down to see the full body of the text.

In figure 5.15, a `ScrollView` is used to enable users to read paragraphs of text that don't fit on the screen. Without it—as in the example on the left, with the text rendered in a `VerticalStackLayout`—only the content that fits on screen is available to users.

Note that, by default, the orientation of the `ScrollView` (i.e., the direction of scrolling) is vertical. You can also specify the direction as horizontal if you wish.

Vertical and horizontal aren't the only options. You can also set the orientation to both or neither. Both, as the name suggests, allow the user to scroll both vertically and horizontally. This option could be useful for showing an image at full scale and allowing the user to pan around it. It can also be a useful accessibility feature. Some users may prefer large type, and being able to scroll the text both vertically and horizontally can be preferable to scrolling vertically through many lines of just one or two words.

Take care with nested scrolling views

Be careful when nesting scrolling views inside each other as it can make the UI difficult to use, or impossible in some cases. An obvious example would be to not place one `ScrollView` inside another. Some more subtle examples could include a `CollectionView` inside a `ScrollView` or a `ScrollView` in a bottom sheet.

As the user is swiping their finger up or down the screen, the results can be unexpected because your app won't necessarily scroll the view that they are expecting. So, perhaps a more precise warning is not to use overlapping control gestures.

If you find yourself using nested scrolling views, rethink your design so that your scrolling views only appear on fixed pages.

The exception is scrolling views where the direction of scroll is perpendicular. If, for example, you have a page that scrolls vertically, you can include a horizontally scrolling `CollectionView` in the page, as there is no ambiguity between directions of scroll for the gestures your user provides.

A popular trend is to use `ScrollView` as an enclosing container for pages. Because devices come in many different shapes and sizes now, it has become impossible for designers to create a UI that looks the same on all kinds of screen aspect ratios. The depth of this problem is illustrated by the design trend away from "pixel-perfect" designs toward design systems. There's a neat summary of this topic you can read here: http://mng.bz/Zq99, and a quick web search for the term "pixel-perfect myth" will turn up plenty of results. You'll get an appreciation for the problem.

> **NOTE** This "pixel-perfect myth" is a good reason why the default approach with .NET MAUI (consistent but not identical, as discussed in chapter 1) can often lead to much better UI and UX. That's not to say you can't achieve a pixel-perfect UI with .NET MAUI (insofar as the term is commonly accepted nowadays), but it's well worth considering whether delivering a consistent experience is more important.

Consider the example in figure 5.16. This design has a bunch of cards in a vertical stack, with a horizontally scrolling collection in the middle.

The original design, shown on the left in figure 5.16, is based around a tall and narrow screen. To adapt it for a squatter, shorter screen, we could either vertically compress the visual elements, resulting in something like the middle option, or we could keep them all the same size and shape but make the whole view scroll, as depicted on the right. We've seen this approach already; it's in the template that we used to build all our apps so far. You can see it in `MainPage.xaml` in the Aloha, World! app.

A fourth option would be to design a responsive UI that has space for visual elements to be repositioned without compromising the elements themselves. This approach works up to a point but has its limits. We'll have a look at this approach in chapter 10.

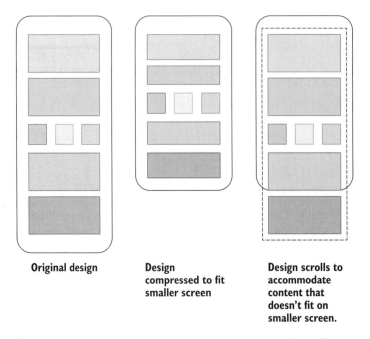

Original design

Design compressed to fit smaller screen

Design scrolls to accommodate content that doesn't fit on smaller screen.

Figure 5.16   A mobile UI design created for a long screen (left). When rendering this UI on a screen with a different aspect ratio that makes the device less "tall," you have two options. The first is to squish the content so that it all fits on screen (middle). The second is to enclose the content in a `ScrollView` (right) so the content appears the same size as the original design and the user can scroll to see content that doesn't fit on screen.

You can choose the approach that works best for you, although the scrolling option is gaining popularity, and the ScrollView in .NET MAUI lets you implement this approach with minimal effort.

5.3   *HorizontalStackLayout and VerticalStackLayout*

The two stack layouts in .NET MAUI are the simplest layouts to use, and probably the easiest for building quick prototypes or trivial apps. VerticalStackLayout and HorizontalStackLayout work in the same way, except for their orientation. They have a collection of type View called Children, and Views are added to the stack and rendered on-screen in the order in which they are added. This means you can add any control or layout to a VerticalStackLayout or HorizontalStackLayout.

We've seen VerticalStackLayout in use already; it's also in the template we've been using and is nested inside the ScrollView. You can see it in MainPage.xaml in the Aloha, World! app.

You can combine VerticalStackLayout and HorizontalStackLayout to create almost any UI. As an example, let's reimagine CellBoutique using cards for the products rather than a CarouselView, as in figure 5.17.

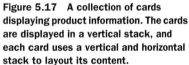

Figure 5.17   A collection of cards displaying product information. The cards are displayed in a vertical stack, and each card uses a vertical and horizontal stack to layout its content.

In the example in figure 5.17, the CarouselView has been replaced with a Collection-View (we could also just use a VerticalStackLayout inside a ScrollView and hard-code the products), and the card template is built entirely using VerticalStackLayout and HorizontalStackLayout. Let's break it down.

Each card will itself be a HorizontalStackLayout, which will allow it to arrange its children horizontally, from left to right. The children will be a VerticalStackLayout to display the product title and description and a Label to display the price. An example is shown in figure 5.18.

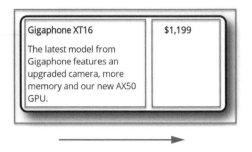

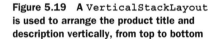

Figure 5.18   **The cards themselves are a HorizontalStackLayout that arrange their child views horizontally on screen, from left to right.**

The first child view of the HorizontalStackLayout that makes up the card is a Vertical-StackLayout that's used to arrange the product title and description, one above the other (figure 5.19).

Figure 5.19   **A VerticalStackLayout is used to arrange the product title and description vertically, from top to bottom**

I've mentioned the importance of layout already; in fact, we can remove all the borders from these cards and rely on layout alone and still have a decent UI. We achieve this using spacing. HorizontalStackLayout and VerticalStackLayout provide a Spacing property, which is used to add a gap between child views in a stack.

Spacing is one of (if not the) most important aspects of layout. It helps to define hierarchy in your UI and relationships between different elements. If we take our current card UI example, we can remove the borders and shadows and rely only on spacing, as in figure 5.20.

In the example in figure 5.20, the borders and shading have been removed. The price has been moved to the left as, without the border, it appears to float without reference. Moving it to the left helps to better define the relationship between the price and the other elements. The space between cards has been increased, and the difference in spacing between each group of elements and the elements within each group leaves no ambiguity about which price, title, and description belong together.

Have a go at refactoring the CellBoutique app to match both of these designs, using the Borders and Shadows that we learned about in chapter 4, and try the layout without borders too. Remember that the cards are only using HorizontalStack-Layout and VerticalStackLayout. You can see the code for my version in the book's online resources.

$1,199   Gigaphone XT16

The latest model from
Gigaphone features an
upgraded camera, more
memory and our new AX50
GPU.

$1,099   Gigaphone XT12

The 'little brother'. Has all the
same hardware as the flagship
XT16 but with a smaller
screen.

$999   Gigaphone AF10

This budget friendly model
won't break the bank, but
doesn't skimp on features
either.

$699   Gigaphone AF05

Our entry level Gigaphone. It
looks cool, but doesn't make
calls or access the internet. It
does play cool jingles though!

**Figure 5.20   This UI uses a combination
of** `VerticalStackLayout` **and**
`HorizontalStackLayout`**. It doesn't
have any borders or shadows but instead
uses spacing to group elements.**

5.4   *FlexLayout*

If you're familiar with web technologies and CSS, you've no doubt heard of the flexible box layout, often just called flexbox. In .NET MAUI, we have a similar layout
called `FlexLayout`.

`FlexLayout` has a lot of similarities with `HorizontalStackLayout` and `Vertical-`
`StackLayout`, but with some important distinctions. The most important difference is
that with the two stack layouts, anything that doesn't fit on screen will simply not be
rendered and is lost to the UI, but `FlexLayout` will wrap items to the next row or col-

umn, depending on the direction specified for the `FlexLayout`. Figure 5.21 shows the difference between `FlexLayout` and a stack layout.

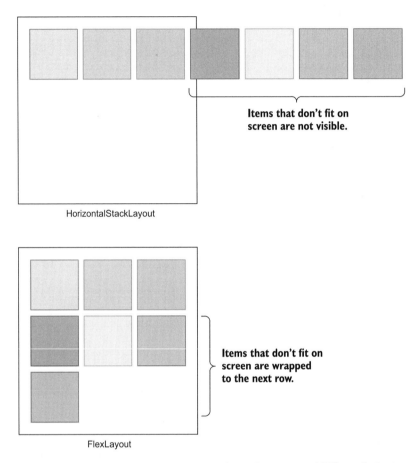

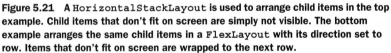

Figure 5.21   A `HorizontalStackLayout` **is used to arrange child items in the top example. Child items that don't fit on screen are simply not visible. The bottom example arranges the same child items in a** `FlexLayout` **with its direction set to row. Items that don't fit on screen are wrapped to the next row.**

`FlexLayout` is almost a direct translation of the CSS flexbox and has similar properties to allow you to arrange child items in either rows or columns and specify the spacing and alignment. We'll look at two different ways of using `FlexLayout` in the next chapter.

Summary

- Grid is a powerful layout, and you can use it to create almost any UI. Grid is used to arrange child views in rows and columns.
- You can use a ScrollView to make more content than fits on screen available to users. You can use ScrollView for a scrolling section of a page or even wrap the whole page in a ScrollView to accommodate different screen sizes.
- HorizontalStackLayout and VerticalStackLayout are simple layouts for arranging child views one after the other, vertically or horizontally. Most simple layouts can be accomplished using a combination of these.
- You can combine layouts in .NET MAUI, and in your real-world apps, you will likely do so. Combining these is the best way to build the UIs your designers give you in .NET MAUI apps.

Advanced layout concepts

This chapter covers

- Using a `Grid` for advanced layouts
- `BindableLayout`
- `AbsoluteLayout`
- Combining layouts to build rich UIs

So far, we've looked at `Grid`, `HorizontalStackLayout` and `VerticalStackLayout`, and `FlexLayout`, and you'll likely find that nearly any UI you're trying to achieve can be accomplished using these. But there are more layout options available in .NET MAUI.

Before we get into new layouts, we'll revisit the `Grid` and see how we can apply it to more complex layouts. In chapter 5, we saw how to use it for a UI that naturally lends itself to a grid pattern, but it's also often the best layout for arranging things that don't initially seem to be a grid. We'll work through an example of a UI using `Grid` in a real-world app to get a better understanding of how flexible and powerful it is.

Sometimes, though, you need just a little bit more, and in .NET MAUI, there's still plenty of room to grow beyond the basics we've explored so far. In this chapter, we'll look at how you can use `BindableLayout` to convert any layout into a collection view, and we'll see how `FlexLayout` is an ideal candidate for this treatment.

After that, we'll move on to `AbsoluteLayout`. `AbsoluteLayout` can be a powerful tool when you need to hit an exact UI target, and we'll see how you can use it for more exact positioning of elements on a screen.

6.1 Thinking in grids

We've seen how we can use a `Grid` to lay things out that naturally lend themselves to a grid pattern. However, as I mentioned in chapter 5, `Grid` is a powerful layout, capable of much more than just displaying squares and rectangles.

When it comes to the overall page or screen layout, `Grid` is the best option for most scenarios. You can achieve nearly any UI using `Grid`. Let's look at a real-world example to see `Grid` in action.

SSW Rewards is an app developed by my company to drive engagement with the developer community. Users can accumulate points and exchange them for prizes, and it also features a profiles section that provides a picture and bio of SSW staff. It is open source, and people are welcome to adapt it for their own uses. Figure 6.1 shows the design for the profiles page in the app.

You might not look at this and immediately see a `Grid`, but once you've been developing .NET MAUI apps for a while, you'll start to see rows and columns in designs like this, almost like Neo seeing the world as green code rain in *The Matrix*. Let's look at how we can start breaking this down (figure 6.2).

The top level of this design is the page, so let's start there. The page is

Figure 6.1 The Profiles page of the SSW Rewards app. There are multiple components to this page, and while it may not immediately look like a grid, the `Grid` layout is used to implement this design.

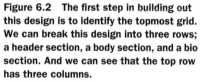

Figure 6.2   **The first step in building out this design is to identify the topmost grid. We can break this design into three rows; a header section, a body section, and a bio section. And we can see that the top row has three columns.**

comprised of three main sections: the header, which contains the name and title and some navigation buttons; the main details section, which includes a picture, a skills summary, a QR indicator (it shows whether the user has scanned this developer and accumulated the points), and some social interaction buttons; and the footer, which contains a short bio about the person.

The first step is easy then—we know we need three rows. You can approximate their relative sizes from this picture. However, because this design was shared with me by the UX team in a design collaboration tool, I have the luxury of knowing the precise relative proportions of these rows. They translate to 2*, 9*, and 3*.

Now we need to determine the columns. Only the top row uses the columns, but that's not a problem, since we can set the ColumnSpan of the remaining two rows to 3 so that they will take up all three columns. The navigation controls can then be placed in columns 0 and 2 of row 0. The column definitions based on the design are *, 5*, *. Next, we need to break down the developer details section of this page, and we can also use a Grid for this (figure 6.3).

Figure 6.3 The grid layout breakdown of the developer details section. We can see that it will have two equally sized columns, with the picture taking up all three rows of the first column. It will also have a `ColumnSpan` of 2 so the picture can overlap other items. The remaining items will be in the second column, with the skills summary in the first row, the QR icon in the second, and the social interaction buttons in the third.

This section will have two columns of equal width. The picture will be in the left column, and everything else will be in the right column. In the right column, the top row will hold the skills summary, the middle row will hold the QR icon, and the bottom row will hold the social interaction buttons.

Determining the relative column widths is straightforward as they both take up an equal share of the width, so they are both *. For the rows, I can determine from the design their relative heights of 5*, 2*, and *. The following listing shows these `Grids`, with their row and column definitions.

Listing 6.1   The `Grid` layout for the SSW Rewards People page

```xml
<?xml version="1.0" encoding="utf-8" ?>
<ContentPage xmlns="http://xamarin.com/schemas/2014/forms"
             xmlns:x="http://schemas.microsoft.com/winfx/2009/xaml"
             BackgroundColor="{StaticResource PeopleBackground}"
```

```
            xmlns:controls="clr-namespace:SSW.Rewards.Controls"
            xmlns:converters="clr-namespace:SSW.Rewards.Converters"
            x:Class="SSW.Rewards.Pages.PeoplePage">
    <ContentPage.Content>
        <Grid RowDefinitions="2*, 9*, 3*"
            ColumnDefinitions="*, 5*, *">

            <Grid Grid.Row="1"
                Grid.Column="0"
                Grid.ColumnSpan="3"
                ColumnDefinitions="*, *"
                RowDefinitions="5*, 2*, *">
            </Grid>
        </ContentPage.Content>
    </ContentPage>
```

Listing 6.1 shows only the `Grid` definitions; it's a complex page, and including all of the views, converters, helpers, and bindings is out of the scope of this section. However, as I mentioned previously, it's open source, so if you want to look at the full source code, you can see it on GitHub at https://github.com/SSWConsulting/SSW .Rewards. We'll also revisit SSW Rewards in appendix B when we look at using the .NET Upgrade Assistant to port a Xamarin.Forms app to .NET MAUI. We'll come back to `Grids` with a hands-on example at the end of this chapter.

6.2   *BindableLayout*

`BindableLayout` isn't a layout itself. It's a static class that can be attached to any layout that will allow it to generate its own content. Essentially, it turns any layout into a collection view.

Using `BindableLayout`, we can specify an `ItemsSource` property for a layout and then use a `DataTemplate` to render each item in the collection, just like with `CollectionView`, as if they were hard-coded child views of the layout we attach `BindableLayout` to. This can work well with `HorizontalStackLayout` or `VerticalStackLayout` and particularly well with `FlexLayout`, as we'll see in an example shortly. It doesn't make much sense to use `BindableLayout` with `Grid`, as views in a `Grid` need the `Row` and `Column` properties to arrange themselves properly.

Using `BindableLayout` with one of the stack layouts or with `FlexLayout` can make a layout similar to `CollectionView`, but `CollectionView` offers functionality you don't get with `BindableLayout`—for example, the ability to select one or more items backed by bindable properties. `BindableLayout` is a good option when you just need a data source for rendering content; `CollectionView` is a better option when you need your user to interact with the collection rather than just the items in that collection.

Let's see how we can use `BindableLayout` with `FlexLayout` to arrange a collection of items on screen. We're going to build an app to give us movie recommendations based on what's currently trending and our chosen genres.

The UI will be straightforward. The user will see a list of trending movies and will have the option to filter the list by genre. Figures 6.4 to 6.6 show the mock-ups for the MauiMovies app.

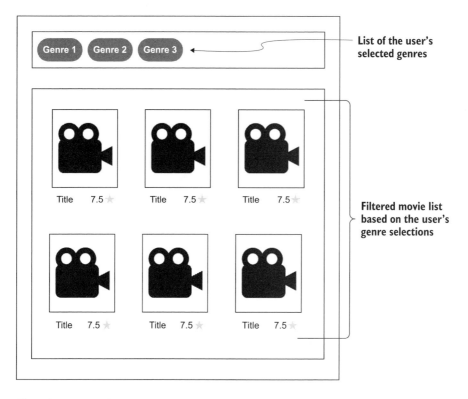

Figure 6.4   The main UI layout for the MauiMovies app. A list of trending movies is shown, with a poster, title, and rating. At the top of the screen is a list of genres the user has chosen to filter by. The user can tap on this list to change their selection.

We're going to use `BindableLayout` with two `FlexLayouts` in MauiMovies: one for the genre list and one for the movie list.

6.2.1   Creating the MauiMovies MainPage

We'll build this app using the free API available from https://www.themoviedb.org. Head over there now and sign up. From within the account settings page, you can request an API key. **Fill out the details to request an API key**; we'll use it in the Maui-Movies app. **Create a new .NET MAUI app from the `blankmaui` template and call it MauiMovies.**

Before we can start building the UI, we'll need to add some types to deserialize the data we get back from the API. If you're using Visual Studio, you can copy JSON to

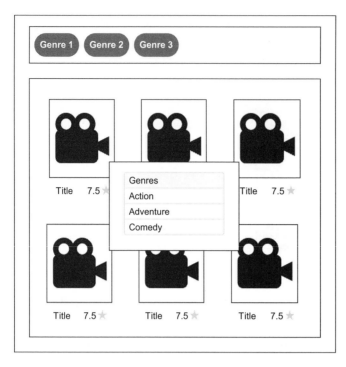

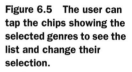

Figure 6.5   The user can tap the chips showing the selected genres to see the list and change their selection.

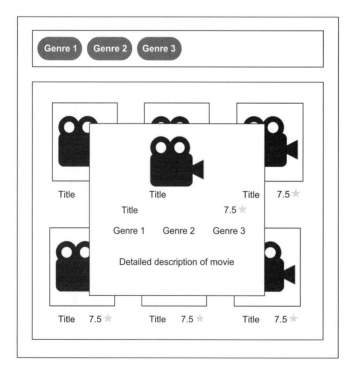

Figure 6.6   The user can tap or click on one of the movies to see more information about it. A popup will show the poster, title, rating, the genres the movie fits into, and the detailed description or blurb.

your clipboard and use the Edit | Paste Special menu to have it automatically converted to C# classes. If not, you can use https://json2csharp.com. In any case, I've already done this, so you don't need to.

First, **create a folder in the project called** `Models` and add a class called `Movie-Result`. The following listing shows the code for this class.

Listing 6.2   The `MovieResult` class

```
namespace MauiMovies;

public class MovieResult
{
    public string original_language { get; set; }
    public string original_title { get; set; }
    public string poster_path { get; set; }
    public bool video { get; set; }
    public double vote_average { get; set; }
    public string overview { get; set; }
    public string release_date { get; set; }
    public int vote_count { get; set; }
    public int id { get; set; }
    public bool adult { get; set; }
    public string backdrop_path { get; set; }
    public string title { get; set; }
    public List<int> genre_ids { get; set; }
    public double popularity { get; set; }
    public string media_type { get; set; }
}
```

Next, add a class to the `Models` folder called `TrendingMovies`. The following listing shows the code for this class.

Listing 6.3   The `TrendingMovies` class

```
namespace MauiMovies;

public class TrendingMovies
{
    public int page { get; set; }
    public List<MovieResult> results { get; set; }
    public int total_pages { get; set; }
    public int total_results { get; set; }
}
```

Add another class to the `Models` folder called `Genre`. The following listing shows the code for this class.

Listing 6.4   The `Genre` class

```
namespace MauiMovies;

public class Genre
{
```

```
    public int id { get; set; }
    public string name { get; set; }
}
```

Next, add a class to the `Models` folder called `GenreList`. The following listing shows the code for this class.

Listing 6.5 The `GenreList` class

```
namespace MauiMovies;

public class GenreList
{
    public List<Genre> genres { get; set; }
}
```

The last class we need to add to the `Models` folder is `UserGenre`. This will subclass the `Genre` class but add a `Selected` property. The following listing shows the code for this class.

Listing 6.6 The `UserGenre` class

```
namespace MauiMovies;

public class UserGenre : Genre
{
    public bool Selected { get; set; }
}
```

Now that we've got all the types we need in place, let's add the functionality to get the data we want from the API. Open the `MainPage.xaml` file in the MauiMovies app and **delete everything between the `<ContentPage...>...</ContentPage>` tags**. Next, open `MainPage.xaml.cs` and **delete the count and the OnCounterClicked method**.

Now we're ready to build the functionality to get movies and genres from the API. The following steps will set us up to build the UI with this data:

1. Add a field for the API key.
2. Add a field for the base URI for the API.
3. Add a field for the top 20 trending movies from the API.
4. Add a field for the list of genres from the API.
5. Add a field for the `HttpClient`.
6. Add a loading property to show an `ActivityIndicator` while we wait for the data.
7. Add a property for the genres the user has selected.
8. Add a property for the movies filtered by genre.

The following listing shows the updated `MainPage.xaml.cs` with the added fields and properties.

Listing 6.7 The updated `MainPage.xaml.cs` with the fields and properties

```
using System.Collections.ObjectModel;
using System.Net.Http.Json;

namespace MauiMovies;

public partial class MainPage : ContentPage
{
    string _apiKey = "[your API key]";
    string _baseUri = "https://api.themoviedb.org/3/";

    private TrendingMovies _movieList;

    private GenreList _genres;

    public ObservableCollection<Genre> Genres { get; set; } = new();

    public ObservableCollection<MovieResult> Movies { get; set; } = new ();

    public bool IsLoading { get; set; }

    private readonly HttpClient _httpClient;

    public MainPage()
    {
        InitializeComponent();
    }
}
```

Next, we need to update the page's constructor. We'll set the page's binding context to itself so the UI can bind to the properties we just created, and we'll instantiate the `HttpClient` with the API's base URI. The following listing shows the updated constructor in `MainPage.xaml.cs` (with the additions in **bold**).

Listing 6.8 The `MainPage.xaml.cs` constructor

```
public MainPage()
    {
        InitializeComponent();
        BindingContext = this;
        _httpClient = new HttpClient { BaseAddress = new Uri(_baseUri) };
    }
```

The last step before we start building the UI is to do the initial data load. Override the page's `OnAppearing` method and make it async. Use the `HttpClient` to retrieve and deserialize the movies and genres from the API. The following listing shows the overridden `OnAppearing` method.

Listing 6.9   The `MainPage.xaml.cs OnAppearing` method

```
protected override async void OnAppearing()
    {
        base.OnAppearing();
        IsLoading = true;
        OnPropertyChanged(nameof(IsLoading));

        _genres = await _httpClient.
    GetFromJsonAsync<GenreList>($"genre/movie/list?
    api_key={_apiKey}&language=en-US");

        _movieList = await _httpClient.GetFromJson
    Async<TrendingMovies>($"trending/movie/week?
    api_key={_apiKey}&language=en-US");

        IsLoading = false;
        OnPropertyChanged(nameof(IsLoading));
    }
```

> Uses the HttpClient to get a list of movie genres from the API and deserialize it into the _genres field

> Uses the HttpClient to get a list of trending movies from the API and deserialize it into the _movieList field

Now that we've got the initialization code finished, we can start laying out the structure for the UI. Figure 6.7 shows the breakdown of the layouts we'll use for MauiMovies.

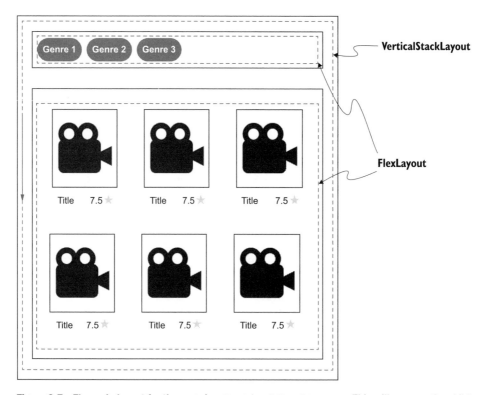

Figure 6.7   The main layout for the page is a `VerticalStackLayout`. This will arrange the child views vertically from top to bottom. The first view to add to the `VerticalStackLayout` is a `FlexLayout` that will show the selected genres. After that, we'll add another `FlexLayout` to show the filtered list of movies.

In the `MainPage.xaml` file, add `VerticalStackLayout` with `Spacing` of 10 and `Padding` of 30. The first item to add to the `VerticalStackLayout` is the genre selection box. To do this, we'll add another `VerticalStackLayout` that will have a `Label` that says "Genres," and a `FlexLayout` underneath it showing the selected genres. We'll use `BindableLayout` to provide the data source for the selected genres, and these will be presented as "chips" or pills.

We can use `Border` for two things: to wrap the whole genre selection box in a nice border and to provide the chip effect. Finally, we will add a gesture recognizer so that when the user taps on the genre selection box, we can present a popup showing the list of available genres for them to choose from. The following listing shows the updated `MainPage.xaml`, with the added genre selection box.

Listing 6.10 `MainPage.xaml` with the genre selection box

```xml
<?xml version="1.0" encoding="utf-8" ?>
<ContentPage xmlns="http://schemas.microsoft.com/dotnet/2021/maui"
             xmlns:x="http://schemas.microsoft.com/winfx/2009/xaml"
             x:Class="MauiMovies.MainPage">

    <VerticalStackLayout Spacing="10" Padding="30">

        <Border Stroke="Black"
                StrokeThickness="2"
                StrokeShape="RoundRectangle 5">
            <VerticalStackLayout Padding="20">
                <VerticalStackLayout.GestureRecognizers>
                    <TapGestureRecognizer NumberOfTapsRequired="1"
                                          Command=
    "{Binding ChooseGenres}"/>
                </VerticalStackLayout.GestureRecognizers>
                <Label Text="Genres:"/>
                <FlexLayout BindableLayout.
    ItemsSource="{Binding Genres}"
                            JustifyContent="SpaceEvenly"
                            Wrap="Wrap">
                    <BindableLayout.ItemTemplate>
                        <DataTemplate>
                            <Border Stroke="CadetBlue"
                                    StrokeShape="RoundRectangle 15">
                                <Label Text="{Binding name}"
                                       TextColor="White"
                                       Padding="10"
                                       BackgroundColor="CadetBlue"/>
                            </Border>
                        </DataTemplate>
                    </BindableLayout.ItemTemplate>
                </FlexLayout>
            </VerticalStackLayout>
        </Border>
    </VerticalStackLayout>
</ContentPage>
```

Binds the TapGestureRecognizer's Command property to a property called ChooseGenres (we'll add this shortly)

Adds a FlexLayout to show the list of selected genres and makes it a BindableLayout with the ItemsSource property bound to the Genres property in the code-behind

Now that we've added the genres, let's add the layout for the actual movies. In Main-Page.xaml, underneath the Border we just added in the VerticalStackLayout, add a ScrollView. Inside this, add a FlexLayout, make it a BindableLayout, and bind the ItemsSource to the Movies collection. Set the JustifyContent property to Space-Between and the Wrap property to Wrap. The following listing shows the code to add to MainPage.xaml, with the added code in **bold**.

Listing 6.11 The movies layout to add to `MainPage.xaml`

```xml
<?xml version="1.0" encoding="utf-8" ?>
<ContentPage xmlns="http://schemas.microsoft.com/dotnet/2021/maui"
             xmlns:x="http://schemas.microsoft.com/winfx/2009/xaml"
             x:Class="MauiMovies.MainPage">

    <VerticalStackLayout Spacing="10" Padding="30">

        ... [Code omitted for clarity]...

        <ScrollView>
            <FlexLayout BindableLayout.ItemsSource
    ="{Binding Movies}"
                        JustifyContent="SpaceEvenly"
                        Wrap="Wrap">
                <BindableLayout.ItemTemplate>
                    <DataTemplate>
                    </DataTemplate>
                </BindableLayout.ItemTemplate>
            </FlexLayout>
        </ScrollView>
    </VerticalStackLayout>
</ContentPage>
```

Adds a FlexLayout, makes it a BindableLayout, and binds the ItemsSource property to the Movies collection

For the DataTemplate, we'll use a VerticalStackLayout to arrange the poster, title, and rating. The title and rating can go into a HorizontalStackLayout underneath the poster, and the poster should have a shadow to add some depth to the UI. The following listing shows the code to add to MainPage.xaml, with the added code in **bold**.

Listing 6.12 The movies layout to add to `MainPage.xaml`

```xml
<?xml version="1.0" encoding="utf-8" ?>
<ContentPage xmlns="http://schemas.microsoft.com/dotnet/2021/maui"
             xmlns:x="http://schemas.microsoft.com/winfx/2009/xaml"
             x:Class="MauiMovies.MainPage">

    <VerticalStackLayout Spacing="10" Padding="30">

        ... [Code omitted for clarity]...

        <ScrollView>
            <FlexLayout BindableLayout.ItemsSource="{Binding Movies}"
                        JustifyContent="SpaceEvenly"
                        Wrap="Wrap">
```

```
        <BindableLayout.ItemTemplate>
            <DataTemplate>
                <VerticalStackLayout WidthRequest="200"
                                     Margin="30"
                                     Spacing="10">
                    <VerticalStackLayout.GestureRecognizers>
                        <TapGestureRecognizer
    NumberOfTapsRequired="1"

                                             Command=
    "{Binding ShowMovies}"/>
                    </VerticalStackLayout.GestureRecognizers>

                    <Image Source="{Binding poster_path}"
                           Aspect="AspectFit">
                        <Image.Shadow>
                            <Shadow Brush="Black"
                                    Opacity="0.6"
                                    Offset="5,5"
                                    Radius="20"/>
                        </Image.Shadow>
                    </Image>
                    <HorizontalStackLayout>
                        <Label Text="{Binding title}"
                               FontAttributes="Bold"
                               WidthRequest="150"
                               LineBreakMode="TailTruncation"/>
                        <Label HorizontalOptions="EndAndExpand"
                               HorizontalTextAlignment="End"
                               WidthRequest="50"
                               Text="{Binding
    vote_average, StringFormat='{0:N1} ☆ '}"/>

                    </HorizontalStackLayout>
                </VerticalStackLayout>
            </DataTemplate>
        </BindableLayout.ItemTemplate>
      </FlexLayout>
    </ScrollView>
  </VerticalStackLayout>
</ContentPage>
```

The main UI is now complete, and we're almost ready to run MauiMovies and see it in action. But first we need to add a little bit more code. The poster_path property that we get from the API is only a partial URL, so we'll need to hydrate that with a base URL for the images. We'll add a field for this base URL and hydrate the poster_path when we load the movies from the API. I got this URL from the API's /Configuration endpoint, which is covered in its documentation.

We also need to add a method to update the Movies ObservableCollection with the filtered movie list. When the page loads, this will be all movies, as the user won't have chosen any genres yet. We also added bindings in the UI to two Commands, so we need to add these, too (although we don't need to do anything with them yet).

The following listing shows the updated `MainPage.xaml.cs` with the added code shown in **bold**.

Listing 6.13 `MainPage.xaml.cs` with the logic to load movies to the UI

```
using System.Collections.ObjectModel;
using System.Net.Http.Json;
using System.Windows.Input;

namespace MauiMovies;

public partial class MainPage : ContentPage
{
    string _apiKey = "[YOUR API KEY HERE]]";
    string _baseUri = "https://api.themoviedb.org/3/";

    string _imageBaseUrl = "https://image.
    tmdb.org/t/p/w500";

    TrendingMovies _movieList;

    GenreList _genres;

    public ObservableCollection<UserGenre> Genres { get; set; } = new();

    public ObservableCollection<MovieResult> Movies { get; set; } = new();

    public ICommand ChooseGenres { get; set; }

    public ICommand ShowMovie { get; set; }

    public bool IsLoading { get; set; }

    HttpClient _httpClient;

    List<UserGenre> _genreList { get; set; } = new();

    public MainPage()
    {
        InitializeComponent();
        BindingContext = this;
        _httpClient = new HttpClient { BaseAddress = new Uri(_baseUri) };
    }

    protected override async void OnAppearing()
    {
        base.OnAppearing();
        IsLoading = true;
        OnPropertyChanged(nameof(IsLoading));

        _genres = await
    _httpClient.GetFromJsonAsync<GenreList>($"genre/movie/list?api_key=
    {_apiKey}&language=en-US »);
```

Adds a field to hold the base URL for images from the API. This value was obtained from the TMDB API configuration endpoint.

```
        _movieList = await
    _httpClient.GetFromJsonAsync<TrendingMovies>($"trending/movie/week?
api_key={_apiKey}&language=en-US");

        foreach (var movie in _movieList.results)
        {
            movie.poster_path = $"{_imageBaseUrl}{movie.poster_path}";
        }

        foreach (var genre in _genres.genres)
        {
            _genreList.Add(new UserGenre
            {
                id = genre.id,
                name = genre.name,
                Selected = false
            });
        }

        LoadFilteredMovies();

        IsLoading = false;
        OnPropertyChanged(nameof(IsLoading));
    }

    private void LoadFilteredMovies()
    {
        Movies.Clear();

        if (_genreList.Any(g => g.Selected))
        {
            var selectedGenreIds = _genreList.Where(g =>
g.Selected).Select(g => g.id);

            foreach (var movie in _movieList.results)
            {
                if (movie.genre_ids.Any(id => selectedGenreIds.Contains(id)))
                {
                    Movies.Add(movie);
                }
            }
        }
        else
        {
            foreach(var movie in _movieList.results)
            {
                Movies.Add(movie);
            }
        }
    }
}
```

We've now got all the code we need to get a list of movies from themoviedb.org and display them in our UI (although we've still got the filtering and movie details to go). Run MauiMovies, and you should see something like figure 6.8.

Movies that do not fit on screen are wrapped to the next row by FlexLayout.

BindableLayout is used to provide the data source to render the movie list.

Figure 6.8   MauiMovies running on Windows. `FlexLayout` **is used to arrange the movies and wrap each movie onto the next line if it doesn't fit. The movies come from an** `ObservableCollection`, **and** `BindableLayout` **is used to bind that collection to the** `FlexLayout`. **Each movie is rendered based on a template that includes the poster, title, and rating.**

With the app running, we can now see the list of movies from the API. We've got two things left to do: filter based on genre and show details for a movie. Even though we can't see it yet, the genre box at the top of the screen is already set up to show a list of chips with the names of the genres the user has chosen for filtering. We just need to give the user a way to choose them.

We're going to use popups for both of these (the genre list and movie details). In the next section, we'll see how to create the genre list and movie details popups.

6.2.2   Creating the popup pages

We'll use popups to display the genre selection list and the movie details. The .NET MAUI Community Toolkit has a nice popup view that we can use for these.

The first step is to **install the** `CommunityToolkit.Maui` **NuGet package** into the MauiMovies project. Before we can start using it, we need to register it in `MauiProgram.cs` by chaining `UseCommunityToolkit()` to the `builder`:

```
builder.UseMauiApp<App>().ConfigureFonts().UseMauiCommunityToolkit();
```

> **NOTE**   The font registrations are left out of this example just to make the code easier to show here. Don't remove them!

Now we need to add the popup pages; let's start with the genre list. The easiest way to create these pages is to add a .NET MAUI `ContentPage` (using the template) and modify it to suit our needs. **Add a new page using the `.NET MAUI ContentPage (XAML)` template and call it `GenreListPopup`.**

Open the `GenreListPopup.xaml.cs` file and change the inherited type from `ContentPage` to `Popup`. You'll need to bring in the `CommunityToolkit.Maui.Views` namespace. You'll see some errors now because of a mismatch with the XAML, so switch over to the `GenreListPopup.xaml` to fix it up.

First, we need to bring in the .NET MAUI Community Toolkit XAML namespace, and we'll assign it to the name `mct`. Then, we can change the type from `ContentPage` to `mct:Popup`. You'll get one more error because the `ContentPage` template includes a `Title` property which `Popup` doesn't have, so delete the `Title` property. `Popup` also lets us define the size in XAML, so we can add this in the opening tag. Finally, delete all the content from the template (the `VerticalStackLayout` and its children), and then you should be all clear of errors and ready to start adding some views. The following listing shows the code for the `GenreListPopup.xaml.cs` file.

Listing 6.14 `GenreListPopup.xaml.cs`

```
using CommunityToolkit.Maui.Views;          ◁—— Brings in the
                                                 CommunityToolkit.Maui.Views
namespace MauiMovies;                            namespace

public partial class GenreListPopup : Popup   ◁—— Updates the class to inherit
{                                                  from Popup instead of
    public GenreListPopup()                        ContentPage
    {

        InitializeComponent();

    }
}
```

The following listing shows the code for the `GenreListPopup.xaml` file.

Listing 6.15 `GenreListPopup.xaml`

```
<?xml version="1.0" encoding="utf-8" ?>      Changes the type
<mct:Popup xmlns="http://schemas.microsoft.com   from ContentPage
➡ /dotnet/2021/maui"                         ◁—— to mct:Popup
         xmlns:x="http://schemas.microsoft.com/winfx/2009/xaml"
         xmlns:mct="http://schemas.microsoft.com
➡ /dotnet/2022/maui/toolkit"                 ◁—— Brings in the .NET MAUI
         Size="600,600"                          Community Toolkit
         x:Class="MauiMovies.GenreListPopup">    namespace (to support
</mct:Popup>                                     the Popup type)
```
Sets the Popup's Size to 600
(width) by 600 (height)

With the basic `Popup` created, let's add some code to handle the genre list that we'll pass through from the main page. The first thing we'll need is to accept the list of genres for the user to select, so update the constructor to take a list of type `UserGenre`. We'll need to add an `ObservableCollection` to hold the `UserGenres` that we receive and to bind to in the UI. To use that binding, we also need to set the `Popup`'s binding context to itself, as in the following listing.

Listing 6.16   The `ObservableCollection` and constructor

```
using CommunityToolkit.Maui.Views;
using System.Collections.ObjectModel;

namespace MauiMovies;

public partial class GenreListPopup : Popup
{
public ObservableCollection<UserGenre> Genres { get; set; }

        public GenreListPopup(List<UserGenre> Genres)
        {
                BindingContext = this;
           this.Genres = new ObservableCollection<UserGenre>(Genres);
                InitializeComponent();
        }
}
```

We will need two event handlers in the code. The first one will handle when a selection changes in the genre list. We can use the event arguments passed to the event handler to get the currently selected items and iterate through the `Genres` collection and, for each entry, check to see whether it is in the selected items. If it is, we mark its `Selected` property as `true`. The changes are shown in the following listing. Note that this is something we can do with `CollectionView` but wouldn't be able to do with `BindableLayout` attached to another layout. We'll also add a field that can be used to track when the user has made a selection change.

Listing 6.17   The `CollectionView_SelectionChanged` method

```
    private bool _selectionHasChanged = false;

    private void CollectionView_SelectionChanged(
 object sender, SelectionChangedEventArgs e)
    {
        _selectionHasChanged = true;

        var selectedItems = e.CurrentSelection;

        foreach (var genre in Genres)
        {
            if (selectedItems.Contains(genre))
            {
                genre.Selected = true;
            }
            else
```

```
            {
                genre.Selected = false;
            }
        }
    }
```

The second event handler will dismiss the popup when the user clicks a button. The popup base class has a `Close()` method we can use, so we'll just call this. We can use this method to return a value to our page that called the popup, so that it knows whether the user has made a selection change. We'll initialize a field with a value of `false` and change it to `true` if the selection changed event handler is called.

In listing 6.18, we use a property inherited from `Popup` called `ResultWhenUserTaps-OutsideOfPopup` to also return the value of this field when the user dismisses the popup by tapping outside rather than using the Confirm button (which we will add shortly). This will need to be set in the constructor.

Listing 6.18 The logic for indicating whether the selection has changed

```
using CommunityToolkit.Maui.Views;
using System.Collections.ObjectModel;

namespace MauiMovies;

public partial class GenreListPopup : Popup
{
    // remaining code omitted

    Public GenreListPopup(List<UserGenre> Genres)
    {
        // remaining code omited

        ResultWhenUserTapsOutsideOfPopup = _selectionHasChanged;
    }

    // remaining code omitted

    private void Button_Clicked(object sender, EventArgs e) => Close(_selec-
      tionHasChanged);
}
```

That's all the logic for this popup, so let's add the UI now. In the `GenreList-Popup.xaml` file, we'll add a `VerticalStackLayout` to arrange all the views. We'll add a Confirm `Button` to the top and then a `CollectionView` to show the available list of genres. The following listing shows the complete code for `GenreListPopup.xaml`.

Listing 6.19 `GenreListPopup.xaml`

```
<?xml version="1.0" encoding="utf-8" ?>
<mct:Popup xmlns="http://schemas.microsoft.com/dotnet/2021/maui"
           xmlns:x="http://schemas.microsoft.com/winfx/2009/xaml"
           xmlns:mct="http://schemas.microsoft.com/dotnet/2022/maui/toolkit"
           x:Class="MauiMovies.GenreListPopup">
```

```
<VerticalStackLayout Spacing="10"
                     Padding="10">

    <Button Text="Confirm"
            Clicked="Button_Clicked"/>

    <CollectionView ItemsSource="{Binding Genres}"
                    SelectionMode="Multiple"
                    SelectionChanged=
    "CollectionView_SelectionChanged">
        <CollectionView.ItemTemplate>
            <DataTemplate>
                <Label Text="{Binding name}"/>
            </DataTemplate>
        </CollectionView.ItemTemplate>
    </CollectionView>

</VerticalStackLayout>
</mct:Popup>
```

> **Delegates the SelectionChanged event to the event handler we created**

We've now got a complete popup for displaying the list of genres and letting the user select one or more genres. As the genres are passed by reference, the user's selection here will be reflected in the MainPage when we go back to it.

The last piece of UI to add for the MauiMovies app is another popup to show movie details. **Use the same process to add another popup called MovieDetailsPopup** (add a ContentPage from the template, update the base class, bring in the Community Toolkit namespace, and change the type in XAML).

We'll need properties for all the key details about the movie: title, description, poster URL, a list of genres, and the rating. We can add a MovieResult as a constructor parameter and assign most of these values based on this parameter. MovieResult only contains a list of genre IDs, though, so we should pass in the list of genres, too, and assign relevant names from here based on the IDs of the genres that apply to the movie.

Finally, we can set the popup's binding context to itself. The following listing shows the complete code for MovieDetailsPopup.xaml.cs.

Listing 6.20   MovieDetailsPopup.xaml.cs

```
using CommunityToolkit.Maui.Views;

namespace MauiMovies;

public partial class MovieDetailsPopup : Popup
{
    public string Title { get; set; }

    public string Description { get; set; }

    public string PosterUrl { get; set; }

    public List<string> Genres { get; set; } = new();

    public double Rating { get; set; }
```

```
public MovieDetailsPopup(MovieResult movie, List<Genre> genres)
{
    Size = new Size(600, 600);

    Title = movie.title;

    Description = movie.overview;

    PosterUrl = movie.poster_path;

    Rating = movie.vote_average;

    foreach (var id in movie.genre_ids)
    {
        Genres.Add(genres.Where(
➡ g => g.id == id).Select(g => g.name).FirstOrDefault());
    }

    BindingContext = this;

    InitializeComponent();
}
}
```

The movie details popup now has all the code it needs to display details about a movie that gets passed into it, so let's create the UI. We'll use a VerticalStackLayout to arrange the views. At the top, we'll use an Image to show the poster. After that, we can use a FlexLayout to show the title and rating. After that, another FlexLayout can show the genres, and at the end, a Label can show the description. The following listing shows the code for MovieDetailsPopup.xaml.

Listing 6.21 `MovieDetailsPopup.xaml`

```
<?xml version="1.0" encoding="utf-8" ?>
<mct:Popup xmlns="http://schemas.microsoft.com/dotnet/2021/maui"
           xmlns:x="http://schemas.microsoft.com/winfx/2009/xaml"
           xmlns:mct="http://schemas.microsoft.com/dotnet/2022/maui/toolkit"
           x:Class="MauiMovies.MovieDetailsPopup">
    <VerticalStackLayout Padding="20"
                         Spacing="20">

        <Image Source="{Binding PosterUrl}"
               HeightRequest="300"
               Aspect="AspectFit"/>

        <FlexLayout JustifyContent="SpaceBetween">
            <Label Text="{Binding Title}"
                   FontAttributes="Bold"/>
            <Label HorizontalTextAlignment="End"
                   Text="{Binding Rating, StringFormat='{0:N1} ☆'}"/>
        </FlexLayout>

        <FlexLayout BindableLayout.ItemsSource=          ⟵─   Adds a FlexLayout for the Genres,
➡ "{Binding Genres}"                                           makes it a BindableLayout, and
                    JustifyContent="SpaceEvenly"               binds the ItemsSource property
                                                               to the list of genre names
```

```
                    Wrap="Wrap">
            <Label Text="{Binding .}"/>          ◄──

        </FlexLayout>

        <Label Text="{Binding Description}"/>
    </VerticalStackLayout>
</mct:Popup>
```

> We don't need a DataTemplate
> as we just want to display a
> Label for each item, and
> because each item is a string,
> we can bind the Text property of
> the Label to the item itself.

This code gives us all the UI components for the MauiMovies app. All that's left to do is wire them all up to the main page.

6.2.3 Showing the popup pages

Let's go back to the main page and wire up some logic to show our new popup. In MainPage.xaml.cs, add a method with a return type of Task called ShowGenreList, and make it async. In this method, instantiate a new GenreListPopup, passing the _genreList field to its constructor. We can show the popup by calling an extension method from the .NET MAUI Community Toolkit called ShowPopupAsync. We'll await the result and then ensure that the result is True (which it will be if the user has made a selection change before closing the popup).

If the result is True, we'll clear the Genres ObservableCollection and then repopulate with the updated _genreList. Then we can call the LoadFilteredMovies method, which will update the UI to show movies that meet the users selected genre criteria. Now that this method exists, we can wire up the ChooseGenres Icommand to call it using an expression body.

Listing 6.22 shows the MainPage.xaml.cs file but only with the added code. The remaining code has been omitted for brevity.

Listing 6.22 The new code in `MainPage.xaml.cs`

```
using CommunityToolkit.Maui.Views;
using System.Collections.ObjectModel;
using System.Net.Http.Json;
using System.Windows.Input;

namespace MauiMovies;

public partial class MainPage : ContentPage
{
    // …

    public ICommand ChooseGenres => new
  Command(async () => await ShowGenreList());

    // ...

    private async Task ShowGenreList()
    {
        var genrePopup = new GenreListPopup(_genreList);   ◄──

        var selected = await this.ShowPopupAsync(genrePopup);   ◄──
```

> Shows the popup by
> calling the ShowPopupAsync
> extension method, passing it
> the GenreListPopup instance,
> and awaits the result

> Instantiates a new
> GenreListPopup,
> passing _genreList
> to its constructor

```
    if ((bool)selected)
    {
        Genres.Clear();
        foreach(var genre in _genreList)
        {
            if (genre.Selected)
            {
                Genres.Add(new Genre
                {
                    name = genre.name
                });
            }
        }

        LoadFilteredMovies();
    }
}
}
```

We've now got all the code we need to filter the movie list based on the user's selection. Run the app and experiment with different genre selections. You should see results similar to figures 6.9 and 6.10.

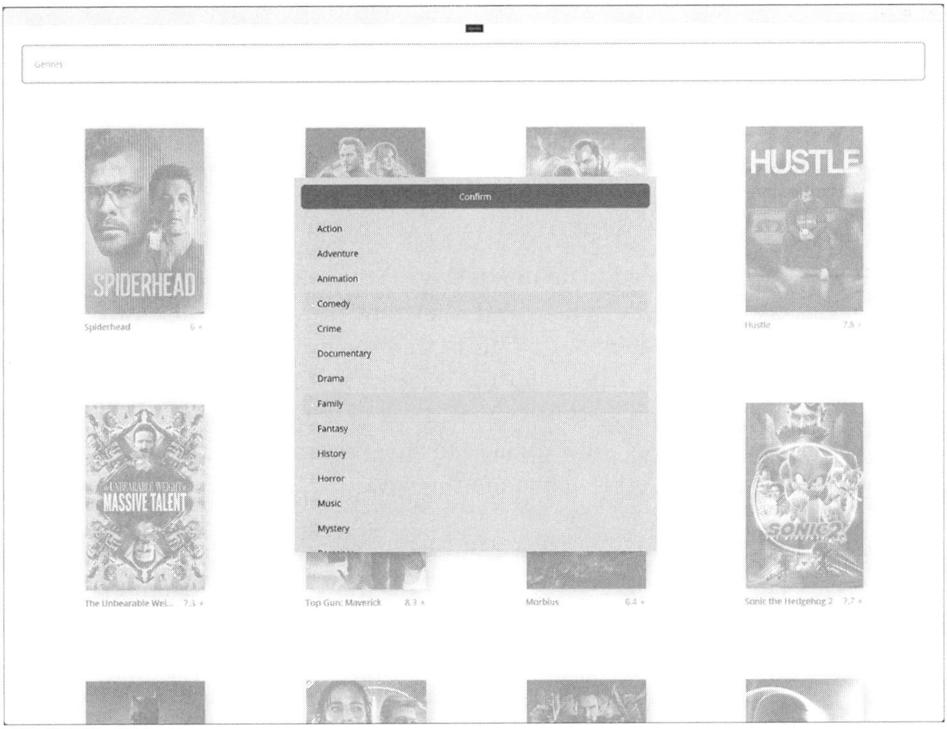

Figure 6.9 MauiMovies running on Windows showing a popup that is displayed by the `ShowPopup-Async` method. A `CollectionView` shows the list of genres, and selecting one or more triggers the `SelectionChanged` event. Dismissing the popup, either by tapping Confirm or tapping on the background outside the popup, returns the `_selectionChanged` value.

Figure 6.10   MauiMovies running on Windows. The user's genre selections are shown in the Genres box, and only movies meeting those criteria are shown.

The last thing we need to do now is show the movie details popup when the user taps or clicks on a movie. We'll need a method we can call that will show a `Movie-DetailsPopup` with the selected movie and the list of genres passed into its constructor, and we'll need to wire up the `ShowMovie ICommand` we already added to this method. The method and the `ICommand` will both need to take the `MovieResult` type.

Listing 6.23 shows these updates to `MainPage.xaml.cs`. Only the new or changed code is shown; the rest is omitted for brevity.

Listing 6.23   The final changes to `MainPage.xaml.cs`

```
using CommunityToolkit.Maui.Views;
using System.Collections.ObjectModel;
using System.Net.Http.Json;
using System.Windows.Input;

namespace MauiMovies;

public partial class MainPage : ContentPage
{
    ...
```

```
    public ICommand ShowMovie => new Command
    <MovieResult>((movie) => ShowMovieDetails(movie));


    ...

    private void ShowMovieDetails(MovieResult movie)
    {
        var moviePopup = new MovieDetailsPopup(movie, _genres.genres);

        this.ShowPopup(moviePopup);
    }
}
```

**Updates the ShowMovie ICommand
using an expression body to set it to a
Command typed to MovieResult, which
will call the ShowMovieDetails method**

Lastly, we'll need to update the `TapGestureRecognizer` attached to the `Vertical-StackLayout` for each movie. The binding we've set for the `Command` property won't work. We've set the binding to the `ShowMovie` method, but the `ShowMovie` method exists on the `MainPage` class, *not* the `MovieResult` class, which is the binding context for the item in the bindable layout.

We can fix this by using the `Source` markup extension and setting a reference to the page. As we've now typed the `Command` to a `MovieResult`, which we also need for the `ShowMovieDetails` method, we will need a `CommandParameter`. This one is easy, though, as we can just set it to the binding for the item itself.

Listing 6.24 shows the changes to the `MainPage.xaml` file. Most of the unchanged code is omitted for brevity, and the changed code is shown in **bold**.

Listing 6.24   The final changes to `MainPage.xaml`

```
<?xml version="1.0" encoding="utf-8" ?>
<ContentPage xmlns="http://schemas.microsoft.com/dotnet/2021/maui"
             xmlns:x="http://schemas.microsoft.com/winfx/2009/xaml"
             x:Name="MoviePage"
             x:Class="MauiMovies.MainPage">

    <VerticalStackLayout Spacing="10" Padding="30">

        ...

        <ScrollView>
            <FlexLayout BindableLayout.ItemsSource="{Binding Movies}"
                        JustifyContent="SpaceEvenly"
                        Wrap="Wrap">
                <BindableLayout.ItemTemplate>
                    <DataTemplate>
                        <VerticalStackLayout WidthRequest="200"
                                             Margin="30"
                                             Spacing="10">
                            <VerticalStackLayout.GestureRecognizers>
                                <TapGestureRecognizer
    NumberOfTapsRequired="1"

                                    Command="{Binding
    Source={x:Reference MoviePage}, Path=ShowMovie}"
```

**Updates the binding for
this Command using the
Source markup extension
to reference the page and
the Path to point to the
ShowMovie property**

```
                                           CommandParameter
   ➥ ="{Binding .}"/>
                              </VerticalStackLayout.GestureRecognizers>
```

**Binds the CommandParameter
property to the item itself, which
is a MovieResult**

```
   ...

      </VerticalStackLayout>
</ContentPage>
```

This code adds the functionality we need to tap or click a movie to see the movie details. If you run MauiMovies now and tap on a movie, you should see something like figure 6.11.

Figure 6.11   MauiMovies running on Windows. The user has tapped on one of the movies to bring up the `MovieDetailsPopup`, which shows a bit more information about the selected movie.

This completes the MauiMovies app! Run the app now and click around, experimenting with changing genres and viewing movie details.

6.3 Absolute layout

AbsoluteLayout lets you use explicit values to position views on the screen. This can be useful, but you have to be cautious with it. Everyone's screen will be a different height and width, so even using explicit values, you can't guarantee the absolute position of a view (figure 6.12).

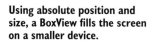

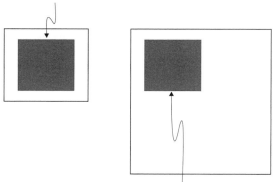

Using absolute position and size, the same BoxView only fills part of the screen on a larger device.

Figure 6.12 Using AbsoluteLayout can have unintended consequences. In this example a BoxView has been added with an absolute position and absolute size. It takes up nearly the whole screen on a smaller device, but just a small part of the top-left corner on a bigger screen.

AbsoluteLayout uses two attached properties, LayoutBounds and LayoutFlags, so that a view can position itself within an AbsoluteLayout. The LayoutBounds is of type Rect, meaning it has four properties: x, y, width, and height.

The first two properties specify the top left position of the view within the Absolute-Layout, and the second two define the size of the view. These properties have default values of 0, 0, Auto, Auto, meaning that if you add any view as a child to an Absolute-Layout, you can omit the LayoutBounds, and the child view will be positioned in the top left and will size automatically to accommodate its contents.

Despite the name, AbsoluteLayout becomes more useful when you use it for proportional sizing and positioning. The LayoutFlags property is an enum that lets you specify which LayoutBounds are proportional and which are absolute (figure 6.13). It provides a lot of flexibility, allowing you to declare whether x, y, or both (position) are proportional; height, width, or both (size) are proportional; all values are proportional; or none are proportional.

To help make sense of this, let's see a simple example. **Create a new .NET MAUI app from the blankmaui template and call it MauiFab.** Wrap the entire contents of the Main-Page in an AbsoluteLayout. Listing 6.25 shows what this should look like, with the added parts in **bold**. The contents of the ScrollView have been omitted for brevity.

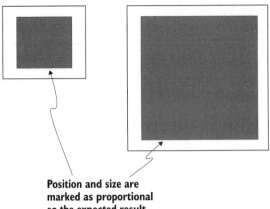

Position and size are
marked as proportional
so the expected result
of near filling the screen
is easier to achieve.

**Figure 6.13 In this example, the
position and size of the BoxView are
proportional to the AbsoluteLayout.
It's easier to achieve the desired effect
(in this case, having a BoxView that
fills most of the screen) using
proportional size and position.**

Listing 6.25 `MainPage.xaml` in `MauiFab`

```
<?xml version="1.0" encoding="utf-8" ?>
<ContentPage xmlns="http://schemas.microsoft.com/dotnet/2021/maui"
             xmlns:x="http://schemas.microsoft.com/winfx/2009/xaml"
             x:Class="FabMaui.MainPage">

    <AbsoluteLayout>
        <ScrollView>
            . . .
        </ScrollView>
    </AbsoluteLayout>
</ContentPage>
```

**An AbsoluteLayout has been
added as the page's Content
property, with the ScrollView
now added as a child.**

We're going to add a simple floating action button (FAB) to this page. To do this, we'll add a `Button` with a height and width of 100 and a corner radius of 50 to make it circular. We'll set the `LayoutFlags` to `PositionProportional`, so that we can ensure it always appears in the same relative position, and set the `LayoutBounds` to put the x and y both at 0.9. As the position is proportional, 0.9 is 9/10 of the way across (for x) and down (for y), so it will be positioned in the bottom right.

Listing 6.26 shows the `MainPage.xaml` with the `Button` added in **bold**. The contents of the `ScrollView` have been omitted for brevity.

Listing 6.26 `MainPage.xaml` with the FAB added

```
<?xml version="1.0" encoding="utf-8" ?>
<ContentPage xmlns="http://schemas.microsoft.com/dotnet/2021/maui"
             xmlns:x="http://schemas.microsoft.com/winfx/2009/xaml"
             x:Class="FabMaui.MainPage">

    <AbsoluteLayout>
        <ScrollView>
```

```
        . . .
    </ScrollView>

    <Button CornerRadius="50"
            Text="Fab!"
            FontSize="Large"
            AbsoluteLayout.LayoutBounds=
➥  "0.9,0.9,100,100"
            AbsoluteLayout.LayoutFlags=
➥  "PositionProportional"/>

    </AbsoluteLayout>
</ContentPage>
```

Sets the Button's
LayoutBounds: 0.9 for x,
0.9 for y, 100 for width,
and 100 for height

Sets the Button's LayoutFlags to
PositionProportional, so that the
position is proportional to the
AbsoluteLayout but the height
and width are absolute

Run the app now, and you should see something like figure 6.14.

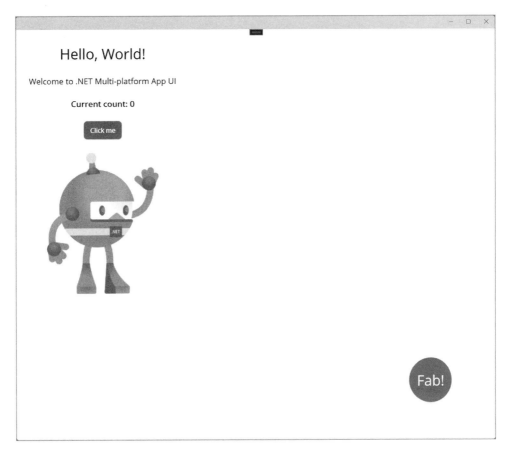

Figure 6.14   **The contents of** `MainPage` **are wrapped in an** `AbsoluteLayout`**, which lets us position a FAB at 90% of the way down and across the screen. But now the rest of the contents are in the top left.**

You can resize the window as much as you like, and the FAB will always stay in the same relative position (figure 6.15).

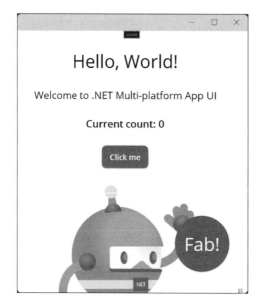

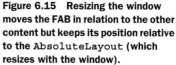

Figure 6.15   Resizing the window moves the FAB in relation to the other content but keeps its position relative to the `AbsoluteLayout` (which resizes with the window).

You'll notice that since we wrapped the `ScrollView` in an `AbsoluteLayout`, it's now positioned in the top left of the window. This is because, as previously mentioned, it's now within an `AbsoluteLayout` and doesn't have any `LayoutBounds` specified. Therefore, it assumes the default values of 0 for the x and y positions at the top left and an automatic size.

There are other ways to create a FAB, and we'll see one in the next section. You'll probably find that you use `AbsoluteLayout` less frequently than other layouts, as most things that you can achieve with it are possible with other layouts. However, it's a powerful tool to have in your belt as a .NET MAUI developer. You can find out much more about `AbsoluteLayout` in the .NET MAUI documentation.

6.4   *Putting it all together*

Throughout the remainder of this chapter, we're going to see how we can use the simple building blocks .NET MAUI provides by combining our familiar layouts and controls to create a rich UI. We'll put ourselves in the shoes of a UI engineer at Microsoft, having received the design for the Microsoft Outlook mobile app, and see how we can use the layouts we've learned to arrange the controls we are now familiar with to implement the design. Figure 6.16 shows the Microsoft Outlook app running on iOS.

We're not going to build any of the functionality Outlook provides. We're just going to recreate the UI of the Inbox screen to sharpen our layout skills in .NET MAUI.

Figure 6.16   Microsoft Outlook running on iOS

UI challenges

A UI challenge is where you take an existing UI design and build it in .NET MAUI (of course, you could do the same with another UI framework). A common approach is to replicate the UI of a well-known, existing app (which we do in this section). Another is to find a fun and interesting concept design and build that; I often see Dribbble.com used as inspiration for these.

(continued)

UI challenges are a popular way to keep your UI building skills sharp. They help you identify and solve UI problems and help you to build out the UI building tools you have in your mental toolkit. Several prominent content creators often post blogs or videos of their UI challenges, showing how they solve problems and create beautiful and functional designs. Two of my favorites are Leomaris Reyes and Kym Phillpotts. I recommend following them both for inspiration and to learn new UI tricks and skills. Also, keep your eye out for others posting their UI challenges online, as well as community events like this one: https://goforgoldman.com/posts/maui-ui-july/. And, of course, do your own!

6.4.1 Adding the app's shared resources

Let's get started! **Create a new .NET MAUI app from the `blankmaui` template and call it OutlookClone.**

Outlook uses Microsoft's Fluent Design system, which includes an icon set. The icons are available in their own repository on GitHub, which you can find at https://github.com/microsoft/fluentui-system-icons in various formats. However, in Outlook-Clone, we're going to use fonts that contain all the symbols, and we'll see how we can use font icons.

I've already grabbed the two font assets we'll use in OutlookClone, and they are available in the chapter's resources folder. **Download the two font files, `FluentSystem-Icons-Filled.ttf` and `FluentSystemIcons-Regular.ttf` and import them into the Resources/Fonts folder**. Next, we need to register the fonts in `MauiProgram.cs`. The following listing shows `MauiProgram.cs` for OutlookClone, with the added font registrations noted in **bold**.

Listing 6.27 `MauiProgram.cs`

```
namespace OutlookClone
{
    public static class MauiProgram
    {
        public static MauiApp CreateMauiApp()
        {
            var builder = MauiApp.CreateBuilder();
            builder
                .UseMauiApp<App>()
                .ConfigureFonts(fonts =>
                {
                    fonts.AddFont("OpenSans-Regular.ttf", "OpenSansRegular");
                    fonts.AddFont("OpenSans-Semibold.ttf",
        "OpenSansSemibold");
                    fonts.AddFont("FluentSystemIcons-
        Filled.ttf", "FluentFilled");
                    fonts.AddFont("FluentSystemIcons-
        Regular.ttf", "FluentRegular");
                });
```

Registers the FluentSystemIcons-Filled.ttf font asset with the name FluentFilled

Registers the FluentSystemIcons-Regular.ttf font asset with the name FluentFilled

```
            return builder.Build();
        }
    }
}
```

These fonts are now registered as application-wide resources, accessible via the names registered for them in MauiProgram.cs. We'll see how to use these icons shortly, but we also need some other application-wide resources: colors. We could specify the colors individually for every control, but this is laborious and unnecessary.

I used a color picker to identify the colors we need. We'll register these in the Resources/Styles/Colors.xml file. We'll look at this in more detail in chapter 10, but for now, update the items shown in the following listing.

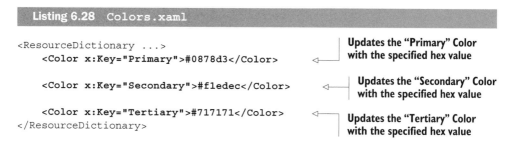

Listing 6.28 Colors.xaml

```
<ResourceDictionary ...>
    <Color x:Key="Primary">#0878d3</Color>        Updates the "Primary" Color
                                                   with the specified hex value

    <Color x:Key="Secondary">#f1edec</Color>      Updates the "Secondary" Color
                                                   with the specified hex value

    <Color x:Key="Tertiary">#717171</Color>       Updates the "Tertiary" Color
</ResourceDictionary>                              with the specified hex value
```

Each of these colors is now available to use as a StaticResource anywhere in the app. Now let's start breaking down the UI.

6.4.2 Defining the UI as a Grid

The first step is to break down the screen into its component parts and figure out how to replicate those parts with .NET MAUI. And the first of these is the screen itself. Figure 6.17 shows how we can use a Grid to break down the top-level components of the Outlook UI, consisting of four rows.

Next, we have the list of messages, and at the bottom, we have the tab bar. In a real-world app, we would use Shell or a TabbedPage to provide these tabs (which we'll look at in chapter 7) or, in other cases, an external control library that includes tabs. In this case, as we're just replicating the UI and not using these for navigation, we'll build the tabs directly into the page.

Looking at this top-level Grid, we can see that the top row (row 0) is slightly larger than the second row (row 1), and that the last row (row 3) is slightly larger still. The middle row (row 2) takes up all the remaining space. I've measured these, and a close enough approximation gives us row heights of 50, 40, *, and 80. This is enough to get started, so let's add the top-level grid to MainPage.xaml. Listing 6.29 shows this initial scaffolding.

Figure 6.17   The Outlook Inbox UI broken down as rows in a `Grid`. We've ignored the status bar and safe area. Using this approach, we can see that we have four rows. The top row has the title and search, and the next row has the focused inbox switch and the filter button. At the bottom, we can see the tab bar, and between the second and fourth rows is the list of messages, which takes up all the remaining space.

Listing 6.29   `MainPage.xaml`

```xml
<?xml version="1.0" encoding="utf-8" ?>
<ContentPage xmlns="http://schemas.microsoft.com/dotnet/2021/maui"
             xmlns:x="http://schemas.microsoft.com/winfx/2009/xaml"
             x:Class="OutlookClone.MainPage">
```

```
<Grid RowDefinitions="50,40,*,80">
  </Grid>
</ContentPage>
```
⊲——⎤ **Adds a Grid with row**
    ⎦ **heights of 50, 40, *, and 80**

6.4.3   Creating the title bar with FlexLayout

We'll use a `FlexLayout` for the top row of the `Grid`, which will let us easily position the child items at the start and end using `SpaceBetween`. Inside this `FlexLayout`, we can use `HorizontalStackLayout` to position the home icon and title at the start and a `Label` to position the search icon at the end (figure 6.18).

Figure 6.18   We can use a `FlexLayout` to arrange the top row, using `SpaceBetween` to position the child views on either side. On the left, we can use a `HorizontalStackLayout` with two `Label`s (one for the icon and one for the title) and a `Label` for the search icon on the right.

As we're going to start using the icons now, we need a simple way to reference the icons we want to use. Usually, when using a font, you just type out the text that you want and let the font display it for you, but we're using glyphs rather than ASCII or Unicode characters. There are a few tools you can use to find the glyph codes you need, but I've already identified the glyphs we need (I used https://andreinitescu .github.io/IconFont2Code/). Table 6.1 shows which glyphs we'll use from which font asset, and for what purpose.

Table 6.1   Glyphs

Icon	Font	Glyph code
Home	FluentFilled	fa38
Search	FluentRegular	fb26
Filter	FluentRegular	f408
Mail	FluentFilled	f513
Calendar	FluentRegular	03de

Using these fonts in XAML is easy. We set the `FontFamily` property of a `Label` to the font we want to use and set the `Text` property to the code of the glyph. When using these codes in XAML, we have to prefix them with the characters &#x and end with ;.

Listing 6.30 shows the updated `MainPage.xaml`, with the inner layout for the top row added. The added lines are shown in **bold**.

Listing 6.30   `MainPage.xaml` with the top row layout added

```xml
<?xml version="1.0" encoding="utf-8" ?>
<ContentPage xmlns="http://schemas.microsoft.com/dotnet/2021/maui"
             xmlns:x="http://schemas.microsoft.com/winfx/2009/xaml"
             x:Class="OutlookClone.MainPage">

    <Grid RowDefinitions="50,40,*,80">

        <FlexLayout Grid.Row="0"
                    HorizontalOptions="FillAndExpand"
                    VerticalOptions="FillAndExpand"
                    BackgroundColor="{StaticResource Primary}"
                    JustifyContent="SpaceBetween">

            <HorizontalStackLayout Margin="5,0,0,0"
                                   Spacing="10">

                <Label Text="&#xfa38;"
                       FontFamily="FluentFilled"
                       TextColor="{StaticResource Primary}"
                       HorizontalTextAlignment="Center"
                       HorizontalOptions="StartAndExpand"
                       VerticalTextAlignment="Center"
                       BackgroundColor="White"
                       VerticalOptions="Center"
                       WidthRequest="30"
                       HeightRequest="30"
                       FontSize="Large"/>

                <Label Text="Inbox"
                       VerticalTextAlignment="Center"
                       HorizontalOptions="StartAndExpand"
                       TextColor="White"
                       FontAttributes="Bold"
                       FontSize="Large"/>

            </HorizontalStackLayout>

            <Label Text="&#xfb26;"
                   FontFamily="FluentRegular"
                   TextColor="White"
                   VerticalOptions="Center"
                   HorizontalOptions="EndAndExpand"
                   HorizontalTextAlignment="End"
                   WidthRequest="40"
                   FontSize="Large"
                   Margin="0,0,5,0"/>
        </FlexLayout>

    </Grid>
</ContentPage>
```

This code gives us nearly everything we need for the top row, but if we run it now, the home icon would be square, and it's round in Outlook. However, we can easily `Clip` the `Label` to make it round. The following listing shows the updated home icon `Label`, with ellipse geometry added to make the icon round. The changes are in **bold**.

Listing 6.31 The updated home icon

```xml
<?xml version="1.0" encoding="utf-8" ?>
<ContentPage xmlns="http://schemas.microsoft.com/dotnet/2021/maui"
             xmlns:x="http://schemas.microsoft.com/winfx/2009/xaml"
             x:Class="OutlookClone.MainPage">

    <Grid RowDefinitions="50,40,*,80">
        <FlexLayout ...>
            <HorizontalStackLayout ...>
                <Label Text="&#xfa38;"
                       FontFamily="FluentFilled"
                       TextColor="{StaticResource Primary}"
                       HorizontalTextAlignment="Center"
                       HorizontalOptions="StartAndExpand"
                       VerticalTextAlignment="Center"
                       BackgroundColor="White"
                       VerticalOptions="Center"
                       WidthRequest="30"
                       HeightRequest="30"
                       FontSize="Large">
                    <Label.Clip>
                        <EllipseGeometry RadiusX="15"
                                         RadiusY="15"
                                         Center="15,15"/>
                    </Label.Clip>
                </Label>
                <Label …/>
            </HorizontalStackLayout>
            <Label …/>
        </FlexLayout>
    </Grid>
</ContentPage>
```

That completes the first row of the `Grid`. You can run OutlookClone now if you like; you will see a blank screen with just the top row. But we're ready to move on to the second row.

6.4.4 Creating the filter bar with FlexLayout

We'll use a `FlexLayout` for the second row too. The focused inbox switch is a custom control, and building that is outside the scope of this exercise, so we're going to use a little artistic license and replace it with a standard `Switch` and a `Label`. We'll place these inside a `HorizontalStackLayout` and use a second `HorizontalStackLayout` at the end of the `FlexLayout` for the filter icon and label (figure 6.19).

Listing 6.32 shows the updated `MainPage.xaml` with the code for the second row added in **bold**. The code for the first row has been omitted for brevity.

Figure 6.19 We can use a `FlexLayout` to arrange the second row, using `SpaceBetween` to position the child views on either side. On the left is the focused inbox switch control, and on the right is a `HorizontalStackLayout` with two child `Label`s: one for the icon and the second for the word *Filter*.

Listing 6.32   The second row of the `Grid`

```xml
<?xml version="1.0" encoding="utf-8" ?>
<ContentPage xmlns="http://schemas.microsoft.com/dotnet/2021/maui"
             xmlns:x="http://schemas.microsoft.com/winfx/2009/xaml"
             x:Class="OutlookClone.MainPage">

    <Grid RowDefinitions="50,40,*,80">
        <FlexLayout …>
...
        </FlexLayout>

        <FlexLayout Grid.Row="1"
                    HorizontalOptions="FillAndExpand"
                    VerticalOptions="FillAndExpand"
                    BackgroundColor="{StaticResource Primary}"
                    Padding="20,5"
                    JustifyContent="SpaceBetween">    ⬅ Sets the JustifyContent
                                                        property to SpaceBetween
                                                        so that the child items are
                                                        positioned at the beginning
                                                        and end of the row
            <HorizontalStackLayout Margin="5,0,0,0">

                <Label Text="Focused"
                       TextColor="White"
                       VerticalOptions="Center"/>

                <Switch/>

            </HorizontalStackLayout>

            <HorizontalStackLayout Margin="0,0,5,0"
                                   Spacing="10">

                <Label Text="&#xf408;"
                       FontFamily="FluentRegular"
                       TextColor="White"
                       VerticalOptions="Center"
                       HorizontalOptions="EndAndExpand"
                       HorizontalTextAlignment="End"
                       WidthRequest="40"
                       FontSize="Large"/>

                <Label Text="Filter"
                       TextColor="White"
                       VerticalOptions="Center"
                       HorizontalOptions="EndAndExpand"
                       HorizontalTextAlignment="End"/>
```

```
        </HorizontalStackLayout>
    </FlexLayout>


  </Grid>
</ContentPage>
```

The header section of OutlookClone is now complete. If you run the app, you'll see a blank screen, with the header section, shown in figure 6.20, at the top.

Figure 6.20   The OutlookClone header section. Two rows are arranged using a `Grid`, and the rows themselves use `FlexLayout` and `HorizontalStackLayout` to position items.

NOTE   Delete all the code from `MainPage.xaml.cs`, apart from the constructor, before running the app.

6.4.5   *Using Grid to create a FAB*

The main section of the page is the message previews on row 2. Each message preview follows a specific layout and uses a data source for each item. The collection of messages is scrollable, and a message can be selected. `CollectionView` is an ideal candidate for this use case (figure 6.21).

We're not going to build the `CollectionView` just yet as we'll need some data to see any contents, which we'll get to shortly. But we can add the FAB. We'll add it to row 2 and position it vertically and horizontally at the end. As we're using a `Button`, which has a `CornerRadius` property, we won't need to do any clipping to make it round. And we'll give it a `Shadow` to make it mimic the real app.

The following listing shows the updated `MainPage.xaml` with the added `Button` in **bold**. Most of the rest of the code has been omitted for brevity.

Listing 6.33   The FAB

```
<?xml version="1.0" encoding="utf-8" ?>
<ContentPage xmlns="http://schemas.microsoft.com/dotnet/2021/maui"
             xmlns:x="http://schemas.microsoft.com/winfx/2009/xaml"
             x:Class="OutlookClone.MainPage">

    <Grid RowDefinitions="50,40,*,80">
        <FlexLayout …>
        ...
        </FlexLayout>

        <FlexLayout …>
            ...
        </FlexLayout>
```

```
        <Button Grid.Row="2"
                BackgroundColor="{StaticResource Primary}"
                HorizontalOptions="EndAndExpand"
                VerticalOptions="EndAndExpand"
                Margin="20"
                HeightRequest="60"
                WidthRequest="60"
                CornerRadius="30"
                FontSize="30"
                Text="+">
            <Button.Shadow>
                <Shadow Brush="Black"
                        Offset="5,5"
                        Radius="10"
                        Opacity="0.5"/>
            </Button.Shadow>
        </Button>
    </Grid>
</ContentPage>
```

Figure 6.21   Using `CollectionView` **for the third row is a no-brainer, but we can see there's a FAB button in the bottom right-hand corner, too. This can be in the same row (there's only one column), and we can use** `HorizontalOptions` **and** `VerticalOptions` **to position it at the end.**

Now that we've got the FAB, the final component before we start populating the messages section is the tab bar footer.

6.4.6   *Building a tab bar with Grid*

To build the tab bar, we'll add a `Grid` to the fourth row (row 3) of the page's top-level `Grid`. It will have three columns, one for each tab, and within each column will be a `VerticalStackLayout` to arrange the tab's icon and label (figure 6.22).

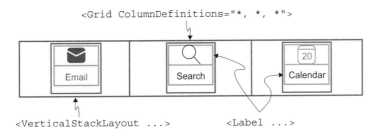

Figure 6.22   The last row is the tab bar. We'll use another `Grid` for this part, with three columns. In each column we'll use a `VerticalStackLayout` with two `Label`s as child items: one for the tab icon and one for the tab label.

Let's start by adding the `Grid`. Listing 6.34 shows the code for `MainPage.xaml` with the tab bar `Grid` added in **bold**. Most of the remaining code has been omitted for brevity.

Listing 6.34   The tab bar

```xml
<?xml version="1.0" encoding="utf-8" ?>
<ContentPage xmlns="http://schemas.microsoft.com/dotnet/2021/maui"
             xmlns:x="http://schemas.microsoft.com/winfx/2009/xaml"
             x:Class="OutlookClone.MainPage">

    <Grid RowDefinitions="50,40,*,80">
        <FlexLayout …>
...
        </FlexLayout>

        <FlexLayout …
...
        </FlexLayout>

        <Button …>
...
        </Button>

        <Grid Grid.Row="3"
              HorizontalOptions="FillAndExpand"
              VerticalOptions="FillAndExpand"
              ColumnDefinitions="*,*,*"
              Padding="5"
              BackgroundColor="{StaticResource Secondary}">
```

```
        </Grid>

    </Grid>
</ContentPage>
```

That defines the high-level layout for the tab bar. Now let's add the VerticalStack-Layout for the first tab. The following listing shows the updated MainPage.xaml, with the added code in **bold**. Some of the code (including the Grid's properties) has been removed for brevity.

Listing 6.35   The first tab

```
<?xml version="1.0" encoding="utf-8" ?>
<ContentPage xmlns="http://schemas.microsoft.com/dotnet/2021/maui"
             xmlns:x="http://schemas.microsoft.com/winfx/2009/xaml"
             x:Class="OutlookClone.MainPage">

    <Grid RowDefinitions="50,40,*,80">
        <FlexLayout …>
...
        </FlexLayout>

        <FlexLayout …
        ...
        </FlexLayout>

        <Button …>
        ...
        </Button>

        <Grid …>
            <VerticalStackLayout HorizontalOptions="Center"
                    Grid.Column="0">

                <Label Text="&#xf513;"
                       FontFamily="FluentFilled"
                       TextColor="{StaticResource Primary}"
                       HorizontalTextAlignment="Center"
                       HorizontalOptions="Center"
                       VerticalTextAlignment="Center"
                       VerticalOptions="Center"
                       WidthRequest="30"
                       HeightRequest="30"
                       FontSize="30"/>

                <Label Text="Email"
                       TextColor="{StaticResource Primary}"
                       HorizontalTextAlignment="Center"
                       HorizontalOptions="Center"
                       VerticalTextAlignment="Center"
                       VerticalOptions="Center"
                       FontSize="11"/>
            </VerticalStackLayout>
```

```
        </Grid>

    </Grid>
</ContentPage>
```

Now that we've got the first tab complete, we can copy and paste the code for the tab to add the second and third tabs. We'll need to change the column, glyph, and text colors.

Listing 6.36 shows the updated MainPage.xaml file with the second and third tabs added in **bold**. The first tab and most of the remaining code have been omitted for brevity. Pay attention to the columns, Text properties, and TextColor properties.

Listing 6.36 The final two tabs

```
<?xml version="1.0" encoding="utf-8" ?>
<ContentPage xmlns="http://schemas.microsoft.com/dotnet/2021/maui"
             xmlns:x="http://schemas.microsoft.com/winfx/2009/xaml"
             x:Class="OutlookClone.MainPage">

    <Grid RowDefinitions="50,40,*,80">
        <FlexLayout …>
        ...
        </FlexLayout>

        <FlexLayout …
        ...
        </FlexLayout>

        <Button …>
        ...
        </Button>

        <Grid …>
            <VerticalStackLayout …>
            ...
            </VerticalStackLayout>

            <VerticalStackLayout HorizontalOptions="Center"
                                 Grid.Column="1">

                <Label Text="&#xfb26;"
                       FontFamily="FluentRegular"
                       TextColor="{StaticResource Tertiary}"
                       HorizontalTextAlignment="Center"
                       HorizontalOptions="Center"
                       VerticalTextAlignment="Center"
                       VerticalOptions="Center"
                       WidthRequest="30"
                       HeightRequest="30"
                       FontSize="30"/>

                <Label Text="Search"
                       TextColor="{StaticResource Tertiary}"
```

```
                    HorizontalTextAlignment="Center"
                    HorizontalOptions="Center"
                    VerticalTextAlignment="Center"
                    VerticalOptions="Center"
                    FontSize="11"/>

        </VerticalStackLayout>

        <VerticalStackLayout HorizontalOptions="Center"
                             Grid.Column="2">

            <Label Text="&#x03de;"
                    FontFamily="FluentRegular"
                    TextColor="{StaticResource Tertiary}"
                    HorizontalTextAlignment="Center"
                    HorizontalOptions="Center"
                    VerticalTextAlignment="Center"
                    VerticalOptions="Center"
                    WidthRequest="30"
                    HeightRequest="30"
                    FontSize="30"/>

            <Label Text="Calendar"
                    TextColor="{StaticResource Tertiary}"
                    FontSize="11"
                    HorizontalTextAlignment="Center"
                    HorizontalOptions="Center"
                    VerticalTextAlignment="Center"
                    VerticalOptions="Center"/>

        </VerticalStackLayout>
    </Grid>

    </Grid>
</ContentPage>
```

That completes the layout for OutlookClone. We still need to add the messages, but you can run it now and immediately see what we're building. If you run the app now, you should see something like figure 6.23.

The last piece of the puzzle is the CollectionView, which will occupy the main section of the page. Before we build that though, let's set up some data to display messages.

6.4.7   *Populating dummy data*

We're not going to build an email client, so we need a way to simulate the data for our inbox. For this, we'll use an API that returns random quotes from *The Simpsons*. The API will give us a quote along with the name of the character who said it and a link to a picture of them. We'll use the name as the sender, the picture for the avatar, and the quote can be both the message and the subject.

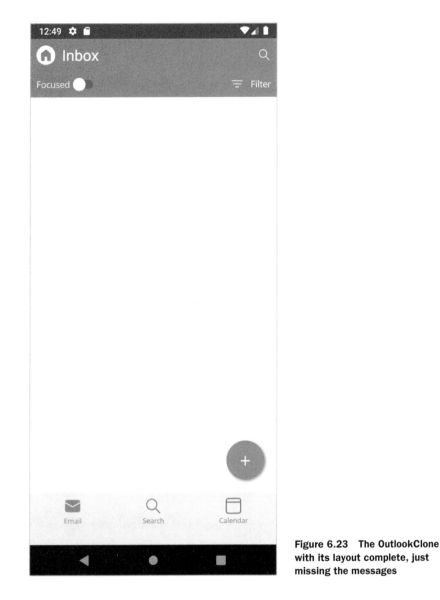

Figure 6.23 The OutlookClone with its layout complete, just missing the messages

The API that we're going to use is https://thesimpsonsquoteapi.glitch.me. By checking the API documentation, we can see that we can call the `quotes` endpoint specifying `count` as a query parameter. An initial call to that endpoint gives us the structure of the JSON data that it returns, and from there, we can create a class to use in our code to deserialize the response from the API.

> **NOTE** As mentioned in section 6.2.1, there are a few ways you can generate the C# classes from the Simpsons quote API's JSON data, including the built-in tooling in Visual Studio or free online converters.

Create a class in the OutlookClone project called Simpson. The following listing shows the code for this class.

Listing 6.37 The Simpson class

```
namespace OutlookClone;

public class Simpson
{
    public string quote { get; set; }
    public string character { get; set; }
    public string image { get; set; }
    public string characterDirection { get; set; }
}
```

Now that we've got this class, we can write some logic to call the API and build a collection of quotes. In the MainPage.xaml.cs file, add an ObservableCollection of type Simpson and add a field for the URI we use to call the API.

Next, override the OnAppearing method and make it async. In this method, we'll instantiate an HttpClient and use it to call the API, returning the data as a collection of the Simpson type we've defined. Then, we can iterate through the results and add each one to the ObservableCollection. The following listing shows the updated MainPage.xaml.cs file with the added code in **bold**.

Listing 6.38 MainPage.xaml.cs

```
using System.Collections.ObjectModel;
using System.Net.Http.Json;

namespace OutlookClone
{
    public partial class MainPage : ContentPage
    {

        private string contentUri = "https://thesimpsonsquoteapi.glitch.me/
    quotes?count=20";

        public ObservableCollection<Simpson> Simpsons = new();

        public MainPage()
        {
            InitializeComponent();
        }

        protected override async void OnAppearing()
        {
            base.OnAppearing();

            var httpClient = new HttpClient();

            var jsonResponse = await
    httpClient.GetFromJsonAsync<List<Simpson>>(contentUri);
```

```
        jsonResponse.ForEach(s => Simpsons.Add(s));
      }
    }
  }
```

Now that we've set up our data source and know the structure of the data we're displaying, we can add the CollectionView and use that structure to define our DataTemplate.

6.4.8 *Displaying the messages with CollectionView*

Now that we've got a data source, let's add the CollectionView to the UI. Open MainPage.xaml and add a CollectionView to row 2 of the page's top-level Grid. You'll need to add it *before* the Button in the same row; otherwise, the CollectionView will get rendered on top of the Button (you can also adjust the z-index of these elements, but for a simple UI like this, it's easier to just add them in the right order).

The following listing shows MainPage.xaml with the CollectionView added. Some of the code has been omitted for brevity, and the added code is shown in **bold**.

Listing 6.39 MainPage.xaml with the CollectionView added

```
<?xml version="1.0" encoding="utf-8" ?>
<ContentPage xmlns="http://schemas.microsoft.com/dotnet/2021/maui"
             xmlns:x="http://schemas.microsoft.com/winfx/2009/xaml"
             x:Class="OutlookClone.MainPage">

    <Grid RowDefinitions="50,40,*,80">
        <FlexLayout …>
        ...
        </FlexLayout>

        <FlexLayout …>
        ...
        </FlexLayout>

        <CollectionView Grid.Row="2"
                        x:Name="MessageCollection"
                        HorizontalOptions="Fill"
                        VerticalOptions="Fill">
            <CollectionView.ItemTemplate>
                <DataTemplate>

                </DataTemplate>
            </CollectionView.ItemTemplate>
        </CollectionView>

        <Button ...>
        ...
        </Button>

        <Grid …>
        ...
        </Grid>
```

```
    </Grid>
</ContentPage>
```

With the `CollectionView` in place, it's time to define the template for the items in the collection. Looking at the original Outlook UI, we can see that there is an avatar image, a sender name, a message subject, a preview of the message body, and a time or day when the message was sent.

We can use a `Grid` for this layout (figure 6.24). The `Grid` will have three columns; the first and last columns will have a width of 50, and the middle column can take up the remaining space. We'll have three rows, with the second row being slightly less high than the top row and the third row being twice the height of the second.

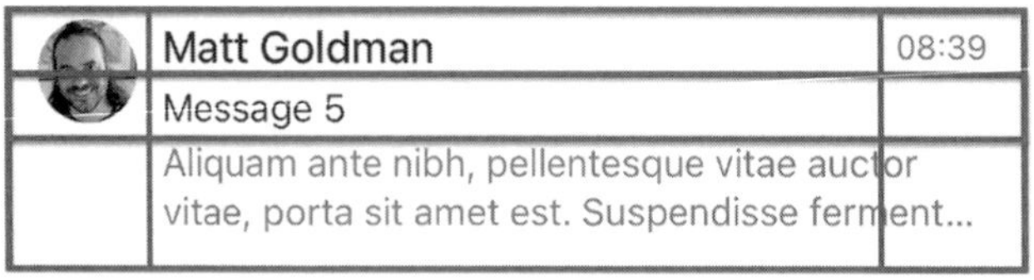

Figure 6.24   The message template for the Inbox can be laid out as a `Grid`, with three columns and three rows. The avatar will reside in the first column and row and will have a row span of 3 (there's nothing else in the first column). The sender's name will go into the first row, second column. The subject will go into the second row, second column, and the message body preview will go into the third row, second column, and will span into the third column. The time or day when the message was sent will go into the first row, third column.

Now that we know how to lay out the message template, let's add this to the `Collection-View`. We haven't set the binding yet, but we know that we're going to use our `Simpson` class as the source data type, so we can bind to properties on that class in the template. The following listing shows the code for the data template, with the added code in **bold**. The rest of the page's code has been omitted for brevity.

Listing 6.40   `MainPage.xaml` with the message template

```
<CollectionView ...>
    <CollectionView.ItemTemplate>
        <DataTemplate>
            <Grid ColumnDefinitions="50,*,50"
                  RowDefinitions="25,20,40"
                  HorizontalOptions="Fill"
                  VerticalOptions="Fill"
                  Padding="10,5,20,5">

                <Image WidthRequest="40"
                       HeightRequest="40"
                       Grid.RowSpan="3"
```

```
                              VerticalOptions="Start"
                              HorizontalOptions="Start"
                              Aspect="AspectFill"
                              Source="{Binding image}">
                       <Image.Clip>
                           <EllipseGeometry RadiusX="20"
                                            RadiusY="20"
                                            Center="20,20"/>
                       </Image.Clip>
                   </Image>

                   <Label Grid.Row="0"
                          Grid.Column="1"
                          Text="{Binding character}"
                          FontSize="18"
                          FontAttributes="Bold"
                          TextColor="Black"/>

                   <Label Grid.Row="1"
                          Grid.Column="1"
                          Text="{Binding quote}"
                          LineBreakMode="TailTruncation"
                          VerticalOptions="Start"
                          TextColor="Black"/>

                   <Label Grid.Row="2"
                          Grid.Column="1"
                          Grid.ColumnSpan="2"
                          Text="{Binding quote}"
                          LineBreakMode="WordWrap"
                          VerticalOptions="Start"
                          TextColor="{StaticResource Tertiary}"/>

                   <Label Grid.Row="0"
                          Grid.Column="2"
                          Text="Saturday"
                          FontSize="12"
                          TextColor="{StaticResource Tertiary}"/>
               </Grid>
           </DataTemplate>
       </CollectionView.ItemTemplate>
   </CollectionView>
```

This completes the layout for the message template. We need to wire up the Items-Source property of the CollectionView, but before we do, I want to make one more addition for a slight UX improvement.

Add an ActivityIndicator to the page's top-level Grid. We'll use this to show that data is loading. We'll place it in row 2 to show where the messages will appear once the data is loaded. We'll control the visibility of the ActivityIndicator in the code-behind.

Listing 6.41 shows MainPage.xaml with the ActivityIndicator added, shown in bold. The rest of the code has been omitted for brevity.

Listing 6.41   `MainPage.xaml` with the `ActivityIndicator`

```xml
<?xml version="1.0" encoding="utf-8" ?>
<ContentPage xmlns="http://schemas.microsoft.com/dotnet/2021/maui"
             xmlns:x="http://schemas.microsoft.com/winfx/2009/xaml"
             x:Class="OutlookClone.MainPage">

    <Grid RowDefinitions="50,40,*,80">

        ...

        <ActivityIndicator Grid.Row="2"
                           Color="{StaticResource Primary}"
                           IsRunning="True"
                           IsEnabled="True"
                           VerticalOptions="Center"
                           HorizontalOptions="Center"
                           x:Name="LoadingIndicator"/>

    </Grid>
</ContentPage>
```

The `MainPage.xaml` UI is now 100% complete. The last steps are to set the `Items-Source` property of the `CollectionView` and show/hide the `ActivityIndicator` as appropriate. We'll do both of these in the code-behind. Make the changes shown in **bold** in the following listing to `MainPage.xaml.cs`.

Listing 6.42   The complete `MainPage.xaml.cs`

```csharp
using System.Collections.ObjectModel;
using System.Net.Http.Json;

namespace OutlookClone
{
    public partial class MainPage : ContentPage
    {

        private string contentUri = "https://thesimpsonsquoteapi.glitch.me/
    quotes?count=20";

        public ObservableCollection<Simpson> Simpsons = new();

        public MainPage()
        {
            InitializeComponent();
            MessageCollection.ItemsSource = Simpsons;
        }

        protected override async void OnAppearing()
        {
            LoadingIndicator.IsVisible = true;

            base.OnAppearing();
```

```
        var httpClient = new HttpClient();

        var jsonResponse = await
httpClient.GetFromJsonAsync<List<Simpson>>(contentUri);

        jsonResponse.ForEach(s => Simpsons.Add(s));

        LoadingIndicator.IsVisible = false;
      }
    }
}
```

The OutlookClone app is now complete. Go ahead and run it, and you should see something like figure 6.25.

Figure 6.25   The completed
OutlookClone app

Replicating app UIs is a fun and challenging way to keep your UI skills sharp with .NET MAUI. There are also a bunch more things we could do with this app, such as add SwipeView to the messages, make the tabs a templated control (we'll see how to do this in chapter 8), or even, if you're feeling ambitious, replicate the focused inbox switch from the original app.

Summary

- Grid is a versatile layout you can use for nearly any UI. You can build complex layouts using a Grid, like SSW.Rewards or even Microsoft Outlook, not just simple rows and columns like MauiCalc.
- With BindableLayout, you can use a data source to add child items to any layout using a DataTemplate, just like with CollectionView.
- FlexLayout is a great layout to use with BindableLayout. HorizontalStackLayout and VerticalStackLayout are good candidates for BindableLayout too, although Grid is not a sensible choice for this.
- With AbsoluteLayout you can gain precise control over where things are positioned on screen and how they are sized. Within an AbsoluteLayout, you can use proportional or absolute sizing and positioning to arrange views.

Pages and navigation

This chapter covers

- How to break your app up into pages using the
  `ContentPage` base class
- How to use the navigation paradigms supported
  by .NET MAUI to navigate between different pages
  in your app
- Using Shell to simplify organizing the pages in
  your app
- Passing data between pages when navigating

So far, we've built a handful of apps, all using a single page. A single page has worked well for the sample apps we've been building and works equally well for several commercial apps in the real world. But often, you need more than one page, for example, to distinguish different areas of an app or logically group functionality. Additional pages become especially necessary with nontrivial apps when they grow too much to cram everything into a single screen. In this chapter, we'll look at navigation paradigms and the different ways that .NET MAUI supports providing multiple pages in your apps and navigating between them.

7.1   *ContentPage*

ContentPage is the most important page type. Other page types are just containers that provide different navigation paradigms that offer a way to present a ContentPage.

ContentPage has a single public property of type View called Content, which is what the page will render on screen. In XAML, the Content property is assigned by placing the XAML element between the opening and closing <ContentPage...> ...</ContentPage> tags, as in listing 7.1. In C#, you can assign it just like any other property, as in listing 7.2.

Listing 7.1   `ContentPage.xaml`

```
<ContentPage xmlns="http://schemas.microsoft.com/dotnet/2021/maui"
             xmlns:x="http://schemas.microsoft.com/winfx/2009/xaml"
             x:Class="MayApp.MyPage">

    <!--Your page's content goes here -->
```
> In XAML, you assign content to the page by writing it between the opening and closing ContentPage tags.
```
</ContentPage>
```

Note that you can also explicitly add the Content property and then add your views to it using the <ContentPage.Content>...</ContentPage.Content> tags. However, this does not need to be explicitly specified. A View added between the <ContentPage> tags will be assigned to the Content property.

Listing 7.2   `ContentPage.xaml.cs`

```
namespace MyApp;

public partial class MyPage : ContentPage
{
    public MyPage()
    {
        InitializeComponent();
        Content = new VerticalStackLayout();
    }
}
```
> In C#, you can assign a View directly to the Content property of a ContentPage

When building a page in a .NET MAUI app, you will choose one of these two approaches (listings 7.1 and 7.2 would not be from the same app).

UI in C#

In this book, while we dip into C# to declare or manipulate UI when necessary, we'll focus primarily on the XAML approach. However, if you are interested in declaring your UI in C# code, you can find out more about it in the .NET MAUI documentation.

Plenty of community-generated resources are also available for learning and using C# declared UI, including markup extensions in the Community Toolkit that let you write your UI in C# using a fluent API. If this approach interests you, I recommend starting with the video by Gerald Versluis, available on his YouTube channel at https://www.youtube.com/watch?v=nCNh9G-Q688.

All the layouts and controls provided in .NET MAUI are derived from the `View` base class, so they can be assigned to the `View` property of `ContentPage`. It's common to assign a layout to the `Content` property of a `ContentPage` or a `ScrollView`, which we discussed in chapter 4. We've seen this approach in every example we've looked at so far, including the page generated by the template, as shown in figure 7.1.

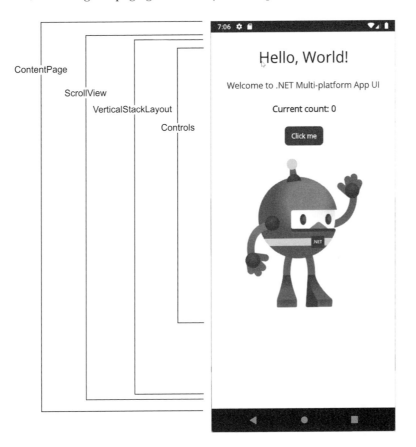

Figure 7.1   A `ContentPage` has a `Content` property to which you can assign a `View`, which means any layout or control. In this case, a `ScrollView` is assigned to the `Content` property, which wraps a `VerticalStackLayout`, which contains all the controls. The `ScrollView` ensures any content that doesn't fit on screen is still available, and the `VerticalStackLayout` enables multiple controls to be added to the page.

As I mentioned, all controls in .NET MAUI are also derived from `View`, so you could, in fact, just add, for example, a `Button` to the `View` property of a `Content-Page`, as in listing 7.3.

Listing 7.3   A page with a single control as its `Content`

```xml
<?xml version="1.0" encoding="utf-8" ?>
<ContentPage xmlns="http://schemas.microsoft.com/dotnet/2021/maui"
             xmlns:x="http://schemas.microsoft.com/winfx/2009/xaml"
             x:Class="AlohaWorld.MainPage">

    <Button Text="Click me"
            FontAttributes="Bold"
            HorizontalOptions="Center" />
</ContentPage>
```

As you can see from figure 7.2, this wouldn't make for a particularly interesting page.

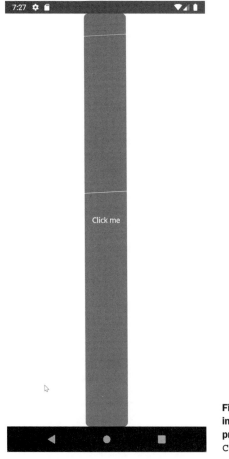

Figure 7.2   A `ContentPage` **with a single** `View`, **in this case, a** `Button`, **assigned to its** `Content` **property by placing the** `View` **between the** `ContentPage`'s **opening and closing tags**

While this is a valid approach to building .NET MAUI apps, it's not a sensible one, and you should stick to assigning either a layout or a `ScrollView` to the `Content` property of your pages.

7.2 Common page properties

In .NET MAUI, a page is a class that inherits the `Page` base class (or in the case of `TabbedPage`, a collection of `Pages`). The `Page` base class has several properties related to rendering a UI on screen, as well as some lifecycle methods and events.

The `Page` base class also has a few properties that are inherited by, and can be useful in, the derived page types. Depending on the navigation paradigm you're using to present your page, these properties may do different things or, in some cases, nothing at all.

These properties are all bindable, meaning you can assign values to them directly or bind them to properties of corresponding types in a binding context. This section lists the most useful and most commonly used of these properties.

> **NOTE** The `IsBusy` property isn't covered here because it does not work reliably and should not be used. Adding your own `ActivityIndicator` is trivial; you should do this instead, as we've seen in MauiTodo and MauiMovies.

7.2.1 IconImageSource

`IconImageSource` lets you specify an image to be displayed as the page's icon. If your page is being presented by either a `FlyoutPage` or `TabbedPage`, the image you specify here will be displayed as the page's icon either in the flyout menu or the tab bar.

7.2.2 Background Images

The `BackgroundImageSource` property of a page lets you specify an image that will be displayed in the background. Layouts, by default, are transparent, so any areas of the page not covered by a control will show the image specified as the background.

Image properties can be provided to specify how the image should be displayed (e.g., filled, tiled, etc.). If you want a tiled background image, `BackgroundImage-Source` can be a good option. However, setting a `BackgroundImageSource` can yield unpredictable results if you want to fit or fill the image.

If you want a filled or fitted background image, you'll get much more reliable results using a `Grid` as a parent layout for your page, placing an `Image` in row and column 0, and setting the `Aspect` property you want. If you don't want to use a `Grid` as your layout, you can still use this approach; simply add the `Image` and your preferred layout, in that order, to your page. You don't even need to define any rows or columns or specify which row and column the `Image` and your layout should go in. By default, the `Grid` will have a single row and column, and views inside a `Grid` will, by default, be in row and column 0.

Let's use this approach to add a background image to MauiMovies. I will use a picture of the Hollywood sign from Pexels.com, a website for free stock images and other creative works; you can find it in the chapter's resources folder or source your own. The following listing shows the changes needed to add the background image, and you can see the result in figure 7.3.

Listing 7.4   `MainPage.xaml` with background image

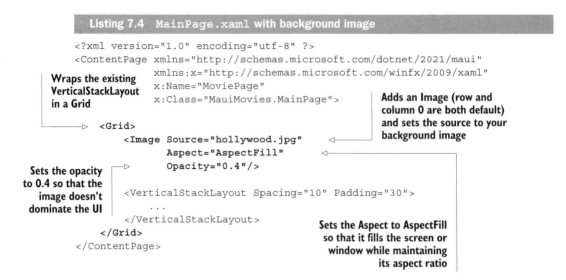

```xml
<?xml version="1.0" encoding="utf-8" ?>
<ContentPage xmlns="http://schemas.microsoft.com/dotnet/2021/maui"
             xmlns:x="http://schemas.microsoft.com/winfx/2009/xaml"
             x:Name="MoviePage"
             x:Class="MauiMovies.MainPage">
    <Grid>
        <Image Source="hollywood.jpg"
               Aspect="AspectFill"
               Opacity="0.4"/>

        <VerticalStackLayout Spacing="10" Padding="30">
            ...
        </VerticalStackLayout>
    </Grid>
</ContentPage>
```

Wraps the existing VerticalStackLayout in a Grid

Adds an Image (row and column 0 are both default) and sets the source to your background image

Sets the opacity to 0.4 so that the image doesn't dominate the UI

Sets the Aspect to AspectFill so that it fills the screen or window while maintaining its aspect ratio

Figure 7.3   A background image added to a page by assigning both the image and the page's layout to a single row and column `Grid` that takes up the whole page. This approach lets you reliably fit or fill the image, which yields unpredictable results when using the page's `BackgroundImageSource` property. Tiling a background image is more reliable when using `BackgroundImageSource`.

7.2.3 Padding

Page has a Padding property of type Thickness. All views have a boundary, and Padding specifies how close to that boundary items inside the view are allowed to get.

Padding differs from Margin in that Padding represents the space inside a view's boundary, whereas Margin corresponds to the space outside a view's boundary (figure 7.4). Specifying the page's Padding property will ensure a gap between the outer boundary of the page and any child items your page displays.

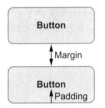

Figure 7.4 Two buttons on a page. The arrow between them represents Margin and specifies how apart views are from other views. The arrow pointing inward represents Padding and specifies how far from a view's boundary its internal elements can be displayed.

7.2.4 Title

Page has a Title property of type string. The Title property is used to show which page of the app is currently being displayed and is shown in the app's toolbar or navigation bar. Figure 7.5 shows what the MainPage of the MauiTodo app would look like with a title set.

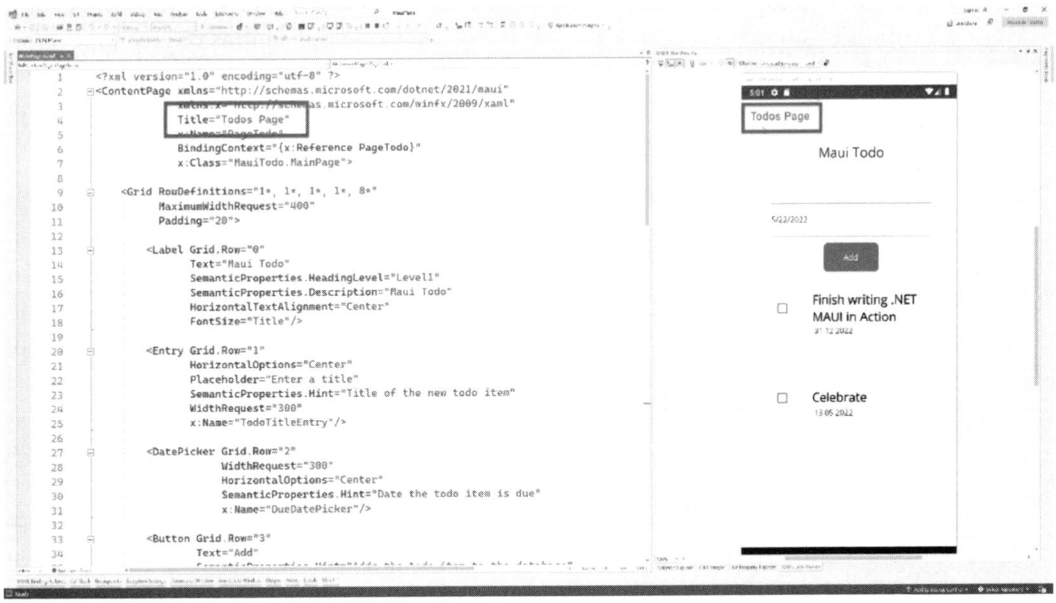

Figure 7.5 The MauiTodo app with the Title property of the MainPage set in XAML, with the title shown in the navigation bar.

NOTE In the example shown in figure 7.5, the MainPage has been enclosed in a NavigationPage. If you only make the change shown in the XAML here, you won't see the same result. We'll see how to do this later in the chapter.

With a single-page app, as the titles of the app and the page are likely the same, displaying the page Title may not be necessary. In fact, due to the limitations of showing this property in the navigation bar, it's probably preferable to use a Label (or graphic of some kind) to show the title of your app or page in the page's content, as we've done in FindMe and MauiTodo.

For a multiple-page app, displaying the page's title in the navigation bar is a quick and familiar way for your user to see where in the app they are. If you are using one of the navigation paradigms covered in this chapter, setting the Title property of the page will automatically make that title display in the navigation bar.

7.2.5   *MenuBarItems*

MenuBarItems is a collection of type MenuBarItem and is used on the desktop target platforms (Windows and macOS) to display a menu. The menu follows the standard presentation paradigm for each OS. So, on Windows, it will appear at the top of the window, and on macOS, it will appear at the top of the screen. The MenuBarItems collection is not rendered on the mobile target platforms (iOS and Android).

A menu is a well-known interaction method for accessing features of an application, dating back to the earliest graphical user interfaces (GUIs). In a mobile app, UIs need to be simplified to cater to both smaller screens and fingers, which are more coarse-grained input devices than a mouse and pointer. But, in a desktop application, a menu is a good choice, especially in line-of-business applications or any application that offers a rich range of features that would be difficult to cram all onto one screen as buttons. We'll see menus in action in chapter 10 when we look at catering your app to use on desktop operating systems.

7.3   *Common page lifecycle methods*

The Page base class provides several methods that are called by event handlers in response to page lifecycle events. Lifecycle events are attached to the lifecycle of the page, as opposed to a direct response to an external action like an interaction from a user or a push notification. Many of these lifecycle events do ultimately originate from a user interaction or some external stimulus. For example, the OnAppearing method is called when a page appears, but a page only appears because a user has navigated to it. However, the method is attached to the lifecycle event of the page, not to the user interaction.

This section covers the lifecycle methods you are most likely to use in your apps. The .NET MAUI documentation has full coverage of all lifecycle methods; you can read more about them at http://mng.bz/e1GP.

7.3.1   OnAppearing

The OnAppearing method is called, as the name suggests, when a page appears. This method is important as it is where you should perform any of your page initialization logic. Like any class, Page and its derived types have constructors, and it can be tempting to perform initialization logic there. But this is not what constructors are for; in a .NET MAUI Page, constructors should only be used for setting initial values of fields.

Anything else that you want to happen when your page appears should be called from the OnAppearing method. A common use case is loading data, which will usually be an asynchronous operation as the data is loaded either from a database or from a web API, and you can't have an asynchronous constructor.

In MauiTodo, we wrote our own Initialize method to do this, but the logic in this method is an ideal candidate for the OnAppearing method. Open the MauiTodo app and edit the MainPage.xaml.cs file. In here, override the OnAppearing method and move in the logic from the Initialize method. Once that's done, you can delete the Initialize method and the call to it from the constructor. Keep the call to base.OnAppearing() and make the method async. The following listing shows the new OnAppearing method.

Listing 7.5   The OnAppearing method in MainPage.xaml.cs

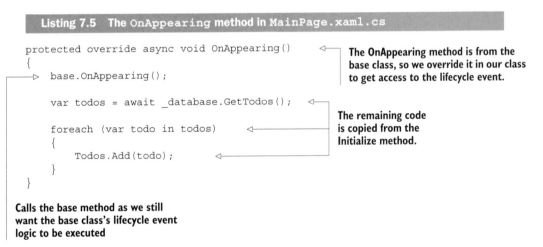

```
protected override async void OnAppearing()
{
    base.OnAppearing();

    var todos = await _database.GetTodos();

    foreach (var todo in todos)
    {
        Todos.Add(todo);
    }
}
```

The OnAppearing method is from the base class, so we override it in our class to get access to the lifecycle event.

The remaining code is copied from the Initialize method.

Calls the base method as we still want the base class's lifecycle event logic to be executed

Not shown in Listing 7.5 is the removal of the Initialize method and the call to it in the constructor (_ = Initialize()), so remember to delete these. You can run the MauiTodo app now and see that it still loads the to-do items from the database when the page appears.

7.3.2   OnDisappearing

As the name suggests, the OnDisappearing method is called when the page disappears. OnDisappearing can be useful for pages that manage a state of some kind, for unsubscribing to events and messages, and for cleaning up resources that are no longer needed when the page is no longer visible.

7.3.3   *OnNavigatedTo and OnNavigatedFrom*

The OnNavigatedTo and OnNavigatedFrom methods perform essentially the same function as the OnAppearing and OnDisappearing methods, respectively, but with one key difference. The OnNavigatedTo and OnNavigatedFrom methods are called before the page appears or disappears, whereas the OnAppearing and OnDisappearing methods are called after.

As we've seen, the OnAppearing method is a good option for loading data. Once the page is visible, you can show an ActivityIndicator (or a custom loading indicator of your own) to display to the user that something is happening in the background. If you performed this action in the OnNavigatedTo method, the app would appear to stall while waiting for the data to load.

You will likely find that using the OnAppearing and OnDisappearing methods are the best fit for most use cases. But in scenarios where you need a quick, synchronous operation before a page appears or disappears, OnNavigatedTo and OnNavigatedFrom will be the better choice.

7.3.4   *OnSizeAllocated*

The OnSizeAllocated method is called whenever the size of the page changes. This can include when the page first loads, when changing orientation, or when a window is resized. The method takes two parameters of type double for width and height.

This method is useful for building responsive UI and resizing or repositioning elements in response to page size changes. For example, we saw in the previous chapter how AbsoluteLayout can use proportional positioning to place a floating action button (FAB) nine tenths of the way down and across the screen or window. However, using OnSizeAllocated lets you write more sophisticated rules about the position and size of your views. For instance, you might like to change both the size and margin of the FAB at certain breakpoints. This would differ from using proportional size and positioning, as you could write some logic to determine which of a set of fixed sizes and positions to apply based on a range of screen or window sizes. You can see an example using this approach in this chapter's code folder.

7.3.5   *BackButtonPressed*

The BackButtonPressed method is called when either the back button on the .NET MAUI navigation bar is used (you'll see this in action later in the chapter) or, if using Android, the Android OS back button is used. BackButtonPressed can be useful if you want to execute some code when this event occurs.

> **NOTE** The BackButtonPressed method should be used for supplementing, rather than changing, the behavior of the back button. If you want to change the behavior of the back button for Android users, you should override the OnBackPressed method in the MainActivity class in the Android platform folder.

Unlike the other lifecycle methods mentioned here, which are all void, `Back-ButtonPressed` has a return type of `bool`. However, as the method is called by an event handler, the return type is moot. You can't, for example, return `false` instead of returning a call to the base method (which would be the default behavior) to cancel navigation.

7.4 Navigation in .NET MAUI

Some apps work well with just a single page, but they tend to get more interesting when they include enough functionality to warrant multiple pages. The apps we've built so far have all been single-page apps, and that's worked well for them. Throughout most of the remainder of this book, we'll be building MauiStockTake, a more complex app that will need multiple pages and, consequently, navigation. MauiStockTake will also rely on some of the more advanced concepts we'll learn throughout the rest of the book.

.NET MAUI supports three main navigation paradigms: hierarchical navigation, tabbed navigation, and flyout navigation. Each of these is supported by a subclass of `Page`, specifically configured to support each navigation paradigm. Additionally, .NET MAUI has Shell, which supports tabbed and flyout navigation as well as route-based navigation. Route-based navigation is especially helpful if you want to support deep linking (letting the host OS navigate to specific parts of your app using a unique URL).

Throughout the remainder of this chapter, we'll get an overview of MauiStockTake, the app that we'll use to build our .NET MAUI skills throughout most of the remainder of the book, and look at the way .NET MAUI supports the navigation that we will need to build a multipage app.

7.4.1 Scenario: The MauiStockTake app

Mildred is the owner of Mildred's Surf Shack, a popular surf store near the beach. Mildred sells surfboards and surfing supplies and rents surfboards to tourists. Mildred uses her sales figures every week to place orders with her suppliers to make sure she always has enough stock of consumables like wax. She also takes an inventory of her stock once a quarter to ensure that her formula is working well.

Once a quarter, Mildred asks two of her staff members to come in overnight to help her take inventory. Each one uses a clipboard, writes their name at the top, and records what they see. The process works but has some problems. First, the way people note down inventory is not consistent, and this compounds the second problem, which is that it's difficult and time-consuming for Mildred to reconcile her and her staff's notes at the end. Finally, the process takes all night, and Mildred's staff don't like working all night any more than she likes paying them overtime.

You are the owner of Beach Bytes, an app development company conveniently situated next door to Mildred's Surf Shack. Mildred thinks you can help her by building an app that makes her stock-taking process more efficient.

7.4.2   *Features of the MauiStockTake app*

The MauiStockTake app is concerned with three main areas, as outlined in Table 7.1.

Table 7.1   Summary of the problem domain for the MauiStockTake app

Problem area	Description
Products	Staff record product names inconsistently and sometimes get them wrong. To avoid this, Mildred wants the app to look up products in her catalog rather than letting her staff enter details arbitrarily. She also wants it to report on the manufacturers so that she can identify where she spends the most money on inventory and, hopefully, negotiate bulk discounts.
Inventory	Recording inventory is the core behavior of the app. Mildred needs to take inventory of how many of each product she has.
Staff	Mildred wants to divide up her work into three areas and assign each area to a member of the team (including herself). She needs to know who is recording what to simplify tracking down any errors. Additionally, when there is a large volume of stock to get through, she might want to rotate the team so that each area is inventoried by at least two people to catch any mistakes early.

Now that we understand the problem, we can start thinking about the solution. Each of these areas will need a page in the app that addresses the problem. Figure 7.6 shows a mock-up for a products page that would address the products' problem area.

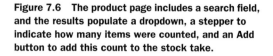

Figure 7.6   The product page includes a search field, and the results populate a dropdown, a stepper to indicate how many items were counted, and an Add button to add this count to the stock take.

The product page will be the heart of the app. We will have a lookup field where Mildred's staff can enter a product name and select the appropriate result from the list. Accordingly, we know we need a product lookup feature. Figure 7.7 shows a login page mock-up that addresses the staff problem area.

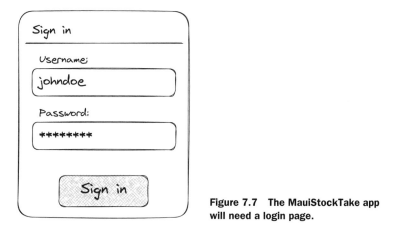

Figure 7.7   The MauiStockTake app will need a login page.

Mildred said she wants to be able to identify who has entered each inventory record, so we need a way for staff to log in to the app—or, at least, enter their name. This means that we will need a user service so that the staff can identify themselves.

Finally, we need a way to review the results of the stock take on each device, and we'll also want to sync them to an upstream service so that they can be consolidated into a single comprehensive report. For both of these, we'll need an inventory service, which will aggregate the inventory counts as they come in, list the results for the user, and sync them to the upstream service. Figure 7.8 shows a mock-up for a report page that can be used to view the aggregated stock counts.

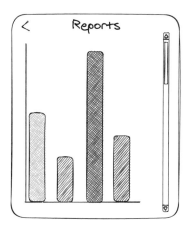

Figure 7.8   The MauiStockTake app will need a reports page.

To accommodate the multiple pages in the app, we'll need to adopt a navigation paradigm so that users can move between the different pages.

7.4.3 *Hierarchical navigation*

In .NET MAUI, NavigationPage is used to provide *hierarchical navigation* by showing ContentPages in a navigation stack. In this case, the term *stack* has its standard definition, meaning it allows elements to be pushed (added) onto the stack and popped (removed) from the stack. In the case of a NavigationPage, the elements that are pushed or popped from the stack are pages (figure 7.9).

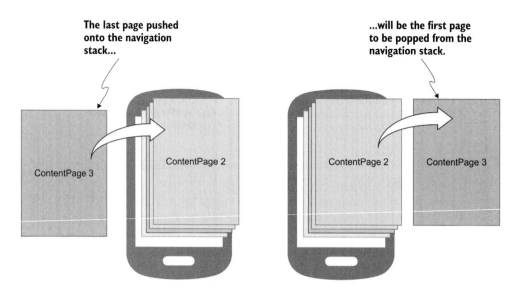

Figure 7.9 In hierarchical navigation, a page can be pushed onto the stack (left) or popped from the stack (right), following a last-in, first-out pattern.

The most recently pushed (or last-in) page to the stack is the page that your user will see on screen. Any class that is derived from the Page base class can be pushed to a navigation stack, including any of the page types listed in this section. With this approach, you can combine navigation paradigms, although this can be confusing for your users, so be careful not to use unfamiliar combinations.

Hierarchical navigation is a good option if you want your app to start with a menu screen. We could use this approach for MauiStockTake by starting with a menu page and offering buttons to navigate to the input page and report page. Tapping one of the buttons would push the relevant page onto the stack. When you use Navigation-Page, a navigation bar is shown at the top that has a back button, which pops the current page to take you back one step in the stack. Figure 7.10 shows how hierarchical navigation could work with MauiStockTake.

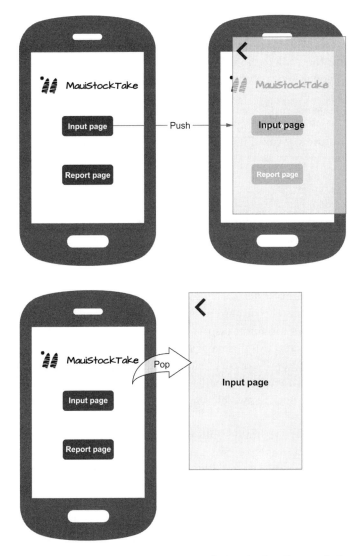

Figure 7.10   MauiStockTake with hierarchical navigation. The app starts with a menu page, offering two buttons that correspond to the available pages in the app. Tapping one of these pushes the corresponding page onto the navigation stack. Tapping the back button (the chevron in the top left) within a page pops the page from the stack, returning you to the previous page.

Hierarchical navigation differs from the other navigation paradigms in one key way. With the other paradigms, pages are bound to a UI control like a tab or a flyout item, and tapping on or clicking them will result in the page being displayed automatically by the framework. With hierarchical navigation, you push pages onto the navigation stack programmatically.

In figure 7.10 we use a `Button` to navigate to a page. If we were implementing this in code, we would use the `PushAsync` method on the `Navigation` class, passing in an instance of the page type we want to navigate to as a parameter:

```
await Navigation.PushAsync(new InputPage());
```

To pop the page from the stack and navigate back to the previous page, we would use the `PopAsync` method:

```
await Navigation.PopAsync();
```

While we won't use it in this book, hierarchical navigation is very popular and is likely what you will use if you have a menu page or landing page in your app.

7.4.4   *Flyout navigation*

With flyout navigation, a menu slides (or "flies") out from the side of the screen and presents a list of pages that can be displayed in the main display area. The user selects a page, which then occupies the main display area while the menu slides back away. Figure 7.11 shows how we could use this navigation paradigm for MauiStockTake.

In .NET MAUI, `FlyoutPage` is used to support the flyout navigation paradigm. `FlyoutPage` has two child properties of type `Page`, one called `Flyout`, which is used for the menu, and one called `Detail`, which the selected page is assigned to and displayed on screen.

You can use a `ContentPage` to build a fully customized flyout menu and assign it to the `Flyout` property of `FlyoutPage`. `ContentPage` gives you a lot of flexibility, although you should be cautious of introducing unfamiliar UX paradigms to your users.

Within your `FlyoutPage`, you will need to supply a collection of type `FlyoutPage-Item` that your user can select from. `FlyoutPageItem` has a property called `Target-Type`, to which you assign the desired page. When your user selects one of these `FlyoutPageItem`, the selected item's `TargetType` property will be assigned to the `Detail` property of the `FlyoutPage`, causing it to be displayed in the main display area of your app.

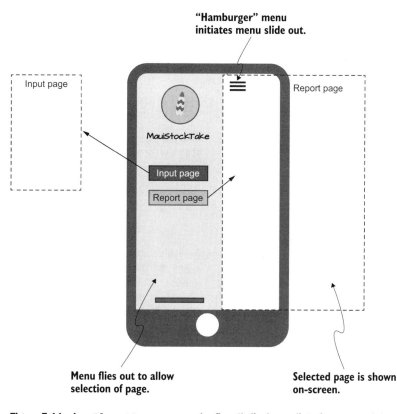

Figure 7.11 In a `FlyoutPage`, a menu (or flyout) displays a list of pages, and the selected page is displayed on the screen.

7.4.5 Tabbed navigation

With tabbed navigation, tabs are used to provide access to the various pages available within the app. A `TabBar` is displayed with a collection of labeled icons, each one representing a page in the app that the user can select. The selected page is displayed in the main display area. By default, on iOS the `TabBar` will be displayed along the bottom of the screen. On Windows and Android, the `TabBar` is displayed at the top, more closely resembling the tabs you're used to seeing in web browsers. Figure 7.12 shows how we could use this navigation paradigm in MauiStockTake.

Tab is a skeuomorphic metaphor that doesn't always hold up (much like the floppy disk icon), as it's rare to see actual tabs. Most UI designs now favor simple icons instead and display them in a bar at the bottom, similar to the default iOS approach.

In .NET MAUI, `TabbedPage` enables the tabbed navigation paradigm. Unlike `ContentPage`, which has a single child `Content` property, `TabbedPage` allows multiple children, each of which must derive from `Page`. These pages are automatically displayed as tabs using the platform default approach, with the icon and text taken from the `Page`'s `Icon` and `Title` properties, respectively.

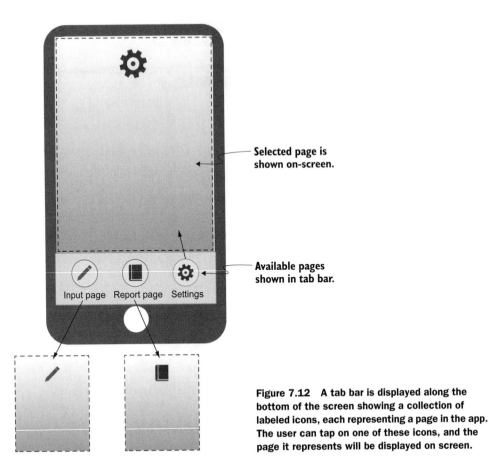

Selected page is
shown on-screen.

Available pages
shown in tab bar.

Input page Report page Settings

Figure 7.12   A tab bar is displayed along the
bottom of the screen showing a collection of
labeled icons, each representing a page in the app.
The user can tap on one of these icons, and the
page it represents will be displayed on screen.

7.5   *Introducing Shell*

In .NET MAUI apps, Shell is a simple way to describe the page navigation hierarchy of
your app in XAML. It provides a simple way to structure your whole app, using flyouts
and tabs to navigate around.

If your app design is based on flyout navigation or tabbed navigation (or both),
Shell can be a better choice than using the page types that support those paradigms.
Shell provides three chief advantages:

- *Whole app mapped in one file*—The Shell file itself is an easy one-stop shop to see
  how your whole app is organized navigationally. It's easy to see how the pages of
  your app fit together and equally easy to shuffle them around if needed.
- *Dependency resolution*—We've already seen how .NET MAUI uses the generic host
  builder pattern, which includes .NET's built-in DI container. Using Shell, any
  dependencies that are constructor-injected into your pages will be automatically
  resolved for you, just like controller dependencies in an ASP.NET Core app.
- *Route-based navigation*—With Shell, each page in your app is reachable via a
  URL, and this ability provides two cool features. The first is that it simplifies

deep linking, enabling your app to be opened externally to a specific page (especially useful for push notifications). The second is that you can use query parameters, meaning you can pass data to your pages as part of the URL.

Complex query parameters in .NET MAUI

Shell was originally introduced in Xamarin.Forms version 4 and included query parameters. If you've previously used Shell in Xamarin.Forms, you'll be pleased to see a significant improvement in .NET MAUI.

In Xamarin.Forms, Shell query parameters were limited to primitive types, so you could easily pass a `string`, `int`, or `bool`, for example. But you couldn't pass a more complex object (unless you used a workaround like serializing it to JSON). If you wanted to route, say, from a product list page to a product details page, you would need to pass the `id` of the product, and your details page (or its `ViewModel`) would be responsible for looking up the details of the product.

With .NET MAUI, Shell lets you pass objects directly as a parameter, so in the previous example, you could route to your product details page and pass the whole product.

Shell lets you combine the flyout and tabbed navigation paradigms in the way that best suits your app.

7.5.1 *The flyout menu*

Shell provides a flyout menu that can be used for navigation as well as providing access to features or functionality that you would expect anywhere across your app. It features a customizable header and footer and allows you to add flyout items for navigation and menu items to execute functionality (figure 7.13).

The header is easy to customize. You can write XAML UI directly inside the `AppShell.xaml` file, or you can use a control template. You can also write your XAML UI directly inside Shell for your footer or use control templates or imported views.

MENU ITEMS

The flyout menu in Shell supports menu items as well as flyout items, meaning you can assign functionality to the items in the flyout rather than having them strictly navigate to a page in the app (think, for example, of a logout button).

Figure 7.14 shows a logout button added to the Shell flyout menu. This is a menu item as it is used to execute some code (the logic to log the user out of the app) rather than to navigate to a page within the app. The `MenuItem` type has a `Clicked` event handler and a `Command`, both of which can be used to call the code you want to execute when the user taps on or clicks the menu item.

FLYOUT ITEMS

Flyout items provide access to pages or groups of pages within your app. The `FlyoutItem` type allows multiple children, meaning you can add a single page or a collection of pages.

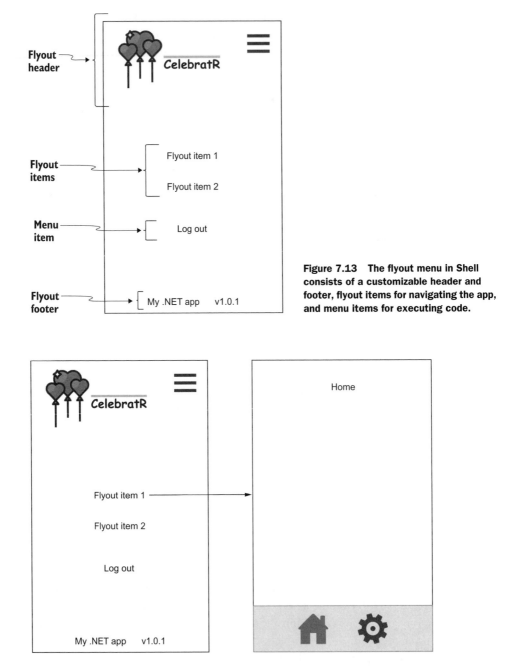

Figure 7.13   The flyout menu in Shell consists of a customizable header and footer, flyout items for navigating the app, and menu items for executing code.

Figure 7.14   A `FlyoutItem` in Shell is configured to show a section of the app. This section contains two tabs: a Home tab and a Settings tab. Users can switch between the two within this Shell section. Opening the menu reveals other flyout items, allowing navigation to other Shell sections.

With Shell, your app is divided into Shell Sections. Each Shell Section can contain one or more pages or collections of pages organized by tabs.

7.5.2 Tabs

Tabs are organized hierarchically in Shell. Unlike with `TabbedPage`, when using Shell, the tabs at the highest tier of the hierarchy (i.e., those that you add first) will always appear at the bottom of the screen, no matter the platform. Pages can be embedded within a tab, which will then be individually tabbed. Tabs at this level of the hierarchy are shown at the top of the screen (figure 7.15).

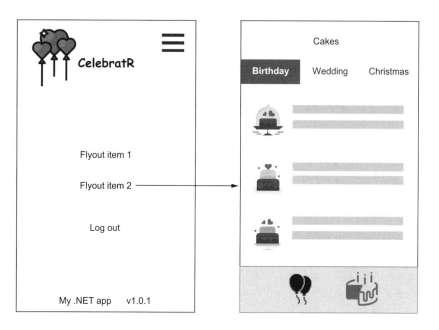

Figure 7.15   Flyout Item 2 navigates to a Shell Section that has two tabs, accessible via a Balloons icon and a Cake icon, both displayed at the bottom of the screen. Within the Cake tab are three additional tabs, providing access to content at the next tier down. These tabs are Birthday, Wedding, and Christmas, accessible at the top of the screen.

For large and complex applications, this ability to partition the app into sections with Shell can be a powerful tool to logically organize your app's content while still ensuring users can easily navigate to the parts they need.

7.5.3 Getting started with MauiStockTake

We're ready to get started building our big project! We'll continue building Maui-StockTake throughout the rest of this book as we learn more about services, architecture, and design patterns. We're going to get started in this chapter by discussing navigation and how to use Shell to build the structure of the app.

DOWNLOADING THE STARTER PROJECT

The MauiStockTake app will need a backend API to query for products and to send inventory counts to. At Beach Bytes, one of your colleagues will focus on this aspect of the solution, allowing you to concentrate on the client app. A prototype of the MauiStockTake API is available for you to download from the chapter's chapter-start folder.

Download the API and have a look at the solution. The solution is based on Jason Taylor's Clean Architecture (CA) template. If you are interested, you can find out more at the GitHub repository, which you can access using this link: https://tinyurl .com/2p9ceh4x. .NET MAUI will integrate with any architecture you like in your .NET solution, but you can find out more about my approach to using .NET MAUI with CA in my talk at https://www.youtube.com/live/K9ryHflmQJE. Or you can ignore it and just run the solution. Once you've confirmed that the solution successfully runs, you can move on to adding the .NET MAUI project.

ADDING THE .NET MAUI APP

Up until now, we've been using the blankmaui template that I gave you. The reason for using this template is that the default template has Shell built in. You can work with this even when not using Shell, but I think it's easier to learn some fundamental principles of .NET MAUI before we start muddying the waters with Shell.

> ### Should I use Shell for every app?
>
> Shell is a good fit for apps using flyout, tabbed navigation, or both, but for some scenarios, it's not the best option.
>
> Line of business desktop applications, for example, don't typically feature this style of navigation, which is more traditionally associated with web or mobile apps. In apps with only a single page, like those we've been building so far in this book, or apps using hierarchical navigation, Shell is unnecessary. Finally, Shell lets you extensively customize the flyout, but you can't customize the tab bar at all, so if your visual design isn't accommodated by what Shell provides, you need to go with a different option.
>
> For many apps though, including MauiStockTake, Shell is perfect.

MauiStockTake will use both tabs and a flyout, and Shell will make it easy for us to build, so this time, we're going to use the default template. **Add a new .NET MAUI project to the MauiStockTake solution and call it MauiStockTake.UI.** The default template is just called .NET MAUI App. If using Visual Studio, the template will look similar to figure 7.16.

NOTE Visual Studio project folders are not mapped 1:1 to file system folders. You'll need to explicitly change the location so that the project is in the Presentation folder on the file system.

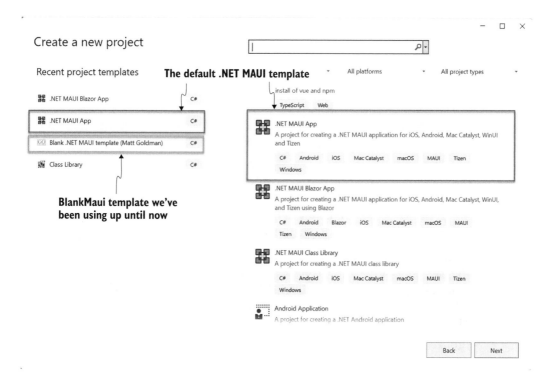

Figure 7.16 The default .NET MAUI App template includes Shell out of the box. The `blankmaui` template we've been using up until now is exactly the same but without Shell.

This template will create a new .NET MAUI app almost identical at this stage to the Aloha, World project. Have a look in solution explorer, and you will see some key differences.

The first difference is that the project includes `AppShell.xaml` and `AppShell.xaml.cs` files. These are the Shell files that define the structure and hierarchy of your app. We'll come back to these shortly.

The next change is how the app bootstraps our main page. In Aloha, World, and all the projects we've built so far, the `MainPage` property in `App.xaml.cs` has been assigned the main page of our app. If you look at `App.xaml.cs` in `MauiStockTake.UI`, you'll see that a new instance of the `AppShell` class is assigned to it instead.

If you open `AppShell.xaml.cs`, you'll see that the root node is of type Shell and has a number of attributes we're familiar with from `ContentPage`. You'll see that it has one child element of type `ShellContent`. This `ShellContent` instance has the following three properties assigned:

- `Title`—This property sets the page title. The title is displayed in the navigation bar when the page is active and in the tab bar when the page is available as a tab.

- ContentTemplate—This is the actual content to be displayed. This is of type DataTemplate, so you could build content directly in your AppShell.xaml file to allocate to it if you wanted. It's more efficient to assign a ContentPage to this property, as has been done here, as the page will only be loaded when navigated to. Once you start factoring a page's dependencies, as we'll see in the next chapter, this can add up to a lot of overhead. In the template, the MainPage type has been assigned from the local namespace, and if you look at the Shell attributes, you'll see that the MauiStockTake.UI root namespace has been added to the local XML namespace, which is where the MainPage class is located.
- Route—This particular Shell content has been assigned the route MainPage. This means that when we navigate with Shell, we can easily get to this page using this route. We'll look at routes and navigation shortly.

We're not going to use the MainPage.xaml file in our app, so we need to replace this item in the Shell with the pages we want to use. We already know what pages we need in the MauiStockTake app, even though we haven't finalized the visual or functional designs. But just knowing the pages is enough to get started building the Shell.

We'll add the pages shortly and then get the Shell structure completed. But before we do, there's one last step in our project setup that will make things easier for us as we go. C# 10 introduced global using statements, which allow us to mark a using statement in any file as global, which then makes the namespace it imports available to any other file in the same project. We can make use of these in .NET MAUI projects to reduce boilerplate code referencing namespaces that we will repeatedly use across different files.

Add a file called GlobalUsings.cs to the root of the project. Depending on how you created this file, there may be some templated code in there. If that's the case, delete it. We'll leave the file blank for now and add namespaces to it as we go. Our solution is now set up and ready for us to start fleshing out the features that Mildred needs in the MauiStockTake app.

ADDING THE INPUTPAGE AND REPORTPAGE

We've got enough of our high-level design in place to start building our app. The app has two functional pages (input and reports), as well as the login page, which will only be used when the user first launches the app. A two-page app lends itself well to a tab bar, but we'll also add a flyout menu that can show some information about the app and the user and provide a logout button.

We know we're going to need a login page, input page, and reports page, so let's add these now. **Create a folder in the MauiStockTake.UI project called** Pages. Add a .NET MAUI ContentPage (XAML) called InputPage, another called LoginPage and a third called ReportPage to this folder.

Remove all the content from each page. In the InputPage and ReportPage, add a VerticalStackLayout with a single Label, with the Text property set to Input Page and `Report Page`, respectively. Do the same with the `LoginPage` but add a button underneath the `Label` that has `Login` as the `Text` property. The XAML for each of these pages is in listings 7.6 to 7.8.

Listing 7.6 `InputPage.xaml`

```
<?xml version="1.0" encoding="utf-8" ?>
<ContentPage xmlns="http://schemas.microsoft.com/dotnet/2021/maui"
             xmlns:x="http://schemas.microsoft.com/winfx/2009/xaml"
             x:Class="MauiStockTake.UI.Pages.InputPage"
             Title="InputPage">
    <VerticalStackLayout>
        <Label Text="Input Page"
               VerticalOptions="CenterAndExpand"
               HorizontalOptions="CenterAndExpand" />
    </VerticalStackLayout>
</ContentPage>
```

Listing 7.7 `LoginPage.xaml`

```
<?xml version="1.0" encoding="utf-8" ?>
<ContentPage xmlns="http://schemas.microsoft.com/dotnet/2021/maui"
             xmlns:x="http://schemas.microsoft.com/winfx/2009/xaml"
             x:Class="MauiStockTake.UI.Pages.LoginPage"
             Title="LoginPage">

    <VerticalStackLayout>
        <Label Text="Login Page"
               VerticalOptions="CenterAndExpand"
               HorizontalOptions="CenterAndExpand" />
        <Button Text="Login"
                HorizontalOptions="Center"
                VerticalOptions="Center" />
    </VerticalStackLayout>
</ContentPage>
```

Listing 7.8 `ReportPage.xaml`

```
<?xml version="1.0" encoding="utf-8" ?>
<ContentPage xmlns="http://schemas.microsoft.com/dotnet/2021/maui"
             xmlns:x="http://schemas.microsoft.com/winfx/2009/xaml"
             x:Class="MauiStockTake.UI.ReportPage"
             Title="ReportPage">

    <VerticalStackLayout>
        <Label Text="Report Page"
               VerticalOptions="CenterAndExpand"
               HorizontalOptions="CenterAndExpand" />
    </VerticalStackLayout>
</ContentPage>
```

We're going to refer to these pages in a few places throughout our app, so add a global using statement for the namespace to the `GlobalUsings.cs` file:

```
global using MauiStockTake.UI.Pages;
```

We're almost ready to add these pages to the Shell, but before we do, we need to import the icons we're going to use for these pages in the tab bar.

IMPORTING REQUIRED ASSETS

We'll need an icon for each of the pages in our tab bar, as well as some other menu item icons for the flyout and a header image. In the book's online resources for this chapter, you'll find five images:

- `icon_input.svg`
- `icon_login.svg`
- `icon_logout.svg`
- `icon_report.svg`
- `surfshack_logo.jpeg`

Download these images and copy them into the Resources/Images folder of the `MauiStockTake.UI` project. Now that we've got the tab icons, let's start building out the tab bar and add the pages to the Shell.

ADDING THE TABBAR

Before we add the tabs for our pages to the app, let's get rid of the boilerplate code that we're not using. **Open `AppShell.xaml`, and delete the existing `ShellContent`:**

```
<ShellContent
        Title="Home"
        ContentTemplate="{DataTemplate local:MainPage}"
        Route="MainPage" />
```

We're not going to use this `MainPage` in our app, so we can delete the `MainPage.xaml` and `MainPage.xaml.cs` files as well. Now that we've got a clean slate, we can add the tab bar. Start by adding this now:

```
<?xml version="1.0" encoding="UTF-8" ?>
<Shell ...>

    <TabBar>

    </TabBar>

</Shell>
```

We want the tab bar to display tabs for the `InputPage` and the `ReportPage`, so we'll add a `Tab` for each of these, and for each `Tab`, we'll assign a `Title` and `Icon`.

Remember, as we saw in section 7.5.2, that a `Tab` can have multiple `ShellContent` children, which would display top tabs within the bottom tab for each page. We're not going to do this, though; we'll add one `ShellContent` child to each `Tab` and assign a page to the `ContentTemplate` property. To do this, we will need to bring in an XML namespace to represent the `Pages` namespace in our app.

The following listing shows the code for `AppShell.xaml`. Add the `TabBar` and the `Tabs` to make your code match listing 7.9.

Listing 7.9   `AppShell.xaml`

```xml
<?xml version="1.0" encoding="UTF-8" ?>
<Shell
    x:Class="MauiStockTake.Maui.AppShell"
    xmlns="http://schemas.microsoft.com/dotnet/2021/maui"
    xmlns:x="http://schemas.microsoft.com/winfx/2009/xaml"
    xmlns:pages="clr-namespace:MauiStockTake.Maui.Pages"
    xmlns:local="clr-namespace:MauiStockTake.Maui">

    <TabBar>
        <Tab Title="Input"
            Icon="icon_input.svg">
            <ShellContent ContentTemplate="{
DataTemplate pages:InputPage}" />
        </Tab>
        <Tab Title="Reports"
            Icon="icon_report.svg">
            <ShellContent ContentTemplate="{DataTemplate pages:ReportPage}"
    />
        </Tab>
    </TabBar>

</Shell>
```

Adds a Tab and sets the Title property to a descriptive title for the page

Sets the Icon property to the appropriate graphics file we imported

Adds a ShellContent, sets the ContentTemplate property using the DataTemplate markup extension, and assigns one of the pages in the app

At this point, the high-level visual structure of our app is defined. Launch the app and confirm that it runs. You should see something like figure 7.17.

Verify that the icons are displayed and that you can tab between the two pages. The label and title should change depending on which page you're on. Once you're happy, delete the `MainPage.xaml` and `MainPage.xaml.cs` files, as we won't be using them anymore.

ADDING THE FLYOUT
We've got a `TabBar` now, which is enough for the user to navigate between the two main pages in the app once they're logged in. But we also want a `Flyout`. We won't use the `Flyout` for navigation, but we'll use it to provide a way to log out of the app and show a header to give the user some information about the app.

Figure 7.17   **The shell of the MauiStockTake app running on Android. At this stage, the** InputPage **and** ReportPage **don't do anything other than display a label with their name. But you can tab between them to verify that the pages are created correctly and the routes are registered.**

The first thing we will want to do is enable the flyout. To do this, **set the** Flyout-Behavior **property of the Shell to** Flyout:

```
<Shell
    x:Class="MauiStockTake.Maui.AppShell"
    ...
    FlyoutBehavior="Flyout">
```

Next, we will want to add a MenuItem to the Shell and set the Text property to Logout and the IconImageSource property to the filename of the logout icon image that we imported. Add this before the closing </Shell> tag:

```
<MenuItem Text="Logout"
          IconImageSource="icon_logout.png" />
```

MenuItem has both an event and a Command that we could wire up, but we don't need this functionality just yet. If you run the app now, the MenuItem looks a bit janky, so we're going to specify the `Shell.MenuItemTemplate` so that we can tweak the layout a little. Inside this tag, we can specify a `DataTemplate`, and in here, we can add our layout, which is a process we've seen used for collections. Each `MenuItem` has an `Icon` and a `Text` property, and we can bind to these in our layout.

The following listing shows the code to add to `AppShell.xaml`. Most of the code has been omitted, and the code to add is shown in **bold**.

Listing 7.10 `Shell.MenuItemTemplate`

```
<?xml version="1.0" encoding="UTF-8" ?>
<Shell ...>


    <Shell.MenuItemTemplate>
        <DataTemplate>
            <Grid ColumnDefinitions="0.2*,0.8*">
                <Image Source="{Binding Icon}"
                       Margin="35,0,0,0"
                       HeightRequest="45" />
                <Label Grid.Column="1"
                       Text="{Binding Text}"
                       Margin="10,0,0,0"
                       VerticalTextAlignment="Center" />
            </Grid>
        </DataTemplate>
    </Shell.MenuItemTemplate>

    ...

</Shell>
```

This isn't the most sophisticated layout; in fact, it's similar to the default layout, but a little more refined. You could be as creative as you like with these, and while we've only got one `MenuItem` in this app, if you have more, the template will apply to all of them.

Before we run the app, let's add the `Flyout` header. We've already got a feel for what a `Flyout` header can look like in the mock-ups we've seen earlier in the chapter (one for MauiStockTake and another for an app called CelebratR).

You can assign an arbitrary layout to `Shell.FlyoutHeader`, so building it will be straightforward. We'll use a `Grid` to position the controls and show an `Image` with the app's logo, clipped to make it circular, and a `Label` underneath with the app's title.

The following listing shows the code for the `Flyout` header. Most of the code has been omitted, and the added code is in **bold**.

Listing 7.11 The Shell `Flyout` header

```
<?xml version="1.0" encoding="UTF-8" ?>
<Shell ...>

    <Shell.FlyoutHeader>
        <Grid RowDefinitions="20,*,*"
```

```
            Padding="20">
        <Image Grid.Row="1"
               Source="surfshack_logo.jpeg"
               WidthRequest="100"
               HeightRequest="100"
               HorizontalOptions="Center"
               VerticalOptions="Center">
            <Image.Clip>
                <EllipseGeometry Center="50,50"
                                 RadiusX="50"
                                 RadiusY="50"/>
            </Image.Clip>
        </Image>
        <Label Grid.Row="2"
               HorizontalOptions="Center"
               VerticalOptions="Center"
               Text="MauiStockTake"/>
    </Grid>
</Shell.FlyoutHeader>

    . . .

</Shell>
```

If you run the app now, you'll notice the hamburger menu in the top left corner. Tap on or click this, and you'll see the `Flyout`, well, fly out. You should see something similar to figure 7.18.

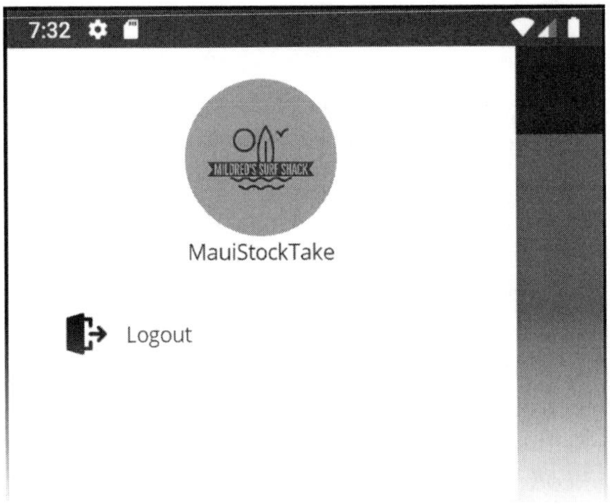

Figure 7.18 The `Flyout` in MauiStockTake. At the top, you can see the Image, which is clipped using `EllipseGeometry`, and underneath that is the `Label` with the app's title. These two together (Image and Label) make up the `Flyout` header. Underneath those, you can see the Logout menu item, which uses the imported icon and is styled using the `Shell.MenuTemplate`.

7.5.4 *Routes and navigation*

So far, we've got two pages in the app, and these are easily accessible via the tab bar. With Shell, most of your pages will be accessed in this fashion—either via a `Tab` or a `Flyout` item. While simplified navigation in this way is the default behavior with Shell (and the main reason why Shell was introduced), it is still possible to navigate programmatically if you need to.

To navigate programmatically with Shell, we use the `GoToAsync` method:

```
await Shell.Current.GoToAsync("myroute");
```

With Shell, you use the `GoToAsync` method with a route rather than an instance of a page (as in hierarchical navigation). To use the route, though, it needs to be registered, which is easy when using `Tab` or `FlyoutItem` as they both have a `Route` property. Let's create a route for the two pages we have so far in our app:

```
<TabBar>
    <Tab Title="Input"
         Icon="icon_input.svg"
         Route="input">
         <ShellContent ContentTemplate="{DataTemplate Pages:InputPage}" />
    </Tab>
    <Tab Title="Reports"
         Icon="icon_report.svg"
         Route="reports">
         <ShellContent ContentTemplate="{DataTemplate Pages:ReportPage}" />
     </Tab>
</TabBar>
```

The pages that we've registered routes for so far are easily accessed via the tab bar, so the routes aren't all that useful. But we have another page that won't be accessible via either tabs or flyout, which is the login page.

As we don't have a tab or flyout item for the `LoginPage`, we will need to use the `GoToAsync` method to access it. And we'll also need a way to register a route for it without specifying the `Route` property of a `Tab` or `FlyoutItem`. We can do this with the `RegisterRoute` method on the `Routing` class. The easiest way to use this method is to pass two parameters: the first is a string to use for the route, and the second is the type of page the route should represent.

We'll register a route for the `LoginPage` now. Open the `AppShell.xaml.cs` file, and register a route for the `LoginPage` in the constructor. The following listing shows the updated constructor for `AppShell.xaml.cs`.

Listing 7.12   The updated `AppShell.xaml.cs` constructor

```
public AppShell()
{
    InitializeComponent();
    Routing.RegisterRoute("login", typeof(LoginPage));
}
```

With this route registered, we can easily navigate to the `LoginPage`, even though it doesn't have a corresponding `Tab` or `FlyoutItem`, using the `GoToAsync` method. We'll revisit `LoginPage` in chapter 8 when we look at authentication.

7.5.5   *Route parameters*

Routing in Shell is similar to the web in that it allows you to pass query parameters. So rather than simply using `GoToAsync` with a route, you could pass values as well (figure 7.19).

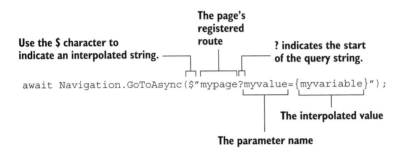

Use the $ character to indicate an interpolated string.

The page's registered route

? indicates the start of the query string.

```
await Navigation.GoToAsync($"mypage?myvalue={myvariable}");
```

The interpolated value

The parameter name

Figure 7.19   The `Navigation.GoToAsync` method with a route and parameter supplied

In the example in figure 7.19, string interpolation is used to pass the value of a string as a parameter to the `mypage` page. You don't have to use string interpolation; we could have hard-coded the value we wanted to pass in that URL. Also, you are not limited to strings. You can also pass the navigation state, which is a dictionary of `<string, object>`, and use the key in the receiving page (or the page's binding context) to get the corresponding value from the dictionary.

To see how this works in practice, we can add a product details page to our app. First, let's add a class to represent products. In `MauiStockTake.UI`, **add a Models folder and, in here, add a new file called `Product.cs`.** This can contain a class called `Product` that will have four properties:

- `id` of type `int`
- `Name` of type `string`
- `ManufacturerId` of type `int`
- `ManufacturerName` of type `string`

Next, **add a XAML `ContentPage` called `ProductPage` to the `Pages` folder. Then register a route for this page in the constructor of `AppShell.xaml.cs`,** right under the line where we register the `LoginPage` route:

```
Routing.RegisterRoute("productdetails", typeof(ProductPage));
```

We could use this page to receive actual product information from our API and display details, but for now, we'll just use it to test that our Shell and routing are set up correctly. We'll add a `Button` to the `InputPage` that says "Go to product" and wire it up to an event handler in the code-behind file. In here, we'll instantiate a mock product that represents the app itself, add it to a dictionary, and then navigate to the `Product-Page`, passing the dictionary as a navigation state parameter.

The following listing shows the updated content of the `InputPage` (the `Content-Page` tags have been omitted). The added code is in **bold**.

Listing 7.13 The updated `InputPage` content

```
<VerticalStackLayout Spacing="50">
    <Label
        Text="Input Page"
        VerticalOptions="Center"
        HorizontalOptions="Center" />

    <Button Text="Go to product"
            WidthRequest="200"
            Clicked="Button_Clicked"/>
</VerticalStackLayout>
```

The following listing shows the event handler to add to the `InputPage.xaml.cs` file.

Listing 7.14 The Go to Product button event handler

```
private async void Button_Clicked(object sender, EventArgs e)
{
    var product = new Product { Name = "MauiStockTake", ManufacturerName =
    "BeachBytes" };

    var pageParams = new Dictionary<string, object>
    {
        { "Product", product }
    };

    await Shell.Current.GoToAsync("productdetails",
    pageParams);
}
```

Uses the GoToAsync method, with the route registered in AppShell.xaml.cs (productdetails) and a dictionary of <string, object> as the navigation state

You could run the app now, and you'll see the Go to Product button in the `InputPage`, and if you tap it now, it will take you to the `ProductPage`. But for the `ProductPage` to display any of the data we're passing, we need to set it up to receive query properties.

To do this, we use the `QueryPropertyAttribute` on the page that we want to receive parameters (or on the page's binding context—we'll see more about this in chapter 9). The `QueryPropertyAttribute` has a constructor that takes two arguments: the first is the name of the property on the page that corresponds to the query property, and the second is the name of the query parameter, or the key of the item in the dictionary, that corresponds to the query parameter (figure 7.20).

In figure 7.20, we can see how we will use this attribute in the `ProductPage`. If we were using a string, as in the example in figure 7.19, the attribute would look like this:

```
[QueryProperty("myPagesString", "myvalue")]
```

The QueryProperty attribute

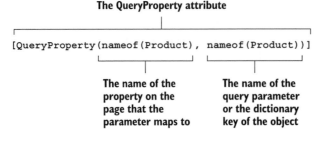

The name of the
property on the
page that the
parameter maps to

The name of the
query parameter
or the dictionary
key of the object

Figure 7.20   The `QueryPropertyAttribute` **is used to
decorate a page or a page's binding context so that the page
can receive URL parameters or navigation state via URL based
navigation in Shell.**

In this example, we must pass a query parameter called `myvalue`, which binds it to a
string called `myPagesString` on the page you are navigating to. We could, of course,
use `nameof` here, too, to avoid typos. You can add as many `QueryPropertyAttributes`
to your pages as you need.

For the `ProductPage`, we'll need to add a `Product` called Product to match the key
in the navigation state. We're going to display the product name and manufacturer
name, so we'll need string properties for these as well as backing fields, and we'll need
to call `OnPropertyChanged` in the setter. The following listing shows the updated Pro-
ductPage.xaml.cs

Listing 7.15   `ProductPage.xaml.cs` updated for navigation state parameters

```
namespace MauiStockTake.Maui.Pages;

[QueryProperty(nameof(Product), nameof(Product))]
public partial class ProductPage : ContentPage
{
    public ProductPage()
    {
        InitializeComponent();
        BindingContext = this;
    }

    Product _product;
    public Product Product
    {
        get { return _product; }
        set
        {
            _product = value;
            ProductName = _product.Name;
            ManufacturerName = _product.ManufacturerName;
        }
    }
}
```

```
string _productName;
public string ProductName
{
    get => _productName;
    set
    {
        _productName = value;
        OnPropertyChanged();
    }
}

string _manufacturerName;
public string ManufacturerName
{
    get => _manufacturerName;
    set
    {
        _manufacturerName = value;
        OnPropertyChanged();
    }
}
}
```

The last step to display the product is to add `Labels` and `Bindings` to the XAML. We can also center the `VerticalStackLayout` and add some spacing. The following listing shows the updated `ProductPage.xaml` file, with the `ContentPage` tags omitted. The updated code is in **bold**.

Listing 7.16   The updated `ProductPage.xaml`

```
<VerticalStackLayout Spacing="50"
                     VerticalOptions="Center">
    <Label Text="{Binding ProductName}"
           FontSize="Title"
           VerticalOptions="Center"
           HorizontalOptions="Center" />

    <Label Text="{Binding ManufacturerName}"
           FontSize="Subtitle"
           VerticalOptions="Center"
           HorizontalOptions="Center" />
</VerticalStackLayout>
```

You can run the app now and should immediately see the Go to Product button. If you tap it, you should be taken to the `ProductPage` and see the details we passed in with the `GoToAsync` method. You can see both images in figure 7.21.

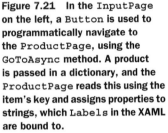

Figure 7.21 In the `InputPage` on the left, a `Button` is used to programmatically navigate to the `ProductPage`, using the `GoToAsync` method. A product is passed in a dictionary, and the `ProductPage` reads this using the item's key and assigns properties to strings, which `Labels` in the XAML are bound to.

Summary

- You can use `ContentPage` to build out navigable parts of your apps.
- `ContentPage` has a `Content` property to which you can assign a layout or control. Assign a layout so that you can add multiple controls.
- Common page lifecycle methods allow you to execute code as part of your app's flow rather than requiring user interaction. You can use this to load data when a page appears or perform other actions you might not want your user to have to initiate.
- You can use tabbed navigation, hierarchical navigation, or flyout navigation in .NET MAUI apps. Or you can combine them.
- You can use Shell to simplify building an app that has multiple pages. Shell lets you define the navigation hierarchy and architecture of the pages in your app in XAML.
- Shell provides automatic navigation for flyout items and tabs, but you can navigate programmatically by assigning routes to pages.
- You can pass data around with navigation in Shell using query strings or a dictionary of `<string, object>` to represent the navigation state.

Part 3

Enterprise development patterns and practices

In this part, everything that we've learned so far comes together as we embark upon our major app project. We'll identify business requirements and map them to features of an app that we'll build to meet them.

We'll learn about the Model-View-ViewModel (MVVM) pattern and how it helps us build robust, maintainable apps, and we'll learn about how we can develop .NET MAUI apps as part of enterprise, full-stack solutions.

In the previous part, we saw how .NET MAUI gives us abstractions of several commonly used controls that can be used to build nearly any app. In this section, we'll take it a step further by seeing how we can build our own controls when we need something .NET MAUI doesn't provide.

We'll see how we can tailor our apps to different platforms, like iOS and Android, and how to tailor them to different device idioms, like mobile and desktop. Finally, we'll wrap up our journey by seeing how we can bring all our hard work to fruition by deploying our apps to the various stores. And, we'll use familiar DevOps tools (in the form of GitHub Actions) to do it.

Enterprise app development

8

This chapter covers

- Moving logic out of the UI and into services
- Authentication
- Using the generic host builder pattern to register services and resources
- Dependency injection
- Full stack architecture patterns for .NET MAUI apps

There's a good chance you've chosen to build an app in .NET MAUI because it fits in with your existing .NET stack. Writing apps in .NET MAUI offers several benefits, but perhaps chief among these is the opportunity to use your existing skills in .NET and easily integrate a .NET MAUI app into an existing solution or code base.

Many of the patterns and practices you're familiar with from other .NET project types can be used in .NET MAUI apps. In this chapter, we'll look at some of these, including abstracting logic into interfaces and implementing that logic in services. We'll also look at some other enterprise patterns in .NET MAUI development, such as dependency injection (DI) and authentication and how we can simplify local development of full-stack, cloud-based solutions with .NET MAUI client apps.

If you already have your cloud or web infrastructure running on .NET and you want to add a mobile or desktop app, .NET MAUI is a no-brainer. In this chapter, we'll look at how MauiStockTake.UI slots into our existing .NET API solution and how we can share code between the different layers of the solution.

8.1   *Moving logic to services*

The MauiStockTake app we began working on in chapter 7 has a page structure and navigation hierarchy defined in its Shell, but it doesn't do anything yet. We need to add some functionality to search for products and an inventory counter.

So far, all the functionality we've been writing in our apps has been in the code-behind files for our XAML pages. This choice is not a smart one for a few reasons, but perhaps the two most important are the following:

- *It tightly couples the UI to business logic*—Writing business logic in the code-behind for a `Page` makes our application more brittle. Changes to the UI can affect the business logic, and vice versa.
- *It doesn't allow code re-use*—Logic written in a `Page` can't be used by other pages. So if, for example, different pages in the app all need to get information about a product, they each have to implement that logic themselves.

In MauiStockTake, we're going to take a different approach and implement the functionality we need in services. This approach will solve both problems, as removing business logic from the UI breaks that coupling and allows the logic to be used wherever it is needed without having to reimplement it.

Before implementing the services, we'll start by defining requirements. We define requirements by determining what functionality we will need in the app and then write interfaces to describe that functionality.

8.1.1   *Defining requirements*

The first thing we want a user to do when they open our app is to log in, so let's start by adding a login `Button` to the `LoginPage`. As well as adding a `Button`, we'll change the layout from a `VerticalStackLayout` to a `FlexLayout` to better arrange the views, and we'll update the text of the `Label` from Login Page to MauiStockTake. Between the `Label` and the `Button`, we can put the app's logo. We'll use the same `surf-shack_logo.jpeg` that we use in the flyout. Finally, we'll wrap the whole layout in a `Grid` and add an `ActivityIndicator` as well, so we can show the user that something is happening while the login is taking place. The following listing shows the updated `LoginPage.xaml` file with the changes in **bold**.

> **Listing 8.1   The updated `LoginPage.xaml`**

```xml
<?xml version="1.0" encoding="utf-8" ?>
<ContentPage xmlns="http://schemas.microsoft.com/dotnet/2021/maui"
             xmlns:x="http://schemas.microsoft.com/winfx/2009/xaml"
             x:Class="MauiStockTake.UI.Pages.LoginPage"
             Title="LoginPage">
```

```
<Grid>
    <FlexLayout JustifyContent="SpaceAround"
                Direction="Column"
                AlignItems="Center"
                HorizontalOptions="Center"
                VerticalOptions="Center">

        <Image Source="surfshack_logo.jpeg"
               WidthRequest="200"
               HeightRequest="200"
               HorizontalOptions="Center"
               VerticalOptions="Center">
            <Image.Clip>
                <EllipseGeometry Center="100,100"
                                 RadiusX="100"
                                 RadiusY="100"/>
            </Image.Clip>
        </Image>

        <Label Text="MauiStockTake"
               FontSize="Title"
               VerticalOptions="Center"
               HorizontalOptions="Center" />

        <Button Text="Login"
                HorizontalOptions="Center"
                VerticalOptions="Center"
                Clicked="LoginButton_Clicked"
                x:Name="LoginButton"/>
    </FlexLayout>
    <ActivityIndicator x:Name="LoggingIn"
                       IsRunning="True"
                       IsVisible="false"/>
</Grid>
</ContentPage>
```

Sets AlignItems to Center so that child items are centered along the main axis (direction of flex flow)

Sets the Direction to Column to arrange the child items vertically

You can see that the login `Button` has a `Clicked` event handler defined, so let's go ahead and add this. The following listing shows the method to add to the `Login-Page.xaml.cs` file.

Listing 8.2   The `LoginButton_Clicked` method

```
private void LoginButton_Clicked(object sender, EventArgs e)
{
}
```

We now have our first *requirement* defined. We have a login `Button`, so we have a requirement for functionality to let the user log in. When we use the dependency inversion principle (see MVVM for SOLID apps in the next chapter), we define requirements where they are consumed (rather than where they are provided). So, we can start by defining an interface to describe the functionality we need to consume on the `LoginPage`. This requirement is summarized in figure 8.1.

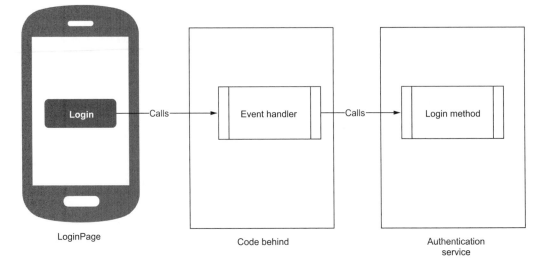

Figure 8.1   The `LoginPage` has a login button. This button triggers an event handler in the code-behind file. The event handler doesn't handle the process of logging in itself; instead, it calls a `Login` method in an authentication service.

In the MauiStockTake.UI project, **create a new folder called `Services` and, in here, create an interface called `IAuthService.cs`**. We know that the implementation of this interface is going to let the user log in, so we can add a method called `LoginAsync`. We'll need to know whether the login was successful, so we should have it return a `bool` (we could handle this a bit more elegantly, but this will suit our needs). Finally, the login process will communicate with the REST API, so we want this communication to happen on a background thread so the UI doesn't freeze while we're waiting for a response. Therefore, we should make the return type a `Task`. The following listing shows the code for the `IAuthService` interface.

Listing 8.3   The `IAuthService` interface

```
namespace MauiStockTake.UI.Services;
public interface IAuthService
{
    Task<bool> LoginAsync();
}
```

We've now defined a namespace that we're going to use in a lot of places throughout our app, so we want add this namespace to our `GlobalUsings.cs` file. **Add the `MauiStockTake.UI.Services` namespace to `GlobalUsings.cs`:**

```
global using MauiStockTake.UI.Services;
```

We can't quite run the app yet as we need to solve two problems. The first is there is no implementation of this interface. The second is while we've registered a route for the LoginPage, we haven't given the user any way to navigate to it.

We'll provide an implementation for the IAuthService in the next section, but for now, we can create a mock implementation. In the Services folder, create a new class that implements the IAuthService interface called MockAuthService. For the implementation of the Login method, simply return a Task result of true. The following listing shows the code for the MockAuthService.

Listing 8.4   MockAuthService

```
namespace MauiStockTake.UI.Services;
public class MockAuthService : IAuthService
{
    public Task<bool> LoginAsync() => Task.FromResult(true);
}
```

Mocking interfaces

We've added the mock implementation for IAuthService so that we won't be held up by not having a real implementation. Defining the requirements in interfaces keeps you from getting blocked while you're building a UI but don't yet have the functionality you depend on, as you can provide a mock implementation in the meantime.

Using a mock implementation won't help you do anything that depends on your user actually being logged in (like authenticating API calls, for example). However, it will allow you to build and run your app and test your UI, and it can also be useful for unit testing later.

Now that we have a mock implementation for the IAuthService interface, we can add some functionality to the LoginButton_Clicked event handler. In the Login-Page.xaml.cs file, add a field for the IAuthService and, in the constructor, assign a new instance of the MockAuthService to it. In the event handler, the first thing we'll do is disable the login button to prevent the user from tapping it while a login is in progress (this won't be a problem for our mock implementation, but it's a good practice). Then we can call the Login method in the authentication service, and if it is successful, place the user into the main guts of the app and, if not, display a warning. Of course, we know that our mock implementation is just going to return true, but we will be well set up for when we provide a real implementation. The following listing shows the full code for the LoginPage.xaml.cs file.

Listing 8.5   LoginPage.xaml.cs

```
namespace MauiStockTake.UI.Pages;

public partial class LoginPage : ContentPage
{
```

```
private readonly IAuthService _authService;        ◁──┐   Adds a field for
                                                       │   the IAuthService
public LoginPage()                                     │   interface
{
    InitializeComponent();                             ┐   Assigns a new instance
    _authService = new MockAuthService();        ◁─────┤   of the MockAuthService
}                                                      │   to the field

private async void LoginButton_Clicked(object sender, EventArgs e)
{
    LoginButton.IsEnabled = false;               ┐   Makes the ActivityIndicator
    LoggingIn.IsVisible = true;            ◁─────┤   visible to show the user a
                                                 │   login is in progress
    var loggedIn = await _authService.LoginAsync();    ◁──┐

    LoggingIn.IsVisible = false;                      Calls the LoginAsync method on
                                                      the IAuthService and assigns the
                                                      result to a temporary variable
    if (!loggedIn)
    {
        await App.Current.MainPage.DisplayAlert("Error", "Something went
wrong logging you in. Please try again.", "OK");
        LoginButton.IsEnabled = true;
    }
    else
    {
        // TODO: navigate back to the app
    }
}
}
```

In the event handler, disables the login button (label pointing to `LoginButton.IsEnabled = false;`)

If the login is not successful, shows a warning to the user, hides the ActivityIndicator, and enables the button

We've got a TODO comment in the code for when the login is successful. That's because at the moment we're not actually showing the LoginPage, so there's nothing to go back from. Logging in is the first thing the user will need to do, so we should show it automatically when the app starts. We've got a route registered for LoginPage, but we should remove this route as we want the LoginPage to appear as part of the app's lifecycle rather than being navigable (you can read more about application lifecycle here: http://mng.bz/e1GP).

We'll use the OnStart application lifecycle method and use hierarchical navigation to push the LoginPage as a modal page onto the navigation stack. Unlike a NavigationPage, a modal page doesn't provide navigation UI (i.e., a back button), which gives the user a cue that the actions in the page should be completed before navigating away from the page. A modal page is well suited for our login scenario. Of course, on Android, you have a hardware or OS-supplied back button, so the user can still dismiss the page, but the cue is still there. You can override this functionality if necessary.

In the `App.xaml.cs` file, override the `OnStart` method and, within the method, push a modal instance of the `LoginPage` onto the stack. The navigation stack is managed by a property called `Navigation` that is inherited by the `Page` class from the `NavigableElement` base class. The app's navigation stack is passed by reference to the page currently assigned to the app's `MainPage` property, so we can use this path to call the navigation methods. The following listing shows the code to add to `App.xaml.cs`.

Listing 8.6 The `OnStart` functionality to add to `App.xaml.cs`

```
protected override async void OnStart()
{
    base.OnStart();

    await MainPage.Navigation.PushModalAsync(
➡   new LoginPage());
}
```

Calls the PushModalAsync method on the Navigation property of the app's MainPage and passes in a new instance of the LoginPage

This code will push a modal instance of the `LoginPage` when the app starts. Once the user has logged in, we can pop this page to return to the main Shell. `LoginPage` also inherits `NavigableElement`, so it also has a `Navigation` property that holds a reference to the app's navigation stack. Therefore, we can call the `PopModalAsync` method on `LoginPage`'s `Navigation` property. Replace the `TODO` comment in `LoginPage.xaml.cs` with the code in following listing.

Listing 8.7 The code to add to `LoginPage.xaml.cs` in place of the `TODO`

```
await Navigation.PopModalAsync();
```

Run the app now, and you should see the `LoginPage` pop up automatically. Click the login button, and the page will disappear, and you'll be back to the app Shell. You can see the result in figure 8.2.

8.1.2 *Implementing the authentication service*

The MauiStockTake API uses IdentityServer, an OpenID Connect (OIDC) compliant framework for ASP.NET Core applications. OIDC, an extension of OAuth2, lets users authenticate using their web browser to obtain a token that can be used to access protected resources. We'll need to build an authentication service in the .NET MAUI app that can sign in our users using IdentityServer and obtain a JSON web token (JWT) that can be used to authenticate calls to the API.

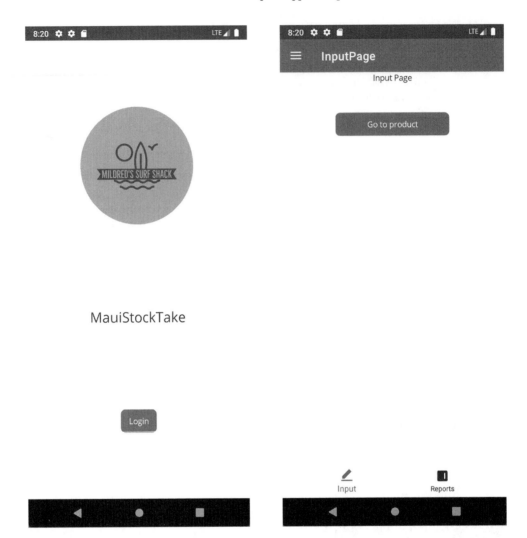

Figure 8.2 On the left, the LoginPage has been pushed as a modal page onto the navigation stack automatically when the app starts. Note the app does not provide a back button. If you click the Login button, the LoginPage is popped programmatically, revealing the existing Shell underneath.

Identity, authentication, and authorization

Identity is a huge topic and way outside the scope of this book, but it's an important topic that you should at least have some familiarity with. Some apps don't require authentication or have any user accounts, but these are a small minority. If you'd like to learn more about identity and authentication, you can check out my video here: https://youtu.be/zOLBNdljhpg.

You don't have to use IdentityServer in your apps. In fact, it's become increasingly popular to outsource identity to a cloud-based identity provider (IDP), like Azure Active Directory B2C or Auth0. We're using IdentityServer here because it's included in the ASP.NET Core templates, so it doesn't require signing up to a third-party service, and you may already be familiar with it. Also, most cloud-based IDPs offer a well-documented and supported client package or SDK that you can install and are very easy to use. They often also take care of some of the functionality we're going to build ourselves, like securely storing refresh tokens.

If you're outsourcing identity in your apps, it will be a lot easier to get started with documented client packages, but if you want to use IdentityServer, the approach here will help. And it will also work with any OIDC-compliant IDP, including most of the commercial cloud offerings.

With OAuth2 authentication, rather than sending a username and password from your app to the IDP, your app opens a web browser at the IDP's login page. This method is considered more secure, as your app never has access to the user's password; they log in to the IDP directly, and once they're logged in, they get redirected to the app with a code that can be used to obtain an access token.

To achieve this authentication in our `IAuthService` implementation, we'll use a combination of the built-in `WebAuthenticator` that comes with .NET MAUI and a NuGet package called `IdentityModel.OidcClient`. `OidcClient` is made by the same people who make IdentityServer, and simplifies the process of parsing the OAuth2 response that IdentityServer returns for a logged-in user. Figure 8.3 shows how this will work in MauiStockTake.

`OidcClient` is used to parse an OIDC response but doesn't provide a way to direct the user to an IDP's login page to authenticate. When creating an `OidcClient` instance, you need to provide an implementation of `OidcClient`'s `IBrowser` interface, which defines a method for performing this action. We'll build an implementation of this interface that uses `WebAuthenticator` to perform the login and then pass the results back to `OidcClient`, which will extract the tokens we need and return them to our authentication service.

> **NOTE** We'll need to use the fully qualified name for `IBrowser`, as .NET MAUI also has an interface called `IBrowser` with a different use case.

When we use an OAuth2 login flow with a web browser, as part of the request, we provide a redirect URI. Once the user successfully authenticates, the IDP returns them to the redirect URI, along with an authorization code, which can be exchanged for tokens. In our case, we don't want to redirect the user to a website but to our app. To do this, we register a custom URL scheme with the operating system so that the OS knows that any URLs bound to addresses starting with that scheme should be sent to our app.

No doubt you are familiar with the `http://` and `https://` URL schemes. When you open a URL, it will be opened with the default application registered with the OS

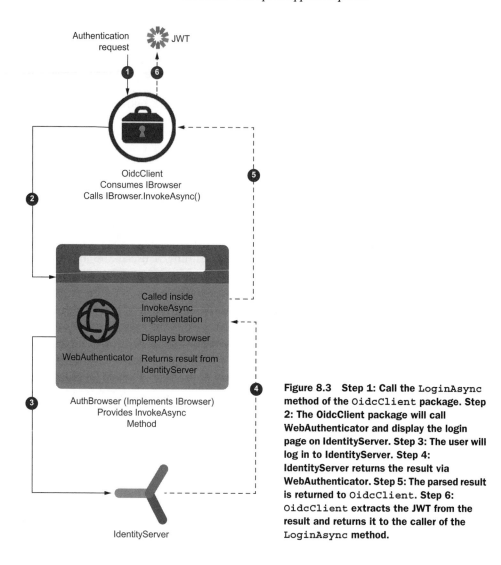

Figure 8.3   **Step 1: Call the** `LoginAsync` **method of the** `OidcClient` **package. Step 2: The OidcClient package will call WebAuthenticator and display the login page on IdentityServer. Step 3: The user will log in to IdentityServer. Step 4: IdentityServer returns the result via WebAuthenticator. Step 5: The parsed result is returned to** `OidcClient`**. Step 6:** `OidcClient` **extracts the JWT from the result and returns it to the caller of the** `LoginAsync` **method.**

for handling the scheme. For HTTP and HTTPS, this will be your default web browser. By using a custom scheme, we can associate it with our app, so any URL beginning with that scheme will be opened in our app. Figure 8.4 shows how we can utilize this scheme to get the authentication response back from an IDP.

For our application, we'll use `auth.com.mildredsurf.stocktake://callback` as the redirect URI. In this case, `auth.com.mildredsurf.stocktake` is the scheme, so we need to register this scheme with our target platforms. The process is slightly different for each platform, and the following sections will walk through the setup for each OS that our app can target.

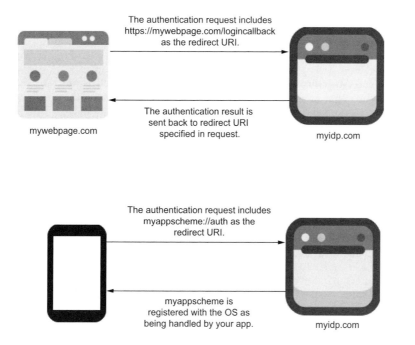

Figure 8.4   When authenticating with an IDP, a redirect URL is supplied. Upon successful authentication, a response is sent back to the redirect URL. For a web application, this redirect is usually the address of the web application where the authentication request originated. For a mobile or desktop app, the URL uses a custom scheme that the OS associated with the app, so the response from the IDP is sent to the app.

ANDROID URL REGISTRATION

Registering a custom URL scheme for Android requires two steps. First, we need to create an `Activity` that will receive the web callback. Second, we need to add an intent to the manifest that will allow us to open the browser.

Let's start with the `Activity`. Add a file in `Platforms/Android` called `WebCallback-Activity.cs` and add the content from the following listing.

Listing 8.8   WebCallbackActivity.cs

```
using Android.App;
using Android.Content;
using Android.Content.PM;

namespace MauiStockTake.UI.Platforms.Android;

[Activity(NoHistory = true, LaunchMode = LaunchMode.SingleTop, Exported =
➥ true)]
[IntentFilter(new[] { Intent.ActionView },
    Categories = new[] { Intent.CategoryDefault, Intent.CategoryBrowsable },
    DataScheme = "auth.com.mildredsurf.stocktake",
    DataHost = "callback")]
```

```
public class WebCallbackActivity : WebAuthenticatorCallbackActivity
{

}
```

Next, we will tell Android that our app will use custom tabs. Custom tabs sit between an embedded webview and switching apps to another browser (you can find out more about them here: https://developer.chrome.com/docs/android/custom-tabs). Add the **bold** code from the following listing to the AndroidManifest.xml file (which, as we saw in chapter 3, can be found in the Platforms/Android folder) before the closing </manifest> tag.

> **Listing 8.9 AndroidManifest.xml**

```
<?xml version="1.0" encoding="utf-8"?>
<manifest xmlns:android="http://schemas.android.com/apk/res/android">
    <uses-sdk android:minSdkVersion="21" android:targetSdkVersion="30" />
    <application android:allowBackup="true" android:icon="@mipmap/appicon"
     android:roundIcon="@mipmap/appicon_round"
     android:supportsRtl="true"></application>
    <uses-permission android:name="android.permission.ACCESS_NETWORK_STATE"
     />
    <queries>
        <intent>
            <action android:name="android.support.customtabs.action.Custom-
    TabsService" />
        </intent>
    </queries>
</manifest>
```

iOS AND MAC CUSTOM URL REGISTRATION

The process for registering a custom URL scheme with iOS and macOS is the same. Repeat the following steps in the platform folders for iOS and Mac Catalyst.

First, register the custom URL scheme in the info.plist file (remember from chapter 3, this can be found in the Platforms/iOS and Platforms/MacCatalyst folders). If using Visual Studio, double-click on the file to open the file with the plist editor and go to the Advanced tab. Expand the URL Types node and click on Add URL type. Add the values shown in Table 8.1.

Table 8.1 The values to add to info.plist

Field	Value
Identifier	`Auth`
URL Schemes	`auth.com.mildredsurf.stocktake`
Role	`Viewer`

If you are not using Visual Studio, or you would simply prefer to add these values manually, open info.plist with a text editor. Inside the <dict>...</dict> tags, add a new entry to the dictionary with a key of `CFBundleURLTypes`. The value will be an array, which will also contain a dictionary. The following listing shows you how to add the entries for the custom URL scheme registration. Add these before the closing `</dict>` tag.

Listing 8.10 Custom URL definition in `Info.plist` for iOS and macOS

```
<key>CFBundleURLTypes</key>
<array>
    <dict>
        <key>CFBundleURLName</key>
        <string>Auth</string>
        <key>CFBundleURLSchemes</key>
        <array>
            <string>auth.com.mildredsurf.stocktake</string>
        </array>
        <key>CFBundleTypeRole</key>
        <string>Viewer</string>
    </dict>
</array>
```

Don't forget to repeat these steps in both the iOS and MacCatalyst platform folders.

WINDOWS CUSTOM URL SCHEME REGISTRATION

To register the custom URL scheme on Windows, we need to update the `Package.appxmanifest` file. Open the file in a text editor (if using Visual Studio, right-click and select View Code or click on the file in Solution Explorer and press F7). Inside the manifest, locate the Applications node and the Application node with the id of App inside it. Add the code from the following listing directly after the `<Application ...>` opening tag.

Listing 8.11 Custom URL definition in `Package.appxmanifest` for Windows

```
<Extensions>
    <uap:Extension Category="windows.protocol">
        <uap:Protocol Name="auth.com.mildredsurf.stocktake">
            <uap:DisplayName>Auth</uap:DisplayName>
        </uap:Protocol>
    </uap:Extension>
</Extensions>
```

Now that we've registered the URL scheme on each platform, we'll need some helper classes to handle the response from IdentityServer.

DEFINING THE IDENTITYSERVER VALUES

When interacting with an OAuth2 IDP, we need a few values defined to help us locate the IDP and specify some details needed for the login interaction. Specifically, we need the URI of the IDP, the client ID (which represents a client defined in the IDP—in this case, our MauiStockTake app), the scopes we request access to, and the redirect

URI. We'll make all these values constant and the class static so that they are easy to access from anywhere in the app.

Add a new class in the root of the MauiStockTake.UI project called Constants. This class will contain several values that we'll use throughout the app. Listing 8.12 shows the code for the Constants class. The code here shows ngrok URLs I have generated for testing (see appendix A). Replace these URLs with your own ngrok URLs (or whatever URLs you are using for testing) when you want to run the app.

Listing 8.12   `Constants.cs`

Adds a string called BaseUrl. This string will be used as the base address for calls to the API.

Adds a string called RedirectUri. This string will be passed to IdentityServer with the login request so a successful login can be returned back to our app. Note that the URL scheme is the scheme we registered earlier in this section.

```
namespace MauiStockTake.UI;

public static class Constants
{
    public const string BaseUrl = "https://8284-159-196-124-207.
    ngrok.io";

    public const string RedirectUri = "auth.
    com.mildredsurf.stocktake://callback";

    public const string AuthorityUri =
    "https://8284-159-196-124-207.ngrok.io";

    public const string ClientId = "com.mildredsurf.
    stocktake";

    public const string Scope = "openid profile
    offline_access MauiStockTake.WebUIAPI";
}
```

Adds a string called AuthorityUri, which we'll use for authentication requests. Note that in this case, it's the same as the API URI because we are running an API with IdentityServer built in.

Adds a string called ClientId. The value here must match a valid client Id in the IDP (the supplied value in the code matches a valid client ID in the API you downloaded).

Adds a string called Scope. This string will hold an array of scopes, which will be space delimited. These scopes must all be valid for the IDP.

ADD THE AUTHBROWSER

The AuthBrowser class will implement the IBrowser interface defined in the Oidc-Client NuGet package, so we need to install this first. **Install IdentityModel.Oidc-Client into the MauiStockTake.UI project.** Next, in the MauiStockTake.UI project, add a folder called Helpers and, in here, add a class called AuthBrowser.

We'll need to declare that AuthBrowser implements the IBrowser interface, but as .NET MAUI also has an IBrowser interface, we'll need to use the fully qualified name including the namespace. IBrowser defines a method called InvokeAsync, so we will need to implement this method.

This method returns a type called BrowserResult. It has a single-string property called Response, which provides the values returned by an IDP formatted in a way that

OidcClient can parse. So, in the InvokeAsync method, we'll invoke WebAuthentica-tor, which will provide the values from the IDP in a dictionary called Properties. We'll write another method to read these and add the values that OidcClient expects to a string formatted in a way it can read. Then we will add this string the Response property of a BrowserResult and return it to the caller. The following listing shows the code for the AuthBrowser class.

Listing 8.13 The `AuthBrowser` class

Calls the AuthenticateAsync method of the WebAuthenticator to open a browser at the IDP login page. The OidcClient will call this method and pass in options that include the IDP URL, but we'll pass in the redirect URI from the constants that we defined.

```
using IdentityModel.OidcClient.Browser;

namespace MauiStockTake.UI.Helpers;

public class AuthBrowser : IdentityModel.OidcClient.
    Browser.IBrowser
{
    public async Task<BrowserResult> InvokeAsync(
    BrowserOptions options, CancellationToken
    cancellationToken = default)
    {
        WebAuthenticatorResult authResult = await
    WebAuthenticator.AuthenticateAsync(new Uri(
    options.StartUrl), new Uri(Constants.RedirectUri));

        return new BrowserResult()
        {
            Response = ParseAuthenticationResult(
    authResult)
        };
    }

    private string ParseAuthenticationResult(
    WebAuthenticatorResult result)
    {
        string code = result?.Properties["code"];
        string scope = result?.Properties["scope"];
        string state = result?.Properties["state"];
        string sessionState = result?.Properties["session_state"];
        return $"{Constants.RedirectUri}#code={code}&
    scope={scope}&state={state}&session_state={
    sessionState}";
    }
}
```

Declares that this class implements the IBrowser interface from the OidcClient package

Implements the InvokeAsync method defined in the IBrowser interface

Returns an instance of the BrowserResult type that OidcClient expects

Assigns a string value to the Response property of BrowserResult, obtained by sending the result from WebAuthenticator to the ParseAuthenticationResult method defined in this class

Returns a formatted string with values from the Properties dictionary of the WebAuthenticatorResult

Defines a class called ParseAuthenticationResult that returns a string and takes in a WebAuthenticatorResult from WebAuthenticator

This code listing completes the AuthBrowser class, which gives us a method of opening a web browser at the IDP login page and returning a formatted result that OidcClient can process. That's all the preparation we need, and we can now build the AuthService.

> **NOTE**   At the time of writing, WebAuthenticator doesn't yet work on Windows, but there is a package called WinUIEx that contains its own WebAuthenticator that can be used instead. I have an example on GitHub, which also links to a video tutorial showing how to use it: https://github.com/matt-goldman/MauiB2C-No-MSAL.

ADDING THE AUTHSERVICE

In the Services folder, **create a class called AuthService**. The AuthService will implement the IAuthService interface, which, at the moment, defines a single method called LoginAsync.

In the AuthService, we're going to implement the LoginAsync method using the OidcClient. When we instantiate this client, it will require some options in its constructor, and we'll build these using a combination of values we set in the Constants class and the IBrowser implementation we created.

The OidcClient will use WebAuthenticator to invoke a browser session and capture the returned session state. The key part we need to authenticate against the API is the access token. Shortly, we're going to see how we can use this access token to make authenticated calls to the API, but for now, we just want to check the result for any errors. If not, we know we've authenticated successfully, have an access token, and can return true from this method or otherwise return false. The following listing shows the code for the AuthService class.

Listing 8.14   The AuthService class

```
using IdentityModel.OidcClient;
using MauiStockTake.UI.Helpers;

namespace MauiStockTake.UI.Services;

public class AuthService : IAuthService          ⟵  Declares that this
{                                                    class implements the
    private readonly OidcClientOptions _options;     IAuthService interface

    public AuthService()                          ⟵  Adds a field to store the
    {                                                 OidcClientOptions
        _options = new OidcClientOptions       ⟵┐
        {                                         │  In the constructor,
            Authority   = Constants.AuthorityUri,    assigns a new instance of
            ClientId    = Constants.ClientId,        OidcClientOptions to the
            Scope       = Constants.Scope,           field using values defined
            RedirectUri = Constants.RedirectUri,     in Constants and the
            Browser     = new AuthBrowser()          AuthBrowser IBrowser
        };                                           implementation
    }
```

```
public async Task<bool> LoginAsync()
{
    var oidcClient = new OidcClient(_options);

    var loginResult = await oidcClient.LoginAsync(
new LoginRequest());

    if (loginResult.IsError)
    {
        // TODO: inspect and handle error
        return false;
    }

    return true;
}
}
```

Implements the LoginAsync method and makes it async

Creates a new instance of the OidcClient using the options stored in the field

Invokes the LoginAsync method of the OidcClient and assigns the result to a temporary variable

Checks to see whether the result is an error, and if it is, returns false or otherwise flows forward to return true

Now that we have a real implementation of the IAuthService, we can go back to the LoginPage code behind and update the constructor. Change the line that assigns the MockAuthService to the IAuthService field to use the real AuthService instead:

```
_authService = new AuthService();
```

If you've followed the setup instructions in appendix A, you can now run the API and use ngrok (or tunnel of your preference) to get a publicly routable URL. Ensure this URL is in your Constants file for both the authority and base URL.

Run the app now, and it should automatically push a modal instance of the login page. If you click the login button, on iOS and Android, you'll see a browser window open within the app, and on Windows and macOS, your default browser will open to the login page of IdentityServer. The API automatically creates a default account with the username administrator@localhost and the password Administrator1!; you can log in with these credentials or register an account for yourself.

Once you log in, if you are on iOS or Android, the browser window will disappear; if you're on macOS or Windows, the browser will ask for permission to open the MauiStockTake app (make sure you approve this). You'll then be back in the app, and the login page will be popped from the stack, just like with the MockAuthService.

If you want, you can put a breakpoint in the AuthService on the line that checks the loginResult to see whether it is an error. You can inspect loginResult, and you should see an access token, an ID token, and a refresh token. Now that our app has a way to obtain an access token, we can build the functionality to make authenticated API calls and make the app do something useful.

8.2   Using the generic host builder and dependency injection

.NET MAUI uses the same generic host builder pattern that's used in other .NET project types, such as console or ASP.NET Core applications. It therefore includes a built-in DI container.

NOTE   If you're not already familiar and comfortable with DI, you can read up on it in *Dependency Injection Principles, Practices, and Patterns* by Steven van Deursen and Mark Seemann (Manning, 2019).

.NET MAUI also includes this built-in DI container. In the `LoginPage` code-behind and in the `AuthService`, we are "newing up" a bunch of dependencies for the login process that we should be able to resolve from the DI container (the `IBrowser` implementation in the `AuthService` and the `AuthService` in the `LoginPage`).

Before we can consume any services or dependencies from the DI container, we need to register them, and to register them, we need to decide their scope. With an ASP.NET Core application, you have a clearly defined HTTP request pipeline, and each request has a scope. This can often inform the service scope you use to register dependencies.

With a UI app, things work slightly differently. As there's no HTTP request pipeline, registering something with `AddScoped` doesn't make any sense because there aren't requests to scope for. This leaves two remaining options: transient or singleton.

With a Shell app in .NET MAUI, pages added to the Shell via XAML or registered for routing (e.g., the `InputPage`, `ReportPage`, and `ProductPage`) are automatically registered in DI with a singleton scope. However, for pages outside of Shell (e.g., our `LoginPage`) and other dependencies like services and ViewModels (which we'll learn about in the next chapter), we need to register them manually. With that in mind, we'll register our dependencies according to the rules in Table 8.2.

Table 8.2   Scope lifetimes for different dependencies in a .NET MAUI app

Dependency type	Scope	Reasoning
Pages	Transient	We should expect a new instance of a page every time we request one. Persisting values across different instances of a page could cause problems, so we're better off persisting state elsewhere and using transient instances of pages.
ViewModels	Transient	Just like pages, our ViewModels should be transient, so we know we've got a clean instance every time we get a new ViewModel.
Services	Singleton	We should only expect one instance of a service for the running lifetime of an app. Instantiating multiple copies of a database or a service responsible for communicating with an API is a waste of resources and can lead to data conflicts. Services should be singletons and can therefore be where we persist app-wide state. We can inject these singleton instances into ViewModels.

Why are we scoping pages differently to Shell?

I mentioned previously that Shell automatically registers pages as singleton but then I suggest registering pages manually as transient. This question is really one of UX and user expectations.

In a Shell app, a user expects to navigate between pages quickly and usually expects to see the same instance of a page as they navigate back and forth. So, the most efficient use of resources is to register the page as singleton and persist it in memory for the lifetime of the app.

With other navigation paradigms, such as hierarchical (and windowed, which we'll discuss in chapter 10), having a single instance of a page or its state can be problematic. The user could expect a fresh instance every time, and persisting seldomly used items in memory throughout the lifetime of the application is inefficient.

Using the Facebook app as an example, the home tab displays the newsfeed, and if it reloaded every time you tab away and then back to it, you would consider this a poor UX. Within the news feed, if you tap on a profile, it isn't navigable within the tabs but rather pushes hierarchically onto the stack. A fresh instance of the profile page makes sense every time; otherwise, it will hold stale data from previous profiles that you have visited

Using the generic host builder pattern, we can register pages, ViewModels, and services as we would in an ASP.NET Core or console app. But with .NET MAUI, we can register other things, too. Over the next few sections, we'll look at each of these.

8.2.1   Registering resources, services, and other dependencies

We already have some experience with registering resources. In chapter 4, we added an LCD font for the MauiCalc app, and in chapter 6, we registered an icon font for the Outlook replica.

In the `MauiProgram` class, we can see that the `CreateMauiApp` method returns a `MauiApp`. This method is called by the framework to create an instance of the app for each target platform. Inside this method, the generic host builder pattern is used to generate the `MauiApp` that gets returned.

Using this pattern, an extension method called `ConfigureFonts` allows us to register the fonts we want in our app. If you've previously used Xamarin.Forms, you'll appreciate how much simpler registering is with .NET MAUI. Other extension methods are used for registering other things, like handlers and animations (we'll learn about both in chapter 11).

We don't need to register any fonts in MauiStockTake, but we do have some dependencies that need to be registered. The host builder in `MauiProgram` is a temporary variable called `builder` of type `MauiAppBuilder`. It has a property called `Services` of type `IServiceCollection`, which we'll use to register dependencies and what the framework will use to resolve them.

Let's work backward. Looking at the `AuthBrowser`, we can see that it has no external dependencies. It implements an interface defined by `OidcClient` and uses the `WebAuthenticator` provided by .NET MAUI. So we can start by registering this interface implementation with the service collection.

In MauiProgram.cs, after the ConfigureFonts call and before the builder is returned from the method, register the AuthBrowser as an implementation of IBrowser with singleton scope:

```
builder.Services.AddSingleton<IBrowser, AuthBrowser>();
```

You will need to bring in the required namespaces, but if you add this line as-is now, you will get an error because of the duplicate IBrowser name in .NET MAUI and OidcClient. To solve this problem, you can use the fully qualified name or, to make it easier to read, declare at the top of the file that in this case IBrowser means the Oidc-Client version:

```
using IBrowser = IdentityModel.OidcClient.Browser.IBrowser;
```

The next link in the chain is the AuthService. AuthService implements the IAuth-Service interface, so we can register this implementation as a singleton as well. Add the following code after the IBrowser registration:

```
builder.Services.AddSingleton<IAuthService, AuthService>();
```

Most pages will be managed by Shell, but the LoginPage is a modal navigation page so we need to register it ourselves. After the AuthService, register the LoginPage with transient scope:

```
builder.Services.AddTransient<LoginPage>();
```

The following listing shows the full code for the updated MauiProgram class.

Listing 8.15 MauiProgram.cs with the dependency registrations

```
using MauiStockTake.UI.Helpers;
using MauiStockTake.UI.Pages;
using IBrowser = IdentityModel.OidcClient.Browser.IBrowser;

namespace MauiStockTake.UI;

public static class MauiProgram
{
    public static MauiApp CreateMauiApp()
    {
        var builder = MauiApp.CreateBuilder();
        builder
            .UseMauiApp<App>()
            .ConfigureFonts(fonts =>
            {
                fonts.AddFont("OpenSans-Regular.ttf", "OpenSansRegular");
                fonts.AddFont("OpenSans-Semibold.ttf", "OpenSansSemibold");
            });

        builder.Services.AddSingleton<IBrowser, AuthBrowser>();
```

```
        builder.Services.AddSingleton<IAuthService, AuthService>();

        builder.Services.AddTransient<LoginPage>();

        return builder.Build();
    }
}
```

That's all the dependencies we have in MauiStockTake at the moment. Now that they're registered, let's see how we can consume them.

8.2.2   Consuming services

We can consume dependencies from the service collection in .NET MAUI using constructor injection, just like in any other .NET application. AuthService has a dependency on IBrowser, but we can only see this dependency by reading the code, as it is not currently constructor injected. But now that it's registered with the service collection, we can constructor inject it and assign the injected instance to the _options field.

In the AuthService, change the constructor to take an injected instance of IBrowser and assign it to the Browser property of the _options field. You will also need to add the same using statement as we added to MauiProgram to resolve ambiguity between the two IBrowser interfaces. The following listing shows the updated constructor for the AuthService.

> **Listing 8.16   The updated** AuthService **constructor**

```
using IBrowser = IdentityModel.OidcClient.Browser.IBrowser;
...
public AuthService(IBrowser browser)
{
    _options = new OidcClientOptions
    {
        Authority   = Constants.AuthorityUri,
        ClientId    = Constants.ClientId,
        Scope       = Constants.Scope,
        RedirectUri = Constants.RedirectUri,
        Browser     = browser
    };
}
```

Now that we've changed the constructor of the AuthService, if you open the Login-Page you will see that we have an error in the constructor. We are currently assigning a new AuthService() instance to the _authService field, but AuthService doesn't have a default constructor anymore. AuthService now has a visible dependency on IBrowser. We could change it to _authService = new AuthService(new AuthBrowser), but it's better to just inject the IAuthService into the LoginPage. This way, the service collection will be responsible for providing the fully resolved IAuthService implementation, and we adhere to the dependency inversion principle by depending on the requirements defined by the `LoginPage` rather than on any specific implementation. The following listing shows the updated constructor for the `LoginPage`.

Listing 8.17 The updated `LoginPage` constructor

```
public LoginPage(IAuthService authService)
{
    InitializeComponent();
    _authService = authService;
}
```

Now that we've changed the constructor for `LoginPage`, we have an error in `App .xaml.cs` in the `OnStart` method. We are passing a new instance of `LoginPage` to the `PushModalAsync` navigation method, but again, we are depending on a default constructor that no longer exists.

   We could solve this problem in a few different ways. For example, we could add a static property of type `IServiceCollection` to `MauiProgram` and assign the `Services` property of the `MauiAppBuilder` to it. Then, we could call it from anywhere in our app to resolve dependencies, but this approach would use the *service locator* antipattern. Alternatively, we could inject `LoginPage` into the `App` class, assign it to a field, and then pass this field to the `PushModalAsync` method.

   However, a better approach is available: we can use the `PageResolver` NuGet package (disclaimer: I am the author of this package). Using this package, you can navigate to pages by type, using the page as a type argument. The plugin will then navigate to a fully resolved instance of the page with all its dependencies.

   Install the `Goldie.MauiPlugins.PageResolver` NuGet package into the Maui-StockTake.UI. We'll need to refer to this package in a couple of places, so let's **add it to the `GlobalUsings` file**:

```
global using Maui.Plugins.PageResolver;
```

Now we can **update the code in `App.xaml.cs`** to use the simplified navigation method and pass the `LoginPage` as a type parameter without having to worry about its dependencies:

```
await MainPage.Navigation.PushModalAsync<LoginPage>();
```

The last step is to register the `PageResolver` with the generic host builder, which will pass it the service collection to resolve dependencies. In `MauiProgram.cs`, append `UsePageResolver()` to the fluent `UseMauiApp` method. The following listing shows the updated method.

Listing 8.18 The updated `UseMauiApp` method

```
builder
    .UseMauiApp<App>()
    .ConfigureFonts(fonts =>
```

```
{
    fonts.AddFont("OpenSans-Regular.ttf", "OpenSansRegular");
    fonts.AddFont("OpenSans-Semibold.ttf", "OpenSansSemibold");
})
.UsePageResolver();
```

Everything is now in place to automatically resolve and consume all of the `LoginPage`'s dependencies. Run the app now, and you should be able to log in just as you could before (you still need your API and tunnel running and may need to update your tunnel URL). There's no change in functionality from what we had before, but the code is now more maintainable.

8.3 *Consuming web services*

Many apps are self-sufficient and don't have any external dependencies, but enterprise apps and most successful consumer apps usually need to communicate with an API. Many technologies like REST, SignalR, GraphQL, and gRPC are available to facilitate this connectivity. We're using REST in MauiStockTake as it's still the most prevalent, but you can see a sample of a chat app using SignalR here: https://github.com/matt-goldman/maui-chat.

When using REST, the API represents resources, and clients interact with them using the HTTP verbs (`GET`, `POST`, `PUT`, `PATCH`, and `DELETE`). Payloads are usually sent in JSON format, which allows APIs and clients to communicate without concern for what technology each implements behind the scenes.

In a .NET application, you can use an extension method in the `System.Net`
`.Http.Json` namespace to call a REST endpoint using `HttpClient` and deserialize the JSON response to a .NET type:

```
var product = await _httpClient.GetFromJsonAsync<Product>("product");
```

In this example, `_httpClient` is an instance of `HttpClient` that has its `BaseUrl` defined (which would make "product" a route).

This is a good approach, and we've used it a couple of times already (in the Outlook replica and MauiMovies). For larger applications, it can become difficult to maintain, but in MauiStockTake, we are using Clean Architecture (CA), which uses NSwag to automatically generate clients for each resource.

Autogenerated clients

Nswag is a convenient tool for generating client class libraries for .NET APIs. For a trivial API like MauiStockTake, it's probably not necessary, but I am using it as it's built into the CA template. As your solutions grow in complexity and the number of routes in the API increases, the value of an autogenerated client increases exponentially.

If you prefer not to use it, you can write your own methods to interact with the API based on the specification. You can explore the API specification by running the WebAPI project and appending /api to the URL, which will bring up the Swagger UI.

> *(continued)*
>
> You are free to choose whichever approach you wish, but I recommend using the autogenerated client. It will make it easier for you to follow along with the code in this chapter and will save time, allowing you to focus on .NET MAUI-specific topics rather than writing REST clients.

The REST client implementations are already taken care of in the MauiStockTake solution. In this section, we'll see how to wire these up in our .NET MAUI app.

8.3.1 Adding the client project

The MauiStockTake solution has a class library project called MauiStockTake.Client. If you look in the `Helpers` folder, you'll see an autogenerated file that contains client classes for interacting with the REST endpoints. In the `Services` folder, you'll find services for the product and inventory resources, along with interfaces that you can inject where you need them that provide a usable wrapper for these clients. We'll look at these in a bit more detail shortly.

We need to add the MauiStockTake.Client project as a dependency on MauiStock-Take.UI. If you're using Visual Studio, right-click **Dependencies** under MauiStock-Take.UI and click **Add Project Reference...** From there, you can check the box next to MauiStockTake.Client and click OK. If you open the `MauiStockTake.UI.csproj` file, you'll see that the following lines are added:

```
<ItemGroup>
    <ProjectReference
      Include="..\MauiStockTake.Client\MauiStockTake.Client.csproj" />
</ItemGroup>
```

If you're not using Visual Studio, you can add these manually to add the project reference.

`MauiStockTake.Client` has a dependency on another project in the solution called `Shared`, which contains data transfer objects (DTOs; covered in more depth in the next chapter) used by the API and the client project. One of these is called `ProductDto` and is almost identical to the `Product` class we created in the `Models` folder of MauiStockTake.UI. We don't need this class anymore, so you can delete the `Product` class and the `Models` folder.

These deletions will cause errors in `ProductPage.xaml.cs` and `InputPage.xaml.cs`, so let's fix them. First, in each page, **remove the `using` statement for the `Models` namespace and replace it with a `using` statement for `MauiStockTake.Shared.Products`.** Next, in both page code-behind files, **update every mention of `Product` to `Product-Dto`.** Build the MauiStockTake.UI project and ensure there are no errors.

8.3.2   *Using a delegating handler*

The MauiStockTake API expects requests to include an access token sent as a header, and requests made to API routes that require this token but do not include it will not be authorized. It's straightforward to add this header to any `HttpRequestMessage`, but it can become a lot to handle if we have to do this every time we call the API.

Instead, we can use a *delegating handler*. A delegating handler can be associated with an `HttpClient` instance and can modify every HTTP request made by that client so that you don't have to do it yourself on every call. Simply call an HTTP method using that client, and the modification will be applied to the request automatically.

In the MauiStockTake.Client project, there's already a delegating handler set up. Look in the `Authentication` folder of the MauiStockTake.Client project, and you'll see a class called `AuthHandler`. This class inherits the `DelegatingHandler` base class and overrides the `SendAsync` method. Inside this method, the logic is simple—add a header to the request that includes the access token and then just call the base method.

Notice that this class also has two additional members. The first is a static string that will hold the value of the access token. The overridden `SendAsync` method uses this to attach to the request, but at the moment, this value is not being populated.

Looking back at our `AuthService` in the MauiStockTake.UI project, we can see that in the `LoginAsync` method, when we get a successful result, we're simply returning `true`. Let's update the code to assign the access token to the static string in the `AuthHandler`. As it's a static string, we can refer to it using the class name and member name without needing an instance.

In the `AuthService`, in the `LoginAsync` method, add a line before we return `true` to assign the value of the access token from the `loginResult` to the `AuthToken` member of the `AuthHandler`. You will also need to bring in the namespace for the `AuthHandler`. The following listing shows the updated `LoginAsync` method, with the added code in **bold**.

> **Listing 8.19   The updated `LoginAsync` method of `AuthService`**

```
using MauiStockTake.Client.Authentication;
...
public async Task<bool> LoginAsync()
{
    var oidcClient = new OidcClient(_options);

    var loginResult = await oidcClient.LoginAsync(new LoginRequest());

    if (loginResult.IsError)
    {
        // TODO: inspect and handle error
        return false;
    }

    AuthHandler.AuthToken = loginResult.AccessToken;

    return true;
}
```

The delegating handler is now ready to modify any HTTP request to include the access token. Now, we need a way for our API client classes to get access to an Http-Client instance that has this handler attached.

8.3.3   *Using IHttpClientFactory*

Microsoft provides a NuGet package called `Microsoft.Extensions.Http` that enables the use of `HttpClient` with DI (this package is already installed in the MauiStock-Take.Client project). Using an extension method in this package, you can call `AddHttpClient` to add a singleton instance of `HttpClient` to the services collection.

You can call this method multiple times to add multiple instances of `HttpClient`, each one serving a different purpose and each referenced with a unique name (you can also register `HttpClient` instances for specific types). When you require an instance of `HttpClient`, you inject the `IHttpClientFactory` interface into your class and call its `CreateClient` method to resolve the named instance of the client you require from the services collection.

Recall that in the `AuthHandler` we had a const string called `AUTHENTICATED_CLIENT`. The purpose of this string is to provide a name that we can refer to throughout the app for the instance of `HttpClient` that will add the token to HTTP requests.

In the root of the MauiStockTake.Client project is a file called `DependencyInjec-tion`, which contains a method called `AddApiClientServices`. Note that in this method, we are adding the delegating handler to the services collection:

```
services.AddSingleton<AuthHandler>();
```

Immediately following this handler, an `HttpClient` instance is registered, named using the const from the `AuthHandler` class, and with the `AuthHandler` added to its handler chain:

```
services.AddHttpClient(AuthHandler.AUTHENTICATED_CLIENT)
        .AddHttpMessageHandler((s) => s.GetService<AuthHandler>());
```

This code registers an instance of `HttpClient` with the services collection, which can be consumed anywhere in the app, that has a handler attached that will append the access token to any HTTP request made using this client.

Chaining delegating handlers

You can do as much as you like to manipulate the `HttpRequestMessage` in a delegating handler before you call the base method to send it. We only have one modification (attaching the access token), but there may be circumstances where you need more. For example, one product I have worked on requires specific headers depending on certain criteria.

You can make all these changes in one delegating handler, but it's better to create specific handlers for each modification. You can call `AddHttpMessageHandler` multiple times to chain handlers.

This approach better adheres to the single responsibility principle and gives you more flexibility. Handlers will be processed in the order that they are added, so with this approach, you can also control the order in which these modifications are applied.

In the MauiStockTake.Client project, look in the Services folder. In it, you can see three files:

- BaseService
- InventoryService
- ProductService

BaseService contains a base class that expects IHttpClientFactory to be injected. The base service contains a field for an instance of HttpClient. The constructor requests an instance of the named client, using the name defined in the AuthHandler, and assigns it to this field:

```
public BaseService(IHttpClientFactory httpClientFactory, ApiClientOptions
➥ options)
    {
        _httpClient = httpClientFactory.CreateClient(AuthHandler.
➥ AUTHENTICATED_CLIENT);

        _baseUrl = options.BaseUrl;
    }
```

You can see here that the constructor also expects a class called ApiClientOptions and uses that to populate a base URL field; we'll talk about this in the next section.

As all services will use the same token, the InventoryService and ProductService inherit this base class. Their constructors must also take the dependencies that the base class requires and pass them through to the base constructor, but they don't need to double-handle requesting the HttpClient instance from IHttpClientFactory.

Looking at the constructor of either the InventoryService or ProductService class, you can see that they use this authenticated client to create an instance of the REST resource-specific client used by each of these services. Using a managed Http-Client instance gives us an access token to make authenticated requests to any endpoint in the API without having to handle it on each individual request.

8.3.4   Adding the remaining MauiStockTake services

In the MauiStockTake.UI project, we've already seen how we can wire up services and dependencies in the IServiceCollection. In MauiProgram, we've registered Auth-Service as an implementation of the IAuthService interface.

The MauiStockTake.Client project also has some interfaces defined as well as some implementations (we looked at their constructors in the previous section). These dependencies are already registered in the DependencyInjection class, so all we need to do to use them in the MauiStockTake.UI project is add this existing dependency registration.

The `AddApiClientServices` method is an extension method on `IService-Collection`, so we can register it in `MauiProgram`. Registration of the service interfaces and their implementations is already done in this method, so adding it in `MauiProgram` will make these services available in the app.

As it's an extension method, we can call it on an existing `IServiceCollection`, rather than passing the `IServiceCollection` in. But the method also expects another parameter of type `ApiClientOptions`. In `MauiProgram`, call this extension method on the `Service` property of the `builder` variable and pass in a new instance of `ApiClient-Options`, with the `BaseUrl` from the `Constants` class assigned to the `BaseUrl` property. The following listing shows the code to add to `MauiProgram`.

Listing 8.20   Registering the client in MauiProgram

```
builder.Services.AddApiClientServices(new ApiClientOptions
{
    BaseUrl = Constants.BaseUrl
});
```

With the MauiStockTake.Client project now registered, we can inject the service interfaces into our classes and use them to talk to the API. Authentication is handled by the `AuthHandler`, and the services are wired up to use an instance of `HttpClient` that uses this handler. In the next chapter, we'll finish building the stock-taking functionality of this app by using these services.

8.4 *Full-stack app architecture*

MauiStockTake is not a standalone mobile and desktop application. It's part of a larger solution that includes cloud/web components and a database, and it requires authentication to secure communication between the .NET MAUI app and the cloud API. In this section, we'll look at how to organize your solution to maximize code sharing and efficiency.

8.4.1 *Project Organization*

As mentioned in the last chapter, the MauiStockTake API is based on the Clean Architecture (CA) template and follows clean architecture principles, but the code-sharing techniques we've covered in this chapter allow you to integrate a .NET MAUI UI into any full-stack .NET architecture. Figure 8.5 shows how the API projects in the solution are organized.

The CA pattern, as applied to the backend API, is beyond the scope of this book, but you can learn more about it by watching Jason Taylor's talk from NDC Sydney here: https://www.youtube.com/watch?v=5OtUm1BLmG0. The particulars of the architecture are not that important; what's important is that we're following the principles and a design pattern to maximize code re-use across our whole stack.

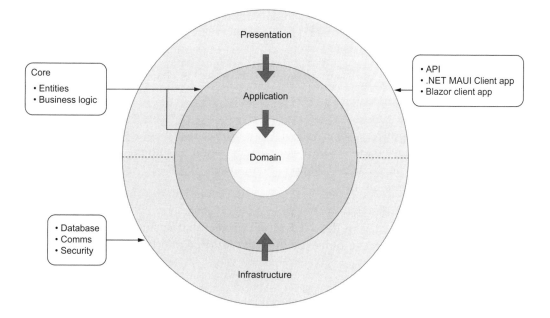

Figure 8.5   With CA, all dependencies point inward. The Core (Domain and Application) contains your entities and business logic. Application depends on Domain, and Domain has no dependencies. Infrastructure and Presentation depend on Application, and the .NET MAUI app is part of Presentation.

You don't have to use Clean Architecture

I used CA for MauiStockTake because it provides a logical, structured way to organize code in your solution. As I use it frequently at work, and have helped Jason to teach it, this familiarity makes it a lower cognitive burden for me to use CA when starting a new project, but more importantly, this structure helps to illustrate how we can share code between the API and the .NET MAUI app.

There are plenty of alternative architectures, though; some may be better suited to your scenario, or you may simply not like the CA approach (many people don't). And that's fine. Vertical slice architecture in particular is currently en vogue. Minimal APIs are also increasing in popularity, and you can find out more about these in *ASP.NET Core in Action* by Andrew Lock (Manning 2023).

Whether you use CA or some other architecture, the principles of sharing code across your stack are the same, and the techniques used here will work just as well with other architectures.

As part of this solution, it makes sense to reuse code by sharing it among the different projects where possible, as we saw in section 8.3. For now, let's focus on the Presentation layer, as this is where our focus will be in building a UI.

The solution is arranged in folders representing the different layers of CA, and looking in the `Presentation` folder, we see

- `WebAPI`
- `MauiStockTake.Maui` (we added this in the last chapter)
- `Client`

WebAPI

The `WebAPI` project is an ASP.NET Core project that provides REST controllers and endpoints that allow the outside world to communicate with the business logic and data in the API. The .NET MAUI app communicates with this over HTTP to interact with the rest of the solution.

MauiStockTake.UI

`MauiStockTake.Maui` is the .NET MAUI project that we added in the previous chapter. In this project, we build the app that Mildred and her team will use when taking inventory.

MauiStockTake.Client

`MauiStockTake.Client` is a class library that contains types and logic that can be used in a .NET UI project for interacting with the API. It contains data transfer objects (DTOs) and services, as well as some autogenerated client code.

Everything in this project is essential for making the MauiStockTake.UI client app work, but it's boilerplate code that is not part of the .NET MAUI app itself. In fact, if we wanted to add a Blazor web app in the future, the Blazor app can reuse this class library, eliminating the need to duplicate code that achieves the same thing.

8.4.2   *Sharing code between projects in the solution*

In CA, it's a strict rule that dependencies point inward. It's also a strict rule that the Domain has no external dependencies. Typically, Application is part of Core along with Domain, and Application *can* have dependencies, just not dependencies that point outward.

Parts of the solution that run perpendicular to the flow of dependencies are referred to as *cross-cutting concerns* (see figure 8.6). In the case of MauiStockTake, we

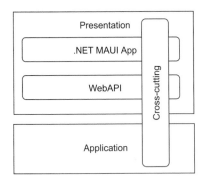

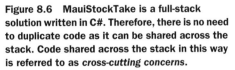

Figure 8.6   MauiStockTake is a full-stack solution written in C#. Therefore, there is no need to duplicate code as it can be shared across the stack. Code shared across the stack in this way is referred to as *cross-cutting concerns*.

have cross-cutting concerns in the form of DTOs that are required by the Application project, the WebAPI project, and the .NET MAUI app (although they are provided to the .NET MAUI app via the API client project).

In MauiStockTake, these DTOs are in a project called Shared (in a solution folder called `Common`). This Shared project is a dependency for the Application project, the WebAPI project, and the MauiStockTake.Client project. Using this approach, we can share code between the back- and frontend effortlessly.

Sharing code in this way provides some significant advantages. It adheres to the "don't repeat yourself" principle, which doesn't just make life easier; it gives us assurances that changes in one part of the solution will be reflected instantly elsewhere. If we change the structure of a DTO, for example, that same DTO is already in use everywhere, so any breaking changes are instantly recognizable. These changes are much more difficult when the layers of the stack are developed independently.

But as we're building a full-stack .NET solution, we can take this a step further. In the future, if we decide to add a web UI to the solution, we can use Blazor, and the MauiStockTake.Client package can be used in the Blazor UI, too. This gives us a full-stack cloud, mobile, desktop, and web solution that maximizes code re-use across the whole stack.

8.4.3 Sharing code between solutions

As a standalone solution, MauiStockTake is already well architected for maximum code re-use. Often, though, the software we build forms part of an enterprise ecosystem. Enterprise logic often forms the core of these ecosystems, providing logic and types that are relevant across the whole enterprise and, in this way, distinct from domain-problem-specific types and questions.

For example, imagine a suite of applications in an enterprise, each one helping with a specific line of business. They would all have their own requirements but would likely share some common functionality. The most obvious example would be user management and authentication.

In addition to business logic, it's important for these applications to maintain a consistent UX to make them feel like part of a cohesive whole, especially with externally facing products. .NET MAUI makes it easy to do this. Figure 8.7 shows an example of how the MauiStockTake app could form part of an enterprise ecosystem.

In this scenario, Mildred's enterprise has a suite of applications, both consumer-facing and internal, that can not only share business logic (where applicable) but also UI and UX. In figure 8.7, the whole ecosystem is broken down into modules that can be shared across solutions. A common approach is to bundle these modules as NuGet packages and host them on a private feed. GitHub offers NuGet package hosting (public and private), and many other products exist that can integrate with your preferred DevOps or CI/CD platform.

At this point, we've reached the nirvana of code sharing in a .NET enterprise ecosystem. We've got business logic and UI that's shared across the whole enterprise, in

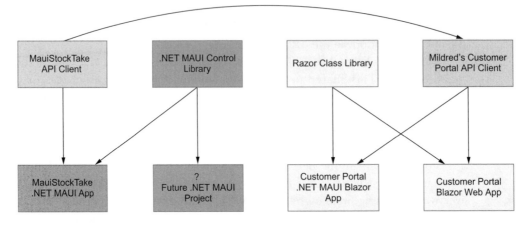

Figure 8.7 **The MauiStockTake app becomes part of an ecosystem if Mildred introduces a customer portal as well, which may require (among other things) an indication of the availability of products. The customer portal would likely have its own API, which could query the MauiStockTake API for this information. The customer portal could be built in Blazor, which would allow its controls to be abstracted back to a Razor class library. The class library could be used by .NET MAUI Blazor to provide the customer portal as an app, too. The controls in the MauiStockTake app could be abstracted back to a .NET MAUI class library to be shared with future apps too, which would maintain the visual consistency of Mildred's brand.**

the cloud, on the desktop, and in the browser. A full-scale enterprise solution like this is beyond the scope of this book, but you can see a demonstration of this approach in my GitHub repo here: https://github.com/matt-goldman/CloudyMobile.

Summary

- Moving logic out of UI and into services lets you share it across a solution.
- You can define requirements for your UI by creating an interface. You can then write a service that implements this interface. This is an example of the dependency inversion principle.
- The WebAuthenticator in .NET MAUI makes it easy to authenticate using OAuth in your apps. It opens the browser session for you and returns the token response to your code.
- You can register a custom URL scheme with the OS for your app, which allows a web browser (or any other application) to route to your app using a URL.
- .NET MAUI uses the generic host builder pattern used across all .NET application types.
- Using the host builder, you can register fonts for use in your .NET MAUI apps.
- The generic host builder pattern gives you access to the built-in services collection. You can use it to register dependencies and inject them into your classes via their constructors.
- You can create a delegating handler that can be configured to automatically attach a header with an access token to any HTTP request made by an `HttpClient`.

- You can register a named instance of `HttpClient`, along with a delegating handler, in the services collection. You can inject `IHttpClientFactory` into any class and use it to get access to the named `HttpClient` instance.
- With .NET MAUI, sharing code across your whole stack is easy. You can place DTOs in a shared project that the front- and backend both have access to.
- You can even share business logic. For example, in MauiStockTake, the client package could be used by a Blazor UI, too.
- Sharing logic and UI across an enterprise is also easy with ASP.NET Core, .NET MAUI, and Blazor, using familiar CI/CD and DevOps tools.

The MVVM Pattern

The Model, View, ViewModel (MVVM) pattern was introduced by Microsoft with Windows Presentation Foundation and has become the standard for apps developed using XAML. It's a popular pattern with enough nuance that entire books have been dedicated to the subject. This chapter will provide an introduction, and as you progress through your .NET MAUI journey, you may find that you want to explore this topic in more depth.

The use of the MVVM pattern is, in some ways, more of an art than a science. You should aim to understand the rules about separating UI logic, presentational logic, and business logic if you are adopting the MVVM pattern in your app. Of course, blind adherence to any pattern is an antipattern, and you should prioritize ensuring that your code is readable and maintainable. But you can't make an informed decision about when to deviate from the pattern if you don't understand it well.

In this chapter, we'll see how we can make our apps simpler to build and maintain by adopting the MVVM pattern. Before we get into the details of the principles of the pattern, we'll look at how, in practice, it can solve real-world problems. Specifically, to help understand the pattern, we'll refactor MauiTodo to solve our outstanding problem of not marking to-do items as done. Once we've seen the practical advantages, we'll dive deeper into the philosophy of the pattern and then refactor MauiStockTake for MVVM and use the MVVM pattern to complete the stock-taking feature.

9.1   Refactoring the MauiTodo app for MVVM

In chapter 3, we saw that databinding can be used to improve our to-do app by binding to a collection and using a template to display each item in the collection. Let's look at how we can go a step further and use the MVVM pattern to solve one significant outstanding problem with MauiTodo. Figure 9.1 shows the current data architecture of MauiTodo, without MVVM.

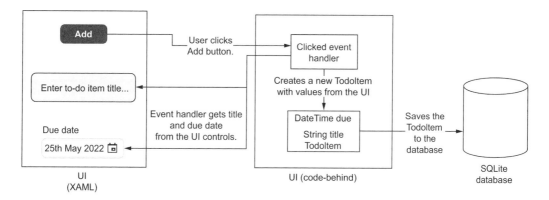

Figure 9.1   Without the MVVM pattern, the UI for the MauiTodoApp handles everything, including communicating with the database. When a user clicks the Add button, the event handler retrieves the new item title and new item due date, creates a new to-do item with these values, and then saves it to the database. The UI cannot currently save changes to the checked state of an item to the database.

An important feature of a to-do app is the ability to mark items as complete. MauiTodo has a `CheckBox` in the data template that renders alongside every to-do item, but it doesn't do anything.

The problem is that while we can add an event handler to the code-behind to respond to `CheckBox` events, we have no way of passing in any parameters—specifically, the to-do item to which the event corresponds. The `CheckBox` control supports a `CheckedChanged` event, which requires a delegate with the following method signature:

```
void CheckBox_CheckedChanged(Object sender, CheckedChangedEventArgs e)
```

If we try to delegate the `CheckedChanged` event of a `CheckBox` to a method with a different signature (the name of the method is not important), we will get an error. This means that we are limited to receiving two parameters: the sender and the event arguments. In this case, the sender is the CheckBox itself, which doesn't give us any information about the to-do item, and the event arguments contain a single Boolean value that tells us whether the CheckBox is checked or unchecked. The latter is useful but still doesn't tell us which to-do item is affected.

There are some hacky ways we could work around this problem, but the better approach is to use a *command instead of an event handler*. Command is an implementation of the ICommand interface, which defines an Execute property—that is, code that will be run when the ICommand is invoked. The constructor for Command accepts a function that gets assigned to the Execute property, which you can declare inline with a lambda expression, or you can pass in a method. A Command can accept parameters, which solves our problem of identifying the to-do item, but CheckBox doesn't have an ICommand property to bind.

Let's start by refactoring MauiTodo. We'll move the code out of the code-behind and into a ViewModel, which will have a command instead of an event handler. Then, we can come back to the problem of a CheckBox lacking an ICommand property. Figure 9.2 shows the new architecture of MauiTodo, using the MVVM pattern.

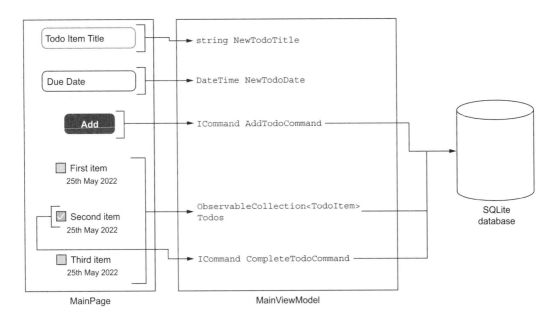

Figure 9.2   After we refactor MauiTodo for MVVM, the code-behind for `MainPage` will do nothing except set the binding context to the ViewModel. All of the controls in the UI will be bound to properties in the ViewModel, and the ViewModel will be responsible for communicating with the database. This approach is cleaner and honors the single responsibility principle.

The first step is to create the ViewModel. A good convention for naming your ViewModels is to use the name of the View and substitute ViewModel for Page or View in the name. We're creating a ViewModel for our MainPage, so we'll call it MainViewModel.

In your MauiTodo project, create a folder called `ViewModels` and create the class `MainViewModel.cs`.

Our `MainViewModel` will implement the `INotifyPropertyChanged` interface. `INotifyPropertyChanged` defines an event handler that notifies the UI when a property on the ViewModel has changed. This step is necessary when using MVVM. As we are no longer directly manipulating properties on the UI, we need to raise an event to inform the UI that a property has changed and the UI should be updated.

In the method that invokes the `PropertyChanged` event, we'll use an attribute called `CallerMemberName` on the method parameter. This will let us call the method without specifying a property name. Instead, when we call it from a property's setter, the name of the property can be automatically inferred. The following listing shows the boilerplate code for the `MainViewModel.cs` file.

Listing 9.1   The initial code for `MainViewModel.cs`

The **OnPropertyChanged** method. We can call this method anywhere in the code and specify a property name to notify the UI to update, or we can call it from a property's Setter without specifying a property name. The **CallerMemberName** attribute will invoke the notification using the name of the caller.

```
using System.ComponentModel;
using System.Runtime.CompilerServices;

namespace MauiTodo.ViewModels;                          ◁── The ViewModel
                                                             implements the
                                                             INotifyPropertyChanged
public class MainViewModel : INotifyPropertyChanged     ◁── interface.
{
    #region INotifyPropertyChanged                      The event handler defined on
    public event PropertyChangedEventHandler            the INotifyPropertyChanged
    PropertyChanged;                              ◁──   interface

    protected void OnPropertyChanged(
    [CallerMemberName] string propertyName = "")
    {
        var changed = PropertyChanged;
        if (changed == null)
            return;
                                                   Invokes the event
                                                   handler, specifying the
                                                   name of the property
        changed.Invoke(this, new PropertyChanged   that has been updated
    EventArgs(propertyName));                 ◁──
    }

    Public void RaisePropertyChanged(params string[]
    properties)                                    ◁──
    {                                                  This method also invokes
        foreach (var propertyName in properties)       the event but lets us supply
        {                                              multiple property names.
            PropertyChanged?.Invoke(this, new
        PropertyChangedEventArgs(propertyName));  ◁──
        }                                              Loops through the list
    }                                                  of property names and
    #endregion                                         invokes the event handler
}                                                      for each one
```

Next, let's add the ViewModel's properties and fields. This step will be largely the same as what we already have in the `MainPage` code-behind but with a few small differences. The fields will be used to hold private data internal to the ViewModel, but properties must be used for binding. We'll add an `ObservableCollection` of type `TodoItem`, a `string` to hold the title of any new to-do item, a `Datetime` to hold the due date of a new to-do item, and an `ICommand` each to add a new to-do item and mark one as complete. The following listing shows this added code, along with the namespaces you need to bring in.

Listing 9.2 The MainViewModel's properties and fields

```
using MauiToo.Models;
using MauiTodo.Data;
using System.Windows.Input;
using System.Collections.ObjectModel;

...

public ObservableCollection<TodoItem> Todos { get; set; } = new();

public string NewTodoTitle { get; set; }

public DateTime NewTodoDue { get; set; } = DateTime.Now;

public ICommand AddTodoCommand { get; set; }

public ICommand CompleteTodoCommand { get; set; }

private readonly Database _database;
```

> Defines a property of type ICommand called AddTodoCommand. Buttons have an ICommand property (that can be data bound), which will be invoked when clicked. This command is in place of the event handler.

> Defines another ICommand called CompleteTodoCommand

Next up, let's add some methods to the ViewModel. We'll add an `Initialize` method, which will get the list of to-do items from the database and populate the `Observable-Collection`. We'll include a method for adding a new to-do item, which will be largely the same as the method in the code-behind, and we'll add a method for marking a to-do item as complete. This method will take a `TodoItem` as a parameter and pass it to the `UpdateTodo` method of the database. The code for these methods is shown in the following listing.

Listing 9.3 The methods to add to MainViewModel

```
private async Task Initialise()
{
    var todos = await _database.GetTodos();

    foreach(var todo in todos)
    {
        Todos.Add(todo);
    }
}
```

```
public async Task AddNewTodo()
{
    var todo = new TodoItem
    {
        Due = NewTodoDue,
        Title = NewTodoTitle
    };

    var inserted = await _database.AddTodo(todo);

    if (inserted != 0)
    {
        Todos.Add(todo);

        NewTodoTitle = String.Empty;
        NewTodoDue = DateTime.Now;

        RaisePropertyChanged(nameof(NewTodoDue),
    nameof(NewTodoTitle));
    }
}

public async Task CompleteTodo(TodoItem todoitem)
{
    var completed = await _database.UpdateTodo(todoitem);

    OnPropertyChanged(nameof(Todos));
}
```

In the code-behind, the method to add to-do items was an event handler, which required a specific signature. Because this method is now invoked by a Command, which has no such requirement, we can change the method type to **Task** and eliminate an async void.

To simplify updating multiple properties in the UI, we've added a second method that invokes the property changed event handler. This method takes an array of strings so we can pass in several property names.

A method for completing to-do items, which we couldn't call before

Finally, let's add a constructor to `MainViewModel`, which will assign a new instance of the database to the private field. We'll also wire up the two `ICommand` properties by assigning them to new instances of the `Command` type, with their respective methods set as the `Execute` property. For the update method, we can use a `TodoItem` as a type argument. The last step is for the constructor to call the `Initialize` method. As this method is async, we'll use the discard operator. The following listing shows the constructor for `MainViewModel`.

Listing 9.4   The `MainViewModel` constructor

```
public MainViewModel()
{
    _database = new Database();

    AddTodoCommand = new Command(async () => await
    AddNewTodo());

    CompleteTodoCommand = new Command<TodoItem>(async
    (item) => await CompleteTodo(item));

    _ = Initialise();
}
```

Assigns the AddNewTodo method to the Execute property of the AddTodoCommand

Assigns the CompleteTodo method to the Execute property of the CompleteTodoCommand

Let's update the code behind-now. We're going to remove nearly all the code, as the functionality we're handling here will be moved to the ViewModel. **Delete all the properties and methods from `MainPage.xaml.cs`**, leaving only the constructor and, from the constructor, **remove all the code except the `InitializeComponent()`** call from the template.

Then, in the constructor after the `InitializeComponent()` call, **add the following line**:

```
BindingContext = new MainViewModel();
```

We learned about the `BindingContext` in chapter 3, and as `ContentPage` inherits `BindableObject`, it has a `BindingContext`. Here we are setting it to be a new instance of `MainViewModel`. Now, anywhere we declare a binding to a source property, it will be a property on this object.

The last step in our MVVM refactor is to update the UI to use the new binding context. The first thing we need to do is remove the binding context assignment from the XAML, as we've now set it in the code-behind. Then, we'll add a property binding for the `Entry` and `DatePicker` controls and replace the event handler on the `Button` with a `Command`. Finally, we'll set a binding for the `ItemsSource` on the `CollectionView` because we are no longer assigning that in the code-behind. Update your `Main-Page.xaml` file to match the following listing.

Listing 9.5   `MainPage.xaml` with MVVM bindings

```
<ContentPage xmlns="http://schemas.microsoft.com/dotnet/2021/maui"
             xmlns:x=http://schemas.microsoft.com/winfx/2009/xaml
             x:Class="MauiTodo.MainPage"
             x:Name="PageTodo">                    ◁──────

    <Grid RowDefinitions="1*, 1*, 1*, 1*, 8*"
          MaximumWidthRequest="400"
          Padding="20">

        <Label Grid.Row="0"
               Text="Maui Todo"
               HorizontalTextAlignment="Center"
               FontSize="Title"/>

        <Entry Grid.Row="1"
               HorizontalOptions="Center"
               Placeholder="Enter a title"
               WidthRequest="300"
               Text="{Binding NewTodoTitle}"/>    ◁──────
```

Removes the binding context assignment from XAML as we're now doing this in code

Binds the Entry to the NewTodoTitle property in the ViewModel. The NewTodoTitle property will be updated whenever the value of the Entry changes, so we don't need to retrieve the value from the control with code anymore.

```
<DatePicker Grid.Row="2"
            WidthRequest="300"
            HorizontalOptions="Center"
            Date="{Binding NewTodoDue}"/>
```

Binds the Datepicker to the **NewTodoDue** property in the ViewModel. The NewTodoDue property will be updated when the value of the Datepicker changes, so we don't need to retrieve the value from the control with code anymore.

```
<Button Grid.Row="3"
        Text="Add"
        WidthRequest="100"
        HeightRequest="50"
        HorizontalOptions="Center"
        Command="{Binding AddTodoCommand}"/>
```

Removes the Clicked event handler reference and adds a Command reference, binding it to the AddTodoCommand in the ViewModel.

```
<CollectionView Grid.Row="4"
                ItemsSource="{Binding Todos}">
    <CollectionView.ItemTemplate>
        <DataTemplate>
            <SwipeView>
                <SwipeView.LeftItems>
                    <SwipeItems Mode="Reveal">
                        <SwipeItem Text="Delete"
                                   IconImageSource="delete"
                                   BackgroundColor="Tomato"/>
                    </SwipeItems>
                </SwipeView.LeftItems>

                <SwipeView.RightItems>
                    <SwipeItems Mode="Reveal">
                        <SwipeItem Text="Done"
                                   IconImageSource="check"
                                   BackgroundColor="LimeGreen"/>
                    </SwipeItems>
                </SwipeView.RightItems>
                <Border Stroke="{StaticResource PrimaryColor}"
                        StrokeThickness="3"
                        StrokeShape="RoundRectangle 10"
                        Padding="5"
                        Margin="0,10">
                    <Border.Shadow>
                        <Shadow Brush="Black"
                                Offset="20,20"
                                Radius="40"
                                Opacity="0.8"/>
                    </Border.Shadow>
                    <Grid WidthRequest="325"
                          ColumnDefinitions="1*, 5*"
                          RowDefinitions="Auto, 25"
                          x:Name="TodoItem">

                        <CheckBox VerticalOptions="Center"
                                  HorizontalOptions="Center"
                                  Grid.Column="0"
                                  Grid.Row="0"
                                  IsChecked="{Binding Done, Mode=
⇒ TwoWay}"/>
```

Note the binding for the **ItemsSource** property of the CollectionView is the same as there is a Todos ObservableCollection in the ViewModel, just as there was in the code-behind.

Removes the Invoked event handlers from the swipe items

```
                                           <Label Text="{Binding
      ▷    ⟹ Title}"

      We don't need to make any changes to the      FontAttributes="Bold"
      bindings in the data template because the      LineBreakMode="WordWrap"
      binding context for the data template is the   HorizontalOptions="StartAndExpand"
      item, and for members of a Collection this     FontSize="Medium"
      doesn't change. Each template still gets passed Grid.Row="0"
      an item from the Collection; the source of the  Grid.Column="1"/>
      Collection is unimportant in this context.
                                           <Label Text="{Binding
      ▷    ⟹ Due, StringFormat='{0:dd MMM yyyy}'}"

                                               VerticalOptions="End"
                                               Grid.Column="1"
                                               Grid.Row="1"/>
                                   </Grid>
                               </Border>
                           </SwipeView>
                       </DataTemplate>
                   </CollectionView.ItemTemplate>
               </CollectionView>
           </Grid>
       </ContentPage>
```

At this point, you should be able to run the MauiTodo app and see it working the same way as before. While the functionality is the same, we now have a much cleaner app; our business logic and UI are cleanly separated. We can now implement features that would be difficult or messy to do before, like setting the Done state of a to-do item from the UI, which we will do in the next section, and making the app easier to maintain overall.

Exercise

We're back to using a discarded `Initialize()` method. See whether you can refactor this to hook back into page lifecycle methods:

1 Assign the new instance of the ViewModel to a private field, then assign the private field as the binding context.
2 Call the `Initialize` method of the ViewModel from the Page's `OnAppearing()` method.

9.2   *Using behaviors to augment your controls*

We've still got one last problem to solve with our to-do app, and that is finding a way to mark to-do items as complete. The model has a Done property, and the UI has a Checkbox, but we still need to figure out a way to connect them.

The problem is that the Checkbox control has a CheckedChanged event that can delegate to an event handler, but it doesn't let us send any custom parameters. We've looked at `Commands` that we can use in MVVM—these do allow parameters, but the `Checkbox` control doesn't have a `Command` property that can be bound.

We can solve this problem by using a *behavior*. Behaviors allow us to extend the functionality of UI controls, which we do by attaching a behavior to a control rather than subclassing the control to our own type. Subclassing controls is useful in some cases but unnecessary here.

A behavior can be attached to any property or method of a control, so we'll attach a behavior to the `CheckedChanged` event of the `Checkbox` and fire a `Command` in response. In listing 9.5, we recapped that in a `CollectionView`, the item itself is the binding context, which means we have access to the to-do item the `Checkbox` corresponds to. Depending on our use case, we could send the `Id` of the to-do item to a method that would mark it as done. In our case, we're going to send the whole to-do item and pass it to the `Update` method in the database. This approach fits our requirements and can also be reused if we decide to add edit functionality in the future rather than writing a bespoke method just for one use case.

Extending a control in this way—calling a `Command` in response to an event being triggered—is a common requirement in MVVM. It's so common, in fact, that there's a ready-built Event to Command Behavior that we can use in the .NET MAUI Community Toolkit. The Community Toolkit is a set of open-source add-ons for .NET MAUI that are, as the name suggests, contributed by the community. These add-ons meet requirements that are so ubiquitous that it makes sense to gather them all in one place for people to use in their .NET MAUI apps, even though they are not part of the core .NET MAUI product.

The Community Toolkit is an invaluable collection of features that you will likely come to depend on in your .NET MAUI apps, and I encourage you to explore it here: https://learn.microsoft.com/dotnet/communitytoolkit/maui. But for now, let's focus on the Event to Command Behavior.

The first thing you need to do is **install the `CommunityToolkit.Maui` NuGet package** into the MauiTodo app. The toolkit requires an initialization line to be added to the host builder in `MauiProgram.cs` (as we saw in MauiMovies), so add that to `MauiTodo` too. We're going to use the `EventToCommandBehavior` in XAML, which is in the `CommunityToolkit.Maui.Behaviors` namespace. Add this namespace to your `Main-Page.xaml` file by adding the following line to the `ContentPage` tag:

```
xmlns:behaviors="clr-namespace:CommunityToolkit.Maui.Behaviors;assembly=
➥ CommunityToolkit.Maui"
```

This code brings in the namespace and gives it an XML namespace reference of `behaviors`. With this in place, we can reference this in our XAML code. Update the `CheckBox` tag to match the following listing.

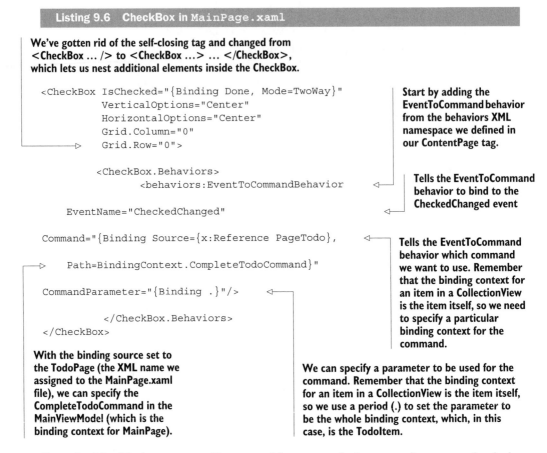

Listing 9.6   CheckBox in MainPage.xaml

We've gotten rid of the self-closing tag and changed from
<CheckBox ... /> to <CheckBox ...> ... </CheckBox>,
which lets us nest additional elements inside the CheckBox.

```
<CheckBox IsChecked="{Binding Done, Mode=TwoWay}"
          VerticalOptions="Center"
          HorizontalOptions="Center"
          Grid.Column="0"
          Grid.Row="0">

    <CheckBox.Behaviors>
        <behaviors:EventToCommandBehavior

EventName="CheckedChanged"

Command="{Binding Source={x:Reference PageTodo},

    Path=BindingContext.CompleteTodoCommand}"

CommandParameter="{Binding .}"/>

        </CheckBox.Behaviors>
</CheckBox>
```

Start by adding the
EventToCommand behavior
from the behaviors XML
namespace we defined in
our ContentPage tag.

Tells the EventToCommand
behavior to bind to the
CheckedChanged event

Tells the EventToCommand
behavior which command
we want to use. Remember
that the binding context for
an item in a CollectionView
is the item itself, so we need
to specify a particular
binding context for the
command.

With the binding source set to
the TodoPage (the XML name we
assigned to the MainPage.xaml
file), we can specify the
CompleteTodoCommand in the
MainViewModel (which is the
binding context for MainPage).

We can specify a parameter to be used for the
command. Remember that the binding context
for an item in a CollectionView is the item itself,
so we use a period (.) to set the parameter to
be the whole binding context, which, in this
case, is the TodoItem.

Run the MauiTodo app now. You can add some to-do items, and you can check the
CheckBox for each to-do item. You could, of course, do this before, but now, if you
add a breakpoint in the Update method of the database, you'll see it gets hit when
you check or uncheck a to-do item. Better yet, if you quit the MauiTodo app and re-
open it, you'll notice that any items you checked to mark as complete will still be
checked. When we check the box and trigger the CheckedChanged event, the Event-
ToCommand behavior is responding and calling the CompleteTodoCommand in the
ViewModel, which, in turn, calls an Update method on the database that persists our
change to disk.

By using a Behavior, we've added functionality to a Control, without having to
subclass the Control or build our own. We can now abstract functionality out of our
View and into our ViewModel; thus, we have solved a critical outstanding problem
with the MauiTodo app.

Exercise

Back in chapter 4 we introduced `SwipeView` to the MauiTodo app, but it only showed a message confirming our intention (to delete or complete a to-do item) rather than doing the action.

In section 9.1, we deleted the `SwipeItem`'s invoked event handler from the `Main-Page` code-behind. So, if you run the app now, you'll get an error as we are still referring to this event handler in the XAML.

Let's complete the swipe feature in MauiTodo.

1 Use the `SwipeView`'s `Command` property to bind to the `CompleteTodoCommand` in the ViewModel.
2 Add a `DeleteTodoCommand` to the ViewModel and use the `SwipeView`'s `Command` property to bind to it.

Once you complete this exercise, you'll be able to add to-do items, mark them as complete (either by checking the box or using the `SwipeView`), or delete them (using the `SwipeView`).

9.3   *What is MVVM?*

MVVM is a software design pattern that promotes organization of code by keeping business logic, presentation logic, and UI separate, as summarised in figure 9.3.

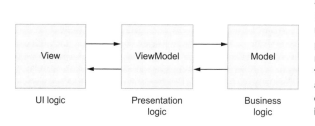

Figure 9.3   With the MVVM pattern, UI logic, which includes layouts and UI behavior like animation and text formatting, belongs in the View. Presentation logic, which includes the UI state such as the values of properties in the UI and logic for responding to user actions, belongs in the ViewModel. Business logic, such as rules for processing user input, or communicating with an API, belongs in the Model.

Using the MVVM pattern, we put the single responsibility principle into practice by keeping the layout and UI behavior in Views, UI state and presentational logic in ViewModels, and business logic in the Model. UI behavior might include things like changing the color of a button or label or animating a UI element. Presentational logic is essentially the UI state—for example, the value entered into an `Entry`. Business logic is how the real-world scenario is modeled in code. It would include models representing real-world objects the app deals with—for example, a model representing a car might have properties for make, model, and year and methods for altering the object's state. Business logic also includes what we do with our models. Examples might include methods for querying a database or API for a list of cars based on certain criteria. In essence, the Model is the problem domain represented in code.

9.3.1   The Model

You will no doubt have come across the term *model* before, but in MVVM, it has a specific meaning that may (or may not) differ from what you are used to. The word *model* is sometimes used to refer to a single class. For example, a Car class might contain properties that represent real properties of a car (like make, model, and year) and, as such, may be considered to model a car.

This definition provides a narrower perspective than in MVVM, where the *Model* refers to the model of your entire problem domain rather than a specific class. Models would include classes that model real-world objects, like the car example, as well as other classes containing domain logic. The classes might include business rules or logic for communicating with a database or REST API. These kinds of classes are sometimes called the service layer or any variation of the application or infrastructure layer. In MVVM, individual models (like the car) and other business logic (like the services) together make up the Model.

Model vs. model: Disambiguation

The word *model* is often used in software development and computer science (and many other fields). In this book, if you see the word capitalized (Model), then I am specifically referring to the Model component of the MVVM pattern. If you see *model* with a lowercase first letter, then I am using the term with a different meaning, which you can infer from the context. The previously mentioned Car class is a model, not a Model.

Classes like Car are often referred to as entities, but to add to the confusion, a common convention in MVVM projects is to put entities in a folder called Models and classes with business logic methods in a folder called Services.

I follow that convention in this book, as I find it easy enough to distinguish between MVVM as an architectural pattern and the organization of files and folders in my solution. You don't have to follow that convention in your own projects, but you'll have to get to grips with that to follow the examples in the book. It will be useful for you to get used to this approach, as you'll likely encounter it in projects you work on or view online.

The Model is comprised of these classes that define objects and functionality that represent the problem domain. In this sense, you can think of the Model as being the same as a domain model in any other .NET application.

9.3.2   The View

We've covered views in detail in earlier chapters, and views, as we described them there, fit the same definition we use in the MVVM pattern. To recap, views come in three flavors: pages, layouts, and controls. Together, these provide the definition of *how* your app's information is displayed to a user, which we refer to as UI logic. UI logic is essentially comprised of layout and behavior. Layout, as a concept, is the definition of what elements go where on screen (as opposed to "a layout," such as a `Grid`, which is how that logic is implemented), and behavior is what those elements do.

For example, a `Page` may contain a `Grid`, inside of which are some `Labels`, an `Entry`, and a `Button`. The `Page`, `Grid`, `Labels`, `Entry`, and `Button` are part of the layout, which is part of the UI logic. An animation that grows and shrinks different `Labels` based on certain conditions is behavior.

9.3.3 The ViewModel

The ViewModel is the heart of the MVVM pattern, as it contains the core logic that controls what the user will see and interact with. ViewModels contain presentational logic, which differs from UI logic in some important ways. Whereas the View defines *how* things are displayed, the ViewModel defines *what* is displayed.

For example, a `Switch` in a view can have a state of on or off (see figure 9.4). This state is presentational logic and belongs in the ViewModel. The color of the switch is UI logic and should be defined in the View.

Figure 9.4 A `Switch` control. In the top example, the switch is in the on position (its state), and its background is green (shown here as light gray; its behavior). In the bottom example, the switch is in the off position, and its background is red (shown here as dark gray). The switch's state should be managed by the ViewModel, and its behavior should be managed by the View.

If you want your switch to appear red when in the off state and green when in the on state, this is UI logic (technically UI behavior). While the *state* of the `Switch` (on/off) should be maintained in the ViewModel, the behavior of that switch, which changes in response to its state, belongs in the View.

ViewModel vs view model: Disambiguation

You may be familiar with the term *view model* (and you'll see me use it in this chapter). It's common to refer to a view model outside of MVVM, and it's important to know that in MVVM, the term *ViewModel* has a different, and very specific, meaning.

Outside of MVVM, the term *view model* can be fluid, but it usually refers to a data transfer object (DTO) that encapsulates all data required for a view rather than a specific model or entity. For example, in a web app that shows a sales leaderboard, you might have a DTO that represents an individual salesperson, another that represents

(continued)

a monthly total, another for a monthly average, etc. Instead of having your web view call each of these individually, the API can return a view model that contains all the data the view needs to render the leaderboard so that a single API call is all that's required. (Incidentally, GraphQL was designed to solve this problem; this discussion is way outside the scope of this book but check out *GraphQL in Action* by Samer Buna [Manning 2021] to find out more about this exciting topic).

In MVVM, the term *ViewModel*, which I will always write as a single word in Pascal-Case, specifically means a class that represents the state of, and provides functionality for, a View. The key difference between an MVVM ViewModel and a view model as a DTO is that a ViewModel contains functionality. A DTO, by definition, cannot.

Figure 9.5 shows a more in-depth example of the relationship between a View, View-Model, and Model.

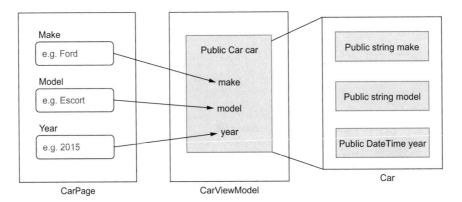

Figure 9.5   A View called CarPage has controls that let the user enter the make, model, and year of a car. The values for these controls are not stored in properties on the View. Instead, databinding is used to bind the values of those controls to properties in a ViewModel. Specifically, the ViewModel has a property called car of type `Car`, and the `Car` type has properties for make, model, and year, and the UI controls are bound to these properties of the `Car` instance in the ViewModel.

9.3.4   *Binding from Views to ViewModels*

The View uses databinding to connect to properties in the ViewModel. As such, the ViewModel holds the values of controls in the View, and the View is only responsible for rendering, rather than storing or processing, information.

ViewModels also contain all the code for interacting with the Model, which keeps this logic out of the View. Views can, of course, do a lot more than just display data or allow data to be edited. Many of the controls we use in .NET MAUI have events, which we can write event handlers for, the simplest example being a `Button`. We've seen before that you can create an event handler to respond to a click, but this method is delegated rather than data bound. Therefore, it must exist in the code-behind file.

There is a way of working around this, which is to delegate the event handler in code rather than in XAML. For example, you could create a method with the right signature in your ViewModel, and then in your View constructor, you can use the following code:

```
MyButton.Clicked += MyViewModel.MyEventHandler;
```

But this approach introduces several problems. First, when we write an event handler for a click event in a code-behind, that code also has access to other UI properties. As an example, in the FindMe app from chapter 3, when the user clicks a Button, we retrieve their name from an Entry in the UI and then use it in the message we share along with location. If this method were in a ViewModel, it would have no access to the Entry to retrieve that name. Another problem, which we solved with MVVM for MauiTodo, is that we often can't pass meaningful parameters with an event handler.

Instead of delegating events that are raised in the View to handlers in ViewModels, in .NET MAUI we use the principle of *commanding*, which solves these problems and gives us more flexibility. Several built-in controls in .NET MAUI have a Command property, which is bindable to a property on a ViewModel of type ICommand (see figure 9.6). .NET MAUI also has built-in implementations of the ICommand interface, and by including these in our ViewModels and binding to them in our Views, we can take all the presentational logic out of our Views, leaving just the necessary UI logic.

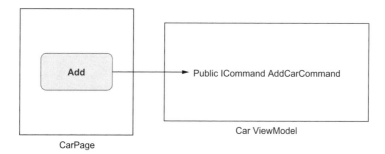

Figure 9.6 The Command property of the Button control in the View is bound to the AddCarCommand property of the ViewModel. When the button is tapped, the ICommand in the ViewModel is called, and any logic defining whether and how it executes code is all handled by the ViewModel.

After moving logic from our View to our ViewModel, we need a way for ViewModels to update controls in the View when the values of bindable properties change. Without MVVM, we could set the values of properties directly on UI controls; now that we are using MVVM, we can't do this.

We've seen before how we can use databinding to bind properties of UI controls to properties of ViewModels. To make this work both ways (i.e., to update the UI when the value of bound property changes), we need to implement the `INotify-PropertyChanged` interface from the `System.ComponentModel` namespace in our ViewModel. `INotifyPropertyChanged` defines a `PropertyChangedEventHandler` event called `PropertyChanged`.

> **NOTE** All Pages in .NET MAUI implement `INotifyPropertyChanged`, which is how we were able to use it in MauiMovies.

When a View binds to a ViewModel, it subscribes to `PropertyChanged` events. When an event is raised for a property that the View is bound to, it will update the corresponding value in the View.

9.3.5 *Putting it all together*

In figure 9.7, we can see an example architecture of an app that interacts with a database of cars that is organized using the MVVM pattern.

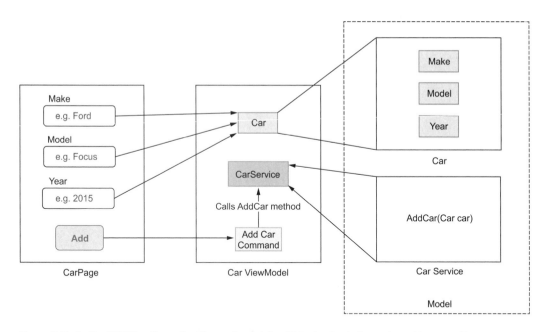

Figure 9.7 In the MVVM pattern, the View only contains UI logic. Controls are bound to properties on a ViewModel, and rather than event handlers, commands are used to trigger actions. The ViewModel maintains the state of the View by exposing properties for the UI to bind to and commands for the UI to call. The Model contains all the business logic, and the ViewModel interacts with the Model. In this example, a `CarService` from the Model is injected into the ViewModel. A `Button` in the View is used to trigger a command in the ViewModel. The ViewModel contains a `Car` object, which has properties bound in the UI. The Add Car Command calls the `AddCar` method in the injected service and passes in the ViewModel's `Car` property as a parameter.

We can see that by following the MVVM pattern, we gain several advantages:

- *Honors the single-responsibility principle*—The View is only responsible for UI. The ViewModel is only responsible for the View state. The classes that make up the Model each serve their own specific function.
- *Easier to maintain*—Because each of these components is loosely coupled, we can change any one of them with little or no effect on any other. Designers or UI developers can work independently of developers working on the presentation logic or business logic. Problems are more easily isolated, and new features are easier to implement.
- *Easier to test*—Because the ViewModel is code only, we can write unit tests that can validate nearly every function of the UI. In fact, we can test any logic we like that exists outside of the View, and in MVVM, that's everything except layout and UI behavior.

Do I always have to use the MVVM pattern?

The MVVM pattern is a tool you will learn to use when it adds value to your work. In some cases, particularly with trivial, one-screen apps, the MVVM pattern is unnecessary. Even for complex apps, there are alternatives to MVVM—in particular, the Model-View-Update (MVU) pattern, which is quite popular. MVU is a state-based pattern with an immutable UI and is a good fit if you prefer to define your UI in C# code rather than XAML.

You can choose to use MVVM, MVU, or neither in your .NET MAUI apps. Which one you use will be up to you and your team. While MVU is considered first class in .NET MAUI, it is not supported out of the box with first-party tooling. That is why MVVM is still considered by many to be the standard pattern for use in .NET MAUI and why it is the pattern used in this book.

If you are familiar with the MVU pattern and are interested in using it in .NET MAUI, check out Gerald Versluis's Getting Started video: https://youtu.be/52RmT2MIFzg.

We'll complete MauiStockTake using the MVVM pattern, which will give you a better appreciation of its use. However, the MVVM pattern is an important topic and one you should endeavor to learn in more depth as you progress through your .NET MAUI journey. As you do, you'll start to gain an intuitive understanding of what belongs where in the MVVM pattern. In the meantime, Table 9.1 provides some examples to help you understand where to place the different components of your app.

Table 9.1   The MVVM pattern: UI definitions and behavior belong in the View, presentational logic belongs in the ViewModel, and business logic belongs in the Model

Logical function	Where it belongs	Example
UI definition	In the View	XAML markup defining a `Button` or `Label`
UI behavior	In the view	Code for animating a button in response to a tap

Table 9.1   The MVVM pattern: UI definitions and behavior belong in the View, presentational logic belongs in the ViewModel, and business logic belongs in the Model *(continued)*

Logical function	Where it belongs	Example
Presentational logic (UI state)	In the ViewModel	Properties representing controls displayed in the UI, for example, a Name string that a Label in the UI is bound to that gets data from a Name property on a User object in the Model
Business logic	In the Model	Properties of a car in a car app (e.g., make, model, year, etc.) or code that calls a search method in a repository or API, passing in user input as a search parameter

9.4   *The MauiStockTake app without MVVM*

It's entirely possible to build the MauiStockTake app without MVVM. In fact, we've built several apps so far throughout this book without using the MVVM pattern (although we've started to use some of the features that enable it, such as databinding and service abstraction). These apps have been trivial compared to MauiStockTake, so building them without MVVM hasn't presented us with any problems (apart from the CheckBox in MauiTodo). Without MVVM, the architecture of the MauiStockTake looks something like figure 9.8.

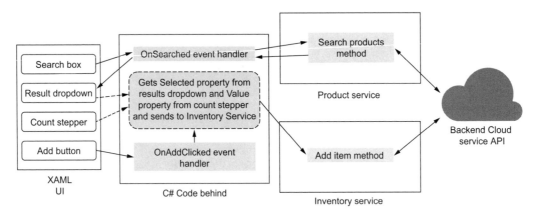

Figure 9.8   Without MVVM, services are injected into the UI. Business logic in the UI gathers data from UI controls and constructs requests for services.

This would work and would give Mildred the functionality she needs. But there are some problems with this approach, which you may have spotted:

- *Violates the single-responsibility principle*—The UI should be responsible for UI only. But in this approach, the UI is managing the application state and executing business logic.

- *Difficult to maintain*—This architecture makes it difficult to identify and fix errors and modify the functionality or add new features. There is tight coupling because business logic is included directly in the UI. Extending logical functionality or changing the UI affect each other directly.

- *Difficult to test*—Business logic in the UI is almost impossible to test in any way other than manually.

You may have spotted other problems with this approach, too. We can solve these problems by adopting the MVVM pattern, which will make it easier for us to write longer-lasting apps with maintainable and adaptive code.

MVVM for SOLID apps

SOLID is a set of object-oriented programming (OOP) principles that help to build clean and maintainable code. SOLID is an acronym that summarizes the principles set out as follows.

Single responsibility principle—The single responsibility principle (SRP) states that any class or method should be responsible for one thing and one thing only. All parts of that class or method should be aligned with that purpose.

Open/closed principle—The open/closed principle states that classes and methods should be open to extension but closed to modification. As such, you extend existing functionality in response to new requirements rather than changing it. In practical terms, this added functionality is achieved using abstract classes and interfaces. Interfaces and base classes should not be modified (closed), but new implementations or derived types can be added freely (open).

Liskov substitution principle—The Liskov substitution principle states that any derived type can stand in for its parent type. Essentially this means that if you inherit a base class, your class must not violate the contract provided by the base class. A derived class must be able to be used anywhere a base class could be.

Interface segregation principle—The interface segregation principle states that an interface (a definition of a dependency) must be tightly focused on only the required functionality for that dependency. For example, if you have a class that needs a `Sum()` method, the dependency for that class should declare a `Sum()` method only, and no other methods like `Subtract()` or `Multiply()`. In this simple example, you may, in fact, also require those other methods in the consuming class, in which case it would make sense to define an `ICalculator` interface that declares all of the basic arithmetic methods. However, remember that C# allows multiple interface inheritance, so you can still write a `Calculator` class that implements all your arithmetic operations defined on different interfaces. This step may not be necessary for a calculator, but in more complex scenarios, it's best to keep interfaces focused on the specific dependency that they define.

Dependency inversion principle—The dependency inversion principle is fundamentally what enables us to write loosely coupled code. It states that we invert dependencies by defining them where we need them rather than where they are provided. The previous `Sum()` example illustrates this: a consuming class knows that it needs a `Sum()`

(continued)

method but doesn't necessarily know (or care) about the Calculator class. This means that the implementation of the Sum() method can be changed without any affect on the class that consumes it.

These explanations are somewhat overly simple and naïve, but hopefully you are familiar with these concepts already. If not, it's well worth investing some time in gaining an understanding and appreciation for them.

As we progress through this chapter, you will see how using the MVVM pattern helps us to write SOLID code.

Later in this chapter, we'll finish the inventory feature in MauiStockTake using the MVVM pattern and see how it addresses these problems.

9.5   *The MauiStockTake app in MVVM*

Earlier in this chapter we looked at what the MauiStockTake app looks like without MVVM. Figure 9.8 shows how the InputPage would work without MVVM, and we saw some of the problems this approach would cause.

Now that we know about the MVVM pattern and how it can help us avoid some of the pitfalls we encounter without it, let's look at what the MauiStockTake app looks like with MVVM. In figure 9.9, the app has been designed using the MVVM pattern, and we can see that UI logic (View), presentation logic (ViewModel), and business logic (Model) are all cleanly separated.

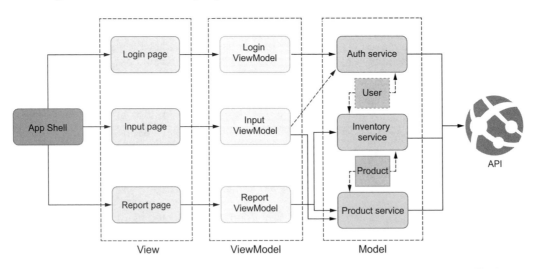

Figure 9.9   The high-level architecture of the MauiStockTake app using the MVVM design pattern. The App Shell defines the overall structure of the app. The LoginPage, InputPage, and ReportPage each have a corresponding ViewModel. The Model consists of services containing business logic and individual models like Product and User (there is one missing for stock count, which we will add later). These services interact with the web API, where the data will be aggregated.

This high-level app architecture is a good starting point, and as the app grows and changes, we can ensure that anything we add or change is aligned with these design principles.

At a more granular level, figure 9.10 shows the View and ViewModel design for the input workflow.

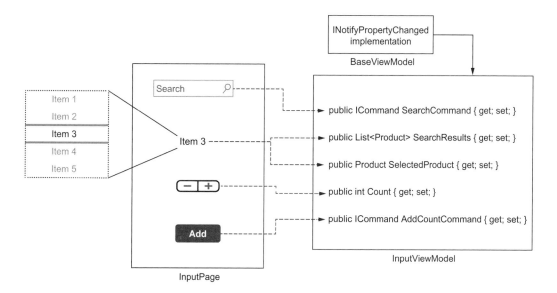

Figure 9.10   The `InputPage` with its associated ViewModel in the MVVM pattern. The `InputViewModel` inherits a common `BaseViewModel`, which contains the `INotifyPropertyChanged` implementation and exposes public properties that controls in the corresponding View are bound to.

When we looked at the MauiStockTake architecture without MVVM at the start of this section, we saw that the UI contained nearly all the logic for the app. There was some functionality that was in services, but the UI was doing the heavy lifting.

In figure 9.9, we've changed this around. The code-behind for the XAML files will do nothing other than set the binding context, and the UI controls will simply bind to a ViewModel.

The `InputPage` has a `SearchBar` where the user can look for the product they want to inventory. The `SearchCommand` property of the `SearchBar` is bound to an `ICommand` property of the ViewModel, which will execute the search using a method in the `ProductService`.

The results of that search are put in an `ObservableCollection`, which a `Picker` in the View is bound to. The user can select an item from the `CollectionView`, and the `SelectedItem` property of the `CollectionView` is bound to a `SelectedProduct` property on the ViewModel. A `Stepper` on the View can be used to indicate how many of the items the user has counted, which is bound to a `Count` property on the ViewModel.

When the user is ready to submit their count, they can click a `Button` that has its `Command` property bound to an `ICommand` on the ViewModel. The `ICommand` will call a method in the `IInventoryService`, which will send the result back to the API.

This meets the core requirements of the app. We still need reporting, but we'll come back to this in the next chapter. Let's get started building the first prototype of the MauiStockTake app.

9.5.1   *The Model*

We started to describe the Model of the MauiStockTake app in chapter 7 (table 7.1), where we looked at the problem areas. In figure 9.9, we can see that the Model for the app consists of the Authentication Service, the Inventory Service, the Product Service, and their associated types.

In MauiTodo, the `TodoItem` and the `Database` comprise the Model. In MauiStock-Take, the Model is made up of the services in the MauiStockTake.Client project and their associated DTOs in the Shared project, as well as the `AuthService` we created in the MauiStockTake.UI project. Table 9.2 shows how the Model represents the problem areas that the MauiStockTake app solves.

Table 9.2   The MauiStockTake Model

Problem Area	Type(s)	Service
Products	`ProductDto`	`ProductService`
Inventory	`StockCountDto, InventoryItemDto`	`InventoryService`
Staff	`User`	`AuthService`

In MauiStockTake, the Model is comprised of services and DTOs that model the problem areas the app is designed to address. For products, the `ProductDto` is the type that represents actual products, and the `ProductService` has business logic for working with the `ProductDto`. For inventory, the `InventoryService` has business logic for working with the `StockCountDto` and `InventoryItemDto`. The `AuthService` has business logic for dealing with users.

When you're writing your own apps, you will create models and services that represent the real-world problem your app addresses. But in MauiStockTake, the Model has already been created.

9.5.2   *The ViewModel*

In this section, we're going to create the ViewModel for the `InputPage`. Just as we did in MauiTodo, the `InputViewModel` will handle all the state and logic for the `Input-Page`, which will have the `InputViewModel` set as its binding context. The `InputPage` will only be responsible for displaying the UI.

The `InputViewModel` will have some properties and methods that are specific to the `InputPage`, but it also has some requirements that will be common to any page in our app. For example, it will need an implementation of INotifyPropertyChanged (as we had in the MauiTodo MainViewModel), as well as a title, a loading indicator, and an instance of INavigation.

> **NOTE** For Shell, you don't need a reference to the app's navigation stack, as you can call Shell.Current.GotoAsync() from anywhere in your app. But you need it for any other navigation paradigm (even in a Shell app, for example, when pushing modal pages).

Rather than replicate these methods and properties, we'll implement them in a base ViewModel that other ViewModels can inherit.

CREATING THE BASEVIEWMODEL

We need to implement the INotifyPropertyChanged interface in our ViewModels so that we can update the UI in response to changes in the state of the ViewModel. In figure 9.10, we saw that in the MauiStockTake app, we'll implement a base class so that this implementation can be reused in multiple ViewModels.

Create a folder in the MauiStockTake.UI project called ViewModels and add a new file called BaseViewModel.cs. We'll make the BaseViewModel class implement the INotifyPropertyChanged interface so that all other ViewModels can derive from the BaseViewModel, and we only have to write the implementation once. Update the BaseViewModel.cs file to match the code in the following listing.

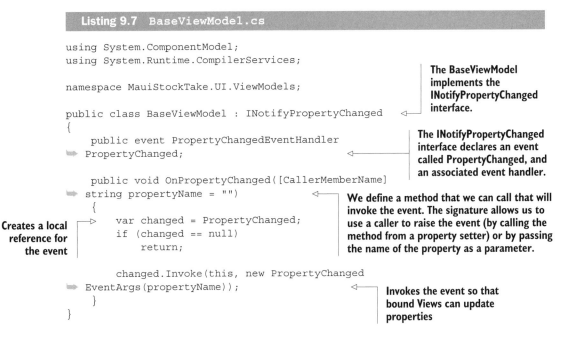

Listing 9.7 BaseViewModel.cs

```
using System.ComponentModel;
using System.Runtime.CompilerServices;

namespace MauiStockTake.UI.ViewModels;

public class BaseViewModel : INotifyPropertyChanged          ◁──  The BaseViewModel
{                                                                  implements the
    public event PropertyChangedEventHandler                      INotifyPropertyChanged
➡ PropertyChanged;                                          ◁──  interface.

                                                                  The INotifyPropertyChanged
                                                                  interface declares an event
                                                                  called PropertyChanged, and
                                                                  an associated event handler.

    public void OnPropertyChanged([CallerMemberName]
➡ string propertyName = "")                          ◁──  We define a method that we can call that will
    {                                                        invoke the event. The signature allows us to
        var changed = PropertyChanged;                       use a caller to raise the event (by calling the
        if (changed == null)                                 method from a property setter) or by passing
            return;                                          the name of the property as a parameter.

        changed.Invoke(this, new PropertyChanged
➡ EventArgs(propertyName));                           ◁──  Invokes the event so that
    }                                                        bound Views can update
}                                                            properties
```

Creates a local reference for the event

The BaseViewModel gives us an implementation of INotifyPropertyChanged, so we can bind a View to any ViewModel that inherits this base class and invoke the handler to notify the UI of changes. We can take our BaseViewModel beyond a simple INotify-PropertyChanged implementation, though. We expect we'll need some other common functionality in all our pages. In MauiStockTake, every page will have a title, so we can add a Title property to the base ViewModel. We will also need a loading indicator, so we can add a property for this, too. We'll need to add backing fields for these and call OnPropertyChanged in the setters for the properties.

We will also want to add an INavigation property to our BaseViewModel. Navigation and control flow is presentation logic, so we want this logic to be managed by the ViewModel rather than the View.

You will see these properties (Title, Navigation, and IsLoading) in base ViewModels in a lot of projects, and in your own apps, you may find there are other common properties you want to implement too. The following listing shows the properties to add to the BaseViewModel class.

Listing 9.8   The BaseViewModel common properties

```
public class BaseViewModel : INotifyPropertyChanged
{

    private string _title;
    public string Title { get => _title; set { _title = value;
OnPropertyChanged(); } }

    private bool _isLoading;
    public bool IsLoading { get => _isLoading; set { _isLoading = value;
OnPropertyChanged(); } }

    public INavigation Navigation { get; set; }

    ...

}
```

TIP   Keep this BaseViewModel handy, as you can refer to it for any of your apps. You can also use the MVVM Community Toolkit to simplify the creation of ViewModels. Learn more about it here: http://mng.bz/pPX2.

We'll use the ViewModels namespace throughout the app, so add it to the Global-Usings.cs file:

```
global using MauiStockTake.UI.ViewModels;
```

CREATING THE INPUTVIEWMODEL
So far, we've built the structure of the app using Shell, and we've built some authentication logic so that we can communicate with a REST API, but we haven't built any of the app's core functionality yet. Let's start doing that now.

View first vs. ViewModel first

I usually build my apps with a ViewModel-first approach rather than a View-first approach. I am a .NET developer, not a UX or UI designer, so I tend to think of the apps I work on from the perspective of functional design rather than visual design. And, in all honesty, my visual design skills leave a lot to be desired, so I find it removes some of the cognitive load when I get around to the visual design if all the functional elements are already in place.

If you're more visually oriented, you might find it easier to build the View first and then the ViewModel. You might also find that some frameworks and libraries either directly require or at least naturally lean toward one approach or the other.

Of course, if you have a UI designer on your team, you may already have the visual design before you write a single line of code, in which case it might be easier to build out the UI first.

But one of the best benefits of the MVVM pattern is that you can do both at the same time. By using MVVM, one developer can work on the Views, and another can work on the ViewModels, without stepping on each other's toes, and you can wire them up once they're ready.

In the `ViewModels` folder, create a class called `InputViewModel` that inherits `BaseViewModel`. From our functional requirements and from figure 9.10, we know that the `InputPage` will need four main controls:

- A `SearchBar` for looking up products
- A `CollectionView` for selecting the desired product from the search results
- A `Stepper` to indicate the number of units of the selected product that were counted
- A `Button` for recording the stock count

We haven't built the UI yet, but given that we know it will need these controls, we can start adding some properties to the ViewModel to support them:

- The `SearchBar` will need a command to execute the search, so add an `ICommand` property and call it `SearchProductsCommand`.
- The `CollectionView` will need a collection to bind to for the search results, so add an `ObservableCollection` of type `ProductDto`. The `CollectionView` will also need a `ProductDto` to bind the selected item to, so add a `ProductDto` property called `SelectedProduct`.
- The `Stepper` will need an `int` to bind to, so add an `int` property called `Count`.
- The `Button` will need a command to save the stock count, so add an `ICommand` property and call it `AddCountCommand`.

If you've added all these properties, your `InputViewModel` should look like the following listing.

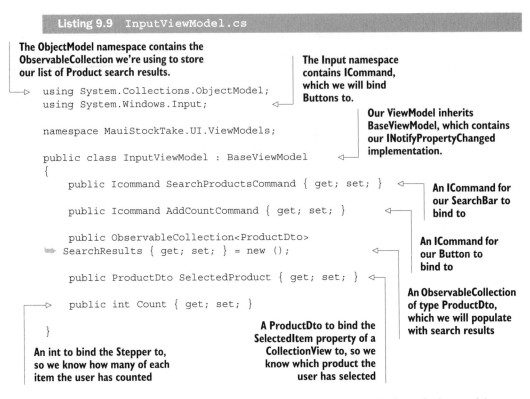

Listing 9.9 `InputViewModel.cs`

The ObjectModel namespace contains the ObservableCollection we're using to store our list of Product search results.

The Input namespace contains ICommand, which we will bind Buttons to.

```
using System.Collections.ObjectModel;
using System.Windows.Input;

namespace MauiStockTake.UI.ViewModels;

public class InputViewModel : BaseViewModel
{
    public Icommand SearchProductsCommand { get; set; }

    public Icommand AddCountCommand { get; set; }

    public ObservableCollection<ProductDto>
    SearchResults { get; set; } = new ();

    public ProductDto SelectedProduct { get; set; }

    public int Count { get; set; }

}
```

Our ViewModel inherits BaseViewModel, which contains our INotifyPropertyChanged implementation.

An ICommand for our SearchBar to bind to

An ICommand for our Button to bind to

An ObservableCollection of type ProductDto, which we will populate with search results

A ProductDto to bind the SelectedItem property of a CollectionView to, so we know which product the user has selected

An int to bind the Stepper to, so we know how many of each item the user has counted

This code completes the definition of the `InputViewModel`. It doesn't do anything yet, we still need to add methods for the commands to execute, but the interface (the bindable properties) for the View is complete. We'll come back and flesh out the functionality soon, but before we can use this ViewModel in a View, we need to register it with the service collection in `MauiProgram` so that we can inject it into the View's constructor. **Add this code after the line that registers the `LoginPage`:**

```
builder.Services.AddTransient<InputViewModel>();
```

9.5.3   *The View*

The corresponding View for the inventory workflow is the `InputPage`. We've already added the `InputPage` as a placeholder, but we need to add the layouts and controls to support this workflow.

CREATING THE INPUTPAGE

The `InputPage` provides the core workflow of our app and provides the functionality that will enable Mildred and her team to dispense with their inefficient paper-and-pen stock takes. At this point, we've got a good understanding of what the page will look like and what it will do, so let's get started.

Let's get everything set up first in the code-behind file. Open `InputPage.xaml.cs` and make the following changes:

1 Remove the `Button_Clicked` event handler.
2 Add a private `readonly` field of type `InputViewModel`, called `_viewModel`.
3 Inject the `InputViewModel` into the page constructor.
4 Assign the injected ViewModel to the field.
5 Assign the page's `Navigation` property to the field's `Navigation` property.
6 Set the page's binding context to the field.
7 Remove the `Products` namespace.

Once you have done these steps, your `InputPage.xaml.cs` file should look like the following listing.

Listing 9.10   `InputPage.xaml.cs`

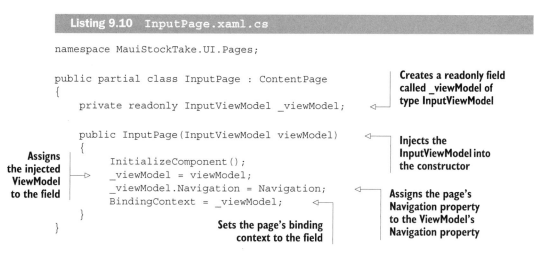

As we're injecting the ViewModel into the `InputPage`, it no longer has a default constructor (i.e., no parameters). Shell won't be able to create an instance of it without resolving it from the service collection, so we'll need to add a registration for it. In `MauiProgram`, after the line where we register the `LoginPage`, **register the `InputPage` as transient**, too.

Now we're ready to start building the UI. **Open the `InputPage.xaml` file, and delete the `VerticalStackLayout` and its contents, leaving only the `ContentPage` tags**. Next, we'll add the following to our page:

- A `Grid` for layout
- A `SearchBar` where the user can enter a search term and search for matching products
- A `CollectionView` to display the list of `SearchResults`
- An `ActivityIndicator` to show that search results are loading
- A `Label` to *show* the number of items the user has counted
- A `Stepper` to *record* the number of items the user has counted
- A `Button` that the user can tap to indicate that they want to save the count

Let's keep things simple and start with the layout. **Add a `Grid` with `Padding` of thickness 20 on all sides and five rows**. Figure 9.11 shows what these rows will hold and how they should be defined.

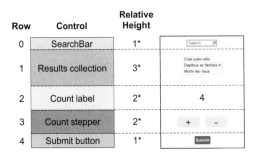

Row	Control	Relative Height	
0	SearchBar	1*	
1	Results collection	3*	
2	Count label	2*	4
3	Count stepper	2*	
4	Submit button	1*	

Figure 9.11   The relative row height and contents for the `Grid` that will make up the `InputPage`. Not shown is the `ActivityIndicator`, which will be in row 0 and have a row span of 5. These settings will make it appear in the center of the `Grid` when it is visible.

The following listing shows `InputPage.xaml` with this added `Grid`.

Listing 9.11   `InputPage.xaml` with the layout added

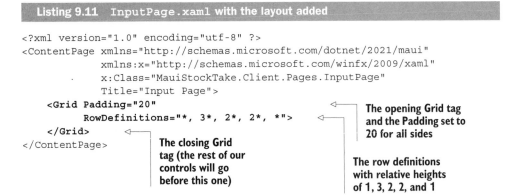

```
<?xml version="1.0" encoding="utf-8" ?>
<ContentPage xmlns="http://schemas.microsoft.com/dotnet/2021/maui"
             xmlns:x="http://schemas.microsoft.com/winfx/2009/xaml"
             x:Class="MauiStockTake.Client.Pages.InputPage"
             Title="Input Page">
    <Grid Padding="20"
          RowDefinitions="*, 3*, 2*, 2*, *">
    </Grid>
</ContentPage>
```

The opening Grid tag and the Padding set to 20 for all sides

The closing Grid tag (the rest of our controls will go before this one)

The row definitions with relative heights of 1, 3, 2, 2, and 1

Now that we've got our page layout, we can start adding some controls. We'll start with the `SearchBar`, which will need its `SearchCommand` property bound to the `Command` we created in the ViewModel, and a `CommandParameter` to pass through the search term. The following listing shows the XAML code for the `SearchBar` control; add this code inside the `Grid` on the `InputPage`.

Listing 9.12   The `SearchBar` control

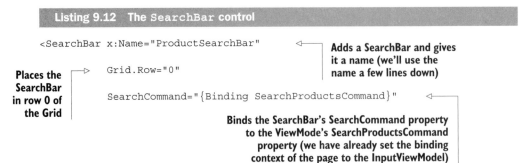

```
<SearchBar x:Name="ProductSearchBar"

           Grid.Row="0"

           SearchCommand="{Binding SearchProductsCommand}"
```

Adds a SearchBar and gives it a name (we'll use the name a few lines down)

Places the SearchBar in row 0 of the Grid

Binds the SearchBar's SearchCommand property to the ViewMode's SearchProductsCommand property (we have already set the binding context of the page to the InputViewModel)

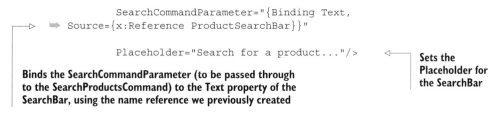

```
            SearchCommandParameter="{Binding Text,
     Source={x:Reference ProductSearchBar}}"

            Placeholder="Search for a product..."/>
```

Binds the SearchCommandParameter (to be passed through to the SearchProductsCommand) to the Text property of the SearchBar, using the name reference we previously created

Sets the Placeholder for the SearchBar

Next, add the `CollectionView` to row 1, which will display the search results. We added an `ObservableCollection` of type `ProductDto` to the `InputViewModel`, so we can bind to it for the `CollectionView`'s `ItemsSource`. We also added a `ProductDto` called `SelectedProduct`, so we can bind the `CollectionView`'s `SelectedItem` property to it. We will also want to add a `DataTemplate` to display the product name and manufacturer name for each item. The XAML code for the `CollectionView` is shown in the following listing.

Listing 9.13   The `CollectionView` control

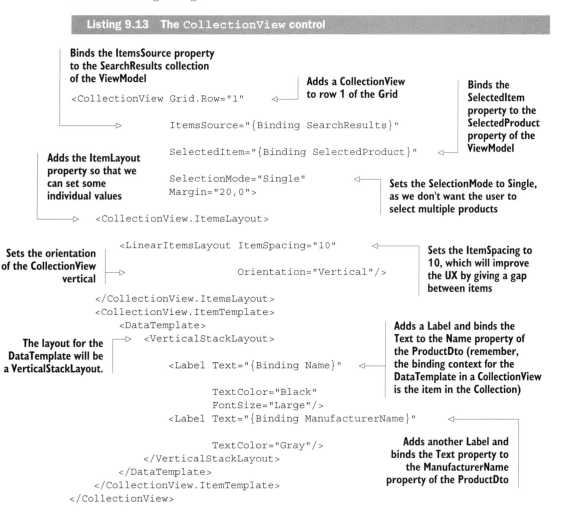

Binds the ItemsSource property to the SearchResults collection of the ViewModel

Adds a CollectionView to row 1 of the Grid

Binds the SelectedItem property to the SelectedProduct property of the ViewModel

Adds the ItemLayout property so that we can set some individual values

Sets the SelectionMode to Single, as we don't want the user to select multiple products

Sets the orientation of the CollectionView vertical

Sets the ItemSpacing to 10, which will improve the UX by giving a gap between items

The layout for the DataTemplate will be a VerticalStackLayout.

Adds a Label and binds the Text to the Name property of the ProductDto (remember, the binding context for the DataTemplate in a CollectionView is the item in the Collection)

Adds another Label and binds the Text property to the ManufacturerName property of the ProductDto

```
<CollectionView Grid.Row="1"

                ItemsSource="{Binding SearchResults}"

                SelectedItem="{Binding SelectedProduct}"

                SelectionMode="Single"
                Margin="20,0">
    <CollectionView.ItemsLayout>

        <LinearItemsLayout ItemSpacing="10"

                            Orientation="Vertical"/>

    </CollectionView.ItemsLayout>
    <CollectionView.ItemTemplate>
        <DataTemplate>
            <VerticalStackLayout>

                <Label Text="{Binding Name}"

                       TextColor="Black"
                       FontSize="Large"/>
                <Label Text="{Binding ManufacturerName}"

                       TextColor="Gray"/>
            </VerticalStackLayout>
        </DataTemplate>
    </CollectionView.ItemTemplate>
</CollectionView>
```

This `CollectionView` gives us a nice way not only to display the list of search results but also for the user to select one to indicate which product they were looking for. The `CollectionView` doesn't include a loading indicator, so let's add an `Activity-Indicator` to the page so the user knows something is happening once they've submitted their search.

We'll add it to the same row of the `Grid` as the `CollectionView`, which will help the user to understand that the results collection is loading when the indicator shows. We'll bind the `IsVisible` property to the `IsLoading` property of the ViewModel, which we can set based on when we're loading data.

The following listing shows the XAML code for the `ActivityIndicator`. Add this code to the `InputPage` after the `CollectionView`.

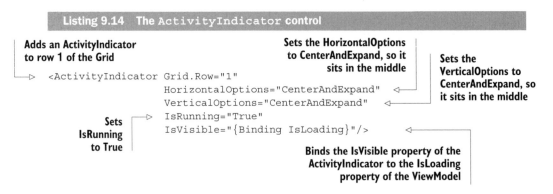

Listing 9.14   The `ActivityIndicator` control

Adds an ActivityIndicator to row 1 of the Grid

Sets the HorizontalOptions to CenterAndExpand, so it sits in the middle

Sets the VerticalOptions to CenterAndExpand, so it sits in the middle

```
<ActivityIndicator Grid.Row="1"
                   HorizontalOptions="CenterAndExpand"
                   VerticalOptions="CenterAndExpand"
                   IsRunning="True"
                   IsVisible="{Binding IsLoading}"/>
```

Sets IsRunning to True

Binds the IsVisible property of the ActivityIndicator to the IsLoading property of the ViewModel

There are two parts to recording a stock count: the product being recorded and the number of items counted. We've added the product part; now, let's move on to the count. We'll add a `Label` to show the current count and a `Stepper` so that the user can increase or decrease the count. The following listing shows the XAML code for these controls.

Listing 9.15   The count label and stepper controls

Adds a Label control and binds the Text property to the Count property of the ViewModel

We want this number to be big, so set the FontSize to Header.

```
<Label Text="{Binding Count}"
       FontSize="Header"
       HorizontalOptions="Center"
       VerticalOptions="Center"
       Grid.Row="2"/>
```

Places the Label in row 2 of the Grid

Sets the HorizontalOptions and VerticalOptions to Center

```
<Stepper HorizontalOptions="Center"
         VerticalOptions="Center"
         Value="{Binding Count}"
         Grid.Row="3"/>
```

Adds a Stepper and sets the HorizontalOptions and VerticalOptions to Center

Places the Stepper in row 3 of the Grid

Binds the Value property to the Count property of the ViewModel

Our `InputPage` is almost finished. The last step is to add a `Button` so the user can indicate that their stock count is ready to be recorded. The following listing shows the XAML code for the `Button` control.

Listing 9.16   The `Button` control

Adds a Button and sets the Text property to
"Add count" (to show what the Button does)

```
<Button Text="Add count"

        Command="{Binding AddCountCommand}"

        Grid.Row="4"/>
```

Binds the Command
property of the Button to
the AddCountCommand
property of the ViewModel

Places the Button in
row 4 of the Grid

Listing 9.16 completes the code for the `InputPage`. Now you can run the app, and you should see something like figure 9.12.

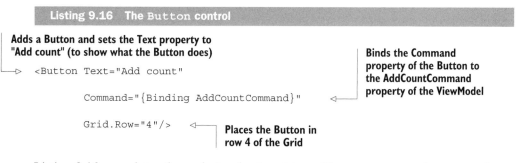

Figure 9.12   The `InputPage` of the MauiStockTake app, seen here running on Android

Finally, we can see our running app! All the controls in the UI are bound to the View-Model. However, while the ViewModel exposes some properties for the UI to bind to, it doesn't provide any functionality. For that, we need to wire up the services, which we will do next.

9.5.4   *Adding the Search functionality*

The `ProductService` will be used by the `InputViewModel` to look up products based on a search term entered by the user. Before we build the `ProductService`, we will define what functionality the ViewModel needs from it.

Open `InputViewModel.cs` and inject the `IProductService` into the constructor. To access it outside the constructor, assign it to a private `readonly` field. The constructor is shown in the following listing.

> **Listing 9.17   The updated `InputViewModel` constructor and field**

```
private readonly IProductService _productService;

public InputViewModel(IProductService productService)
{
        _productService = productService;
}
```

Add a reference to `MauiStockTake.Client.Services` to `GlobalUsings.cs` to import the namespace for this service. Next, **add a new private method of type `Task` called `UpdateSearchResults`** that takes a parameter of type `string` called searchTerm). Make the method async so that it doesn't block the UI while search results are being retrieved from the API.

Inside the method, we want to do the following steps:

1   Set the `IsLoading` property (inherited from the `BaseViewModel`) to true. We'll bind the `ActivityIndicator` in the UI to this property.
2   Clear the `SearchResults` `ObservableCollection` so that only results for the current search are shown. As `ObservableCollections` automatically notify the UI of changes to their content, we clear the collection rather than creating a new instance.
3   Call the `SearchProducts` method we just defined and assign the result to a temporary variable.
4   Set `IsLoading` back to `false` to hide the `ActivityIndicator`.
5   Iterate through the list of search results, and add each one to the `Observable-Collection`.

The code for this method is shown in the following listing.

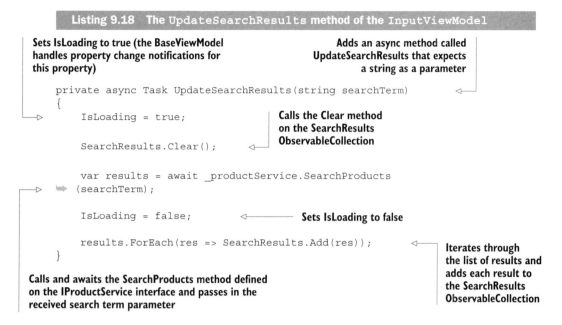

Listing 9.18   The `UpdateSearchResults` method of the `InputViewModel`

Sets IsLoading to true (the BaseViewModel handles property change notifications for this property) · Adds an async method called UpdateSearchResults that expects a string as a parameter

```
private async Task UpdateSearchResults(string searchTerm)
{
    IsLoading = true;                    Calls the Clear method
                                         on the SearchResults
    SearchResults.Clear();               ObservableCollection

    var results = await _productService.SearchProducts
    (searchTerm);

    IsLoading = false;        Sets IsLoading to false

    results.ForEach(res => SearchResults.Add(res));       Iterates through
}                                                         the list of results and
                                                          adds each result to
Calls and awaits the SearchProducts method defined       the SearchResults
on the IProductService interface and passes in the       ObservableCollection
received search term parameter
```

The last step to make the app work is to wire up the `SearchProductsCommand` to use this method. **Add the following line to the InputViewModel constructor:**

```
SearchProductsCommand = new Command<string>(async (term) => await
    UpdateSearchResults(term));
```

Note that the `Command` here is typed to `string`, which allows the `Command` binding to send a `CommandParameter`.

Run the app and try searching for a product. You should see an `ActivityIndicator` spinning while the app is loading results from the API. If you've entered a term that matches a product in the database, you'll see some results (the chapter's resources folder contains a full list of products in the MauiStockTake database), similar to the images in figure 9.13.

9.5.5   *Adding the inventory functionality*

Now that we successfully have our app searching for products, we need a way to record stock count results. If you've explored the app a little, you might notice that the `Stepper` buttons (+ and −) don't seem to do anything. Both the `Stepper` and the `Label` are bound to the `Count` property, but the `Count` property doesn't notify the UI of changes. The value is set when we tap the + and − buttons, but that change is not reflected in the UI.

We can fix this problem by updating the `Count` property in the `InputViewModel` to use a backing field and raise a property changed notification when it gets updated. Update the `Count` property in your `InputViewModel` to match listing 9.19.

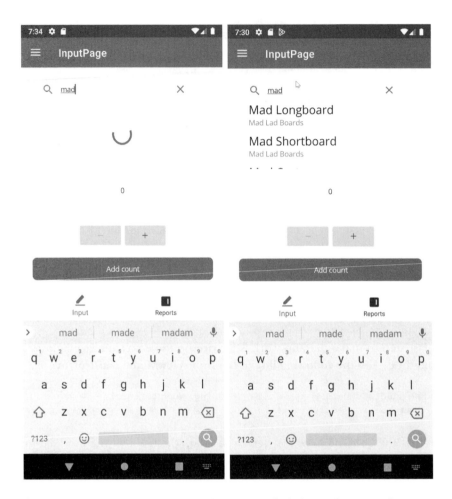

Figure 9.13   MauiStockTake searching for and then displaying products, seen here running on Android

Listing 9.19   The `InputViewModel` Count property

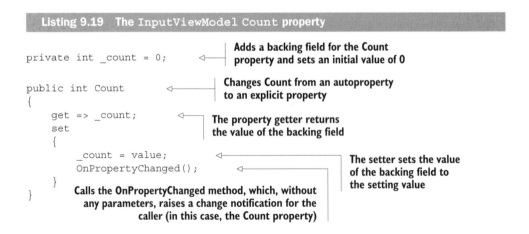

```
private int _count = 0;          ◁─┐  Adds a backing field for the Count
                                     │  property and sets an initial value of 0

public int Count      ◁──────────┐  Changes Count from an autoproperty
{                                 │  to an explicit property
    get => _count;     ◁───────┐  The property getter returns
    set                        │  the value of the backing field
    {
        _count = value;        ◁─────────────────┐  The setter sets the value
        OnPropertyChanged();   ◁──────────────┐   │  of the backing field to
    }                                         │   │  the setting value
}
```

Calls the **OnPropertyChanged** method, which, without any parameters, raises a change notification for the caller (in this case, the Count property)

If you run the app again now, you should see the count indicator changing in response to the Stepper.

Now that we've got a product and a count, we need to record them. This functionality is provided by the IInventoryService, so let's inject it into the InputViewModel constructor, as in the following listing (with changes in **bold**).

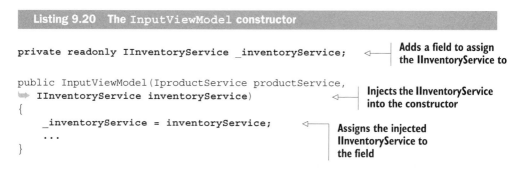

Listing 9.20 The InputViewModel constructor

```
private readonly IInventoryService _inventoryService;     ◁——  Adds a field to assign
                                                                 the IInventoryService to

public InputViewModel(IproductService productService,
  IInventoryService inventoryService)                     ◁——  Injects the IInventoryService
{                                                                into the constructor
    _inventoryService = inventoryService;    ◁——
    ...                                              Assigns the injected
}                                                    IInventoryService to
                                                     the field
```

Next, let's add the method to add a stock count using the IInventoryService. This method will need to do the following:

- Verify that the user has selected a product, and display an alert if they haven't
- Send the stock count to the API using the IInventoryService
- Display a message to the user indicating whether the action was successful

The following listing shows the AddCount method to be added to the InputViewModel.

Listing 9.21 The InputViewModel AddCount method

Makes the method async so it doesn't lock up the UI.

We are not doing any validation, so we need to ensure a Product has been selected. If not, we display an alert and then return from the method.

```
private async Task AddCount()    ◁——
{
    if (SelectedProduct is null)    ◁——
    {
        await App.Current.MainPage.DisplayAlert("Product Required", "You
  have not selected a product to record a count for", "OK");
        return;
    }

    IsLoading = true;    ◁——

    var added = await _inventoryService.AddStockCount(
  SelectedProduct, Count);    ◁——

    IsLoading = false;    ◁——
```

Sets the loading indicator to true so that the user can see that something is happening while the app talks to the API.

Calls the AddStockCount method on the IInventoryService and passes it the SelectedProduct and Count properties; awaits the result and assigns it to a temporary variable

Now that the communication with the API has completed, sets the loading indicator to false

```
    if (added)                              ⟵
    {
        await App.Current.MainPage.DisplayAlert(
➥  "Added", "Stock count has been added to
➥  inventory", "OK");
    }                                       ⟵
    else
    {
        await App.Current.MainPage.DisplayAlert(
➥  "Error", "Something went wrong, please try
➥  again.", "OK");                  ⟵
    }
}
```

Checks to see whether the addition of the count was successful so we can give appropriate feedback to the user

Displays a success message if the addition succeeded

Displays a failure message if the addition failed

The last step is to assign the new method to the `Execute` property of the `AddCount-Command`. **Add the following line to the constructor:**

```
AddCountCommand = new Command(async () => await AddCount());
```

At this point, the stock take workflow is functionally complete. You can run the app, search for products, and record a stock count. However, two UX bugs remain to be fixed. First, the count only allows input via the `Stepper`, which could be tedious if the user wants to record a count in the 10s or hundreds (anything greater than 10 will be annoying to have to enter via the `Stepper`). We'll come back to this problem in chapter 11. The other problem, which we should tidy up now, is that the search results stick around after recording a stock count. Ideally, the form will reset after recording data, ready for the next stock count.

There's not much left to do to get this working. We'll need to make a small change to the `InputPage` XAML and a small change to the `InputViewModel`. Currently, the `SearchBar` control calls a `Command` on the ViewModel and sends its `Text` property as a `Command` parameter. Instead, we'll bind the `Text` property to a property on the View-Model and use it to call the `SearchProducts` method on the `IProductService`. Then, we'll simply set it to an empty `string` to clear the search term and clear the `Observable-Collection` of search results.

Let's start by updating binding properties, and then we can clear the form. **Add a string property called `SearchTerm` to the `InputViewModel`. Then, update the Upda-teSearchResults method** to use this rather than a parameter and **update the command definition in the constructor**. Next, **add a method called `ResetForm`**. In this method, we will

1 Clear the `SearchResults` collection
2 Set the `Count` to 0
3 Set the `SelectedProduct` to `null`
4 Set the `SearchTerm` to an empty string
5 Raise a property changed notification for the `SearchTerm` property

Once we've added the method, we can call it from the `AddCount` method to reset the form once the count has been successfully recorded. The following listing shows the full code for the updated `InputViewModel`, with changes in **bold**.

Listing 9.22 The updated `InputViewModel`

```
public class InputViewModel : BaseViewModel
{
    ...

    public string SearchTerm { get; set; }

    public InputViewModel(IProductService productService, IInventoryService
    inventoryService)
    {
        ...

        SearchProductsCommand = new Command(async
        () => await UpdateSearchResults());

    }

    private async Task UpdateSearchResults()
    {
        IsLoading = true;

        SearchResults.Clear();

        var results = await _productService.
    SearchProducts(SearchTerm);

        IsLoading = false;

        results.ForEach(res => SearchResults.Add(res));
    }

    private async Task AddCount()
    {
        ...

        if (added)
        {
            await App.Current.MainPage.DisplayAlert("Added", "Stock count
    has been added to inventory", "OK");
            ResetForm();
        }
        else
        {
            ...
        }
    }

    private void ResetForm()
    {
        SearchResults.Clear();
```

Adds the
SearchTerm
property

Removes the string
parameter from the
Command assignment to the
SearchProductsCommand

Removes the method
parameter from
UpdateSearchResults

Updates the call to the
SearchProducts method do use
the ViewModel's SearchTerm
property, rather than a value
passed to the method

After a successful
count addition, calls
the ResetForm method

Adds a ResetForm
method with a void
return type

Clears the SearchResults
ObservableCollection

```
Count = 0;
SelectedProduct = null;
SearchTerm = string.Empty;
OnPropertyChanged(nameof(SearchTerm));
      }
   }
```

Now that we've updated the ViewModel to reset the form after successfully adding a stock count, we need to make a small change to the UI. The `SearchBar` control currently sends a command parameter; we need to remove it and bind the `Text` property to the `SearchTerm` property on the ViewModel. Listing 9.23 shows the updated XAML code for the `SearchBar` control in the `InputPage`. The added binding is in **bold**, but note the removed command parameter is not shown (it has been replaced by the `Text` binding).

Listing 9.23   The updated `SearchBar` control

```
<SearchBar x:Name="searchBar"
           Grid.Row="0"
           TextColor="{StaticResource PrimaryColor}"
           SearchCommand="{Binding SearchProductsCommand}"
           Text="{Binding SearchTerm}"
           Placeholder="Search for a product..."/>
```

That completes everything we need for the stock take workflow (except, perhaps, improving the UX for entering large numbers). Go ahead and run the app and make sure you can search for products and record stock counts. You should see something like figure 9.14.

9.6   *Reviewing the MauiStockTake app so far*

Congratulations on building your first functional real-world .NET MAUI app! Up until this chapter, all the examples we've been building have been simple demos. MauiTodo is something of an exception, although it's still very simple. MauiStockTake is our first major project.

We've built the MauiStockTake app using the MVVM pattern. Using this approach, we have a clean separation between our UI logic, presentation logic, and business logic. Using the `InputPage` and the stock take workflow as an example, we have UI logic in the `InputPage`, presentation logic in the `InputViewModel`, and business logic in the models (`ProductDto` and `StockCountDto`) and services (`IInventoryService`, `IProductService`, `IAuthService`, and their implementations).

Each of these pieces has been built independently and can be maintained independently. We could completely change the look of the UI without having to rebuild any other part of the app. Likewise, we could switch out the REST API for GraphQL,

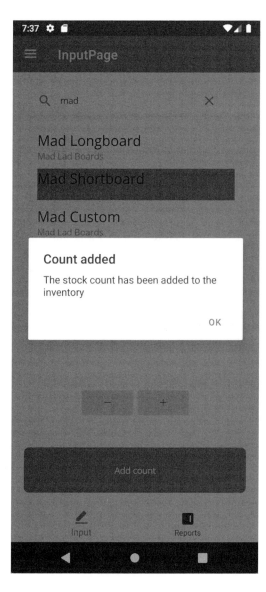

Figure 9.14 A successful stock count recording in the MauiStockTake app, seen here running on Android

and all we would have to do is update the functionality inside the service implementations. No other parts of the app, including the interfaces, would have to change.

We've followed the principle of dependency inversion (defining dependencies where we intend to consume them), starting with the UI. The InputViewModel is designed to expose the functionality and state required by the InputPage. I've cheated a little to simplify things in that I've provided you with interfaces that provide functionality required by the InputViewModel. I actually built the InputViewModel first, defined the interfaces as I was building it, and then built the implementations afterward.

The MVVM pattern isn't the only way to build apps with .NET MAUI, but it is the most popular—and for good reason. MVVM helps us build maintainable apps. The MauiStockTake app is architected for maintenance, making it simple to grow and change.

There's still more functionality to add, and there are a few things we can do to improve our app. We'll keep building on MauiStockTake over the next chapters, but before we move on, treat yourself to a slice of cake. You've earned it.

Summary

- We use the MVVM pattern in .NET MAUI to improve separation of concerns. UI logic goes in the View, presentation logic goes in the ViewModel, and business logic goes in the Model.
- By separating these concerns, we have code that is more maintainable and more testable.
- We can use command binding to execute functionality in ViewModels from Views.
- `INotifyPropertyChanged` defines events that tell Views to update their content. We implement this interface on ViewModels to raise this event and update the UI when a state in the ViewModel changes.
- Use the dependency inversion principle to define functionality where you intend to consume it rather than where it's provided, starting with your View.
- Use dependency injection and the `ServiceCollection` in the host builder to manage dependencies throughout your app.
- You can extend any controls with behaviors by adding functionality to the control without having to subclass it.
- The .NET MAUI Community Toolkit contains many useful features developers utilize in their apps.
- `EventToCommandBehavior` lets us respond to events with proprietary parameters.

Styles, themes, and multiplatform layouts

This chapter covers

- Styling controls
- App themes and light/dark mode
- Triggers and visual states
- Features of different device paradigms

Back in chapter 1, we looked at the importance of maintaining a consistent UX throughout your app and across different platforms, and we touched on it again in chapter 5. Whether you strive for the "pixel perfect" approach or just want your app to feel like your app, wherever it is used, keeping your UI consistent is critical and helps users understand how your app works.

For example, using a primary and secondary color helps your users to understand the purpose of a button, as does using specific button shapes (for example, it's common to use a circular floating action button to indicate an additive action). On the other hand, using too many different shaped or colored buttons could lead to confusion. Let's see an extreme example in figure 10.1.

With the example on the left, while having two identical buttons dilutes the call to action and the coupon button should probably be in a secondary style, it's easy to see that there is a button you can tap to apply a 25% discount to your order. On

Buttons are consistent, and the user can easily tell what to do.

Buttons are not consistent, and the user can't easily tell that the star is a button.

Figure 10.1   Two versions of an app UI. In both cases, a button is presented, which the user can tap to apply a 25% discount to their order. In the example on the left, the button looks like all the other buttons in the app, and the user can easily tell what to do. On the right, the button looks completely different, and it is not easy to tell that the star is a button that can be tapped.

the right, while the star may seem more visually striking, it's not consistent with the app's design language and gives no indication to the user that it can be tapped to apply the discount.

This example is extreme, but even small variations in the presentation of controls can cause confusion. In this chapter, we'll see how you can use styles to ensure that the look and feel of your controls is the same throughout your app and across different platforms (even if they are not identical). We'll also see how you can use themes; the most common themes are light and dark, and users often like to choose between light and dark modes or let the app synchronize with the light or dark mode of the OS.

Maintaining consistency across device types and OSes is important, but it's also important to leverage the UX expectations users have for different paradigms. We'll see in this chapter how you can take advantage of UX features users have come to expect on desktop and mobile devices.

10.1   *Creating a consistent look and feel*

We've made some small changes to the way controls look in our .NET MAUI apps so far, but we haven't changed the overall *style* of an app. We want MauiStockTake to reflect the surfing look and feel of Mildred's business, so let's update the app's styles to match.

In chapter 1 (and again in chapter 5), we looked at the *consistent* but not *identical* approach to UI, which is achieved in .NET MAUI using styles. Let's see how we can apply styles to MauiStockTake.

10.1.1 *Styles*

All controls in .NET MAUI have properties that can be customized to change their appearance. Some of these, like `TextColor` on the `Label` and `Entry` controls, are properties of the control itself (although, as you can see, some controls have properties with the same names). Others, like `HorizontalOptions` and `WidthRequest`, are inherited from the `View` and `VisualElement` base classes.

You can modify any of these properties on any control in your app. But applying these modifications each time you add a control is not only laborious, but it also introduces the risk of human error, which could undermine the consistency we're striving for. To avoid this problem, we can use styles.

Styles are collections of customizations for a specific control type. The .NET MAUI templates we have been using have some styles already built in, which is why, for example, the `Button` looks roughly the same on each platform. Let's see how these default app-wide styles are defined and how we can use them to customize the MauiStockTake app.

STYLING BUTTONS

In both the default template and the `blankmaui` template, a set of styles have been defined (we'll look at implicit vs. explicit styles in a few pages). If you open `App.xaml`, you can see that two additional files are loaded into the app's resource dictionary. Both are in the `Resources/Styles` folder; one is called `Colors.xaml`, and the other is called `Styles.xaml`. These files contain a collection of colors used throughout the app and a collection of default styles (which, in turn, uses the colors defined in `Colors.xaml`). As they are loaded into the app's resource dictionary, they are applied across the whole of the app.

Let's start by updating the colors. In `Colors.xaml`, update the `Primary` and `Secondary` values to match those in listing 10.1 and add the additional `PrimaryBackground` and `SecondaryBackground` color definitions.

> **Listing 10.1   Color definitions to add to the `Colors.xaml` resource dictionary**

```
<Color x:Key="Primary">#215377</Color>
<Color x:Key="Secondary">#8dacb9</Color>
<Color x:Key="PrimaryBackground">#8dacb9</Color>
<Color x:Key="SecondaryBackground">#b4bcc7</Color>
```

If you run the app now, you'll notice the change in `Button` color right away. The two background colors we've added are for styling the `Page`, which we'll get to shortly, but let's take a look at how those `Button` colors are applied.

Open the `Styles.xaml` file and look for the style with a `TargetType` of `Button`. Styles must define a `TargetType` and can then use `Setters` to define how properties of that target type should look. For this style with a `TargetType` of `Button`, we can use a `Setter` for any property of a `Button` that we want to control.

For the `Button` style, there is a `Setter` for the `BackgroundColor` property that uses `AppThemeBinding`, which we'll look at in the next section. However, we can see in this

Setter that when the app is running in light mode, the BackgroundColor property of a Button will be set to the Primary color defined in the Colors.xaml file, and when the app is running in dark mode, it will be white. You can see the setter for this property here:

```
<Setter Property="BackgroundColor" Value="{AppThemeBinding Light={
    StaticResource Primary}, Dark={StaticResource White}}" />
```

There are two changes we want to make to the Button style to match Mildred's brand guidelines. First, we want to add a Setter for the HeightRequest property and make it 50, so that every button in the app is the same height. Second, we want to change the CornerRadius setter from 8 to 25, which is half of the height and will give us perfectly rounded edges on every Button.

Add the Setter for HeightRequest now. Depending on your IDE or code editor, you might notice that Intellisense gives you the list of properties as you type. Then, **change the Value in the Setter for CornerRadius**. Finally, **update the Setter for MinimumWidthRequest and set the Value to 100**. If you run the app now, you'll see the updated Button style on the LoginPage, as in figure 10.2.

STYLING PAGES

Pages aren't as customizable as other views, but they do have some properties that you might like to make consistent across your app. One of these is Padding; you may also want to tailor your app to different platforms and device types.

For MauiStockTake, we're going to customize the page background to give us a gradient that's aligned with the beachy, surfing theme of Mildred's brand. In Styles.xaml, look for the style with a TargetType of Page. There is already a Setter here for the BackgroundColor property; we're going to delete this and replace it with a Setter for the Background property.

What is the difference between Background and BackgroundColor?

The VisualElement base class in .NET MAUI, from which all views are derived, has both a Background and a BackgroundColor property. They are similar in that they both set the background of a view but differ in that BackgroundColor is of type Color and Background is of type Brush.

Brushes allow you to "paint" an area (such as the background of a view). However, in addition to allowing just a single color (with the SolidColorBrush, which, in the case of Background, is identical in function to setting the BackgroundColor property), you also have a LinearGradientBrush and a RadialGradientBrush.

We've mentioned brushes before, and we're going to use them here to set a gradient as the Background property of a Page. If you just want a single color, you can set the Background property and use a SolidColorBrush, but a simpler approach is to set the BackgroundColor property.

We'll use gradient brushes again in the next chapter.

Figure 10.2 The Login button on the LoginPage is now styled and meets the branding guidelines for this app. Even though we haven't customized the button directly, the app's styles have been applied to give us the visual style we wanted.

Because `Background` is of type `Brush` and we want to assign a gradient to it, we won't be able to use the inline `Value` property in the `Setter`. Instead, we'll add it explicitly using tags. With this approach, we can assign a `LinearGradientBrush` to the `Value` property and specify its `StartPoint` and `EndPoint` properties. These are of type `Point` and made up of an x and y value, each of which is between 0 and 1 and represents a proportion of the view's width and height, respectively. Starting at the top left with `0,0`, a value of `0.5,0.5` would be the center of the view, and `1,1` would be the bottom right, as you can see in figure 10.3.

Our `Page` gradient is going to run from bottom left to top right, so we'll add a `StartPoint` of `0,1` and an `EndPoint` of `1,0`. The `StartPoint` and `Endpoint` define the

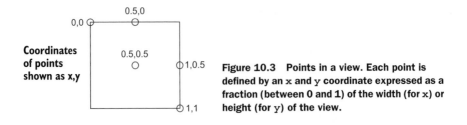

Figure 10.3   Points in a view. Each point is defined by an x and y coordinate expressed as a fraction (between 0 and 1) of the width (for x) or height (for y) of the view.

axis of the gradient—the line from start to finish along which the gradient will run. In addition to the axis, we also need to define *gradient stops,* which specify colors at positions along the axis. GradientStop has two properties: Color and Offset. Color is the color to assign to that position, and Offset is a fractional position along the axis, ranging from 0 to 1.

You can specify as many gradient stops as you like, but for MauiStockTake we are going to provide just two, using the PrimaryBackground and SecondaryBackground values we specified in the Colors.xaml file. We'll add the PrimaryBackground to the start of the axis by giving it a value of 0 and place the SecondaryBackground at the end of the axis by giving it a value of 1.

The following listing shows the Setter to add to the style with a TargetType of Page in the Styles.xaml file. Delete the Setter for the Background property and add the Setter from this listing.

Listing 10.2   The background setter for the Page style

```
<Setter Property="Background">
    <Setter.Value>
        <LinearGradientBrush StartPoint="0,1" EndPoint="1,0">
            <GradientStop Color="{StaticResource
➥ PrimaryBackground}" Offset="0"/>
            <GradientStop Color="{StaticResource
➥ SecondaryBackground}" Offset="1"/>
        </LinearGradientBrush>
    </Setter.Value>
</Setter>
```

Run the app now, and you should see the LoginPage automatically inheriting the Background property we've defined in this style, as in figure 10.4.

STYLE HIERARCHY

Styles are added to a resource dictionary, which can either be the app's resource dictionary (which is the case with the built-in styles) or a page's resource dictionary. Control properties are applied hierarchically, with Styles defined in the app's resource dictionary applied first, then those in the Page's resource dictionary, and,

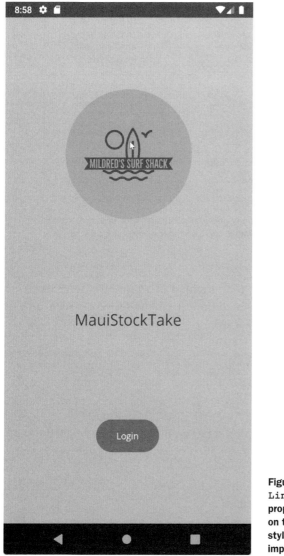

Figure 10.4 The `LoginPage` has a `LinearGradient` as its `Background` property. This gradient hasn't been set on this page but has been applied to a style that targets the `Page` type and is imported at the app level.

finally, any properties explicitly defined on the control. Figure 10.5 illustrates this hierarchy.

You can see from figure 10.5 that if you apply a style at the app level, it will apply to all matching controls in the app. If you apply a style at the page level, it will apply to all matching controls on that page and will override app-level styles. Properties defined on a control override any app or page styles.

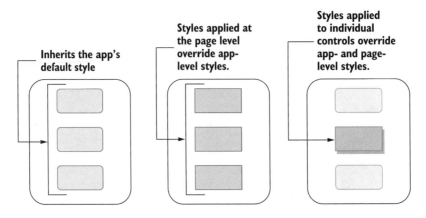

Figure 10.5 Control property values are applied hierarchically, with app-level styles applied by default, page-level styles overriding app-level styles, and values set directly on controls overriding any styles.

Styles that are narrower in scope (i.e., defined at a more granular level) take precedence over broadly scoped styles. In addition to the scope of the style, an explicit style will take preference over an implicit style.

IMPLICIT VS. EXPLICIT STYLES

The styles that we've looked at so far are *implicit* styles. Implicit styles are defined against a target type, and every view of that type that is hierarchically in the scope of the style will apply it.

You can also use *explicit* styles. An explicit style is defined almost identically to an implicit style, except that it adds a *key*. A key is an identifier by which a resource can be referred to. A view will not apply an explicit style unless the style is explicitly assigned to it using, unsurprisingly, the Style property.

The count label is a little bland at the moment, and also not particularly easy to read. Let's use an explicit style to improve it.

> **NOTE** In a real-world app, it would make much more sense to apply these properties directly to *the view*. The value gained from creating a style is when it applies to more than one control.

In the Styles.xaml file, let's create a new explicit style that targets the Label type and give it a key of CountLabelStyle. The count label already has some properties defined (FontSize, HorizontalOptions, and VerticalOptions), so we can start by adding these to our style. Lastly, we can specify the TextColor property and set it as the app's Primary color. The following listing shows the style to add to the Styles.xaml file.

Listing 10.3 The `CountLabelStyle` style

```
<Style TargetType="Label" x:Key="CountLabelStyle">
    <Setter Property="FontSize" Value="64"/>
```

```
    <Setter Property="HorizontalOptions" Value="Center"/>
    <Setter Property="VerticalOptions" Value="Center"/>
    <Setter Property="TextColor" Value="{StaticResource Primary}"/>
</Style>
```

Once you've added this style, we can remove the properties defined here from the count label and assign the style instead:

```
<Label Grid.Row="2"
    Text="{Binding Count}"
    Style="{StaticResource CountLabelStyle}"/>
```

Once you've made these changes, run the app; it should look something like figure 10.6.

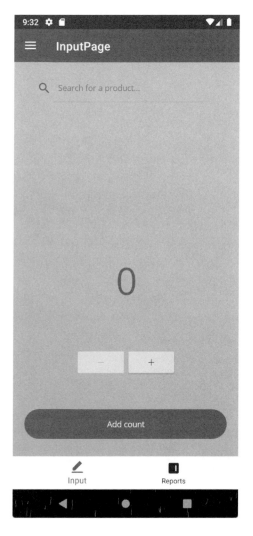

Figure 10.6 An explicit style is applied to the count label to control its horizontal and vertical position, the font size, and the text color. These customizations can be applied to any view with a matching target type (in this case, Label) by using the Style property and referencing this explicit style.

One thing that still doesn't fit in here is the tab bar. In figure 10.6, you can see that it has a white background that doesn't fit in with the rest of the app, so let's update the style for `Shell` to make this match. In `Styles.xaml`, find the style for `Shell` and the `Setter` for `Shell.TabBarBackgroundColor`. Delete the `Value` and replace it with `{StaticResource PrimaryBackground}`. Run the app again, and you should see the tab bar blend into the page background, as in figure 10.7.

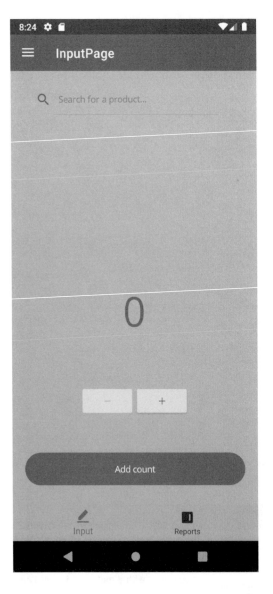

Figure 10.7   The tab bar background in MauiStockTake is now consistent with the rest of the app and is controlled by a `Setter` in the app's `Styles`.

10.1.2 Themes

As developers, we're used to being able to customize the theme or appearance of apps we use. Visual Studio Code, by far the world's most popular developer tool (according to the Stack Overflow developer survey; see: http://mng.bz/OxWo), allows extensive customization and theming, with themes being among the most downloaded extensions.

Customizable color themes or palettes are common in many apps, but even those that don't offer them nearly always offer an option to switch between light mode and dark mode. I conducted a Twitter poll to help understand how important this feature is, and while this is by no means a scientific study, the results, seen in figure 10.8, provide a clear indication that light and dark mode support is generally considered to be important.

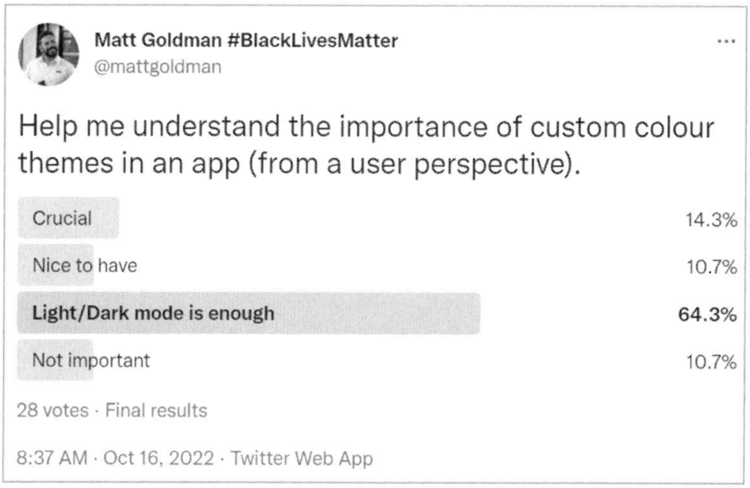

Figure 10.8   A short Twitter poll asking for opinions about color themes in apps. The responses overwhelmingly indicate that providing a light and dark mode should be a priority.

In this section, we'll see how you can provide support for light and dark modes in your app and how you can respond to the system theme. We'll also look at how you can offer a range of color themes for users to choose from.

LIGHT MODE AND DARK MODE

Mildred and her team will often be taking inventory at night, so it's a good idea to add dark mode support to MauiStockTake so that they don't get unnecessary eye strain. Fortunately, support for light and dark modes comes built into the templates in .NET MAUI. Without changing anything, if you create a new project using either the default or `blankmaui` templates or open one of the projects from earlier chapters, you'll notice that the colors in the app change when you change your device from dark mode to light mode, or vice versa.

Let's update the dark mode colors for MauiStockTake. Open `Colors.xaml` and add the color definitions from the following listing.

Listing 10.4   Dark mode color definitions for MauiStockTake

```
<Color x:Key="PrimaryDark">#7b98aa</Color>
<Color x:Key="PrimaryDarkBackground">#141d31</Color>
<Color x:Key="SecondaryDarkBackground">#212f51</Color>
```

Now that we've got some dark mode colors defined, we can update the app's styles to use these colors. You may have spotted some of the styles using a markup extension called `AppThemeBinding`. `AppThemeBinding` lets you respond to the system's light and dark modes, specifying a different value for each mode.

If you look through `Styles.xaml`, you'll see lots of examples, and you may spot plenty of opportunities for customizing the light and dark mode behavior of your apps. For MauiStockTake, we'll use `AppThemeBinding` to control the light mode and dark mode of the following:

- Page background
- Activity indicator
- Button
- Flyout background
- Tab bar
- Navigation (title) bar

Start with the style for `ActivityIndicator`; for light mode, it currently uses the `Primary` color, but for dark mode, it uses `White`. **Change the dark mode color** to the `Primary-Dark` color we've defined.

We can **do the same thing in the style for `Button` with the `Setter` for the Background property**. For the `TextColor` `Setter`, **remove the `AppThemeBinding` and just set the Value to the `White` `StaticResource`**, as the `Button`'s `Background` is no longer white in dark mode, and white text will contrast just as well with `PrimaryDark` as with `Primary`.

The `Setter` for the `Background` property that we added to the `Page` style has two gradient stops, each one referring to a color in the resource dictionary. It's easy enough to change these to use `AppThemeBinding`. Let's do that, but let's also take it a step further by making the whole gradient brush a resource.

Cut the whole `LinearGradientBrush` from between the `<Setter.Value>` **tags and paste it into the `Colors.xaml` file**. You'll see that there are already some `SolidColor-Brush` resources defined here. For our gradient, once we've pasted it, all we need to do is add a key like these other brushes. **Give it a key of `BackgroundGradient` and then update the gradient stops to use `AppThemeBinding`**. Keep the existing colors for light mode, and add the new dark mode background colors we added in listing 10.4. Your new gradient brush resource should look like the following listing.

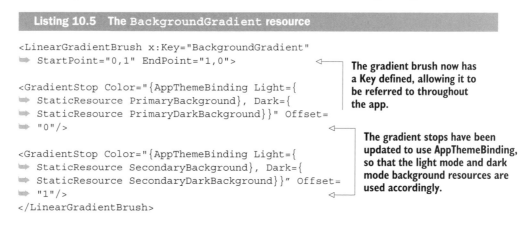

Listing 10.5 The `BackgroundGradient` resource

```
<LinearGradientBrush x:Key="BackgroundGradient"
   StartPoint="0,1" EndPoint="1,0">

<GradientStop Color="{AppThemeBinding Light={
   StaticResource PrimaryBackground}, Dark={
   StaticResource PrimaryDarkBackground}}" Offset=
   "0"/>

<GradientStop Color="{AppThemeBinding Light={
   StaticResource SecondaryBackground}, Dark={
   StaticResource SecondaryDarkBackground}}" Offset=
   "1"/>
</LinearGradientBrush>
```

The gradient brush now has a Key defined, allowing it to be referred to throughout the app.

The gradient stops have been updated to use AppThemeBinding, so that the light mode and dark mode background resources are used accordingly.

Now that the gradient background is a defined resource, we can simplify the `Setter` for the `Background` property of the `Page` style. **Make the `<Setter ...>` a single line self-closing tag and set the `Value` to the `BackgroundGradient` `StaticResource`.** The `Setter` should now look like this:

```
<Setter Property="Background" Value="{StaticResource BackgroundGradient}"/>
```

Next, let's fix the tab bar. In the previous section, we removed the `AppThemeBinding` for `Shell.TabBarBackgroundColor` and replaced it with the `PrimaryBackground` static resource. **Let's add the `AppThemeBinding` back in and use `PrimaryBackground` for light mode and `PrimaryDarkBackground` for dark mode.** The `Setter` for `Shell .TabBarBackgroundColor` should look like this:

```
<Setter Property="Shell.TabBarBackgroundColor" Value="{AppThemeBinding
   Light={StaticResource PrimaryBackground}, Dark={StaticResource
   PrimaryDarkBackground}}" />
```

The flyout background also needs to be updated. This is a simple change: **add a `Setter` for `Shell.FlyoutBackgroundColor` and use `AppThemeBinding` to set `Primary-Background` as the light value and `PrimaryDarkBackground` for dark**. The `Setter` should look like this:

```
<Setter Property="Shell.FlyoutBackgroundColor" Value="{AppThemeBinding
   Light={StaticResource PrimaryBackground}, Dark={StaticResource
   PrimaryDarkBackground}}"/>
```

The last change to make for `Shell` is to update the `Setter` for the `BackgroundColor` property. This value is used to set the background of the navigation bar that holds the menu button and title. It's already got `AppThemeBinding`; we can leave `Primary` as the value for light mode, but let's **change the dark mode value from `Gray950` to `SecondaryDarkBackground`**. This will make both the top and bottom bars blend in with the background gradient. But as the gradient runs at a diagonal, a slight border will be visible, giving a nice UI effect.

The final thing we should update is the explicit style we created for the `CounterLabel`. **Update the `Setter` for the `TextColor` property to use `AppThemeBinding`, keeping the `Primary` `StaticResource` for light mode and using `PrimaryDark` for dark mode.** With all these changes made, your InputPage should look similar to figure 10.9.

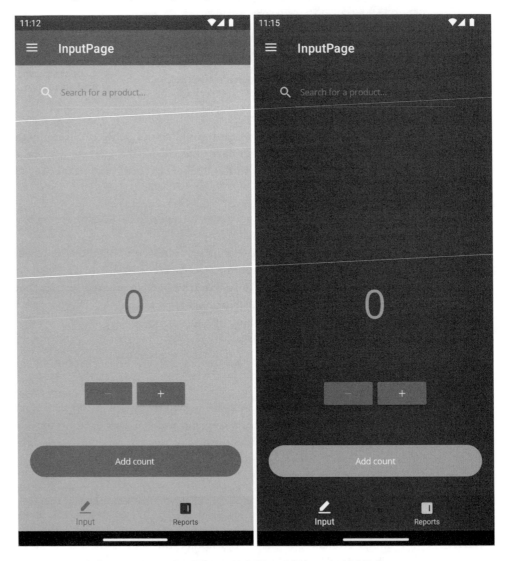

Figure 10.9   MauiStockTake running light mode (left) and dark mode (right). Because `AppThemeBinding` is used, this mode is not selected within the app but is bound to the light or dark theme of the OS.

You can see in `Styles.xaml` there is scope to customize many more styles, but the `AppThemeBinding` markup extension can be used anywhere, not just for setting colors. For example, we could use a different version of the company logo on the login screen for dark mode if we wanted or even have different values for labels.

CUSTOM THEMES

You can go beyond light and dark modes and offer full themes for your apps. Figure 10.8 shows that this feature doesn't seem as highly demanded as light and dark mode support. Although it's worth noting that this poll is far from a rigorous scientific study and was conducted on an app that does, in fact, offer customizable themes.

We've been using the `StaticResource` markup extension to refer to colors in the app's merged resource dictionary. As the name suggests, the value is considered static, so it does not change at run time. However, if you use its `DynamicResource` counterpart, the UI will change at run time to reflect changes in the source value. With this approach, you can swap out the color palette at run time, and using `DynamicResource`, your views will automatically update to reflect the new colors, as seen in figure 10.10 (shown here in various shades of gray).

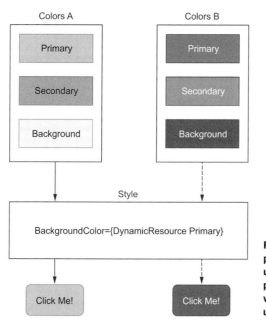

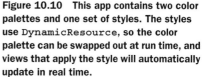

Figure 10.10   This app contains two color palettes and one set of styles. The styles use `DynamicResource`, so the color palette can be swapped out at run time, and views that apply the style will automatically update in real time.

The .NET MAUI documentation covers this approach to theming apps, and you can read about it here: http://mng.bz/Y1vK. There is a limitation, though: `AppTheme-Binding` and `DynamicResource` don't work together. It will work well if you want to provide your own user-selectable color schemes (using just `DynamicResource`, as per the example in the documentation), but it won't allow you to bind to OS light mode and dark mode changes.

We can work around this limitation by using a *theme*, which is a resource dictionary with a combined color palette and set of styles bundled together. Because a theme doesn't depend on DynamicResource, the styles in the theme can use AppThemeBinding. Figure 10.11 shows an example of a theme (shown here in various shades of gray).

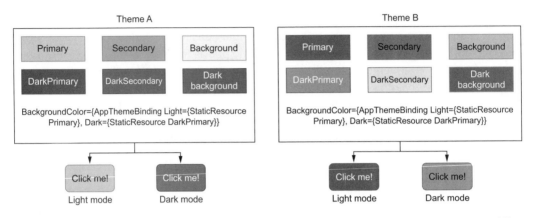

Figure 10.11   A theme contains both colors and styles. If we want to change the theme, we can swap out the whole theme rather than just changing the color palette. Because it is using `StaticResource` rather than `DynamicResource`, it can also use `AppThemeBinding` and support light and dark mode.

If we want to change the theme, we can load a new one, which will contain both colors and styles. Because we're not just swapping out the colors, we have no dependence on DynamicResource, so we can happily use AppThemeBinding to support light mode and dark mode. For MauiStockTake, Mildred has asked that we provide a sandy theme to go alongside the default theme and for both to support automatic light mode and dark mode in response to OS changes.

Start by creating a new folder inside the Resources folder called Themes and add two new resource dictionaries, one called DefaultTheme and another called Sandy-Theme. You can do this in Visual Studio by selecting the .NET MAUI Resource Dictionary (XAML) template or using the .NET CLI with the following command:

```
dotnet new maui-dict-xaml -na MauiStockTake.UI.Resources.Themes -n
⇒ SandyTheme
```

> **WARNING**   Make sure you use the template, rather than just creating a XAML file. When you use the template, it also includes a C# code-behind, which, critically, calls InitializeComponent() in the constructor. This is required, as per the previously linked documentation.

With these files created, we can build the themes by combining our existing color palettes and styles. **Copy everything from the Colors.xaml file** between the <Resource-Dictionary..>...</ResourceDictionary> tags (so, all the color and brush definitions) to the top of the DefaultTheme.xaml file between the ResourceDictionary tags in there. **Next, copy all the styles from the `Styles.xaml` file** and paste them into `DefaultTheme.xaml` after the color definitions and before the closing `Resource-Dictionary` tag.

Repeat this process to create the Sandy theme (copy the colors and styles into the `SandyTheme.xaml` resource dictionary). The two themes are currently identical, so let's update the Sandy theme so that it's got the right colors. We don't need to change much: update the `SandyTheme.xaml` file with the colors shown in the following listing.

Listing 10.6   The colors to update for the Sandy theme

```
<Color x:Key="Primary">#6b433b</Color>
<Color x:Key="PrimaryDark">#d9ceb6</Color>
<Color x:Key="Secondary">#ede8dd</Color>
<Color x:Key="PrimaryBackground">#cdb08a</Color>
<Color x:Key="SecondaryBackground">#dadccb</Color>
<Color x:Key="PrimaryDarkBackground">#251f13</Color>
<Color x:Key="SecondaryDarkBackground">#453b24</Color>
```

Now that we've got our two themes, we need to set one as default and provide the user with a way to switch between them. We can set the default by removing the `Colors.xaml` and `Styles.xaml` files from the resource dictionary in `App.xaml` and replacing them both with the new default theme:

```
<ResourceDictionary Source="Resources/Themes/DefaultTheme.xaml" />
```

Run the app for a quick check to make sure everything works the same as before. We haven't changed anything qualitative yet; we've just combined the styles and colors into a theme, so you shouldn't notice any difference.

We'll add a `MenuItem` to the Shell to allow the user to change the theme. **Download the `icon_palette.svg` file from this chapter's folder in the book's online resources and import it into the `Resources/Images` folder in** `MauiStockTake.UI`; we will use this as the icon for this menu item. We already have a `MenuItem` for logging out; add the `MenuItem` in the following listing to `AppShell.xaml` before the logout menu item.

Listing 10.7   The Change Theme menu item

```
<MenuItem IconImageSource="icon_palette.png"
    x:Name="ThemeMenuItem"
    Clicked="ThemeMenuItem_Clicked"/>
```

For this `MenuItem`, we've set the `IconImageSource` property, added an event handler, and given it a name. We haven't set the `Text` property as it will need to change depending on what the current theme is. We'll set its initial value in the `AppShell.xaml.cs` constructor and then change it as needed in the event handler. **Add this line to the `AppShell.xaml.cs` constructor**:

```
ThemeMenuItem.Text = "Switch to Sandy Theme";
```

To track which theme is currently in use, let's add an enum with all the available themes. We only have two for now, but we can easily add more in the future. If we add more, it's a good idea to provide a settings page where the user can choose; our current approach will only allow toggling between two themes, but that's fine for now. In MauiStockTake.UI, add a file called Theme.cs in the Helpers folder and add the code from the following listing.

Listing 10.8   The Theme enum

```
namespace MauiStockTake.UI.Helpers;
public enum Theme
{
    Default,
    Sandy
}
```

To track the theme currently in use, add a static property to the App class. **Add the following to App.xaml.cs:**

```
public static Theme Theme { get; set; } = Theme.Default;
```

This gives us a static instance of the Theme enum with the default value already set. The final step to managing the theme is to write the event handler. In AppShell.xaml.cs, we'll add an event handler called ThemeMenuItem_Clicked (we've already specified this in the XAML), which will perform the following steps:

1 Check the static enum to see which theme is currently in use.
2 Set the enum to the other value.
3 Update the text of the menu item.
4 Load the merged resource dictionary from the App class.
5 Clear the dictionary.
6 Load the alternate theme.

The code for this event handler is shown in the following listing.

Listing 10.9   The ThemeMenuItem_Clicked event handler

```
private void ThemeMenuItem_Clicked(object sender, EventArgs e)
{
    if (App.Theme == Theme.Default)
    {
        App.Theme = Theme.Sandy;
        ThemeMenuItem.Text = "Switch to Default Theme";
        ICollection<ResourceDictionary>
        mergedDictionaries = Application.Current.
        Resources.MergedDictionaries;
        if (mergedDictionaries != null)
        {
            mergedDictionaries.Clear();
            mergedDictionaries.Add(new SandyTheme());
```

The XAML files added in App.xaml are in a merged dictionary; adds a reference to this here.

Clears the current merged dictionary to remove the current theme

Loads the desired theme into the merged dictionary

```
        }
    }
    else
    {
        App.Theme = Theme.Default;
        ThemeMenuItem.Text = "Switch to Sandy Theme";
        ICollection<ResourceDictionary> mergedDictionaries = Application.
➥ Current.Resources.MergedDictionaries;
        if (mergedDictionaries != null)
        {
            mergedDictionaries.Clear();
            mergedDictionaries.Add(new DefaultTheme());
        }
    }
}
```

Run the app now, and it should start with the default theme. If you open the menu, you'll see the new Switch Theme menu item, and you should be able to change between the two themes and have them both respond to light and dark modes. Figure 10.12 shows these themes on Android.

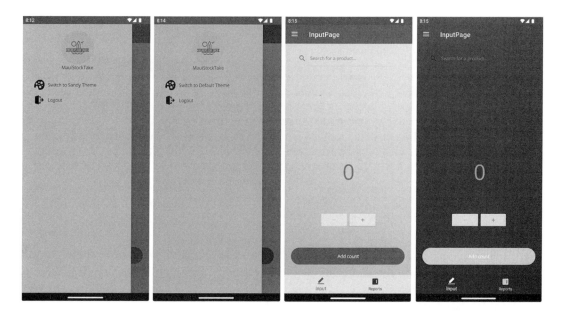

Figure 10.12   The flyout now has a theme-switching menu item. Note how the text changes depending on the currently selected theme (shown here in various shades of gray). Note also how the Sandy theme responds to light mode (left) and dark mode (right) changes, just like the default theme does.

We now have two themes, both using `AppThemeBinding` to support light and dark modes, that can be switched out at run time. This approach is somewhat heavy handed, and if you don't need to support *both* light and dark mode *and* multiple color palettes, you're better off using *either* AppThemeBinding *or* DynamicResource. But this approach gives you both, which the other approaches do not.

10.2   *Responding to state changes*

The UI we've built so far in this book has been relatively static, meaning once the UI has been defined, it doesn't change. But in some cases, we may want the UI to be more dynamic and change in response to changes in the state of the app.

This is what is meant by UI behavior. For example, in chapter 7 we looked at a Switch as an example, and how its background color could change in response to its state. In .NET MAUI, there are a few ways that we can make our UI dynamic in response to state changes.

> **Orientation changes**
>
> The most efficient way to respond to orientation changes is to design your apps to be responsive. This means using layouts that can adapt to different orientations and screen sizes, which can be accomplished using the layouts provided in .NET MAUI.
>
> However, if you want to explicitly change aspects of a page depending on orientation, the best approach is to use the OnSizeAllocated method we mentioned in chapter 7. You can override this method and compare the passed-in height and width values to determine the orientation.
>
> What you do from there is up to you: you could hide or show different views, change font sizes, etc. Another approach is to set the value of an enum and bind properties in your XAML to it so that they can respond to orientation changes. The benefit of this approach is that it works for window resizing too. If we were to use this with the MauiCalc app that we built in chapter 5, we could show a scientific layout on mobile when it's in landscape and on desktop when the window is wider than it is taller (or wider than a minimum required width) and a basic mode layout on mobile when the device is in portrait or on desktop with a taller, rather than wider, window.

10.2.1   *Triggers*

In the InputViewModel in MauiStockTake, we've got a validation check in the AddCount method to ensure the user has selected a product before allowing them to submit the count. This is a good check that prevents saving bad data, but there are two things we can improve. The first is to add a check to prevent submitting a count of zero. The second is that, rather than waiting until the user tries to submit bad data and then showing a dialog, we can just disable the submit button until the data is good to go. And we can achieve both changes with *triggers*.

In .NET MAUI, triggers allow you to define, in XAML, a way for your UI to respond to events or state changes. Triggers use Setter to define the property and value that you want to control, just like in a style. Triggers come in a few different flavors, but the two you are most likely to use are

- *Property triggers*—Property triggers let you define a change in the appearance of a control when one of the properties on that control meets a certain condition. A property trigger would work well for the previously mentioned `Switch` example.
- *Data triggers*—Data triggers let you define a change in the appearance of a control when a property on any control in the view or a property in the binding context has a certain value. We'll use data triggers for the UX changes we're making to MauiStockTake.

The important thing to note about these triggers is that they will apply the specified modification to a control when the specified condition is met and revert that modification when that condition is no longer satisfied.

> **NOTE** These triggers are different from event triggers, which do not revert the change. You can read more about the full range of triggers and their differences at the documentation here: http://mng.bz/GyDR.

Let's start by removing the existing check. In `InputViewModel`, in the `AddCount` method, **delete the `if` block that checks whether `SelectedProduct` is null**. Now let's add our two data triggers to the `InputPage.xaml` file.

We can expand both the `Stepper` and `Button` controls so they are no longer self-closing tags, and for each, we can declare its `DataTriggers` collection. We'll add a data trigger with a `Setter` that sets the `IsEnabled` property to `False` to both.

With a trigger, just like with a style, you need to define a target type, so it will be different for each one. We also need to provide a binding (the source data that the data trigger is bound to) and a value (the condition for the bound property to meet to activate the trigger). For the `Stepper`, this will be the `SelectedProduct` property of the `ViewModel`, and for the `Button`, it will be the `Count` property.

The `Count` property is already bound to the UI (there is a `Label` that shows its value), so it already has an explicit backing field, and its setter calls the `OnProperty-Changed` method. We need to do the same thing for the `SelectedProduct` property, so let's do this first. The following listing shows the updated `SelectedProduct` property declaration.

Listing 10.10 The updated `SelectedProduct` declaration

```
private ProductDto _selectedProduct;          ◁——  Adds a backing field
public ProductDto SelectedProduct             ◁——  for SelectedProduct
{
    get => _selectedProduct;                        Expands the property
    set                                             to define the getter
    {                                               and setter
        _selectedProduct = value;
        OnPropertyChanged();          ◁——  In the setter, calls the
    }                                        OnPropertyChanged
}                                            method to update the UI
```

Now that we've got a property that raises a property changed event, we can bind the UI to it. For the data trigger we're adding to the Stepper, we've set the IsEnabled property to false. Let's bind that to the SelectedProduct property to activate when its value is null. That way, the Stepper will be disabled when no product is selected and will be enabled once the user selects a product.

Because we're binding to a value that can be null (in fact, it always will be when we set the binding), we can use a *binding fallback* to set the initial value when the bound property is null. Binding fallbacks are a useful tool that you can read more about in the .NET MAUI documentation here: http://mng.bz/zXzX, but understanding them is not essential for now. The following listing shows the updated code for the Stepper in InputPage.xaml.

Listing 10.11   The updated Stepper code in `InputPage.xaml`

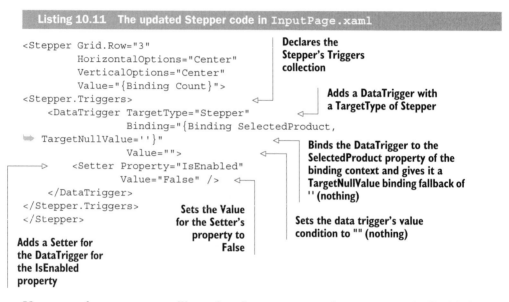

If you run the app now, you'll see that the Stepper on the InputPage is disabled until you search for a product and select one from the list.

Let's add the data trigger for the Button now. It will be almost identical to the data trigger we added to the Stepper; the differences will be the target type, the binding, and the value. The target type will be Button instead of Stepper, and the binding will be the Count property. The Count property is of type int, which has a default value of 0, so the value in the data trigger will be 0. The following listing shows the code for the updated Button in the InputPage.xaml file.

Listing 10.12   The updated `Button` code in `InputPage.xaml`

```
<Button Grid.Row="4"
        Text="Add count"
        Command="{Binding AddCountCommand}">
    <Button.Triggers>
```

```
<DataTrigger TargetType="Button"
             Binding="{Binding Count}"
             Value="0">
    <Setter Property="IsEnabled"
            Value="False"/>
</DataTrigger>
    </Button.Triggers>
</Button>
```

The binding for the Button data trigger is simple and just binds to the Count property.

The Value of the Count property must be 0 to activate this trigger.

With these changes made, you can run the app and should see that the Stepper is deactivated until you've selected a product. The Button to add the count is disabled until the Count is any number other than 0, and consequently, it is also disabled until a product is selected (a product must be selected to change the value of Count and enable the Button).

Triggers can do more than just enable and disable controls. As they use Setters, just like a style, they can modify any aspect of a control or view. Also, just like with a style, a trigger can have multiple Setters and can be used to specify a condition that modifies several aspects of a control.

10.2.2   Visual state manager

Triggers are a great way to dynamically change the appearance of controls in response to events or data changes in your app. Using triggers, you can combine Setters to customize a control based on different conditions.

Sometimes you can logically group Setters in a trigger to define the appearance of a control under a specified set of conditions. But in this case, a more efficient approach is to define a *visual state* for the control.

Visual states in .NET MAUI are managed by the *visual state manager* (VSM), a built-in tool that automatically alters the appearance of a view in response to the visual state that view is in. There are five built-in common visual states in .NET MAUI known as the "common states":

- Normal
- Disabled
- Focused
- Selected
- PointerOver

We've already seen these in action: the normal state is how controls look most of the time, and disabled is what a control looks like when the IsEnabled property is set to false (as we saw in the previous section). We've seen the selected state used in CollectionView a few times, notably in MauiTodo and in the product search results in MauiStockTake.

The selected state for the product search results CollectionView is a bit of a visual anomaly; it's not in keeping with Mildred's branding guidelines and looks out of place in all four of the app's themes. Figure 10.13 shows the currently selected state in MauiStockTake.

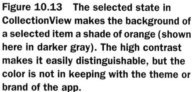

Figure 10.13 The selected state in CollectionView makes the background of a selected item a shade of orange (shown here in darker gray). The high contrast makes it easily distinguishable, but the color is not in keeping with the theme or brand of the app.

As versatile as triggers are, using them to modify the appearance of the selected item in a collection presents, at the very least, a logical challenge; but VSM makes this problem a lot simpler to solve. Let's use VSM to update the background color of the selected product in MauiStockTake.

VSM is applied in a `Style`, with VSM used as the `Setter`'s property, rather than the property of a control. As it's embedded within a `Style`, it's applied using the same hierarchy that we looked at in section 10.1.1. We're going to modify the background color of `VerticalStackLayout` (the layout used in the `CollectionView` data template), so we want to make sure we scope it accordingly.

In `InputPage.xaml`, **add a resource dictionary to the `CollectionView` used to display the product search results, and in here, add a style with a target type of `VerticalStackLayout`.** In this `Style`, we're going to add a `Setter`, with the property set to `VisualStateManager.VisualStateGroups`.

Visual state groups are used to organize sets of visual states in VSM. As mentioned, .NET MAUI comes with a built-in visual state group called `CommonStates` that defines the previously listed five visual states. Visual states in a visual state group are mutually exclusive, meaning only one visual state in a group can be active at a time. A view cannot, for example, be both `Normal` and `Selected`.

Visual states in different groups can be active simultaneously, so if you need to, you can define multiple visual state groups. You can read more about defining custom visual states at the documentation here: http://mng.bz/0KBl.

Within the `Setter` in our `Style`, we first need to declare the visual state group list. We've only got the `CommonStates` visual state group as we haven't defined any custom states, so we'll embed this in the list. In this group, we'll need to define the `Normal` and `Selected` states. For `Normal`, we'll tell VSM to do nothing because, unlike with a trigger, VSM does not revert the changes when the state is no longer active.

For the `Selected` state, we'll add a `Setter` for the `BackgroundColor` property and set it to the `Secondary` static resource. Remember that this `Setter` is embedded within a `Style` that targets `VerticalStackLayout`, so the properties we have access to here are those of the specified target type. The following listing shows the updated code for the `CollectionView` in `InputPage.xaml` that includes the VSM `Style` (nonrelevant code has been omitted).

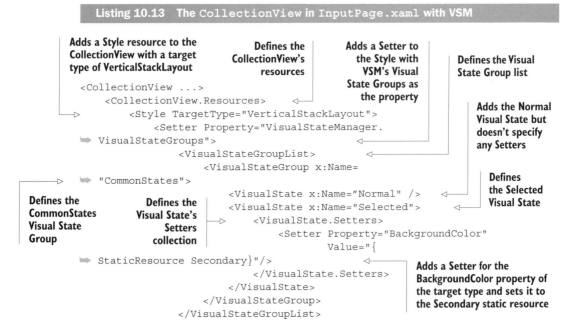

Listing 10.13   The `CollectionView` in `InputPage.xaml` with VSM

Adds a Style resource to the CollectionView with a target type of VerticalStackLayout

Defines the CollectionView's resources

Adds a Setter to the Style with VSM's Visual State Groups as the property

Defines the Visual State Group list

Adds the Normal Visual State but doesn't specify any Setters

Defines the CommonStates Visual State Group

Defines the Visual State's Setters collection

Defines the Selected Visual State

Adds a Setter for the BackgroundColor property of the target type and sets it to the Secondary static resource

```
<CollectionView ...>
    <CollectionView.Resources>
        <Style TargetType="VerticalStackLayout">
            <Setter Property="VisualStateManager.
VisualStateGroups">
                <VisualStateGroupList>
                    <VisualStateGroup x:Name=
"CommonStates">
                        <VisualState x:Name="Normal" />
                        <VisualState x:Name="Selected">
                            <VisualState.Setters>
                                <Setter Property="BackgroundColor"
                                    Value="{
StaticResource Secondary}"/>
                            </VisualState.Setters>
                        </VisualState>
                    </VisualStateGroup>
                </VisualStateGroupList>
```

```
            </Setter>
        </Style>
    </CollectionView.Resources>
    <CollectionView.ItemsLayout>
        ...
    </CollectionView.ItemsLayout>
    <CollectionView.ItemTemplate>
        ...
    </CollectionView.ItemTemplate>
</CollectionView>
```

Run the app now and search for a product. If you make a selection, you will see that the background color of the selected item is now updated. Figure 10.14 shows the result for the default theme in light mode, but you should see the appropriate `Secondary` color for whichever theme you are running.

Figure 10.14   The VSM has been used to update the `Style` for `VerticalStackLayout`, the layout used in the data template of the product search results `CollectionView`. For the `Selected` visual state, the `BackgroundColor` property is set to the `Secondary` static resource, providing a consistent look rather than the default.

Because VSM uses `Styles`, we can clean up the `InputPage` a bit by moving the `Style` out of the `CollectionView`'s resources and into the theme files. We don't want it to apply to every `VerticalStackLayout`, so we can use a key to make it an explicit `Style`. This has the added benefit that we can reuse it in other `CollectionViews` throughout our app.

Cut the `<Style...>...</Style>` tags and everything in between from the `CollectionView`'s resources and paste it into each of the theme files (wherever you like, but after the gradient brush we defined earlier is probably a good spot). **Give it a key of `ProductSelector`**.

Unlike with `Triggers`, changes that are applied when a visual state is entered are not reverted when the conditions for the visual state are no longer met. Therefore, we need to define the `Normal` visual state as well as any state that we want to customize. However, if we don't want to customize the `Normal` visual state (i.e., we want to retain the default appearance of the control), we can simply provide the `Normal` state without defining any setters. The following listing shows how the `Style` should look in each of the theme files.

Listing 10.14 The `VerticalStackLayout` VSM `Style` in the theme files

```
<Style TargetType="VerticalStackLayout" x:Key=
   "ProductSelector">
     <Setter Property="VisualStateManager.VisualStateGroups">
        <VisualStateGroupList>
           <VisualStateGroup x:Name="CommonStates">
              <VisualState x:Name="Normal" />
              <VisualState x:Name="Selected">
                 <VisualState.Setters>
                    <Setter Property="BackgroundColor"
                    Value="{StaticResource Secondary}"/>
                 </VisualState.Setters>
              </VisualState>
           </VisualStateGroup>
        </VisualStateGroupList>
     </Setter>
</Style>
```

Adds the ProductSelector key to the Style copied from the CollectionView

Now you can go back to the `CollectionView` in `InputPage.xaml` and remove the `<CollectionView.Resources>...</CollectionView.Resources>` tags, and everything in between. Add the explicit `Style` to the `VerticalStackLayout` in the `Collection-View`'s data template. The `CollectionView` should now look like the following listing.

Listing 10.15 The final `CollectionView` in `InputPage.xaml`

```
<CollectionView ...>
    <CollectionView.ItemsLayout>
    ...
    </CollectionView.ItemsLayout>
    <CollectionView.ItemTemplate>
        <DataTemplate>
```

The Resources have been removed from the CollectionView.

```
                <VerticalStackLayout Style="{
➥ StaticResource ProductSelector}">                    Adds the explicit
                    ...                                 Style to the
                </VerticalStackLayout>                  VerticalStackLayout.
            </DataTemplate>                             The Style uses VSM.
        </CollectionView.ItemTemplate>
</CollectionView>
```

Run the app again and make sure you still get the `Secondary` background color on selected products in the `CollectionView`. By moving the `Style` and making it explicit, we've cleaned up the UI code and made it reusable, which helps to maintain the consistent look and feel throughout the app.

10.3 *Multiplatform Apps*

.NET MAUI apps can run on a huge range of devices: laptop and desktop computers, phones, tablets, watches, and TVs. Sometimes the apps that you build will be targeted to a specific category of device, but often your app will need to work across many of these different device *idioms*.

Different device idioms have different UX paradigms. For example, touch and swipe gestures are ubiquitous on mobile devices, and while you can often achieve the same result with a mouse click and drag, these may not be as implicitly discoverable to desktop users, who expect to interact with your app in different ways.

There are several approaches to providing different UX for different device idioms. You can get the current idiom in code at any time by calling `DeviceInfo.Current .Idiom`. This code returns a custom struct that is essentially an enum (and can be treated as such) that will give a value of `Phone`, `Tablet`, `Desktop`, `TV`, `Watch`, or `Unknown`. You can then use this output to execute idiom-dependent logic or manipulate your UI as required. Brady Stroud has a cool sample showing this approach, using the idiom to load a different view for desktop versus all other platforms. You can see it in action in his GitHub repo here: https://github.com/bradystroud/MauiMail.

Another approach is to use compiler directives, which don't support different idioms but do let you specify a platform (note you can use `DeviceInfo.Current.Platform` to get the platform, too). You can see this approach in use in David Ortinau's WeatherTwentyOne sample, available in his GitHub repo here: https://github.com/davidortinau/WeatherTwentyOne.

This approach not only provides a more granular experience but also prevents code that is only intended to run on one platform from being compiled to other platforms. This approach is useful for apps like Verinote, mentioned in chapter 1, that have functionality available on desktop that shouldn't be available on a mobile device—someone attempting to circumvent security measures can't access functionality that simply isn't there. In this section, we're going to focus on the layout and how you can customize the appearance of the app for different platforms in XAML.

10.3.1 Adding the report page

Let's start by adding the report page. When we call the inventory from the API, there's a lot of information that might be useful to a desktop user but would overwhelm a small screen. We want to optimize the screen real estate we have for each platform. So, the report page will need to behave differently on different device idioms.

ADDING THE REPORTVIEWMODEL

We'll continue to follow the Model, View, ViewModel (MVVM) pattern with the `ReportPage`, so we'll put the functionality into a ViewModel. By following the View-Model first approach (see the sidebar "View First vs. ViewModel First" in chapter 9), we can build out this functionality (and even write tests for it) before even adding the UI.

In the `ViewModels` folder, **add a class called `ReportViewModel` that inherits `BaseViewModel`**. In this ViewModel, we'll need an `ObservableCollection` of type `InventoryItemDto` to bind the UI to, and we'll need to inject the `IInventoryService` into the constructor so that we can call the API to get the current inventory.

Add a method called `Init`. We'll call this method from the `ReportPage`'s `OnAppearing` method and add another method called `Refresh` that calls the `IInventoryService`, clears and then populates the `ObservableCollection`, and sets the `IsLoading` property from the `BaseViewModel` as required.

In the `Init` method, we can check a flag called `initialized` that has a default value of `false`. If it's `true`, we can just return from the method; otherwise, we can call `Refresh`. This approach will let us reuse the `Refresh` method, which we'll need to do later in this section and also if we later want to add `pull-to-refresh`.

This technique could be useful for other pages, so **add the `initialized` bool to the `BaseViewModel` and mark it as protected** (so it can be accessed from derived types). The following listing shows the code for the `ReportViewModel` class.

Listing 10.16 `ReportViewModel.cs`

```
using System.Collections.ObjectModel;
using MauiStockTake.Shared.Inventory.Queries;

namespace MauiStockTake.UI.ViewModels;
public class ReportViewModel : BaseViewModel
{
    private readonly IInventoryService _inventoryService;

    public ObservableCollection<InventoryItemDto> Inventory { get; set; }
    = new();

    public ReportViewModel(IInventoryService inventoryService)
    {
        _inventoryService = inventoryService;
        IsLoading = true;
    }
```

```
public async Task Init()
{
    if (initialized)
        return;

    initialised = true;

    await Refresh();
}

private async Task Refresh()
{
    IsLoading = true;
    Inventory.Clear();

    var inventory = await _inventoryService.GetInventory();

    foreach (var item in inventory)
    {
        Inventory.Add(item);
    }

    IsLoading = false;
}
}
```

Now that we've added the ReportViewModel, let's register it in the service collection so that we can inject it into our report page. In MauiProgram.cs, after the line that registers the InputViewModel, **add a line to register the ReportViewModel**:

```
builder.Services.AddTransient<ReportViewModel>();
```

That's all the logic we need to add for now, so let's move on to the UI.

ADDING THE REPORTPAGE UI

We've already got the ReportPage in MauiStockTake, but it's blank. Before we add the UI, let's add a field for the ReportViewModel to the code-behind and, in the constructor, inject the ViewModel, assign the page's Navigation property to the ViewModel's Navigation property, and set the ViewModel as the binding context. Then, override the base OnAppearing method, make it async, and call the ViewModel's Init method. The following listing shows the updated code for ReportPage.xaml.cs.

Listing 10.17 ReportPage.xaml.cs

```
namespace MauiStockTake.UI.Pages;

public partial class ReportPage : ContentPage
{
    private readonly ReportViewModel _viewModel;

    public ReportPage(ReportViewModel viewModel)
    {
```

```
        InitializeComponent();
        viewModel.Navigation = Navigation;
        _viewModel = viewModel;
        BindingContext = _viewModel;
    }

    protected override async void OnAppearing()
    {
        base.OnAppearing();

        await _viewModel.Init();
    }
}
```

We're almost ready to build the UI, but as `ReportPage` no longer has a default constructor, we need to register it for dependency injection. **In `MauiProgram.cs`, after the line that registers the `InputPage`, add a line to register the `ReportPage`:**

```
builder.Services.AddTransient<ReportPage>();
```

Now that we've wired everything up, let's add the UI. The main layout for this page will be a `CollectionView`, bound to the `Inventory` property of the ViewModel, but we'll wrap it in a `Grid` so that we can overlay an `ActivityIndicator` bound to the `IsLoading` (inherited) property on the ViewModel.

We'll explicitly set the `CollectionView`'s `ItemsLayout` property as `LinearItemLayout` so that we can specify the `ItemSpacing` as 30 to give us a bit of space between inventory items. Then, in the `DataTemplate`, we'll use a `Border` and `Shadow` to give us a card-like effect and then a `Grid` to lay out the product name and the number currently counted in inventory. We'll use `AppThemeBinding` for the various colors on the card so that they work with both themes in light and dark mode. The following listing shows the updated `ReportPage.xaml` file.

Listing 10.18 `ReportPage.xaml`

```xml
<?xml version="1.0" encoding="utf-8" ?>
<ContentPage xmlns="http://schemas.microsoft.com/dotnet/2021/maui"
             xmlns:x="http://schemas.microsoft.com/winfx/2009/xaml"
             x:Class="MauiStockTake.UI.Pages.ReportPage"
             Title="ReportPage">
    <Grid>
        <ActivityIndicator HorizontalOptions="Center"
                           VerticalOptions="Center"
                           IsEnabled="True"
                           IsRunning="True"
                           IsVisible="{Binding IsLoading}"/>
        <CollectionView HorizontalOptions="Center"
                        Margin="30"
                        ItemsSource="{Binding Inventory}">
            <CollectionView.ItemsLayout>
                <LinearItemsLayout ItemSpacing="30"
                                   Orientation="Vertical"/>
```

```
                    </CollectionView.ItemsLayout>
                    <CollectionView.ItemTemplate>
                        <DataTemplate>
                            <Border StrokeShape="RoundRectangle 10"
                                    Stroke="Transparent"
                                    BackgroundColor="{AppThemeBinding Light={
    StaticResource PrimaryBackground}, Dark={StaticResource
    PrimaryDarkBackground}}">
                                <Grid ColumnDefinitions="4*, *"
                                      Margin="20">
                                    <Label Grid.Column="0"
                                           TextColor="{AppThemeBinding
        Light={StaticResource Primary}, Dark={StaticResource PrimaryDark}}"
                                           FontSize="24"
                                           Text="{Binding ProductName}"/>
                                    <Label Grid.Column="1"
                                           FontSize="24"
                                           TextColor="{AppThemeBinding
        Light={StaticResource Primary}, Dark={StaticResource PrimaryDark}}"
                                           HorizontalTextAlignment="Center"
                                           Text="{Binding Count}"/>
                                </Grid>
                                <Border.Shadow>
                                    <Shadow Brush="{AppThemeBinding
        Light={StaticResource SecondaryBackground}, Dark={StaticResource
    SecondaryDarkBackground}}"
                                            Offset="-5,-5"
                                            Radius="10"
                                            Opacity="0.8"/>
                                </Border.Shadow>
                            </Border>
                        </DataTemplate>
                    </CollectionView.ItemTemplate>
                </CollectionView>
        </Grid>
</ContentPage>
```

We're not doing anything new here; we've seen similar card views in other apps we've built, and we've seen AppThemeBinding earlier in this chapter. This logic gives us a basic layout that will work well on mobile. If you run the app now and open the report page, you should see something similar to figure 10.15.

This layout works well on a phone, but it has two problems on desktop (or tablet). The first is that it looks terrible (you can run it now on Windows or macOS to see how it looks on desktop). The second is that the minimal information that we've pared down to for the mobile display isn't an efficient use of screen real estate.

10.3.2 *Multiplatform layouts*

We've seen how you can use the DeviceInfo API to get information about the current platform or idiom your app is running on (in fact, you can get a lot more information from the API). This approach is good if you need it in your C# code, and in XAML, we can use markup extensions, such as OnIdiom. Using OnIdiom, you can specify different

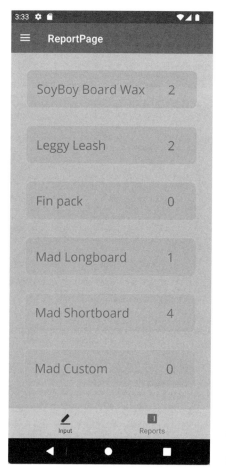

Figure 10.15   The `ReportPage` running on Android. The card layout works on a small screen and presents only the minimal information required, which is the product name and current inventory count.

values for different platforms directly in XAML for any property of any view. Let's look at the example in figure 10.16.

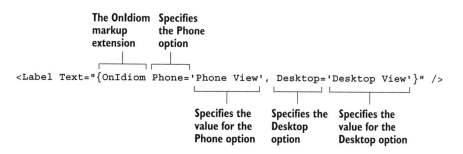

Figure 10.16   The `OnIdiom` markup extension is used to specify different values depending on the device idiom. In this example, different strings are assigned to the `Text` property of a label depending on whether it is running on a desktop or a phone.

Like the `DeviceIdiom` struct, `OnIdiom` lets you specify values for `Phone`, `Tablet`, `Desktop`, `Watch`, or `TV`, but instead of `Unknown`, it has an option for `Default`. So, you don't necessarily need to specify a value of each idiom; you can specify your standard value and just change it for the idiom you want to modify.

Let's start by updating some of the spacing. **In the `LinearItemsLayout` tag, change it from 30 to 10 for desktop, 30 for phone, and a default value of 20**. That line should now look like this:

```
<LinearItemsLayout ItemSpacing="{OnIdiom Desktop=10, Phone=30, Default=20}"
```

For the `Margin` property in the `Grid`, change from 20 to a default value of 0 and 20 on phone. That line should now look like this:

```
Margin="{OnIdiom Phone=20, Default=0}">
```

Next, let's change the `BackgroundColor` of the `Border` so that it only shows the bound color on phone. **Wrap current `AppThemeBinding` as a value for `Phone` and set the default to `Transparent`.** That line should now look like this:

```
BackgroundColor="{OnIdiom Phone={AppThemeBinding Light={StaticResource
⇒ PrimaryBackground}, Dark={StaticResource PrimaryDarkBackground}},
⇒ Default=Transparent}">
```

This code will give us a better layout for desktop, but ideally, we'd display the information in tabular form and expose more of the data. We can use the `OnIdiom` markup extension to specify a different number of columns. We'll use two for phone, as we have been doing, but five for desktop so that we can show the product name, manufacturer name, count, date counted, and who counted it.

On phone, as we only have two columns, we want the second column to show the count, but on desktop, as we have more columns to play with, we can move the count further along and show the manufacturer name in the second column, by specifying a different binding depending on the idiom. To add the extra columns, we can simply add the `Labels` we need, placing them in the appropriate columns, and we can use `OnIdiom` to set the `IsVisible` property depending on whether we're on phone or desktop.

As we're now displaying this information as a table, we should add some headers. We can specify the `CollectionView.Header` property, and in here, we'll add a `Grid` with five columns, with the same definitions as the desktop view in the data template. We'll use `OnIdiom` to make the whole `Grid` invisible on phone but visible on desktop.

Inside this `Grid`, we can add five `Labels`, which will be almost identical to the `Labels` in the data template. The differences will be that the `FontAttributes` will be set to bold, and the column headers will be hard-coded.

The last bit of flair to include for desktop is to add a data trigger to the `Label` that shows the date counted. As the value is a `DateTime`, the DTO has a default value of `DateTime.Minimum` if no explicit value is returned from the database. This happens when no counts have been recorded for that item, so we can use a data trigger to set the `Text` property of the `Label` to `No stock counted` when this occurs.

> **NOTE** You could achieve the same result by binding the data trigger to the `Count` property and using `0` as the value. But this approach demonstrates the versatility of data triggers.

The following listing shows the updated code for `ReportPage.xaml`, including all the `OnIdiom` markup extensions and the added data trigger.

Listing 10.19 The final `ReportPage.xaml` code

```xml
<?xml version="1.0" encoding="utf-8" ?>
<ContentPage ...>
    <Grid>
        <ActivityIndicator .../>
        <CollectionView ...>
            <CollectionView.ItemsLayout>
                <LinearItemsLayout ItemSpacing="{OnIdiom Desktop=10, Phone=
30, Default=20}"

                                    Orientation="Vertical"/>
            </CollectionView.ItemsLayout>
            <CollectionView.Header>
                <Grid IsVisible="{OnIdiom Phone=False,
Desktop=True}"

                      ColumnDefinitions="2*, 2*, *, 2*, 2*">
                    <Label Grid.Column="0"
                           Text="Product"
                           FontSize="24"
                           FontAttributes="Bold"/>
                    <Label Grid.Column="1"
                           Text="Manufacturer"
                           FontSize="24"
                           FontAttributes="Bold"/>
                    <Label Grid.Column="2"
                           Text="Count"
                           FontSize="24"
                           FontAttributes="Bold"/>
                    <Label Grid.Column="3"
                           Text="Counted By"
                           FontSize="24"
                           FontAttributes="Bold"/>
                    <Label Grid.Column="4"
                           Text="Counted On"
                           FontSize="24"
                           FontAttributes="Bold"/>
                </Grid>
            </CollectionView.Header>
```

Uses OnIdiom to specify the item spacing for different idioms

The entire Grid header can be made visible on desktop but hidden on phone. That way, no additional idiom specificity is required for the controls in this view.

The Border is there to provide the card view on phone. On desktop, this is tabular so we can make the background transparent.

```
<CollectionView.ItemTemplate>
    <DataTemplate>
        <Border StrokeShape="RoundRectangle 10"
                Stroke="Transparent"
                BackgroundColor="{OnIdiom Phone={AppThemeBinding
Light={StaticResource PrimaryBackground}, Dark={StaticResource
PrimaryDarkBackground}}, Default=
Transparent}">
```

On phone, we only have two columns, but on desktop, we have five.

```
            <Grid ColumnDefinitions="{
OnIdiom Phone='4*, *', Desktop='2*, 2*, *, 2*, 2*'}"
```

The Grid needs a margin on phone for the card view. On desktop, this is a table row, so the margin is not required.

```
                  Margin="{OnIdiom Phone=20, Default=0}">
                <Label Grid.Column="0"
                       TextColor="{AppThemeBinding
Light={StaticResource Primary}, Dark={StaticResource PrimaryDark}}"
                       FontSize="24"
                       Text="{Binding ProductName}"/>
                <Label Grid.Column="1"
                       FontSize="24"
                       TextColor="{AppThemeBinding
Light={StaticResource Primary}, Dark={StaticResource PrimaryDark}}"
                       HorizontalText
```

On phone, the count label should be centered. On desktop, it should be left aligned (default) to match the header and other columns.

```
Alignment="{OnIdiom Phone=Center}"
                       Text="{OnIdiom
Phone={Binding Count}, Desktop={Binding ManufacturerName}}"/>
                <Label Grid.Column="2"
                       TextColor="{AppThemeBinding
Light={StaticResource Primary}, Dark={StaticResource PrimaryDark}}"
                       FontSize="24"
                       Text="{Binding Count}"
                       IsVisible="{OnIdiom
Phone=False, Desktop=True}"/>
```

The remaining columns will only be visible on desktop and hidden on phone.

```
                <Label Grid.Column="3"
                       FontSize="24"
                       TextColor="{AppThemeBinding
Light={StaticResource Primary}, Dark={StaticResource PrimaryDark}}"
                       Text="{Binding CountedByName}"
                       IsVisible="{OnIdiom Phone=False,
Desktop=True}"/>
                <Label Grid.Column="4"
                       FontSize="24"
                       TextColor="{AppThemeBinding
Light={StaticResource Primary}, Dark={StaticResource PrimaryDark}}"
                       Text="{Binding CountedAt}"
                       IsVisible="{OnIdiom Phone=False,
Desktop=True}">
```

On desktop, the value of the second column will be the manufacturer's name (as the count will be in the next column). On phone, we are only showing product name and count, so count needs to be in the second column.

```
                                        <Label.Triggers>
                                          <DataTrigger TargetType="Label"
                                                       Binding="{Binding CountedAt}"
                                                       Value
```

="1/1/0001">

A data trigger can be used to provide an alternative value when the DateTime is set to the default of DateTime.Minimum.

```
                                            <Setter Property="Text"
                                                    Value="No stock counted"/>
                                          </DataTrigger>
                                        </Label.Triggers>
                                      </Label>
                                    </Grid>
                                  <Border.Shadow>
                                    <Shadow Brush="{AppThemeBinding
                  Light={StaticResource SecondaryBackground}, Dark={
              StaticResource SecondaryDarkBackground}}"
                                            Offset="-5,-5"
                                            Radius="10"
                                            Opacity="0.8"/>
                                  </Border.Shadow>
                                </Border>
                              </DataTemplate>
                          </CollectionView.ItemTemplate>
                      </CollectionView>
                  </Grid>
</ContentPage>
```

Run the app now on desktop and go to the report page. You should see all the information displayed in a nice tabular view, like figure 10.17.

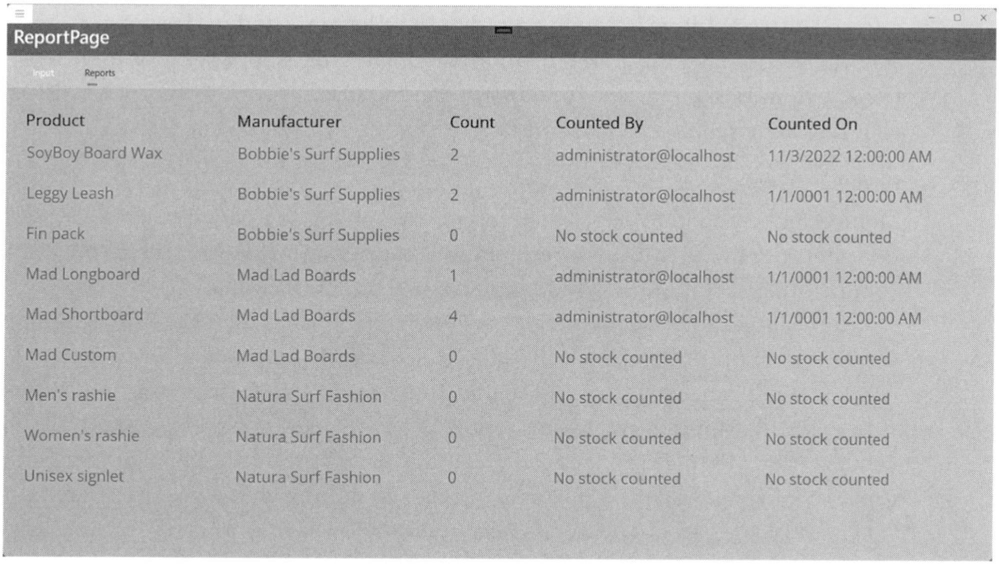

Product	Manufacturer	Count	Counted By	Counted On
SoyBoy Board Wax	Bobbie's Surf Supplies	2	administrator@localhost	11/3/2022 12:00:00 AM
Leggy Leash	Bobbie's Surf Supplies	2	administrator@localhost	1/1/0001 12:00:00 AM
Fin pack	Bobbie's Surf Supplies	0	No stock counted	No stock counted
Mad Longboard	Mad Lad Boards	1	administrator@localhost	1/1/0001 12:00:00 AM
Mad Shortboard	Mad Lad Boards	4	administrator@localhost	1/1/0001 12:00:00 AM
Mad Custom	Mad Lad Boards	0	No stock counted	No stock counted
Men's rashie	Natura Surf Fashion	0	No stock counted	No stock counted
Women's rashie	Natura Surf Fashion	0	No stock counted	No stock counted
Unisex signlet	Natura Surf Fashion	0	No stock counted	No stock counted

Figure 10.17   The ReportPage running on Windows. The OnIdiom markup extension is used to change the way the information is displayed, providing additional information and a tabular layout compared to the simple card view shown on phones.

Run the app again on Android or iOS; you should note no change from before, and it should look the same as in figure 10.15.

If you look at the examples linked to at the start of this section, you can see how you can load different views for different idioms and platforms. Using the approach here, you can see that we can customize the display for different platforms and idioms, all within the same view.

Exercise

There is one final change we need to make to the report page. The CollectionView won't respond to theme changes, so we need a way to tell it to refresh when the theme has changed. To do this, you can use the WeakReferenceMessenger in the MVVM Community Toolkit. You can read about it in the documentation (http://mng .bz/KedZ) or in James Montemagno's video (https://youtu.be/vD17OetzGXc). You can also see my solution in the chapter-complete folder.

WARNING If you have come from Xamarin.Forms, you might be tempted to use MessagingCenter for the exercise; however, MessagingCenter has been deprecated and will be removed from .NET MAUI in .NET 8. Use Weak-ReferenceMessenger in your apps now instead.

10.3.3 *Features of desktop apps*

Providing a desktop-specific layout is the most important thing you can do to provide a good UX for desktop users. It will give your app a professional feel that distinguishes it from "lift and shifted" mobile apps that have been ported to desktop.

But you can take this a step further by utilizing the UX paradigms users have come to expect on desktop OSes: fundamentally, menus, and windows. Let's finish off this chapter by seeing how you can add these to your .NET MAUI app.

MENUS

Menus can be added to pages in an app by specifying the page's MenuBarItems collection. Because the menu bar is only shown on desktop, you don't need to use OnIdiom (or any other technique) to hide it on mobile or other idioms.

Menus are added at the top level by specifying a MenuBarItem, and these menus can be made up of MenuFlyoutItems, which display text and offer an action to execute, or MenuFlyoutSubItems, which let you group MenuFlyoutItems into submenus.

Let's add a menu now to the report page. In the ReportPage.xaml file, add the ContentPage.MenuBarItems tags before the Grid and add a MenuBarItem with Text property of Help. Add a single MenuFlyoutItem in here with a Text property of About.

MenuFlyoutItem has a Clicked event and a Command property. You can use either of these to execute an action when your user clicks on the menu item, with either an event handler in your code-behind or a command in your binding context. The following listing shows the menu added to the report page.

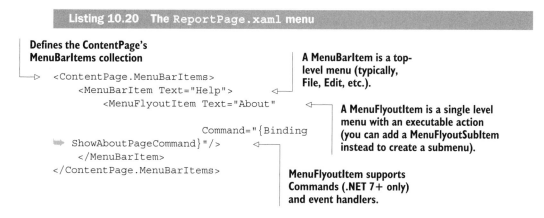

Listing 10.20   The `ReportPage.xaml` menu

**Defines the ContentPage's
MenuBarItems collection**

```
<ContentPage.MenuBarItems>
    <MenuBarItem Text="Help">
        <MenuFlyoutItem Text="About"

                      Command="{Binding
    ShowAboutPageCommand}"/>
    </MenuBarItem>
</ContentPage.MenuBarItems>
```

**A MenuBarItem is a top-
level menu (typically,
File, Edit, etc.).**

**A MenuFlyoutItem is a single level
menu with an executable action
(you can add a MenuFlyoutSubItem
instead to create a submenu).**

**MenuFlyoutItem supports
Commands (.NET 7+ only)
and event handlers.**

You can run the app now if you like, and if you navigate to the report page, you'll see the Help menu displayed in the top left, as in figure 10.18, next to the title bar. If you try to click on the About menu item now, it won't work, but in the next section, we'll add the About page and get the app to display it in a window.

Figure 10.18   The `ReportPage` with a Help menu added. The Help menu has a single menu item called About.

WINDOWS

When you launch a .NET MAUI app on Windows or macOS, an initial window is created, and the app's `MainPage` is loaded into this window. In the `blankmaui` template, we assigned a content page to this property, and in the default template Shell is assigned to it, which becomes the content of the app's main window.

But you can also create additional windows and assign your own pages to them programmatically. Let's add a page to make the About menu work. **In the Pages folder in MauiStockTake, add a new XAML page called AboutPage.** The content of this page should be a VerticalStackLayout with spacing 30 containing three Labels. All three Labels should be centered and have horizontal text alignment. Assign the first Label's text property Welcome to MauiStockTake, v1.0 to the second, and Copyright Mildred's Surf Shack 2023 to the third. Assign them the font sizes of Header, Title, and Large, respectively.

Now that we've got a page to show in the About window, let's add a method to the ReportViewModel to show it. We'll need to create a new instance of the Window type, and we can pass a ContentPage to its constructor (or directly assign one to its Page property). It's a good idea to set the Title property, as well as the Height and Width. When we're ready, we can call Application.Current.OpenWindow and pass in our Window instance. The method to add to ReportViewModel should look like the following listing.

Listing 10.21 The ShowAboutPage method in ReportViewModel

```
public void ShowAboutPage()
{
    var newWindow = new Window(new AboutPage())
    {
        Title = "About",
        Width = 300,
        Height = 300
    };
    Application.Current.OpenWindow(newWindow);
}
```

Add the ShowAboutPageCommand property (of type ICommand) to the ReportViewModel:

```
public ICommand ShowAboutPageCommand { get; set; }
```

Then, in the constructor, assign the method to it via a new Command instance:

```
ShowAboutPageCommand = new Command(ShowAboutPage);
```

Windows are a staple of desktop apps, but they are also supported on iOS and Android (depending on your system). What we've done so far will work fine for Windows and Android, but there are a couple more steps necessary to enable multiwindowing on macOS and iOS. The first thing we need to do is create a SceneDelegate. A Scene in iOS and Mac Catalyst is a running instance of your app and is responsible for managing your app's windows and UI.

   The following listing shows the code for the `SceneDelegate` to add into the iOS and MacCatalyst platform folders in MauiStockTake. Take care to update the namespace accordingly.

> **Listing 10.22 The `SceneDelegate.cs` file**

```
using Foundation;

namespace MauiStockTake.UI.Platforms.[iOS/MacCatalyst];

[Register("SceneDelegate")]
public class SceneDelegate : MauiUISceneDelegate
{
}
```

◁── **Removes the square brackets and just keeps the appropriate platform namespace**

   The final step is to update the `info.plist` file to declare that you're using multiple scenes. Add the key and dictionary in the following listing to the `info.plist` file in both the iOS and MacCatalyst platform folders.

> **Listing 10.23 The multiwindow key to add to `info.plist`**

```
<key>UIApplicationSceneManifest</key>
<dict>
  <key>UIApplicationSupportsMultipleScenes</key>
  <true/>
  <key>UISceneConfigurations</key>
  <dict>
    <key>UIWindowSceneSessionRoleApplication</key>
    <array>
      <dict>
        <key>UISceneConfigurationName</key>
        <string>__MAUI_DEFAULT_SCENE_CONFIGURATION__</string>
        <key>UISceneDelegateClassName</key>
        <string>SceneDelegate</string>
      </dict>
    </array>
  </dict>
</dict>
```

   Run the app now and go to the `ReportPage`. Click on the Help menu and then the About menu item. It should open your `AboutPage` in a new window, just like in figure 10.19.

Figure 10.19   The `AboutPage` for MauiStockTake shown in a new wndow. It is just a `ContentPage`, like the other `ContentPages` in our app, but it's been assigned to the `Page` property of an instance of the `Window` class. This instance can then be shown using the `OpenWindow` method.

Summary

- `Styles` are collections of `Setters` that modify the values of properties on a control.
- Styles can be implicit or explicit. With implicit styles, you can apply visual changes to all instances of a control in your app. With explicit styles, you can limit the changes only to specific instances.
- A hierarchy is used to determine the final appearance of a control. App-wide `Styles` are applied first, but page-specific `Styles` take precedence. Layout or control-specific `Styles` take higher precedence than page `Styles`, and explicit `Styles` override any other `Style`. Property values set directly on a control override any value in a `Style`.
- You can bind to the device's light or dark mode setting using `AppThemeBinding`. This makes it easy to provide light and dark mode views for your app.
- You can use `DynamicResource` to change themes and colors at run time.
- Data triggers let you respond to changes in your app's state at run time. You can change any property of any layout or control in response to a state or value change anywhere in your app.
- `VisualStateManager` lets you group `Setters` into a visual state. Visual states are collected in visual state groups. Five states called common states come built into .NET MAUI (`Normal`, `Selected`, `Disabled`, `Focused`, and `PointerOver`), but you can define your own, too.

- .NET MAUI apps can run on a range of different devices, including laptop and desktop computers, phones, TVs, and watches. Which one of these the app is running on is called the *device idiom*.
- There are several ways to modify your app for different platforms. You can use compiler directives to control what code gets compiled to which platforms, and the `DeviceInfo` API can provide the current platform or idiom at run time.
- The `OnIdiom` markup extension can let you define different views and layouts for different platforms, all within the same XAML file.
- Different UX paradigms are common on different idioms. With .NET MAUI, you can have menus and multiwindows in your apps to cater to desktop users.

Beyond the basics:
Custom controls

This chapter covers

- Building reusable components with templated controls
- Creating your own bindable properties
- Modifying the default controls with handlers
- A recap on code sharing

.NET MAUI comes with enough controls to let you build almost any UI. Functionally, there is very little that you can't do using just the standard controls, and they are highly customizable through styles and various styling properties. But, sometimes, you need to go a little further.

In .NET MAUI you have a few ways to build or customize controls, from bundling controls into a reusable component, to customizing the platform implementations that come in the box, to drawing your own controls and graphics with the `Microsoft.Maui.Graphics` library.

> **NOTE** `Microsoft.Maui.Graphics` is a powerful library capable of sophisticated image generation and manipulation. Drawing your own controls is only a small subset of what it's capable of. If you're interested in learning more, see http://mng.bz/9D8o.

In this chapter, we'll look at the first two of these three approaches. We'll start by building our own control by reusing the built-in controls, and we'll also see how we can modify the way that .NET MAUI displays the built-in controls by default.

11.1   Using ContentView

Componentization is a core feature of every modern UI framework. While you can build your whole UI using the elementary controls that come in the box, a more efficient approach is to combine these controls into reusable components.

If you've worked with any modern UI framework before, you'll be familiar with this approach; it's used in Blazor, Angular, React, Flutter, and countless others. The terminology differs across frameworks, but it's usually some variation of "reusable components." In .NET MAUI, these reusable components are built using ContentView.

Let's look at an example from MauiStockTake. On the input page, we need to allow users to record how many of a specific item they have counted, and we need to display this count to the user. This functionality is provided by combining two controls, as shown in figure 11.1.

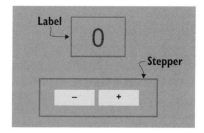

Figure 11.1   Label and a Stepper are used to display the current count and allow the user to input the current count, respectively. Anywhere else this functionality is required, we need to add both controls again.

We have a UX problem with the app, as we mentioned earlier, which is that it's problematic for larger numbers, especially anything greater than 10. Can you imagine trying to enter 546 using just a stepper? We can build a custom control that will solve this UX problem. A common solution to this problem is to provide an input field with a Stepper built into it, as in figure 11.2.

Figure 11.2   An input field for entering numerical values. The user can type a number in and use the up and down arrows to increase and decrease the value, respectively.

This stepper works well in forms on the web and can work on desktop too, but it isn't particularly touch-friendly and, therefore, isn't a great choice for mobile. Instead, we can combine it with the existing design to create a custom stepper control with an editable value field built in, as shown in figure 11.3.

Figure 11.3   A templated control made up of two Buttons and an Entry. The Buttons can be used to increase or decrease the value of a bound property, and the Entry can be used to edit it directly.

We could just build these controls directly into the UI, and while dropping an `Entry` and a couple of `Button`s onto a page as and when we need them isn't particularly laborious, building a templated control lets us reuse the UI and saves us having to solve the problem every time we encounter it. And the more complex the UI, the more value there is in making it a reusable component.

TIP   Be on the lookout for opportunities to bundle parts of your UI for reuse. Don't repeat yourself!

11.1.1 *Building the custom stepper layout*

Let's get started building the custom stepper control. **Add a folder to `MauiStock-Take.UI` called `Controls`.** In here, we're going to add a .NET MAUI ContentView (XAML). You can do this from the context menu in Visual Studio or using the .NET CLI.

Add a new `ContentView` called `MildredStepper`. The layout for this control will be a `Grid`, with one row and three columns (one for each `Button` and one for the `Entry` in the middle). The `Width` of the `Button` columns will be `50`, and the `Width` of the `Entry` column will be `120` (to accommodate larger numbers). We'll vertically and horizontally center everything and use a large font size (42 point) for the number, the same as what we have now for the `Label` that displays the count.

We'll need event handlers on all three controls so that we can set a value property. The last thing we need to do is set `MinimumWidthRequest` for the `Button`s to `50`. `MinimumWidthRequest` is set in the theme as `100` (from the default `Style`), so we need to override it so that the buttons can fit inside their columns. The following listing shows the code for the custom stepper's layout.

Listing 11.1   The custom stepper layout

```xml
<?xml version="1.0" encoding="utf-8" ?>
<ContentView xmlns="http://schemas.microsoft.com/dotnet/2021/maui"
             xmlns:x="http://schemas.microsoft.com/winfx/2009/xaml"
             x:Class="MauiStockTake.UI.Controls.MildredStepper">
    <Grid ColumnDefinitions="50,120,50">
        <Button Grid.Column="0"
                Text="-"
                Clicked="MinusButton_Clicked"
                x:Name="MinusButton"
                VerticalOptions="Center"
                HorizontalOptions="Center"
                MinimumWidthRequest="50"/>
        <Entry Grid.Column="1"
               x:Name="ValueEntry"
               FontSize="42"
               HorizontalTextAlignment="Center"
               TextChanged="ValueEntry_TextChanged"
               VerticalOptions="Center"
               HorizontalOptions="Center"/>
        <Button Grid.Column="2"
                Text="+"
```

```
                    Clicked="PlusButton_Clicked"
                    x:Name="PlusButton"
                    VerticalOptions="Center"
                    HorizontalOptions="Center"
                    MinimumWidthRequest="50"/>
        </Grid>
</ContentView>
```

The `Buttons` and the `Entry` all have event handlers defined, so we need to add them in the code-behind. We'll need a property to store the value, and when the Text-Changed event is fired, we'll need to get the `Text` value of the `Entry`, parse it to an `int`, and assign it to the property. When one of the `Buttons` is clicked, we'll need to increase or decrease the value of the property and then cast it to a `string` and assign it to the `Text` property of the `Entry`. The following listing shows the code for `Mildred-Stepper.xaml.cs` file.

> **Listing 11.2 The `MildredStepper.xaml.cs` file**

```
namespace MauiStockTake.UI.Controls;

public partial class MildredStepper : ContentView
{
    public int Value { get; set; }

    public MildredStepper()
    {
        InitializeComponent();
         ValueEntry.Text = "0";
    }

    private void MinusButton_Clicked(object sender, EventArgs e)
    {
        Value--;
        ValueEntry.Text = Value.ToString();
    }

    private void PlusButton_Clicked(object sender, EventArgs e)
    {
        Value++;
        ValueEntry.Text = Value.ToString();
    }

    private void ValueEntry_TextChanged(object sender,
➥ TextChangedEventArgs e)
    {
        if (int.TryParse(e.NewTextValue, out var value))
        {
            Value = value;
        }
    }
}
```

Now that we've built our custom stepper control, we can use it in the input page. When adding things to our XAML files that are not part of the standard .NET MAUI controls and markup extensions, we need to add an XML namespace (just as we have done for `Behaviors` in the .NET MAUI Community Toolkit).

We currently have two rows of the `Grid` allocated for this functionality (one for the `Label` and one for the `Stepper`). We only need one row with our custom control, so we need to adjust the row definitions and the row allocation for the add count `Button` (previously in row 4; it will now be row 3). The following listing shows the updates to make to the `InputPage.xaml` file.

> **Listing 11.3   The updated `InputPage.xaml` file**

```xml
<?xml version="1.0" encoding="utf-8" ?>
<ContentPage xmlns="http://schemas.microsoft.com/dotnet/2021/maui"
             xmlns:x="http://schemas.microsoft.com/winfx/2009/xaml"
             x:Class="MauiStockTake.UI.Pages.InputPage"
             xmlns:controls="clr-namespace:
  MauiStockTake.UI.Controls"
             Title="InputPage">
    <Grid Padding="20"
          RowDefinitions="*, 3*, 4*, 1*">
        <SearchBar .../>

        <CollectionView Grid.Row="1" ...>
            ...
        </CollectionView>

        <ActivityIndicator Grid.Row="1" .../>

        <controls:MildredStepper Grid.Row="2"
                                 HorizontalOptions="Center"
                                 VerticalOptions="Center"/>

        <Button Grid.Row="3"
            ...
        </Button>
    </Grid>
</ContentPage>
```

Adds an XML namespace to refer to the Controls namespace in the app that contains the custom stepper control

Adjusts the row definitions. Previously, there were five rows. Rows 2 and 3 had definitions of 2 and 2*; we've combined these into a single row of 4*.*

Adds the custom stepper control to row 2, referencing it using the XML namespace imported at the top of the file; vertically and horizontally centers it

Moves the Button from row 4 to row 3 (row 4 isn't defined anymore)

You can run the app now, and you'll see that the `Label` and `Stepper` have been replaced with our new custom control. You can click the plus and minus `Buttons` to increase and decrease the count, and you can click directly into the `Entry` to edit the number directly.

This setup is good so far, but the `Stepper` and `Label` that this control has replaced had bindings to the ViewModel; our custom control doesn't have that. This feature is pretty important, and we'll fix that in section 11.2. But before we do, let's add a couple of UX improvements.

11.1.2 *Improving the custom stepper's UX*

There are a couple of small changes we can make to the custom stepper control that will significantly improve the UX. The first is that it's possible to enter a negative number, either via the `Entry` or using the `Buttons`. Let's start by putting a check on the minus `Button` to ensure it doesn't decrease the number to less than 0.

In the `MinusButton_Clicked` event handler, **add a check to ensure the value is greater than 0 before decreasing it**:

```
private void MinusButton_Clicked(object sender, EventArgs e)
{
    if (Value > 0)
    {
        Value--;
        ValueEntry.Text = Value.ToString();
    }
}
```

Once the number reaches 0, clicking on the minus `Button` won't do anything. Let's add a simple check to the `Entry` event handler, too. Before we parse the number, let's check to see whether the new value begins with "-". If it does, we can reset the `Text` property of the `Entry` back to the current value and exit out of the event handler. **Add the following code inside the event hander before parsing the new value**:

```
if (e.NewTextValue.StartsWith("-"))
{
    ValueEntry.Text = Value.ToString();
    return;
}
```

This will prevent users from accidentally trying to record a negative stock count.

Validation

Usually in a UI app, you would validate all user input. What we've done here is *almost* validation, but it's not quite for one reason: we don't provide any feedback to the user.

Validation can take many forms, for example, ensuring an entered value is a number between a certain range, checking that it's in an approved list, verifying that it's an email address, and so on. With validation, a user is not prevented from entering an invalid number but rather is informed that the entry is invalid and prevented from submitting the form.

We've done the last part already (disabled the add count button), but we're not giving the user any feedback. In .NET MAUI, you have a lot of options for implementing validation. We could expand what we've done already by adding a `Label` to the UI that displays a warning message and only make it visible when the validation has failed.

(continued)

Additional validation can be done with bindable properties, which we're going to look at in the next section. But the best way to get started is to look in the .NET MAUI Community Toolkit. The toolkit has a handful of common validations included as behaviors that are simple to implement in your .NET MAUI apps. To find out more, see http://mng.bz/jP6p.

The second UX improvement is to provide the user with the right keyboard when they enter values directly. When you run the app, if you edit the value in the custom stepper, you'll use the regular keyboard, which has a full set of keys and a small row of buttons along the top. We only want numbers entered here, and we can make this easier for the user by giving them a numeric keyboard. To do this, **set the `Keyboard` property of the `Entry` in the `MildredSTepper.xaml` file to `Numeric`.** If you run the app again now, you will see a numeric keypad when editing this field.

Improving input UX in .NET MAUI

You can improve the UX in many cases by providing the right keyboard for your user. If you need the user to input numbers, use the numeric keyboard. The email keyboard provides quick access to the @ symbol and common top-level domains. The keyboard types you can use are `Default`, `Chat`, `Email`, `Numeric`, `Plain`, `Telephone`, `Text`, and `URL`.

You can also improve input UX in other ways. For example, for a password field, you can set `IsPassword` to `true`, and it will mask the input as the user types it, transforming their entered characters into asterisks.

The .NET MAUI Community Toolkit includes a `MaskedBehavior`, which can be attached to an `Entry` to make the input match a specific pattern. `MaskedBehavior` is particularly useful for credit card numbers or specific telephone number formats. You can find out more about it here: http://mng.bz/Wzmw.

Note that these are UX improvements only; a user can still bypass them, which is why it's important to combine them with the previously mentioned validation techniques.

Our custom stepper control is now almost complete. The last thing we need to do is provide a way to get the value out of the control and into the parent page or layout.

11.2   *Bindable properties*

A core concept in .NET MAUI is *bindable properties*. These are an extension of the class properties you are familiar with in .NET (i.e., a public class member with a getter and setter) but with additional functionality that enables, among other things, data binding.

NOTE Bindable properties provide a lot more functionality, and to get an idea of everything they can do, I recommend looking through the documentation here: http://mng.bz/8r8B.

In chapter 3, when we first looked at data binding, we noted that data binding occurs from a source to a target, as in figure 11.4.

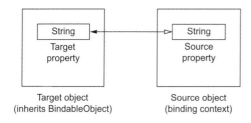

Figure 11.4 A binding occurs from a source object (the binding context) to a target object. The target object (the view) must inherit `BindableObject`, and the target *property* must be a bindable property.

The target of a binding must inherit the `BindableObject` base class. The custom stepper we have created is a `ContentView`, which is a descendant of `BindableObject`. But the target *property* of a binding must be a bindable property (the source of a binding can be a regular property, as we have seen with the ViewModels we've been using so far).

For example, we previously bound the `Value` property of a `Stepper` and the `Text` property of a `Label` (the targets) to properties in a ViewModel (the sources). `Stepper.Value` and `Label.Text` are bindable properties. The `Value` property in the `Mildred-Stepper` control is a property but not a *bindable* property, which means that if we tried to add this to the input page it wouldn't work:

```
<controls:MildredStepper Value="{Binding Count}">
```

But we need this functionality, so we need to make `Value` a bindable property. We're going to wrap the inner workings of our control and expose a value externally via a bindable property, as shown in figure 11.5.

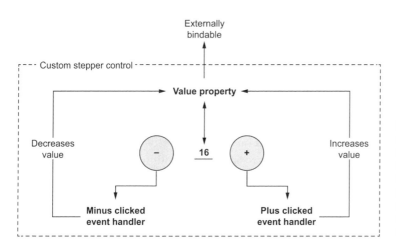

Figure 11.5 The two `Buttons` and the `Entry` that make up the custom stepper control all manipulate or are manipulated by values in the code-behind. But a single property is exposed externally as a bindable property, meaning we can get and set it with a binding.

Our custom stepper is a simple example, and while we need to create a bindable property to make the value accessible externally, this "wrapping" can be even more valuable in complex scenarios. Imagine, for example, a templated control that lets you edit details about a person (first and last name, date of birth, etc.) but exposes a unified `PersonDTO` class as a bindable property, as in figure 11.6.

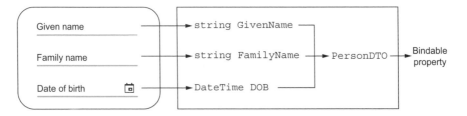

Figure 11.6 **A custom control that contains input fields for the given name, family name, and date of birth. These fields directly set values of properties in the code-behind, but a single bindable property is exposed that wraps all three properties into a single data transfer object (DTO).**

For now, we'll focus on our simpler use case and create a bindable property for the `Value` property in the custom stepper.

11.2.1 *Adding the Value property*

Adding bindable properties to a control in .NET MAUI requires following some conventions. The static `Create` method on the `BindableProperty` class is used to create bindable properties, which must be created with the `static` and `readonly` modifiers.

Remember that bindable properties back regular properties (instead of fields). The name of a bindable property must match the name of the property it is backing, with the `Property` suffix. In our custom stepper, we have a property called `Value`, so the bindable property that will back it must be called `ValueProperty`.

The `Create` method has three required parameters:

- The name of the property that it backs
- The return type (i.e., the type of the property that it backs)
- The declaring type (i.e., the type of the custom control that the bindable property belongs to)

With this information, we can create the bindable property for the value in our custom stepper, using the code shown in figure 11.7.

We can use this code to make `Value` a bindable property on the custom stepper control, but there's another step we need to make the binding work. The getter and setter of the regular `Value` property need to call the `GetValue` and `SetValue` methods, respectively. These methods are inherited from the `BindableObject` base class.

The `GetValue` and `SetValue` methods need to be added to the getter and setter of a property to return and set the value. The `GetValue` method takes a single parameter:

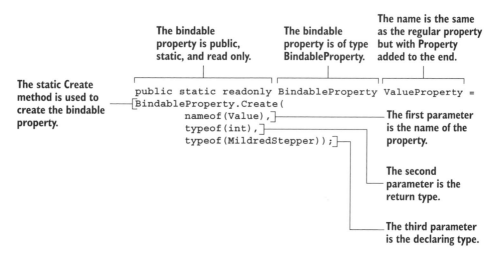

Figure 11.7 The static `Create` method on the `BindableProperty` type is used to create instances of bindable properties. These must be public, static, and read-only. The `Create` method requires the name of the property, the type of the property, and the type of the control the property belongs to. The name of the bindable property must match the name of the property, with `Property` appended.

the name of the bindable property. `GetValue` returns `object`, so you need to cast the result to the type of your property (`int` in the case of the `Value` property in the custom stepper).

`SetValue` takes two parameters: the name of the bindable property and the value that you want to assign to the bindable property. With this information in mind, we can add the bindable property and update the `Value` property to work with it, as shown in the following listing.

Listing 11.4 The `BindableProperty` and updated property

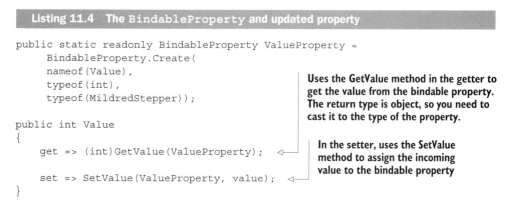

```
public static readonly BindableProperty ValueProperty =
    BindableProperty.Create(
    nameof(Value),
    typeof(int),
    typeof(MildredStepper));

public int Value
{
    get => (int)GetValue(ValueProperty);

    set => SetValue(ValueProperty, value);
}
```

Uses the GetValue method in the getter to get the value from the bindable property. The return type is object, so you need to cast it to the type of the property.

In the setter, uses the SetValue method to assign the incoming value to the bindable property

With the bindable property added, the custom stepper is now ready to use. Go back to the input page and add the binding from the `Value` property of the `MildredStepper` to the `Count` property of the page's binding context. The following listing shows the updated control in the input page.

Listing 11.5   The `MildredStepper` with the binding added

```
<controls:MildredStepper Grid.Row="2"
                HorizontalOptions="Center"
                VerticalOptions="Center"
                Value="{Binding Count}"/>
```

If you run the app now, you'll see the custom stepper on the page. You can increase and decrease the count using the plus and minus buttons and edit the value directly, as shown in figure 11.8. You should be able to record a stock count and, if you go to the reports page, see that the count is successfully saved with the value from the custom stepper.

Figure 11.8   The `InputPage` with the custom `Mildred-Stepper` control added. On the left, the count has been changed by using the plus and minus buttons. On the right, the value has been edited directly, and the numeric keyboard makes it easy for the user to enter the correct type of data.

11.2.2 *Adding the IsEnabled property*

As you can see in figure 11.8, the custom stepper is enabled by default, and changing the count subsequently enables the add count `Button`, meaning we could submit a count with no product selected and get an error. Before we introduced our custom control, we controlled the `IsEnabled` property of the standard `Stepper` using a `Data-Trigger`, which would disable the control when the `SelectedProduct` property of the binding context was null and enable it once a product has been selected. When using custom controls to improve UX, it's important not to compromise any existing functionality, so let's reintroduce this feature.

ADDING THE BINDABLE PROPERTY

MildredStepper is of type ContentView, which already has an IsEnabled property inherited from the VisualElement base class. We can bind to this from the containing view and get and set its value this way, but it doesn't currently support the functionality we need for our data trigger. We could add a different property with a different name, but this wouldn't be consistent with the existing convention used by controls in .NET MAUI.

We can work around this by using the new keyword. We can add the bindable property as we would any other bindable property, and although it already exists on a base class, we can add the new modifier to hide the inherited member. There is also an IsEnabled property that the bindable property backs, so we can reuse this and refer to it in the Create method, without needing to add it again. The following listing shows the new bindable property to add to MildredStepper.xaml.cs.

> **Listing 11.6   The new bindable property for the IsEnabled property**

Uses the existing base IsEnabled property

Uses the Create method to create an instance of BindableProperty but adds the new modifier as well as static and readonly

```
public static new readonly BindableProperty
    IsEnabledProperty = BindableProperty.Create(
        nameof(IsEnabled),
        typeof(bool),
        typeof(MildredStepper));
```

Sets the return type and the declaring type

So far, the only thing that's changed here is the addition of the new keyword, and functionally, this bindable property is no different from the inherited one. To bring back the functionality that we need for the data trigger, we need to make a couple of changes:

- *Change the default value*—The default value of bool is false, but the data trigger we are using needs to change the value to true. Remember that data triggers revert their changes when the condition is no longer met. So, if the trigger sets IsEnabled to false, when the SelectedProduct is no longer null, it would revert to its default value, which is also false. We need it to revert to true.
- *Add a change handler*—When the value of the IsEnabled property changes, we want to programmatically enable or disable the Buttons and Entry within our templated control. By adding a change handler, we can inspect the new value and the old value and respond accordingly.

ADDING DEFAULT VALUES

Primitive types in .NET all have a default value (for example, false for bool or 0 for int). With a regular property you can override the type's default and assign a default value to the instance, either when you declare it or in a class constructor. However, with bindable properties, you need to assign the default value in the Create method.

So far, we've specified three arguments for the Create method; to specify a default value, we just provide it as the fourth argument. Update the bindable property declaration to include a default value of true. The following listing shows the updated bindable property declaration for the IsEnabled bindable property.

> **Listing 11.7   The bindable property declaration with a default value provided**

```
public static new readonly BindableProperty IsEnabledProperty =
    BindableProperty.Create(
        nameof(IsEnabled),
        typeof(bool),
        typeof(MildredStepper),
        true);
```

Sets the default value of the IsEnabled property to true. The default for bool is false, but we want it to be true so that the data trigger can set it to false based on the SelectedProperty being null.

With this change, the default value of the bindable property will be true, which is what we need to support the data trigger we will add later in this section.

ADDING A CHANGE HANDLER

The BindableProperty.Create method allows you to specify a delegate to be invoked when the value of the property changes, with a parameter called propertyChanged. So far, we've been using positional arguments in the Create method, but property-Changed is not the next argument in the sequence, so we'll need to supply it as a named argument.

Before we add the argument, let's build the delegate, which needs to be a static method with a specific signature. The method will specify three parameters:

- A BindableObject, which will be the calling templated control. In this case, the instance of MildredStepper that the BindableProperty instance belongs to
- An object, which will represent the old value (the value of the property before the change)
- An object, which will represent the new value (the value of the property after the change)

These parameters will cover any bindable property of any bindable object, so they need to be cast to the specific types needed for any given property. It's also a good idea to ensure they are the correct type, and for the bindable object, we can do both at once.

Getting both the old value and the new value means you can compare them and act accordingly. But, in our case, we're only concerned with the new value. We need to cast it to a bool and set the corresponding property on the bindable object to the new value. We don't need to check the value; we can simply set the IsEnabled property of the individual controls (the Entry and the two Buttons) on the bindable object to whatever value we've received. The following listing shows the On IsEnabledChanged method to add to MildredStepper.xaml.cs.

Listing 11.8 The `OnIsEnabledChanged` **method**

Checks that the bindable object the method has received is the right type and casts it to a variable

Adds the On IsEnabledChanged method and makes it static. It must take a BindableObject parameter, an object parameter for the old value, and an object parameter for the new value.

```
private static void OnIsEnabledChanged(BindableObject
➡ bindable, object oldValue, object newValue)

{
    if (bindable is MildredStepper mildredStepper)
    {
        mildredStepper.IsEnabled = (bool)newValue;

        mildredStepper.ValueEntry.IsEnabled =
➡ mildredStepper.IsEnabled;
        mildredStepper.PlusButton.IsEnabled =
➡ mildredStepper.IsEnabled;
        mildredStepper.MinusButton.IsEnabled =
➡ mildredStepper.IsEnabled;
    }
}
```

Casts the new value to the right type (in this case, bool) and assigns it to the corresponding property on the bindable object (in this case, IsEnabled)

Sets the IsEnabled property of the child controls to the IsEnabled property on the bindable object, which will disable or enable them as required

Now that we've got the method, all that remains is to assign it to the `IsEnabledProp-erty` in the `Create` method using a named argument. The following listing shows the updated code for the `IsEnabledProperty` declaration.

Listing 11.9 The `IsEnabledProperty` **declaration with the** `propertyChanged` **delegate**

```
Public static new readonly BindableProperty IsEnabledProperty =
➡ BindableProperty.Create(
    nameof(IsEnabled),
    typeof(bool),
    typeof(MildredStepper),
    true,
    propertyChanged: OnIsEnabledChanged);
```

Assigns the OnIsEnabledChanged method to the propertyChanged parameter using a named argument

With that, the `IsEnabled` bindable property and the `MildredStepper` control are complete. The final step is to add the data trigger back into the input page.

ADDING THE DATATRIGGER

The process for adding the data trigger for the custom stepper is the same as it was for the stock `Stepper`. We define the control's `Triggers` collection and add a `DataTrigger` with a `TargetType`, `Binding`, and `Value`. Then, we add a `Setter` with a `Property` and a `Value`. The difference is that, as the control is not in the standard XAML namespace, we need to include the XML namespace when defining the `Triggers` collection and the `TargetType`. The binding, value, and setter are identical to what we used with the stock `Stepper`. The following listing shows the updated code for the `MildredStepper` in `InputPage.xaml`, with the data trigger included.

Listing 11.10   MildredStepper with the DataTrigger added

```
<controls:MildredStepper Grid.Row="2"
                         HorizontalOptions="Center"
                         VerticalOptions="Center"
                         Value="{Binding Count, Mode=TwoWay}">
    <controls:MildredStepper.Triggers>
        <DataTrigger TargetType="controls:MildredStepper"

                     Binding="{Binding SelectedProduct, TargetNullValue=''}"
                     Value="">
            <Setter Property="IsEnabled"
                    Value="False" />
        </DataTrigger>
    </controls:MildredStepper.Triggers>
</controls:MildredStepper>
```

Includes the namespace when referring to the control when defining the triggers and the target type

This completes the work for the custom stepper control. If you run the app now, you should see the custom stepper disabled, as in figure 11.9, until you search for and select a product. Once you do this, the stepper will be enabled, and you can set a count and, subsequently, submit it.

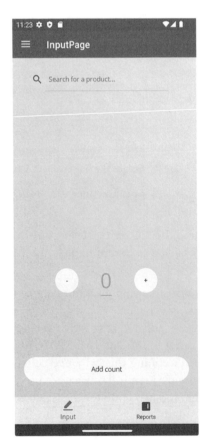

Figure 11.9 The custom stepper is disabled by a DataTrigger when the SelectedProduct in the binding context is null. Searching for and selecting a product enables the custom stepper.

An easier way to create bindable properties

In previous chapters, we saw how the `INotifyPropertyChanged` interface is used to notify the UI that properties have changed in their binding context. This process is more complex than in some other UI frameworks, but it can be simplified with source generators in the MVVM Community Toolkit. Instead of writing the property and the field and invoking the `PropertyChanged` event in the setter, you simply declare the field and decorate it with an attribute. To find out more about this awesome feature, check out this video from James Montemagno: https://youtu.be/aCxl0z04BN8.

Creating bindable properties is significantly more laborious, and unfortunately, the .NET MAUI Community Toolkit doesn't include such a source generator for bindable properties (although, at the time of writing, there is an open proposal and spec for one). However, there is a package available that does exactly this. You can find out more about it here: https://github.com/rrmanzano/maui-bindableproperty-generator.

I recommend that you continue to create bindable properties manually until you can do so without referring to this book or the documentation to ensure that you have a thorough understanding of how they work. But once you do, switching to this package could be a significant time saver.

11.3 Modifying platform controls with handlers

The new custom stepper control we have added provides a significant UX improvement, especially for inputting large numbers. After a round of testing, Mildred's staff have found that they prefer the functionality over the standard `Stepper`, but the UI is unpopular. Mildred asked her designers to suggest improvements, and they have asked you to make the `Entry` in the middle of the stepper a bit less conspicuous.

Figure 11.10 compares how the custom stepper currently looks across the supported platforms. Each platform takes a slightly different approach to how it renders an `Entry` and, therefore, how the stepper is rendered.

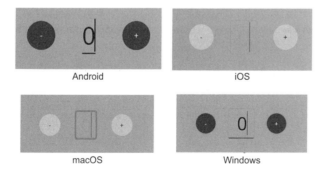

Android

iOS

macOS

Windows

Figure 11.10 The custom stepper is similar on each platform but with some variations. On all platforms, the Entry is prominent, which makes it discoverable but unsightly, particularly when just the buttons are used.

In the last chapter, we saw how we can use styles and control properties to change the appearance of out-of-the-box controls; but there is no property exposed by .NET MAUI to control the border of an `Entry` control. When we encounter situations like this, we can override the way that the .NET MAUI control abstraction is implemented on the target platforms, and we do this by customizing the control's *handler*.

11.3.1 *Handler architecture*

The cross-platform controls that we have been using in our .NET MAUI apps are represented by abstractions, meaning that each is essentially a conceptual definition of a UI control. *Virtual views* implement these abstractions as the controls we use in .NET MAUI apps, and *handlers* map the abstractions to *native views*—their specific implementations on each platform. Each handler has a property called `PlatformView` that represents the native control. Handlers are the glue that binds together the cross-platform controls to platform-specific implementations and are the core technology that lets us write cross-platform apps in .NET MAUI. Figure 11.11 shows the architecture of handlers in .NET MAUI.

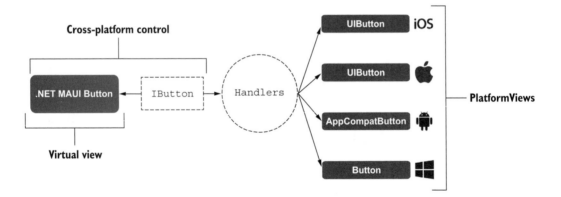

Figure 11.11   Cross-platform controls are described by interfaces, and virtual views implement them as controls in the .NET MAUI UI layer. Handlers map the abstractions to platform-specific implementations.

Handlers define *mappings* in a dictionary that describes how these cross-platform properties are applied on each platform. For example, a `Button` in .NET MAUI has several properties we can modify, including `BackgroundColor`. A handler maps the .NET MAUI `BackgroundColor` property, which is of type `Microsoft.Maui.Graphics.Color` to the platform-specific property, which, on iOS and macOS, for example, is of type `UIKit.UIColor`.

> **NOTE** One handler exists for each control and each platform. For example, there is one `Button` handler for Android, one for iOS, one for Windows, and one for Mac Catalyst.

Each platform implements UI controls differently, but when building .NET MAUI apps, we're not usually concerned about the platform-specific implementation details. Sometimes, though, to get a finer-grained level of control over how UI elements are displayed, we need to override them.

We can also create our own handlers to create our own cross-platform controls to gain access to platform-specific controls that have not been exposed in .NET MAUI. If you find a platform-specific control that you need access to in your .NET MAUI app, you can read more about this approach in the documentation here: http://mng.bz/EQjj. For our custom stepper, we will only need to modify existing mappings.

11.3.2 Overriding handler mappings

When we need to modify the appearance of a control beyond what is provided by the cross-platform abstraction, we can override the handler mappings. Each handler has a mapper, and each mapper provides three methods for overriding the mappings:

- `PrependToMapping`—The changes you specify here are applied *before* the default mappings in the handler. This can be a good option if you're adding mappings that aren't currently defined.
- `ModifyMapping`—This changes existing mappings defined in the hander.
- `AppendToMapping`—The changes you specify here are applied *after* the default mappings in the handler. This means that changes here will take precedence over the defaults.

> **When do I use each method?**
>
> The `PrependToMapping` method can be useful if you want to map properties that aren't already mapped by the default handler mappings but you *don't* want your mappings to override anything in the defaults.
>
> `ModifyMapping` can be useful if you have a deep understanding of the existing mapping dictionary and want to change the way the default mappings are defined.
>
> `AppendToMapping` gives you the most assurance that your customizations will be applied and is the method you should use in almost all cases. It's unlikely that you'll need to use one of the other methods in most cases.

All three methods have the same two parameters. The first is a key; mappings are defined in dictionaries. So, if you're using the `ModifyMapping` method, you must use the key for the default mapping (in .NET MAUI, these are defined as the name of the property on the relevant interface). For the other two methods, you can use whatever `string` key you like.

The second parameter is an `Action`, which has two arguments that get passed in for you. The first is the handler that the mapper belongs to (i.e., the platform-specific instance of the handler), and the second is the view that the handler corresponds to. Figure 11.12 shows a sample of adding a handler mapping to a view.

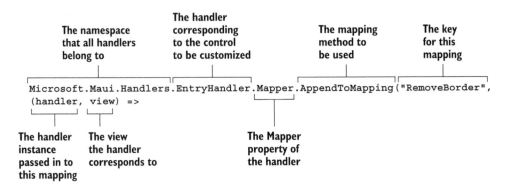

Figure 11.12   This code opens a lambda expression for appending mappings to the handler for the cross-platform `Entry` control. The mappings for this control to platform-specific controls are in the `EntryHandler`, which is in the `Microsoft.Maui.Handlers` namespace. The `AppendToMapping` method has been used, which is on the `Mapper` property of the handler. The key for this mapping profile is `RemoveBorder`, but if it was using the `ModifyMapping` method instead, an existing key in the mapping dictionary would need to be used. The `Action` gets two arguments passed in: the handler instance and the view being customized.

You can implement your handler mappings in a few places. One common approach is to put them in `MauiProgram` as part of the app's startup logic; another is to put the handler logic in the relevant platform folders. A third approach, as we will use later in this chapter, is to keep the handler mapping with the control that we are modifying.

An important thing to remember is that, once executed, your handler modifications will apply to *all* instances of the control throughout the app, and where you put your handler logic determines when that logic gets executed. For example, if you put it in `MauiProgram`, it will be executed before any views are rendered, and the modifications apply to all instances of the view as soon as the app starts. If you put it somewhere else, it will be executed once that code path is reached, at which point *all* instances of the control the handler is responsible for will be modified.

If you don't want to apply a modification to all instances of a control, you can subclass it and check within your handler logic whether the affected view is an instance of the base class or of your subclass. We will take this approach later in this chapter.

With a subclassed control, my preferred approach is to keep the handler mappings in the constructor. This ensures that any time an instance of my control is rendered, the handler logic will be executed, and it keeps all the rendering logic for the custom control in one place. If I wanted to alter all instances of a control, I would put the handler mappings in `MauiProgram`, and if I wanted to modify a control on one platform only, I would put the handler logic in that platform folder. Let's see how we can put this into action to make the modifications Mildred is requesting for her app.

11.3.3 Implementing custom handler logic

For the custom stepper, we need to modify the `Entry` control, but the mapping dictionary in the `EntryHandler` applies to *all* instances of `Entry`. Once we apply the mappings, they will apply across the board, which isn't what we want. Instead, let's subclass the `Entry` type, and in our `AppendToMapping` method, we'll check to make sure we're only applying it to the desired type.

Create a class called `BorderlessEntry` in the `Controls` folder of `MauiStock-Take.UI` that subclasses `Entry`. Add a private void method called `ModifyEntry` and call it from the constructor. Inside the `ModifyEntry` method, call the `AppendToMapping` method on the `EntryHandler`'s `Mapper`, and give it a key of `RemoveBorder`. The following listing shows the boilerplate code for the `BorderlessEntry`.

Listing 11.11 The `BorderlessEntry` class

```
namespace MauiStockTake.UI.Controls;
public class BorderlessEntry : Entry       ◁──  Subclasses the Entry control so we can
{                                                have our own version to customize
    public BorderlessEntry()
    {
        ModifyEntry();          ◁──┐  Calls the ModifyEntry method
    }                              └  from the constructor

    private void ModifyEntry()
    {
      Microsoft.Maui.Handlers.EntryHandler.Mapper.
➡ AppendToMapping("RemoveBorder", (handler, view) =>      ◁──┐
        {                                                     │
        });                Calls the AppendToMapping method on the Mapper
    }                      property of the EntryHandler and gives our mapping
}                          a key of 'RemoveBorder'; names the handler and
                           view arguments passed to the lambda expression.
```

At this point, we could start adding our customizations. However, as we're applying these to the `EntryHandler`, as soon as an instance of `BorderlessEntry` is constructed, these customizations will apply to everything the `EntryHandler` is responsible for—in other words, every instance of the `Entry` control.

Instead, let's add a conditional check inside the mapping logic to ensure we're only applying this to instances of `BorderlessEntry` and not any instance of `Entry`. The following listing shows the check to add inside the mapping code.

Listing 11.12 The conditional check in the mapping code

```
Microsoft.Maui.Handlers.EntryHandler.Mapper.AppendToMapping("RemoveBorder",
➡  (handler, view) =>
{
    if (view is BorderlessEntry)      ◁──  Adds a check to wrap all of our customization
    {                                      logic in a conditional check to ensure we apply
    }                                      the customizations only to our custom
});                                        subclassed control and not all instances of Entry
```

The last thing that we need to do before we start applying our customizations is to add some compiler directives so that we can separate the logic for each instance of the handler (i.e., each platform-specific handler). There are other ways we could have done this; for example, we could have used partial classes and added the modifications inside the platform holders. But this approach lets us keep all the logic for each custom control in one place. The following listing shows the compiler directives to add inside the `if` conditional block.

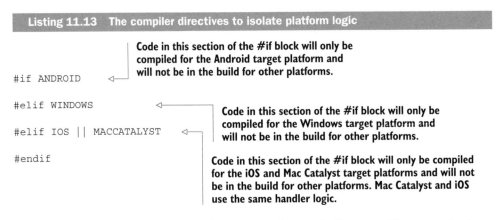

Listing 11.13   The compiler directives to isolate platform logic

```
#if ANDROID
```
Code in this section of the #if block will only be compiled for the Android target platform and will not be in the build for other platforms.

```
#elif WINDOWS
```
Code in this section of the #if block will only be compiled for the Windows target platform and will not be in the build for other platforms.

```
#elif IOS || MACCATALYST
```

```
#endif
```
Code in this section of the #if block will only be compiled for the iOS and Mac Catalyst target platforms and will not be in the build for other platforms. Mac Catalyst and iOS use the same handler logic.

The `BorderlessEntry` is now ready for us to apply our platform-specific customizations.

ANDROID

As we previously saw, the lambda expression gets two arguments passed in. One is the view being customized, and the other is the platform-specific handler instance. The handler instance has a property called `PlatformView` that gives us access to the native control that the handler maps to. In the case of Android, this is an `AppCompatEditText` widget.

To get rid of the borders and the underline on Android, all we need to do is set the `Background` property of the `AppCompatEditText` widget to `null` and call its `SetBackgroundColor` method, passing in `Android.Graphics.Color.Transparent` as an argument. We use the fully qualified name for the color because we've already got compiler directives inside the mapper; if we start adding them to the `using` statements too, the code will get messy. The following listing shows the two lines to add inside the `ANDROID` section of the compiler directive `#if` block.

Listing 11.14   The Android-specific customizations

```
handler.PlatformView.Background = null;
handler.PlatformView.SetBackgroundColor(Android.
➥Graphics.Color.Transparent);
```

The PlatformView in this case is AppCompatEditText, which has a Background property that we need to set to null.

AppCompatEditText has a SetBackgroundColor that accepts an Android.Graphics.Color as an argument. We're setting it here to Transparent and using the fully qualified name, so we don't need to bring Android-specific using statements into shared code.

How do I know what changes to make to platform-specific mappings?

Working with handlers is a breeze, especially compared to the renderers' architecture it replaces in Xamarin.Forms. The difficulty comes from knowing which native controls are being mapped to and what properties on them to change.

You will develop this skill as you progress as a .NET MAUI developer, particularly as you learn more about the target platforms. Eventually, you may find that you have your own library of platform customizations that you curate, but there are a few ways you can figure out what changes you need to make to mappings.

A good way to explore this is with IntelliSense. If you're using an IDE like Visual Studio, IntelliSense will tell you which properties and methods are available. Sometimes, it will be obvious what kinds of values you can assign to them; other times, you can look them up in, say, the Android developer documentation. You can also hover your mouse over `PlatformView`, or its properties, in the editor to see which native control is in use; you can then look up what its properties are or even find documentation or guides on how to perform the specific customization you're trying to achieve. Then, all you need to do is translate it into a mapping in the handler, but this is usually easier than the first part.

However, it's likely that most of the modifications you will need in your apps are already well-documented by the community. Even if you can't find something .NET MAUI specific, you'll almost certainly find it for Xamarin.Forms. While Xamarin.Forms uses a different architecture, translating renderers to handlers is usually a simple task. In fact, there's an example of translating the `BorderlessEntry` we're creating here from a Xamarin.Forms renderer to a .NET MAUI handler linked in appendix B.

The .NET MAUI community is one of the best things about .NET MAUI development. It's an active and vibrant community full of people who love sharing knowledge and supporting their peers. When you need to customize a handler, your favorite search engine will almost certainly turn up a relevant blog post, video, or discussion. And if not, you can always reach out to the .NET MAUI community using the links in the Other Online Resources section.

Eventually, you'll likely start figuring these out for yourself, using a combination of IntelliSense, platform documentation, and your growing skill set. When you do, consider documenting your findings. Blog posts and videos are popular, and there are regular community showcase events where people share these kinds of things. The community will thank you, and you may also thank yourself when you come back and refer to it later!

This code removed the `Entry` chrome, which looks great when using the stepper buttons. But there are none of the usual UX cues a user expects when editing text fields. Before we make the changes to the other platforms, let's add a `Border` around the `Entry` in the custom stepper. We'll set the `StrokeThickness` to 0 so that it's not usually visible and use a data trigger to show it when the `Entry` has focus (i.e., when a user taps on or clicks into it). We can use the `OnPlatform` markup extension so that it only shows on Android. The following listing shows the changes to the `MildredStepper` `.xaml` file to add the border.

Listing 11.15   The conditional border to add to `MildredStepper.xaml`

```xml
<?xml version="1.0" encoding="utf-8" ?>
<ContentView ...>
    <Grid ...>
        ...
        <Border Grid.Column="1"
                Stroke="{StaticResource Primary}"
                BackgroundColor="Transparent"
                Margin="10"
                StrokeThickness="0"
                StrokeShape="RoundRectangle 5">
            <Border.Triggers>
                <DataTrigger TargetType="Border"
                             Binding="{Binding Source={x:Reference
    ValueEntry}, Path=IsFocused}"
                             Value="True">
                    <Setter Property="StrokeThickness"
                            Value="{OnPlatform Android=1}"/>
                </DataTrigger>
            </Border.Triggers>
            <Entry x:Name="ValueEntry" .../>
        </Border>
        ...
    </Grid>
</ContentView>
```

This completes the modifications necessary for Android; let's move on to iOS and macOS.

macOS AND iOS

Back in chapter 3, we saw that .NET MAUI apps run on macOS through Catalyst, which runs iOS apps on macOS, while still giving access to macOS features when needed. Because of this, the customizations for iOS and macOS are the same, and we can put them into the same conditional compiler block.

On iOS and macOS, the `PlatformView` is a `UITextView`. We'll set its `Background-Color` property to `UIColor.Clear` in the `UIKit` namespace and its `BorderStyle` property to `UITextBorderStyle.None`, also in the `UIKit` namespace. We also need to set the `BorderWidth` property from the `UIView` base class that `UITextView` inherits to 0. The following listing shows the code to add to the macOS and iOS conditional compiler block.

Listing 11.16   The macOS and iOS customizations

```
handler.PlatformView.BackgroundColor = UIKit.UIColor.Clear;
handler.PlatformView.Layer.BorderWidth = 0;
handler.PlatformView.BorderStyle = UIKit.UITextBorderStyle.None;
```

This completes the changes we need to make for iOS and macOS, so let's move on to Windows.

WINDOWS

The `PlatformView` on Windows is a `TextBox` in the `Micorosft.UI.Xaml.Controls` namespace. It has a `Background` property, which we need to set to `null`, and a `Border-Thickness` and `FocusVisualMargin` property, which we need to set to a new instance of `Microsoft.UI.Xaml.Thickness`. This takes an `int` in its constructor that defines its thickness value, so we'll pass in `0`. The following listing shows the code to add to the Windows conditional compiler block.

Listing 11.17 The Windows customizations

```
handler.PlatformView.BorderThickness = new Microsoft.UI.Xaml.Thickness(0);
handler.PlatformView.Background = null;
handler.PlatformView.FocusVisualMargin = new Microsoft.UI.Xaml.Thickness(0);
```

The `BorderlessEntry` class is now complete, and while it removes the border from the `Entry` on Windows, the focus underline will still appear. We can't remove it using a handler; instead, we need to modify the resource dictionary in the `App.xaml` file in the `Windows` platform folder. The Windows `App.xaml` file contains a root node of `maui:MauiWinUIApplication`. Add the code in the following listing to the `App.xaml` file between these tags.

Listing 11.18 The code to add to `App.xaml` in the Windows platform folder

```
<maui:MauiWinUIApplication.Resources>
    <Thickness x:Key="TextControlBorderThemeThickness">0</Thickness>
    <Thickness x:Key="TextControlBorderThemeThicknessFocused">0</Thickness>
</maui:MauiWinUIApplication.Resources>
```

These properties are not exposed via the `PlatformView`, so it's the only place we can make this change. This introduces a new problem, though: as we are not applying this to a specific subclass, *every* `Entry` will now be completely borderless on Windows and will lose the focused underline. While we're only using the `Entry` control as part of other controls in MauiStockTake, on Windows, the `SearchBar` (which we have at the top of the input page) uses the `TextBox` control, which this change applies to, under the hood, so it will be affected.

We could resolve this problem by subclassing the WinUI `TextBox` control in the Windows platform folder. Then, we could apply this Windows-specific style change to the subclass rather than the base `TextBox`. Finally, we could create an entirely new mapping (rather than modifying the existing one) that maps our subclassed `Borderless-Entry` to our subclassed `TextBox` derivative.

However, as we're not using `Entry` anywhere else, this process is not necessary for MauiStockTake, and an easier approach is to just fix up the `SearchBar` for now. Let's add a `Border` around it but use the `OnPlatform` markup extension to give the `Border` a `StrokeThickness` of `0` on all the other platforms.

Making tradeoffs

In MauiStockTake, we don't have any explicit instances of the `Entry` control, so sacrificing the borders and underlining isn't a huge problem. We can accept that compromise to achieve the desired effect with a control that we *do* use.

As the app grows, we will likely find we will use the `Entry` in other places. When this happens, we have a choice to make: we can either revert this change on Windows and accept that the custom stepper doesn't 100% match the design (but maybe it's close enough) in exchange for using the `Entry` control as it is provided out of the box, or we can create a custom entry control, for example, introducing our own border or underline focus effects, which we would then use everywhere in the app instead of the standard control. I made a video showing this approach with a `Material` style custom entry control, available free (with sign-up) on Manning's liveVideo platform here: http://mng.bz/N2j7.

On larger apps, this latter approach is likely what you'll be doing anyway. Many companies have their own specific branding and style guides and want all their controls, across all their aps and platforms, to look a certain way. In .NET MAUI apps, you may be creating controls to achieve this and sharing them via control libraries, as we mentioned in chapter 8 and will revisit later in this chapter.

The following listing shows the border code to add to `InputPage.xaml`.

Listing 11.19   The Border workaround for `SearchBar` in `InputPage.xaml`

```xml
<?xml version="1.0" encoding="utf-8" ?>
<ContentPage ...>
    <Grid ..>
        <Border StrokeShape="RoundRectangle 5"
                Stroke="{StaticResource Primary}"
                BackgroundColor="Transparent"
                StrokeThickness="{OnPlatform WinUI=1, Default=0}">
            <SearchBar .../>
        </Border>
        ...
    </Grid>
</ContentPage>
```

This completes the borderless entry control; all we need to do now is drop it into the custom stepper.

11.3.4 *Updating the custom stepper*

The custom stepper control has an `Entry` in the central column of its `Grid`. Because the `BorderlessEntry` is a subclass of `Entry`, we can just drop it in as a direct replacement (recall the Liskov Substitution Principle mentioned in the sidebar "MVVM for SOLID apps" in chapter 9). The only thing we need to do first is to add an XML namespace in the XAML so that we can refer to the custom control, and then we can just do a direct replacement, referencing the `BorderlessEntry` via the XAML namespace. The following listing shows code changes for the `MildredStepper.xaml` file.

Listing 11.20   `MildredStepper.xaml` updated to use the new `BorderlessEntry`

```xml
<?xml version="1.0" encoding="utf-8" ?>
<ContentView xmlns:controls="clr-namespace:
    MauiStockTake.UI.Controls" ...>
    <Grid ...>
        ...
        <controls:BorderlessEntry

            x:Name="ValueEntry"
            Keyboard="Numeric"
            FontSize="42"
            HorizontalTextAlignment="Center"
            TextChanged="ValueEntry_TextChanged"
            VerticalOptions="Center"
            HorizontalOptions="Center"/>
        ...
    </Grid>
</ContentView>
```

> Adds an XML namespace for the Controls namespace in the MauiStockTake.UI project

> Replaces the standard Entry control with the BorderlessEntry control in the controls XML namespace

With that final change, the custom stepper is now complete. Run the app, and you should see the updated `MildredStepper` on the input page, as in figure 11.13.

Figure 11.13   The custom stepper with the `BorderlessEntry`, shown here on Android. On the left, the number has been changed using the stepper buttons. On the right, the number is being edited directly, and a border is shown.

On Windows, there is a hover effect (called `PointerOver` in the `VisualStateManager`, as we saw in chapter 10) and a focus effect. We could remove these, too; however, they lend themselves well to the discoverability of the control, so we'll keep them in (and lament their absence on the other platforms!).

11.4   Creating and sharing control libraries

You can create custom controls using templated controls, by drawing controls with the Microsoft.Maui.Graphics library, by customizing native controls with handler mappings, or combinations of all of them. Often these custom controls will be used to conform to a company's branding or style guide or even its design language system. When this is the case, it's useful to be able to reuse these controls across multiple apps, and even when not, sometimes you develop a useful control (or set of controls) that you think is worth reusing.

In chapter 8, we looked at sharing code within a solution, but we also mentioned sharing code across an enterprise. If you're building .NET MAUI apps, it makes sense to share reusable controls in control libraries. For example, if Mildred's Surf Shack wanted to introduce some more apps, it would make sense to move the custom stepper into a control library that can be shared with other apps. Figure 11.14 shows an updated version of the code-sharing diagram from chapter 8 to highlight this.

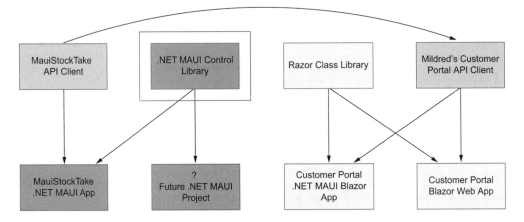

Figure 11.14   Components of the enterprise app ecosystem at Mildred's Surf Shack. The .NET MAUI Control Library is highlighted by a box. It would make sense to move the custom stepper (and any other custom controls) into here so that it can be used by the stock-taking app as well as any other apps in the enterprise.

Naming controls

It's common to see controls with names like `CustomStepper`. This name isn't particularly descriptive, and it's better to use more meaningful names. For example, it's easy to tell just from the name what `BorderlessEntry` is and what it does.

It's also common for developers to name controls after themselves or their company—for example, `GoldieEntry` or `SSWButton`. This is OK when you're building and curating (or even sharing) your own control library, but if you're building apps for or on behalf of another business, it's better to name the controls in a way that is meaningful for them, as in the example of the `MildredStepper`.

`MildredStepper` may not provide information about its specific customizations, but it does tell you that it's a variation of a `Stepper` control that fits in with Mildred's brand. This name is better than `CustomStepper`, as it's more specific and, therefore, less likely to clash with controls in other libraries. It's also better than an app-specific name like `StockTakeStepper`, especially if it gets moved to a control library and used in more than one app at Mildred's Surf Shack.

Sharing controls with .NET MAUI is straightforward. If we wanted to share the `Mil-dredStepper` control with other apps, the first thing we would do is create a .NET MAUI class library. There is a .NET template for this that you can use from Visual Studio or the .NET CLI, which is like a regular class library but with all the .NET MAUI dependencies already wired up. Figure 11.15 shows the new project dialog for the .NET MAUI class library project template.

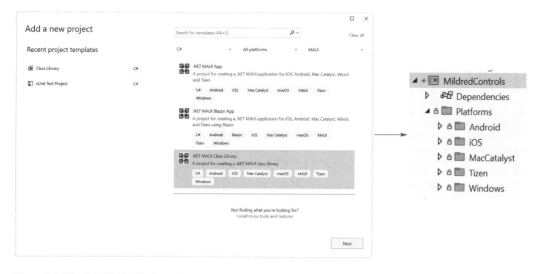

Figure 11.15   A .NET MAUI class library with all .NET MAUI dependencies wired up. It includes the platform folders where you can keep platform-specific code.

We could then move (or re-create) the `MildredStepper` control to this library and then add a dependency on this library in the MauiStockTake app. We'd have to update the namespace, but otherwise, there would be no difference.

.NET makes it easy to share class libraries across an enterprise too. The whole library can be packaged with NuGet, which is configurable as part of the build, as shown in figure 11.16.

Once the project has been built, you can copy it to a shared folder, which can be added as a NuGet source. A better approach, though, is to have the NuGet package created and distributed as part of your CI/CD pipelines. If it's a control library that you're sharing publicly, the best place is www.nuget.org. In other scenarios, GitHub can host both private and public NuGet feeds, as can Azure DevOps and several other for-purpose NuGet solutions.

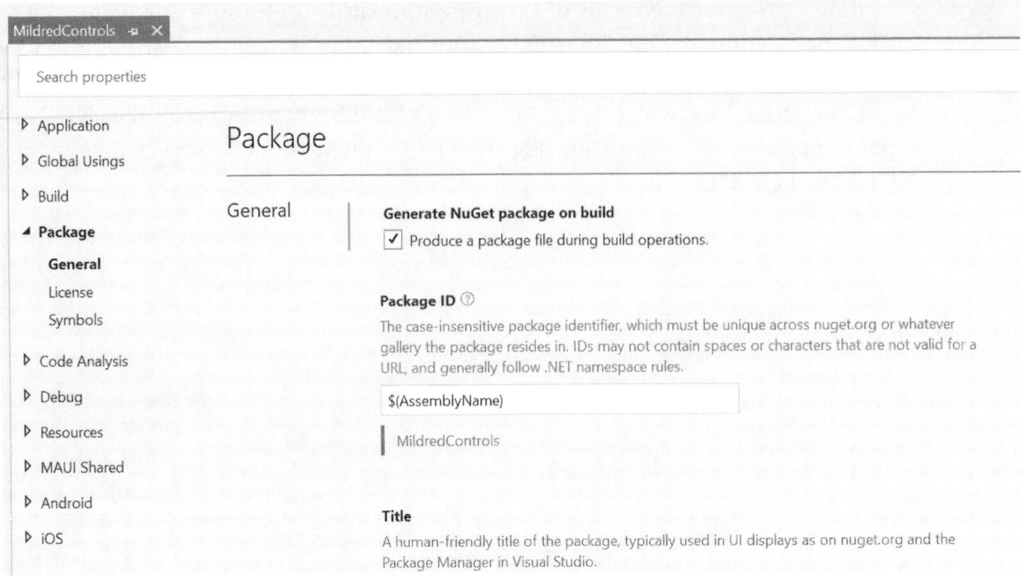

Figure 11.16 Creating a NuGet package from a class library, including a .NET MAUI class library, can be configured as part of your build process.

Summary

- Templated controls in .NET MAUI let you "componentize" views. Templated controls are created using the `ContentView` template.
- Custom controls should always improve UX. If you remove or override some functionality, you should either re-add it or replace it with something better.
- Validation, and particularly meaningful feedback about failed inputs, will significantly improve your app's UX.
- Templated controls use bindable properties to enable data binding between their containing view and their internal data.
- Bindable properties are created using the static `BindableProperty.Create` method. The properties that they back must use the `GetValue` and `SetValue` methods in their getter and setter to get and set values of the corresponding bindable property.
- Bindable properties must follow the naming convention of [property that they back]`Property`; for example, `IsEnabledProperty` backs a class property called `IsEnabled`.
- .NET MAUI maps cross-platform controls to native controls using handlers. Handlers contain dictionaries of property mappings that map the properties of cross-platform controls to the native platform controls.
- .NET MAUI class libraries are an awesome way of sharing controls between apps in an enterprise or with the community.

12

Deploying apps to production with GitHub Actions

This chapter covers

- Preparing your apps to be used by other people
- Providing your own icon and splash screen
- The Apple, Google, and Microsoft developer programs
- Continuous integration and continuous delivery with GitHub Actions

Congratulations! You have built a complete, nontrivial app in .NET MAUI. Building apps is fun, but sadly, very few people get paid to build apps just for fun; usually, there's an expectation that you will deliver a working app to users.

We've come a long way since the start of this book. We began with "Aloha, World!," and we've built a location-sharing app, a to-do app, a movie recommender, and now an enterprise stock-taking app. Getting to where we are now has been a long journey, and the last, and arguably most important, step is to get our app deployed. Once you have a build of your app that's ready to deploy to your users, there are a few final pieces of polish you need, outside of the app's functionality, before you have a finished product.

Once all the pieces are in place, the last step is deployment. As a professional app developer, you will need a CI/CD pipeline and automated build and deployment; as part of an enterprise app development team, they are an essential component of delivering quality software. In this chapter, we'll see how we can add those last pieces of polish to our app, and as an enterprise software development team at Beach Bytes, we'll use GitHub Actions to create repeatable, reliable builds that we can deliver to the various stores through automation.

12.1   App icons, splash screens, and app identifiers

The icon is the first part of your app that anyone will ever see. The various store listings will feature the icon prominently, and once it's installed onto a device, users will see the icon before even launching the app. Having a unique icon stands out both in the store and on the device, helping users find and launch your app quickly, so it's important to replace the default .NET icon. Mildred's design team has given us an icon to use, which you can see in figure 12.1.

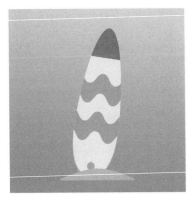

Figure 12.1   An app icon for MauiStockTake that's aligned with the surfing theme of Mildred's business

This icon has been provided as two SVG files: `icon-bg.svg` and `icon-fg.svg`. Both of these files can be found in the chapter 12 resources folder. We don't need to worry about merging these, as .NET MAUI composes an app icon for you based on a foreground file and a background file, as shown in figure 12.2.

Figure 12.2   An app icon can be composed of a foreground image layered on top of a background.

12.1.1 *Replacing the default app icon*

If you open `MauiStockTake.UI.csproj`, you'll see there is an icon defined in an `ItemGroup` marked with a comment that says `App Icon`. To define an app icon in .NET MAUI, you add the `MauiIcon` item and set `Include` to the file you want to use as your icon. You can use the `ForegroundFile` property to layer another image over the top.

Download the two icon files from the chapter 12 resources folder and copy them into the `Resources/AppIcon` folder in the `MauiStockTake.UI` project. We could update the `.csproj` file to refer to the two new filenames, but the most reliable way to use new files is to keep the default names. **Delete the `appicon.svg` and `appiconfg.svg` files**, then rename `icon-bg.svg` to `appicon.svg` and `icon-fg.svg` to `appiconfg.svg`.

To ensure the new icons get deployed successfully, clean and rebuild your project, delete the app from your device or simulator/emulator, and then run it again. If you stop the app, you should see its icon has been updated, as in figure 12.3.

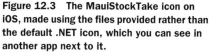

Figure 12.3   The MauiStockTake icon on iOS, made using the files provided rather than the default .NET icon, which you can see in another app next to it.

12.1.2 *App icon composition*

We've used two layers to compose our icon, but, in fact, you can build an icon out of four layers, as shown in figure 12.4.

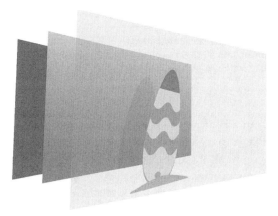

Figure 12.4   An app icon in .NET MAUI can be composed of four layers: a background color, an icon, a foreground icon, and a tint color.

The four layers that can be used to compose an app icon in .NET MAUI are

- A background color, specified by the `BackgroundColor` property
- An icon, specified with the `Include` property
- An icon foreground, specified with the `ForegroundFile` property
- A tint color, specified with the `TintColor` property

The background color ensures that your icon will be a solid bitmap even if there are transparencies in any of your layers, which is useful as iOS does not allow transparency in app icons. Both the `BackgroundColor` and `TintColor` properties can be specified using either hex colors or by using a statically defined .NET MAUI color (e.g., `Red`). For MauiStockTake, we're only using the `Include` and `ForegroundFile` properties, so you can delete `Color`, which is included by default.

12.1.3 App icon resizing

As your app icon is shown in a lot of places, it needs to be provided in a variety of sizes. This includes sizes for different device sizes and resolutions (from watches to TVs and everything in between), as well as store listings, search results, and notifications, as shown in figure 12.5.

Figure 12.5   An app icon is used in multiple places, including store listings, store details pages, device home screens, and notifications. It needs to be provided in sizes to accommodate all these scenarios and many different device sizes, including watches, phones, laptops, and TVs.

Historically, generating the icon in all these different sizes has been a pain point of mobile development. Websites like https://appiconmaker.co can help, but even after you've generated copies of the icon in all the right sizes, you still have to import them all, which has also been a laborious process in the past. .NET MAUI makes resizing much simpler by letting you add an icon, which is automatically resized and imported in all the different size specifications for each platform.

Resizetizer

Resizetizer is a package that was created by Jonathan Dick on the .NET MAUI team. Originally written for Xamarin.Forms and later rewritten for .NET MAUI, resizetizer automatically scales an image for all required device resolutions. It's used not only to generate the app icon but also to automatically generate different scaled versions of your images.

If you've worked with Xamarin.Forms in the past, you'll know how difficult it was to import and manage image assets. You had to provide different versions for each resolution and, for Android, copy them to the correct device resolution folder, as well as update the appropriate asset catalog. A Visual Studio extension called MFractor simplified this process, but managing images without this paid add-on was a pain.

With .NET MAUI, this is all taken care of for you. Simply add an image file to the `Resources/Images` folder (or otherwise specify the image's `BuildAction` as `MauiImage`), and .NET MAUI will use Resizetizer to generate all the required image assets for you.

Resizetizer will resize any image format, but it's best to use SVG where possible. Scaling of bitmap images can lead to pixelated or blurred results, but SVGs can be scaled up or down without any loss of fidelity. However, the resized images are all PNG files, so you must refer to images using the `.PNG` extension in your code, irrespective of the original format.

Having these icons resized automatically is an awesome feature, but if you want some extra control, you can specify a `BaseSize` property (in fact, if you use a bitmap image type, you *must* specify the `BaseSize` property for the image to be automatically resized). You can also disable resizing altogether by setting the `Resize` property to `false`.

You can find out more about these properties and about app icons in general in .NET MAUI, including, for example, how to specify different icons per platform, by consulting the documentation: http://mng.bz/D4ja.

12.1.4 *Replacing the default splash screen*

Splash screens in .NET MAUI are composed in almost the same way as app icons, including autoscaling, with the exception that they only use one image layer. If you look in `MauiStockTake.UI.csproj`, you should be able to find the `MauiSplashScreen` item. We'll replace it with a design from Mildred's team, too.

> **TIP** If your team doesn't include a designer or you don't have access to a design department, check out https://www.svgrepo.com and https://www.reshot.com (this is where I sourced MauiStockTake's icon and splash screen). They provide a massive range of attribution-free SVG images under the Creative Commons (or similar) license that you can use in your apps. For something unique, https://www.fiverr.com is a great resource that I have used for multiple personal projects.

Download the `splash.svg` file from the chapter 12 resources folder and copy it to the `Resources/Splash` folder in MauiStockTake.UI, overwriting the one that's already there. In `MauiStockTake.UI.csproj`, we're keeping the filename, but we need to update a couple of properties. **Change the `Color` property to #74A0B7 and change the `BaseSize` to 256,256.** Run the app now, and you should see the updated splash screen, as shown in figure 12.6.

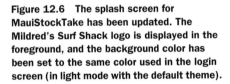

Figure 12.6   The splash screen for MauiStockTake has been updated. The Mildred's Surf Shack logo is displayed in the foreground, and the background color has been set to the same color used in the login screen (in light mode with the default theme).

Updating an app's icon and splash screen is a relatively simple process, but it instantly transforms your app from a development project to a professional product.

> **NOTE** If you do not see the expected results with the splash screen, try uninstalling the app from your device or emulator/simulator and clean and rebuild the project before redeploying.

12.1.5 *Application identifiers and version numbers*

Each app needs a unique identifier to differentiate itself from other apps, both on devices and in the store ecosystems. The name alone is not sufficient, and more importantly, using an identifier distinct from the name allows the name to be changed.

On Android, iOS, and macOS, a bundle ID is used. This is written in reverse-DNS format and typically identifies the app publisher and the app itself. For MauiStock-Take, we'll set this to com.mildredssurfshack.mauistocktake.

WARNING These identifiers are case-sensitive.

NOTE The publisher in this case should always be the business that the app is created for. Here, we are using Mildred's Surf Shack as the publisher, not Beach Bytes. By the same token, the developer account (covered later in this chapter) used to publish the app should be owned by Mildred's Surf Shack, not Beach Bytes.

On Windows, the application is identified with a GUID, which is generated automatically by the template when you create a new .NET MAUI project, so we don't need to update it. But let's fix up the bundle ID for the other platforms, and while we're at it, we can fix up the display name of the app too.

Open MauiStockTake.UI.csproj, and update the ApplicationTitle and ApplicationId items, as shown in the following listing.

Listing 12.1 The app identifiers

Removes the .UI suffix and leaves the display name as MauiStockTake. The .UI suffix is useful to identify the project in the solution but is not a good user-facing part of the name.

The template will add the name of the project to the ApplicationId by default, but it also includes the .UI suffix, which we don't need, and it includes the generic companyname component. Update these to better reflect the publisher and app name.

```
<!-- Display name -->
<ApplicationTitle>MauiStockTake</ApplicationTitle>

<!-- App Identifier -->
<ApplicationId>com.mildredssurfshack.mauistocktake
 </ApplicationId>

<ApplicationIdGuid>F31A0539-B7DB-4874-94A9-489AA23BDF47
 </ApplicationIdGuid>
```

The ApplicationGuid is automatically generated by the template and does not need to be changed (yours will be different).

If you run the app now, you'll note that you have two versions of the app on your device or emulator/simulator because now that you've changed the identifier, the OS considers it to be a different app. You can safely uninstall the old one, or if you can't easily determine which is which, just delete both until the next time you deploy.

The application ID lets the store ecosystems and devices identify your app, but they also need to distinguish different versions of your app. This allows you to provide updates when you have new features and bug fixes. Just like app identifiers, version identifiers have a reference version, used to identify the version of the app (analogous to the ApplicationId), and a display version, used to indicate to the user which version they are using (analogous to the ApplicationTitle).

These version identifiers are handled differently on the different platforms, but .NET MAUI provides a unified way of setting them, also in the .csproj file. In

`MauiStockTake.UI.csproj`, find the two properties next to the `Versions` comment, as shown in the following listing.

> **Listing 12.2   Application versions**

```
<!-- Versions -->
<ApplicationDisplayVersion>1.0</ApplicationDisplayVersion>
<ApplicationVersion>1</ApplicationVersion>
```

`ApplicationDisplayVersion` is the version displayed to users, and `Application-Version` is the property used by operating systems and stores to identify new builds. It's useful to be able to set these independently. For example, you may go through several builds that you need to deploy to test users, and you'll need to increment the version number so that they get the new build, but you may not want to update the display version until you have a new public version that you're shipping.

You don't need to update either of these now. With a proper application identifier, custom icon, and custom splash screen, your app has the final bits of polish it needs to start distributing it to users.

12.2   *Deploying apps with GitHub Actions*

There are several ways to build and deploy your apps to the various stores. We can use the `dotnet publish` command in the .NET CLI, or we can right-click-publish in Visual Studio (on macOS or Windows). I've got a comprehensive guide to manually deploying your apps on my blog, which you can see here: https://goforgoldman.com/posts/maui-app-deploy/.

If you haven't published mobile or desktop apps via the stores before, I recommend working through the blog posts and understanding the process of manually deploying apps. In all cases, you need to upload at least one build manually, and for Windows, you have to actually publish (i.e., release to the public) your app before you can use automation to deploy it.

However, as with any enterprise application, the best approach is to use automated build tools and deploy your app with a CI/CD pipeline. We're going to use GitHub Actions for this, as it's one of the most popular and likely what you will use in your professional work. In any case, while there may be some slight variations with other tools, the workflows we create in this chapter should be straightforward and easy to translate to other platforms.

If you've never used GitHub Actions before, you'll still be able to follow this chapter and should be able to grasp what we cover. For a better understanding of some of the concepts we don't dive into, I recommend the 20-minute GitHub Actions course on Microsoft Learn: http://mng.bz/lWnB.

> **NOTE**   You will need a GitHub account to work through the rest of this chapter and will need to set up a repository for your app. See http://mng.bz/Bm8r.

12.2.1 Setting up the workflow

Part of the popularity of GitHub Actions workflows is due to the simplicity of setting them up and maintaining them. You simply add a YAML file to your code repository in a certain location, and GitHub will automatically execute the instructions in the file. YAML (short for "YAML Ain't Markup Language") is a human-readable data serialization format that is commonly used for CI/CD pipelines. If you're not familiar with it, don't worry; it's designed for simplicity, and you'll have no problem following the example in this chapter.

To add a GitHub Actions workflow, in the root of your repository, create a folder called `.github` and, in here, another folder called `workflows`. We place our GitHub Actions workflows in this folder (defined in YAML), and GitHub will automatically execute them.

Create the `workflows` folder now and, in here, create a file called `build-and-deploy.yaml`.

> ## Working with YAML files
>
> The easiest way to work with YAML files is with a text editor (especially a developer-focused one like Visual Studio Code). This is part of the simplicity of YAML: it's just text files that are very easy to structure and read.
>
> Visual Studio 2022 introduced a feature that lets you work on GitHub Actions within your solution. Historically, this wasn't possible, as the period prefix on the `.github` folder marks it as hidden, but this new update lists GitHub Actions in Solution Explorer.
>
> At the time of writing, this is a preview feature, and **I do not recommend installing preview versions of Visual Studio** if you are working with .NET MAUI—at least not on your main development machine. Preview updates to .NET MAUI are included with preview versions of Visual Studio and can introduce breaking changes, even to stable versions, that can be very difficult to recover from.
>
> VS Code is my preferred way of working with YAML (in fact, it's my preferred way of working with any code that isn't .NET) and is the tool I recommend for working through this chapter.

We're going to add three high-level sections to our GitHub Actions workflow file:

- *Name*—This is the name of the workflow. In this case, we can call it `Build and Deploy MauiStockTake`.
- *On*—This section defines the triggers that will cause the workflow to be run. You can specify which branches and which activities (e.g., pull request or code push) will trigger the workflow, as well as the `workflow_dispatch` trigger, which allows the workflow to be run manually.
- *Jobs*—This section defines the actual work that the workflow will do. Ours will consist of three jobs: one to build the Android app, one to build the iOS app, and one to deploy the builds to the stores.

We need to use some sensitive data in our workflow, such as passwords and signing keys, and we can take advantage of GitHub Actions secrets for this. Using secrets, GitHub securely stores and encrypts data to make it available in workflows. The workflow engine is also smart enough to recognize when a secret is in use and redacts it in any console or log output. Figure 12.7 shows an outline of the three jobs in our workflow.

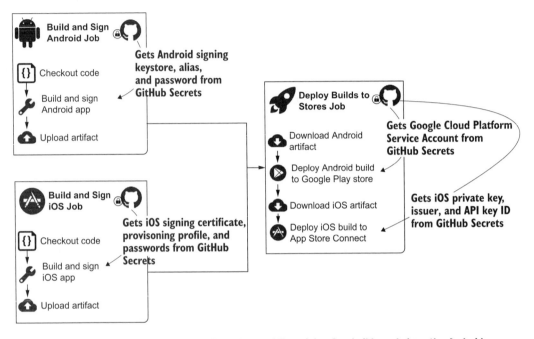

Figure 12.7   The GitHub Actions workflow is made up of three jobs. One builds and signs the Android app, another builds and signs the iOS app, and a third one deploys the two signed builds to their respective stores. The deploy job is dependent on the two build jobs, so they must complete successfully for it to run. All jobs depend on GitHub Actions secrets for signing keys, passwords, and other sensitive data.

To set up the workflow, we need to define the name and the triggers; then we can add the jobs. Open the `build-and-deploy.yaml` in your text editor, and to define the workflow's name, on the first line, add:

```
name: Build and Deploy MauiStockTake
```

YAML files use a combination of colons, whitespace, and indentation to indicate the structure of the data. Colons are used to separate keys and values, while whitespace and indentation are used to indicate nested elements and lists.

Next, up let's add the triggers. The triggers in a GitHub Actions workflow are identified by the on key, so we'll add on: and then indent the following lines to indicate that they're part of this section. We'll add two sections to this:

- push—This trigger indicates that the workflow should run when code is pushed to the nominated branches. It will also be triggered when a pull request is completed to the nominated branches (i.e., when the code is merged).
- workflow_dispatch—This trigger indicates that the workflow can be triggered manually from the GitHub website.

Tests

In a real-world app, you would also typically include unit tests (or other pertinent tests). You could add another workflow that includes the pull_request trigger that would run your tests. You could then make passing tests a requirement for merging pull requests.

Alternatively, you can also include all the triggers in the one workflow and define within each job what conditions must be met for them to run. For example, your tests and builds might always run, but your deploy would only run when code is merged into your main branch.

For the push trigger, we'll nominate the main branch so that the workflow won't run every time we push a commit to our feature branches. We don't need this for the workflow dispatch trigger; it will always be run manually against the main branch. With the triggers added, the build-and-deploy.yaml file will now look like the following listing.

Listing 12.3   The build-and-deploy.yaml file

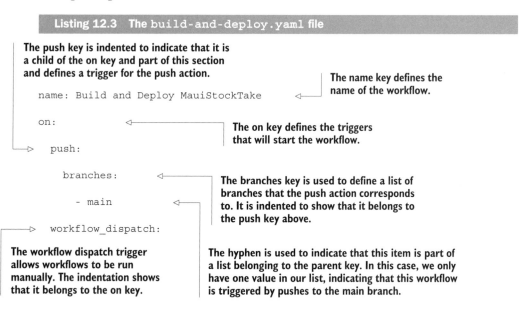

Our workflow is now named and has its triggers defined, so we're now ready to start adding jobs.

12.2.2 Build and sign the Android job

The first job we will add to our workflow is to build and sign the Android app. This job is summarized in figure 12.7, but it will actually consist of six steps, as shown in figure 12.8.

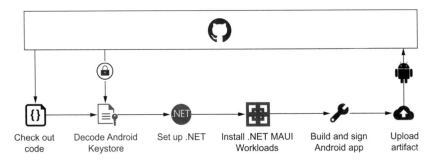

Check out   Decode Android   Set up .NET   Install .NET MAUI   Build and sign   Upload
code   Keystore   Workloads   Android app   artifact

Figure 12.8   The first step in this job checks out the code from the repo. The next will retrieve the Android signing keystore from GitHub Actions secrets and convert it from a base64 string. The next two steps set up dependencies (.NET and the .NET MAUI workloads). After that, the next step creates a signed build, and the final step uploads the signed build to GitHub, ready for the deploy job to pick it up later.

To sign Android apps, we need a keystore. If you've followed the steps in the previously linked blog post or otherwise created a keystore using Visual Studio, you can find this keystore file on Windows in `%LocalAppData%\Xamarin\Mono for Android`, and you can find it on macOS in `~/.local/share/Xamarin/Mono for Android/`. You can also create the keystore from the command line using the `keytool` command:

```
keytool -genkeypair -v -keystore mauistocktake.keystore -alias
    mauistocktakekey -keyalg RSA -keysize 2048 -validity 10000
```

This will create a keystore using the RSA algorithm with a 2048-bit key size. You will be prompted to provide some details and a password. You will end up with a file called `mauistocktake.keystore`.

> **WARNING** From Google's point of view, this key store *is* your Android app. If you lose the key store or the password, you will not be able to upload new versions of your app to Google Play. I have heard of Google support helping people around this, but it is not something you should depend on.

The keystore, password, and alias are confidential and must be secured, which means we can't check the keystore into the repo, and we can't put the password and alias in plain text in the workflow. Fortunately, we can use GitHub Actions secrets to protect these for us; however, secrets can only be strings, and we need to store files as well as strings. To overcome this, we can encode the files as base64 strings and upload them that way.

In the Android job, the second step is decoding the keystore, from the base64 encoded string to a file. We're going to run this job on a Windows agent and use PowerShell to decode the string to a file. To ensure consistency, we can use PowerShell to encode the file.

> **NOTE** If you are using macOS, you can follow the instructions for base64 encoding files in section 12.2.3, or you can install PowerShell Core onto your Mac.

The following listing shows the PowerShell commands to execute to convert your keystore file to a base64 encoded string.

Listing 12.4   Converting files to base64 in PowerShell

```
$keystore = Get-Content mauistocktake.keystore -Encoding Byte
$base64 = [System.Convert]::ToBase64String($keystore)
$base64 | Out-File keystore_file_b64.txt
```

Note that this is not a script; it's three individual commands to run and assumes that your keystore file is called `mauistocktake.keystore`. Once you have run it, you'll have a text file called `keystore_file_b64.txt`. The content of this file is the keystore itself encoded as a base64 string, which you will be able to upload to GitHub.

Now that all our secrets are prepared for this job, let's upload them to GitHub. **Go to the Settings tab of your code repository. Expand Secrets and variables** on the left and **click Actions**. Upload the Android secrets using table 12.1 as a guide, following the GitHub Actions convention of uppercase words separated by underscores.

Table 12.1   The secret names and values to store in GitHub Actions secrets for the Android job

Secret name	Value
ANDROID_KEYPASSWORD	The password for the signing key within the keystore (it's the password you used when creating the keystore)
ANDROID_KEYSTORE	The keystore file encoded as a base64 string
ANDROID_KEYSTOREALIAS	The alias of the keystore
ANDROID_KEYSTOREPASSWORD	The password for the keystore (it's the password you used when creating the keystore)

> **NOTE** When uploading files to secrets encoded as base64 strings, remove any extra line breaks from the end. The secret should end on the last character of the base64 string.

Now that we have the secrets set up for the steps in the Android job, let's start adding the steps. The first thing to do is to define the `jobs` section within the workflow and then the job by giving it a key. We can then give the job a title and define what kind of agent will be used to run it. In this case, we'll use a Windows runner hosted by GitHub as the agent. The following listing shows the code to add to the `build-and-deploy.yaml` file. Add this code after the `workflow_dispatch` line, with an extra line break in between.

Listing 12.5   The Android job definition

```
jobs:
  build-android:

    name: Build Android

    runs-on: windows-latest
```

As we've seen before, indentation is used to indicate structure and hierarchy in a YAML file, so here we can see that we have a `jobs` section, and in here, we have a job defined with the `build-android` key. This job has a `name` property (this is friendlier than the key and will be shown in the workflow results) and a `runs-on`, which we have defined as `windows-latest`, meaning it will run on a GitHub-hosted Windows agent running the latest version.

The actions in GitHub Actions are the steps that we will add in the next section of the workflow file. Actions can be run in one of two ways. The first is with the `run` command, which lets you execute arbitrary shell commands. You can, of course, use these to call your own scripts or executables.

NOTE   The default shell for Windows runners is PowerShell; for Linux runners, bash; and for MacOS runners, zsh, but you can use a different shell if you need to.

You can also run predefined actions published by users on GitHub. These are run with the `uses` key instead of `run` and referred to in the format `[user]/[repo]@[version]`, as shown in figure 12.9.

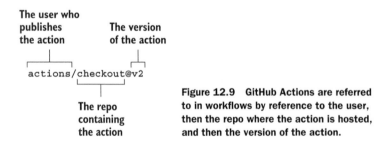

Figure 12.9   GitHub Actions are referred to in workflows by reference to the user, then the repo where the action is hosted, and then the version of the action.

GitHub hosts several common actions, from a user account called actions. You can see them all by browsing the repositories from the profile https://github.com/actions, and many other users make actions available, some of which we'll use in our workflow. You can explore the publicly available actions for use in GitHub workflows at the GitHub marketplace: https://github.com/marketplace?type=actions.

The first step in the workflow is to check out the code, and GitHub provides an action for this. In the second step, we'll retrieve the base64 encoded keystore from GitHub Actions secrets and convert it to a file, which we'll do using shell commands. Secrets can be accessed using a placeholder syntax, in the format `${{ secrets.[YOUR_SECRET_NAME] }}`.

We'll use a GitHub Action to set up .NET in the third step, and in the fourth step, we'll use shell commands to install the .NET MAUI workloads we need to build our app. The following listing shows the steps section of the Android job with the first four steps.

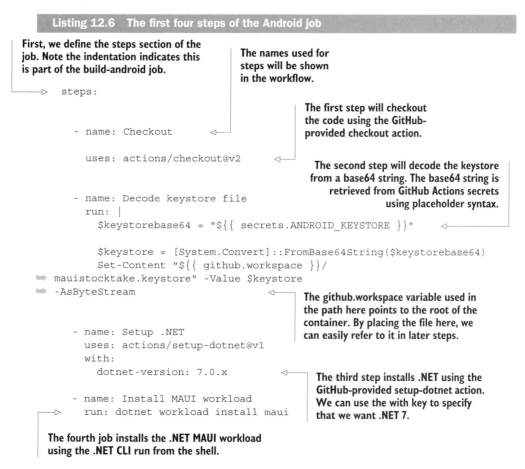

Listing 12.6   The first four steps of the Android job

First, we define the steps section of the job. Note the indentation indicates this is part of the build-android job.

The names used for steps will be shown in the workflow.

```
steps:

  - name: Checkout

    uses: actions/checkout@v2

  - name: Decode keystore file
    run: |
      $keystorebase64 = "${{ secrets.ANDROID_KEYSTORE }}"

      $keystore = [System.Convert]::FromBase64String($keystorebase64)
      Set-Content "${{ github.workspace }}/
mauistocktake.keystore" -Value $keystore
-AsByteStream

  - name: Setup .NET
    uses: actions/setup-dotnet@v1
    with:
      dotnet-version: 7.0.x

  - name: Install MAUI workload
    run: dotnet workload install maui
```

The first step will checkout the code using the GitHub-provided checkout action.

The second step will decode the keystore from a base64 string. The base64 string is retrieved from GitHub Actions secrets using placeholder syntax.

The github.workspace variable used in the path here points to the root of the container. By placing the file here, we can easily refer to it in later steps.

The third step installs .NET using the GitHub-provided setup-dotnet action. We can use the with key to specify that we want .NET 7.

The fourth job installs the .NET MAUI workload using the .NET CLI run from the shell.

This puts all the pieces in place we need to build and sign the Android app. For this step, we're going to call the .NET CLI from a shell command. We'll simply call `dotnet publish` and use the `Release` configuration, specifying the Android target framework. We've seen most of the pieces of this in chapter 2; in this case, we're substituting `publish` for `build`. The anatomy of the `dotnet publish` command is shown in figure 12.10.

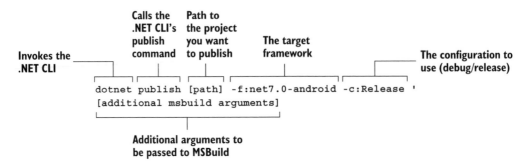

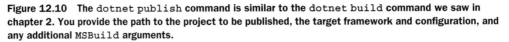

Figure 12.10 The `dotnet publish` command is similar to the `dotnet build` command we saw in chapter 2. You provide the path to the project to be published, the target framework and configuration, and any additional `MSBuild` arguments.

Under the hood, the `dotnet publish` command uses `MSBuild`, and `MSBuild` accepts the arguments we need to sign the Android build. Arguments are passed to `MSBuild` by using the `p:/[argument]` syntax, and we will need to pass the following arguments:

- `AndroidKeyStore`—A Boolean flag to indicate that we will be using a keystore
- `AndroidSigningKeyStore`—The path to the keystore itself, so it will be the keystore file in the `github.workspace` directory
- `AndroidSigningKeyStorePass`—The password to the keystore file
- `AndroidSigningKeyPass`—The password for the signing key inside the keystore
- `AndroidSigningKeyAlias`—The alias that identifies the signing key within the keystore

The `dotnet publish` command doesn't support these arguments directly, but we can pass them through to `MSBuild` to get the desired effect. With this information, we're ready to add the build and sign step to our workflow. You can see this step in the following listing.

Listing 12.7   The build and sign Android step

```
   - name: Build
     run: dotnet publish
➭ src/Presentation/MauiStockTake.UI/MauiStockTake.UI.csproj `
       -f:net7.0-android -c:Release /p:AndroidKeyStore=True `
       /p:AndroidSigningKeyStore="${{ github.workspace }}
➭ /mauistocktake.keystore" `
       /p:AndroidSigningKeyPass=${{ secrets.ANDROID_KEYPASSWORD }} `
       /p:AndroidSigningKeyAlias=${{ secrets.ANDROID_KEYSTOREALIAS }} `
       /p:AndroidSigningStorePass=${{ secrets.ANDROID_KEYSTOREPASSWORD }}
```

NOTE   Backticks (`` ` ``) are used to wrap long commands over multiple lines.

The final step for the Android job is to upload the signed AAB file to GitHub, ready to be pulled down by the deploy job. GitHub provides an action called `upload-artifact` that serves exactly this purpose, so we'll use the uses key instead of run to invoke this action. Some actions take additional parameters, and we can pass these using the with key. The parameters we will use with the upload-artifact action are name and path. The name property will specify the name to use to retrieve the artifact in a later job, and the path specifies the path to the file to be uploaded. This gives us the final step in the Android job, which you can see in the following listing.

```
- name: Upload Android artifact
  uses: actions/upload-artifact@v3.1.0
  with:
    name: mauistocktake-android-build
    path: src/Presentation/MauiStockTake.UI/bin/Release/
➥ net7.0-android/*Signed.aab
```

NOTE I'm using an asterisk (*) in the file path rather than specifying the full AAB filename. This is just for convenience, but it also lets me easily adapt this to other workflows for other apps. You could also use a glob pattern like **/*.aab, which would make it work with any repo, but for the avoidance of doubt it's better to be at least a little specific.

This completes the Android job. You can run the workflow now and should see a green tick for the Android job. If it fails, check the log for any errors and address them as necessary.

12.2.3 Build and sign iOS job

The job to build and sign the iOS app is similar to the Android job in that we check out the code, decode a file (in this case, the distribution certificate as opposed to the keystore), build and sign the app, and upload the build to be picked up later by the deploy job.

NOTE If you're not already familiar with manually building, signing, and deploying iOS apps, I recommend reading up on it on my website here: https://goforgoldman.com/posts/maui-app-deploy-2/.

The iOS job has some subtle differences, though. In addition to the signing certificate, we also need to decode and install the provisioning profile. You can see a summary of the steps for the iOS job in figure 12.11.

We will also make a choice about where to run the iOS job. As it requires a macOS agent to run, a self-hosted runner is a better choice than a GitHub-hosted runner. You can see the instructions for setting up a self-hosted runner here: http://mng.bz/d1Yv. The workflow will also run on a GitHub-hosted runner with a couple of small changes. I'll include these, too, but they will be commented out. Uncomment these if you're using a GitHub-hosted runner.

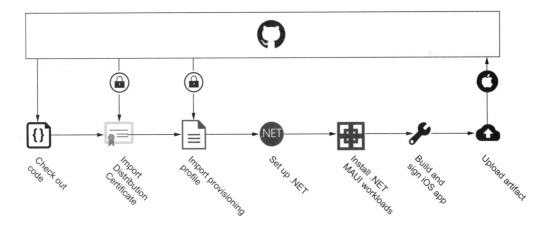

Figure 12.11   The iOS build and sign job is similar to the Android job but decodes (and installs) a distribution certificate instead of a keystore. It will also need to decode and import the provisioning profile.

Self-hosted vs. GitHub-hosted runners

GitHub Actions workflows can run on Linux, Windows, or macOS agents. These can be hosted by GitHub, or you can host them yourself and link them to your repository or organization.

For workflows that require macOS, I recommend a self-hosted runner rather than a GitHub runner due to the limits imposed by GitHub. For most accounts, you get 2,000 minutes per month (the Enterprise plan gets you 50,000), but this is the baseline for Linux runners. For Windows runners, a 2× penalty is imposed, and for macOS, it is 10×. This means that a job that takes 50 minutes will eat a quarter of your monthly quota in one hit.

Workflows can fail and sometimes have unpredictable results; consequently, it's easy to burn through your entire quota without getting a single successful build. By using a self-hosted runner, you avoid these problems as you don't have any time limits in this sense (a single workflow run cannot exceed 35 days, but if your workflows run this long, you've got other problems).

It may be that you specifically want to use GitHub as a build agent *because* you don't have a Mac. Using a GitHub-hosted runner can be a potential workaround; however, the previously mentioned problems will be exacerbated if you haven't had the opportunity to test your build on a Mac before pushing it to GitHub. While it's theoretically possible to develop, build, and deploy a .NET MAUI app to iOS or macOS without a Mac, your developer experience will be much smoother if either you or someone on your team has one.

An entry-level Mac Mini is a good investment; they are relatively inexpensive, will make your life as a developer much easier if you're targeting macOS or iOS, and can double as a self-hosted runner for GitHub Actions.

Let's add the iOS job to the workflow. To start, it will be almost identical to the Android job: it will have a key to identify it in the file, a `name`, and a `runs-on` property. We'll set `name` to `Build iOS` and `runs-on` to `self-hosted`. You can change this if you've named your runner something different or `macos-latest` if you want to run it on GitHub. If you do run it on GitHub, add a timeout property; this is essential as if something goes wrong with your workflow, it could get stuck running and will blow out your available GitHub Actions minutes.

After that, just like with the Android job, we'll check out the code from the repo. The following listing shows the start of the build iOS job.

Listing 12.9   The setup for the `Build iOS` job

```
build-ios-mac:

    name: Build iOS
    runs-on: self-hosted
    # timeout-minutes: 30      ◁——

    steps:
      - name: Checkout
        uses: actions/checkout@v2
```

> **If you're running this on GitHub, set a timeout for the job. This will prevent the job from burning through your allocation of minutes if something goes wrong.**

Before we can proceed any further, we need to set up the secrets that the `Build iOS` job will need. Let's start with the certificate. As with the keystore in Android, it is a file, so we will need to encode it to a bse64 string to store it in GitHub Actions secrets. But first, we need to export it from the Keychain app. **Open the Keychain Access app** and find your distribution certificate. You can do this easily by searching for `Apple Distribution`.

Once you've found the certificate, select it and the corresponding private key (it should be listed directly below it), **right-click them, and select Export 2 items…** Ensure that the .p12 format is selected (you can also change the name if you want, but it doesn't matter as we won't be using this file in the workflow), and **click Save**. You'll be prompted to enter and confirm a password; keep these safe, as we will need to upload them to GitHub. You will also need the name of the certificate for use in the workflow; double-click on the certificate to see its details and highlight the whole name (starting with `Apple Distribution…` and ending with the team name [the random string] and closing bracket). Copy this and paste it somewhere so you can refer to it later.

The `.p12` file contains both the certificate and the private key and, as such, should be considered sensitive and handled accordingly (once I've uploaded the base64 encoded version, I delete it; I can always export it again). We'll use some zsh commands to encode the file to ensure consistency with the environment that will be used to decode them.

> **TIP**   The Terminal app that ships with macOS is OK, but you can get a better experience with an enhanced terminal. iTerm is a popular terminal app, but I've become a big fan of Warp. Find out more here: https://warp.dev.

The zsh shell includes a `base64` command that we can use to encode the certificate. It takes an input and an output parameter, denoted by `-i` and `-o`, respectively, that identify the file to be encoded and the resulting output file. Encode the certificate and private key using the following command:

```
base64 -i certificate.p12 -o certificate-base64.txt
```

In addition to the certificate, we need the provisioning profile. This is a little more straightforward to obtain as you can simply download it from the Apple Developer website (go to https://developer.apple.com, click on Account to log in, then go to Profiles). Download the correct distribution profile and use the `base64` command to convert it to a base64 encoded string:

```
base64 -i MauiStockTake_iOS_Distribution.mobileprovision -o profile-base64.txt
```

Now that we've got all our secrets, let's add them to GitHub. Table 12.2 shows you the secret names to use and the values to copy in for each.

Table 12.2   The secret names and values to store in GitHub Actions secrets for the iOS job

Secret name	Value
`APPLE_CERT`	The certificate and private key. Copy the content from the `certificate-base64.txt` file.
`APPLE_CERT_PASSWORD`	The password for the `.p12` file that you set when you exported it.
`APPLE_CERT_NAME`	The name of the certificate that you copied from Keychain Access.
`APPLE_PROFILE`	The provisioning profile. Copy the content from the `profile-base64.txt` file.
`APPLE_PROFILE_NAME`	The name of the distribution profile, as it appears on the Apple Developer website.

Now that the secrets are in GitHub, let's add the remaining steps. The first two after checkout will be to decode and install the certificate and to decode and install the provisioning profile. We can use the same `base64` command that we used in our terminal, but with the `–decode` flag to indicate that we want to decode a base64 string rather than encode some data to one.

For both these steps, we'll use the `run` key and supply shell commands. For both steps, on the first line, we can `echo` the content of the relevant secret, pipe it to the `base64` command, and then output it to a file. For the certificate, we can use the `security` command to import the certificate, and for the profile, we will need to create the appropriate directory and then copy the profile to it. The following listing shows the two steps to import the certificate and provisioning profile.

Listing 12.10   The steps to import the ceritifcate and provisioning profile

```
      - name: Import Distribution Certificate
        run: |
          echo ${{ secrets.APPLE_CERT }} | base64 --decode >
➥ DistributionCertificate.p12
          security import DistributionCertificate.p12 -k ~/Library/
➥ Keychains/login.keychain -P ${{ secrets.APPLE_CERT_PASSWORD }}

      - name: Import Provisioning Profile
        run: |
          echo ${{ secrets.APPLE_PROFILE }} | base64 --decode >
➥ MauiStockTake_iOS_Distribution.mobileprovision
          mkdir -p ~/Library/MobileDevice/Provisioning\ Profiles
          cp MauiStockTake_iOS_Distribution.mobileprovision
➥ ~/Library/MobileDevice/Provisioning\ Profiles/
```

The remaining four steps are the same as the last four steps in the Android workflow: we set up .NET, install the .NET MAUI workload, build and sign the app, and then upload the artifact. The differences are in the build and sign step; the target framework will be iOS instead of Android, and the MSBuild arguments that we pass will be different.

Before we move on to these steps, there's one extra step that's required for a GitHub-hosted runner, and that is to specify the XCode version. If you're using a self-hosted runner, you just need to ensure the correct version of XCode is installed.

At the time of this writing, the version you need to sign iOS apps built with .NET MAUI is 14.1, but you may need to update this in the future. Listing 12.11 shows the step to select the XCode version. It is commented so you can copy it into your workflow regardless of whether you're self-hosting or running on GitHub. If you're running on GitHub, uncomment this step.

Listing 12.11 also includes the steps to set up .NET and install the .NET MAUI workloads (they are identical to those in the Android workflow). Include these irrespective of which runner you are using.

Listing 12.11   The select XCode version step

```
    #   - name: Set XCode Version
    #     if: runner.os == 'macOS'
    #     shell: bash
    #     run: |
    #       sudo xcode-select -s "/Applications/Xcode_14.1.app"
    #       echo "MD_APPLE_SDK_ROOT=/Applications/Xcode_14.1.app" >>
➥ $GITHUB_ENV

      - name: Setup .NET
        uses: actions/setup-dotnet@v1
        with:
          dotnet-version: 7.0.x

      - name: Install MAUI workload
        run: dotnet workload install maui
```

As previously mentioned, the publish step is the same as in the Android workflow, just with the target framework and MSBuild arguments changed. The MSBuild arguments we need for iOS signing are

- ArchiveOnBuild—A flag that tells MSBuild to create an .ipa file (an iOS archive) on build, so it will be set to true.
- RuntimeIdentifier—While we are providing the target framework, we also need to tell MSBuild the runtime identifier so it can be matched against the profile. Specify this as ios-arm64.
- CodesignKey—The name of the certificate that we copied from Keychain Access (not the name of the file). We've already added this as a secret, so we'll refer to that secret here with the placeholder syntax.
- CodesignProvision—The name of the provisioning profile. We have also added this as a GitHub secret so we can refer to it here with the placeholder syntax.

Just like with the Android build, these arguments are passed through to MSBuild with the /p: flag. The following listing shows the remainder of the steps for the iOS job. All of these steps are the same as the Android job, except for the minor changes to the Build step and the file path and glob to upload the artifact.

Listing 12.12   The remaining steps for the iOS job

```
- name: Setup .NET
  uses: actions/setup-dotnet@v1
  with:
    dotnet-version: 7.0.x

- name: Install MAUI workload
  run: dotnet workload install maui

- name: Build
  run: dotnet publish
src/Presentation/MauiStockTake.UI/MauiStockTake.UI.csproj `
    -v:diag -f:net7.0-ios -c:Release `
    /p:ArchiveOnBuild=true `
    /p:RuntimeIdentifier=ios-arm64 `
    /p:CodeSignKey="${{ secrets.APPLE_CERT_NAME }}" `
    /p:CodesignProvision="MauiStockTake iOS Distribution"
- name: Upload iOS artifact
  uses: actions/upload-artifact@v3.1.0
  with:
    name: mauistocktake-ios-build
    path: src/Presentation/MauiStockTake.UI/bin/
Release/net7.0-ios/ios-arm64/publish//*.ipa
```

The dotnet publish command is the same as in the Android job, except the target framework is net7.0-ios, and the MSBuild arguments are iOS specific, rather than Android specific.

The upload artifact step is the same as in the Android job, except the file path and glob pattern match the signed .ipa file.

We now have a workflow that builds and signs our Android app and our iOS app. All that's left is to deploy it to the stores.

12.2.4 Deploy to stores job

The final job in the workflow will deploy the signed builds to the Google Play Store and to App Store Connect. The Google Play Store and App Store Connect have APIs that we can use to upload these artifacts programmatically, and there are community-provided actions that we can use in the job that call them. Figure 12.12 shows a summary of the main steps in the deploy job.

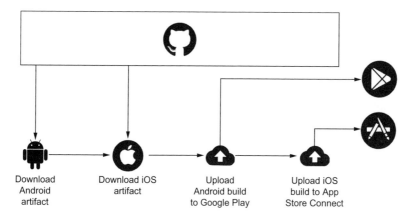

Download   Download iOS   Upload   Upload iOS
Android   artifact   Android build   build to App
artifact   to Google Play   Store Connect

Figure 12.12   The deploy job is relatively simple and has four main steps: download the Android artifact, download the iOS artifact, upload the Android artifact to Google Play, and upload the iOS artifact to App Store Connect.

NOTE   There's one additional step not shown in figure 12.12, but this is just to put one of the filenames into an environment variable for later reference.

To use these APIs, we need to generate credentials that can be used to upload our builds. We'll step through these first and then come back to the workflow.

GENERATING GOOGLE CREDENTIALS

To use the Google API, we need to create a service account in the Google Cloud Platform (GCP). The first step is to link a GCP project to the Google Play Console. I cover these steps in the article I linked to earlier in the chapter—specifically, at the start of the section on deploying from Visual Studio (http://mng.bz/rWMe). It's a good idea to complete the end-to-end process detailed in the linked article to ensure that you can successfully deploy a build before you burn through any of your GitHub Actions minutes.

Once that's done, on the **API Access** page in the Google Play console, scroll down to the **Credentials** section. Next to the **Service Accounts** subheading is a link that says **Learn How to Create Service Accounts**. This will open a dialog that details the steps you need to follow, along with a link to the appropriate area of GCP. What's not listed is the **role** you need to assign to the service account; scroll through the list of roles until you get to the Service Accounts category, select the **Service Account User** role, and complete the steps as described.

> **WARNING**   I've seen some recommendations to use the Owner role, as this will guarantee that the service account has the necessary permissions. But this violates the principle of least privilege and is a security risk.

Once you've created the service account, you should see it listed in a table. Click on the service account link to see its details, then click on the **Keys** tab. Expand the **Add Key** dropdown and select **Create New Key**. A dialog will appear offering you two options. Accept the recommendation for **JSON** and click **Create**. The GCP will now generate a JSON file and automatically trigger a download.

Upload the content of the JSON file as a GitHub secret. As it's JSON, it's just a text string and doesn't need to be base64 encoded. Add it as a secret named GCP_SERVICE _ACCOUNT and don't forget to remove any line breaks from the end.

CREATING APPLE CREDENTIALS

We'll need to create App Store Connect API credentials to upload our build. Log in to App Store Connect and go to the **Users and Access** section. Go to the **Keys** tab and click on the plus (**+**) button. Enter a suitable name, such as MauiStockTake Upload Key, and from the **Access** dropdown, select **App Manager**.

Click the **Generate** button and then click on the **Download API Key** link next to your newly created key in the table. You'll see a warning saying that an API key can only be downloaded once (if you lose it, you'll have to generate another one); click the **Download** button. App Store Connect will download a file with a .p8 extension, but it's just a text file, so you can open it in any text editor.

You'll also need the **Issuer ID** from this screen; conveniently, it's got a **Copy** button next to it that you can click to copy it to your clipboard. You also need the **Key ID**; when you want to copy this, simply highlight it and copy it as you would any other text you've selected.

We've now got all the details we need for the Apple upload step. Table 12.3 shows the secret names to use in GitHub Actions secrets and what values to assign them.

Table 12.3   The secret names and values to store in GitHub Actions secrets for the Apple upload step

Secret name	Value
APPSTORE_ISSUER_ID	The issuer ID you copied from App Store Connect
APPSTORE_API_KEY_ID	The key ID you copied from App Store Connect
APPSTORE_API_PRIVATE_KEY	The content of the .p8 file that you downloaded

Now that we've got all of the Google and Apple secrets, we're ready to complete the workflow.

COMPLETING THE WORKFLOW

As described in figure 12.12, the deploy job will consist of four main steps. One of these steps, the step to upload to App Store Connect, depends on macOS, so we'll also run this job on our self-hosted runner (or a macOS runner if you need to run it on GitHub).

The job will start the same way as the others: with a key, a `name` property, and a `runs-on` property. We'll add one other key, which is `needs`, under which we can list the jobs that must complete successfully before this one. This serves two purposes: first, it allows some jobs to be run in parallel, and second, and more importantly, it saves us from running this job unnecessarily if either of the build and sign jobs has failed. The following listing shows the start of the deploy job.

Listing 12.13 The start of the deploy job

```
deploy-all:

  name: Deploy builds to stores

  runs-on: self-hosted

  needs:             ◁──────────

    - build-android-windows
    - build-ios-mac
```

> **We've added the needs key this time and specified the two build and sign jobs. That will prevent this job from running if either of those jobs fails.**

Next, we'll add the steps, and the first two steps will download the Android and iOS artifacts. For this, we will use a GitHub-provided action, which acts as the inverse of the upload artifact action, using the name that we used in those upload steps to identify the artifacts. The following listing shows the start of the steps portion of the job.

Listing 12.14 The first two steps of the deploy job

```
steps:
  - name: Download Android artifact
    uses: actions/download-artifact@v2
    with:
      name: mauistocktake-android-build  ◁──

  - name: Download iOS artifact
    uses: actions/download-artifact@v2
    with:
      name: mauistocktake-ios-build      ◁──
```

> **Artifacts are identified by name, so we use the same name to download them that we used to upload them.**

Now that we've got the artifacts, let's start uploading them. We'll upload the Android build first with a community-provided action called `upload-google-play`. There are a few ways that you can use this action, but we're going to provide the following parameters:

NOTE   Parameters in GitHub workflows are passed using the with keyword.

- serviceAccountJsonPlainText—This is the JSON content that we downloaded as the service account key. As it's plain text (rather than a file), we can pass it straight from the GitHub secret.
- packageName—This is the bundle ID.
- releaseFiles—This is the path to the signed AAB file(s) we want to upload. We don't need to know the specific path as we can use a glob pattern.
- track—The *release track* to upload the build to (e.g., internal testing, production, etc.).
- status—This can be marked as in progress for a staged release (which also requires you to provide a percentage). We'll just mark this as complete to indicate that it should be rolled out to all eligible users concurrently.

The following listing shows the step that uploads the Android build to Google Play.

Listing 12.15   The Android upload step

```
- name: Upload Singed AAB
  uses: r0adkll/upload-google-play@v1
  with:
    serviceAccountJsonPlainText: ${{ secrets.GCP_SERVICE_ACCOUNT }}
    packageName: com.mildredssurfshack.MauiStockTake
    releaseFiles: ./*Signed.aab
    track: internal
    status: completed
```

The next logical step is to upload the iOS build, and for this, we'll use another community-provided action called upload-testflight-build. Unlike the Android upload job, this action doesn't accept a glob pattern for the file to be uploaded, so we'll insert an interim step first that gets the path to the file and sets it as an environment variable. The following listing shows the step to add to get the iOS build file path.

Listing 12.16   Set the iOS file path as an environment variable

```
- name: Get ipa filename
  run: echo "IPA_FILENAME=$(ls -R *.ipa)" > $GITHUB_ENV
```

We're now ready to add the final step, which is to upload the iOS build. The upload-testflight-build action takes the following parameters:

- app-path—The file path for the .ipa archive. We'll use the environment variable we set in the previous step.
- issuer-id—The issuer ID, which we have set as a GitHub secret.
- api-key-id—The API key ID, which we have set as a GitHub secret.
- api-private-key—The private key that we got as a .p8 file and have set as a GitHub secret.

The following listing shows the upload iOS step.

Listing 12.17   The upload iOS step

```
- name: Upload app to TestFlight
  uses: apple-actions/upload-testflight-build@v1
  with:
    app-path: ${{ env.IPA_FILENAME }}
    issuer-id: ${{ secrets.APPSTORE_ISSUER_ID }}
    api-key-id: ${{ secrets.APPSTORE_API_KEY_ID }}
    api-private-key: ${{ secrets.APPSTORE_API_PRIVATE_KEY }}
```

With the iOS upload step in place, this completes the workflow. You can find the full workflow in the chapter 12 resources folder.

At this point, you should be able to run the workflow and successfully deploy builds to the two stores. If your workflow has completed successfully, you should see some nice ticks, as in figure 12.13.

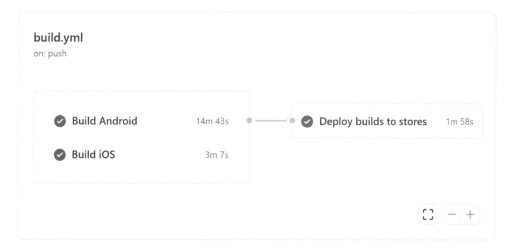

Figure 12.13   A successfully completed workflow run shows a tick for each job.

12.3 *Next steps*

At this point, you've completed an end-to-end development cycle of an enterprise app. You've identified the business requirements, designed and built the app, integrated it into an enterprise architecture, and used a CI/CD pipeline to deploy the build to the stores. This is typical of a real-world scenario and is not too far removed from working on an enterprise app development team (the only things missing are the agile process and QA/testing).

If you've enjoyed this journey, and I hope that you have, the good news is that there's still plenty left to learn. For example, in this chapter, we've looked at automated build processes for Android and iOS (and the iOS process can be easily adapted for macOS). We haven't covered Windows deployment to the Microsoft store because, at the time of this writing, automated deployments of WinUI builds are not as reliable as I would like to be comfortable including them in this book. WinUI is a relatively new technology, so some teething problems are to be expected. If you're targeting Windows desktop, this is an area to keep an eye on.

There are also many features of .NET MAUI that we haven't covered (animation, for example), and many that, while we have covered them, we've only scratched the surface. But, at this stage, you've walked through the process of developing an enterprise app, and you're well-equipped to pick up anything else you need as you go.

Summary

- Adding custom icons and splash screens is easy in .NET MAUI using layered SVGs. Leaving the default icon or splash screen is the hallmark of a work-in-progress, so a well-designed icon or splash screen adds professionalism and polish.
- App icons and, in fact, all images in .NET MAUI are automatically resized for each screen resolution. Using SVG images will ensure these are crisp on all devices.
- Your app is specifically identified by a bundle ID. On Windows, this is a GUID; on Android, iOS; and macOS, a reverse-DNS formatted string.
- Microsoft, Apple, and Google have developer programs. You must join these to distribute your apps via their digital storefronts. Apple's developer program requires an annual membership fee. Microsoft and Google both have a one-time fee; however, Microsoft will deactivate your membership if you are not actively releasing apps or updates.
- Sign Android apps with a self-signed certificate. The Google Play developer console will expect any new versions of the app to be signed with the same certificate. Visual Studio can manage this for you, but you should export the keystore and store it securely.
- Sign iOS apps and macOS apps with a distribution certificate provided by Apple. Visual Studio can automate requesting this certificate for you. Multiple distribution certificates and profiles can be used for any app; these are managed on the Apple Developer website.
- Using GitHub actions makes it simple to create a reusable workflow to build and deploy your apps to the Google Play store and iOS App Store.
- GitHub Actions workflows are defined in YAML files. YAML is a text format that uses indentation to denote structure and hierarchy.
- GitHub Actions workflows are divided into jobs, which are divided into steps. Workflows can define triggers that specify what causes the workflow to be run.

- The steps of a job can be shell commands (which, in turn, means you can execute arbitrary code) or can be predefined actions provided either by GitHub or the community.
- Workflows can be run on GitHub-hosted runners or self-hosted runners. Self-hosted runners are a better option for macOS jobs, as macOS incurs a 10× penalty when running on GitHub.

appendix A
Setting up your environment for .NET MAUI development

Getting started with .NET MAUI is a straightforward experience. You can use either Windows or macOS to develop apps with .NET MAUI, and in this appendix, we'll walk through the steps of installing the right dependencies for each of these OSes.

A.1 Setup on Windows

1 Install the latest version of Visual Studio 2022. Any edition is fine, including the free Community edition. There are no features that you would need for .NET MAUI development that are only in the paid editions. If you already have Visual Studio installed, open the Visual Studio installer and proceed to step 2.

2 Ensure that you select the .NET Multi-platform App UI development workload. This will set up everything you need to develop apps with .NET MAUI (figure A.1).

3 After you have installed Visual Studio (or added the .NET MAUI workload if you already had it installed), install the blank .NET MAUI project template by running the following command from your terminal of choice:

```
dotnet new --install Goldie.BlankMauiTemplate
```

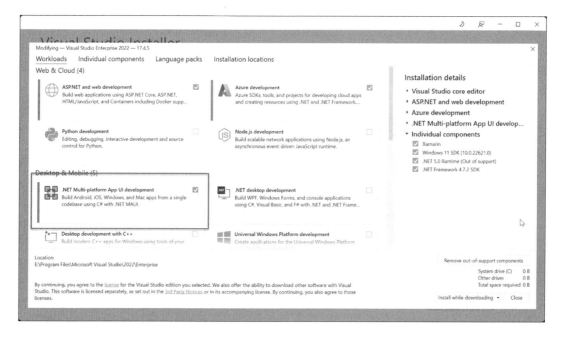

Figure A.1 Select the .NET Multi-platform App UI development workload in the Visual Studio installer

A.2 Setup for Mac

Get the latest version of Visual Studio for Mac from https://www.visualstudio.microsoft .com/vs/mac/.

1 Download and run the installer.
2 Ensure you select the CrossPlatform .NET MAUI workload (figure A.2).
3 After you have installed Visual Studio (or added the .NET MAUI workload if you already had it installed), install the blank .NET MAUI project template by running the following command from your terminal of choice:

```
dotnet new --install Goldie.BlankMauiTemplate
```

A.3 Developing full-stack apps locally

Running many of the apps in the book is as easy as hitting F5 (or clicking the Run button or using `dotnet run` in the CLI). Some of the sample apps talk to a REST API on the public internet to retrieve data, so they are easy for our apps to reach.

When you develop a full-stack solution, your API will eventually be hosted on the public internet. But while you're building the app, it's much easier to run the API locally on your development machine. This is especially helpful if you're working on a full vertical slice (a complete feature that has functionality across all layers of the stack) and need to debug the API and the mobile app at the same time.

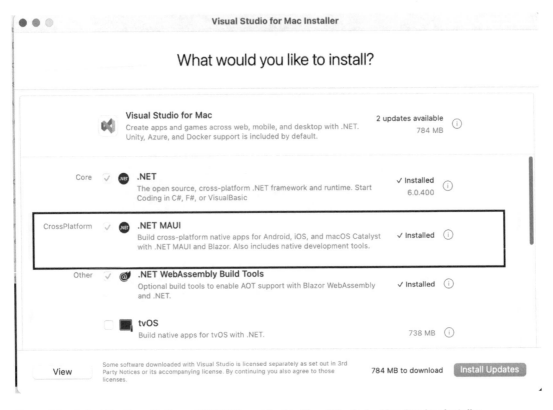

Figure A.2 Select the CrossPlatform .NET MAUI workload in Visual Studio for Mac Preview installer.

A.3.1 *Full-stack local development challenges*

Connecting to an API running on your development machine presents two challenges. The first is how your app can access the API. When it's publicly hosted, it has a URL that your app can reach, but this isn't the case for your local development machine. Depending on your target framework, there are different ways you can get around this. For macOS, Windows, and the iOS simulator, you can use `localhost` or the loopback IP address (127.0.0.1) to access your API. As the Android emulator runs a full OS, this address routes to itself, but the emulator provides a special address to access the host machine (10.0.2.2). If you're running your app on a physical Android or iOS device, you would have to use the IP address of your development machine on your local network, and you would also need to configure your firewall to allow external connections to your API.

The second challenge is around SSL certificates. When you run your API, you can easily instruct your machine to trust the self-signed development certificate using

```
dotnet dev-certs https -trust
```

You can read more about ASP.NET Core developer certificates on Scott Hanselman's blog post here: http://mng.bz/V16W. This works well for ASP.NET Core, but getting your .NET MAUI app to trust this certificate can be tricky, and the method is different for each OS. It can also be unreliable, and Microsoft recommends bypassing security checks for SSL certificates in your code while debugging.

Unfortunately, this last point presents a roadblock for the apps we build in this book because we'll be using the OS's default web browser for authentication (see section 8.1.2), and we can't control the browser's certificate-handling behavior from our code.

A.3.2 Setting up ngrok

If you want to build and test your app on a number of different devices, rather than go through the trouble of installing the certificate each time and changing your code to point to a different URL depending on where it's running, it's much easier to use a reverse proxy or tunnel.

These tools establish a tunnel from your development machine to a server on the internet that sends traffic back across the tunnel. A tunneling tool creates a publicly routable URL that you can use to access your local development machine. The most popular of these tunneling tools is ngrok as it offers a free tier and is easy to set up and use.

> ### You don't have to use ngrok
>
> There are plenty of alternatives to ngrok available. I use Packetriot but have chosen to use ngrok here because Packetriot is not as easy to set up and is not differentiated on the free tier (I have a paid subscription). Cloudflare is also a popular choice.
>
> If you already have another reverse proxy or tunneling solution, you can skip this section and use whatever you are comfortable with.

Go to https://ngrok.com, and click on the Sign Up button. After signing up for a free account, follow the download instructions for your host operating system.

Download and install ngrok and then go back to the website and click on the Your Authtoken tab. Follow the instructions here to add your auth token to your installed ngrok configuration.

Once you've got ngrok installed and authorized, you can set up a tunnel. Run your API project, and it will start up on your local machine with HTTPS running on port 5001.

NOTE   if you want to run on a different port, you can edit the configuration in the `launchsettings.json` file in the `Properties` folder of the API project.

If you've got Swagger setup up (the MauiStockTake API that you will download in chapter 7 uses Swagger) you can verify that the WebAPI project is running by opening a browser and going to the Swagger page (for MauiStockTake, this will be https://localhost:5001/api). This should bring up a Swagger page with information about the API endpoints and schema, similar to figure A.3.

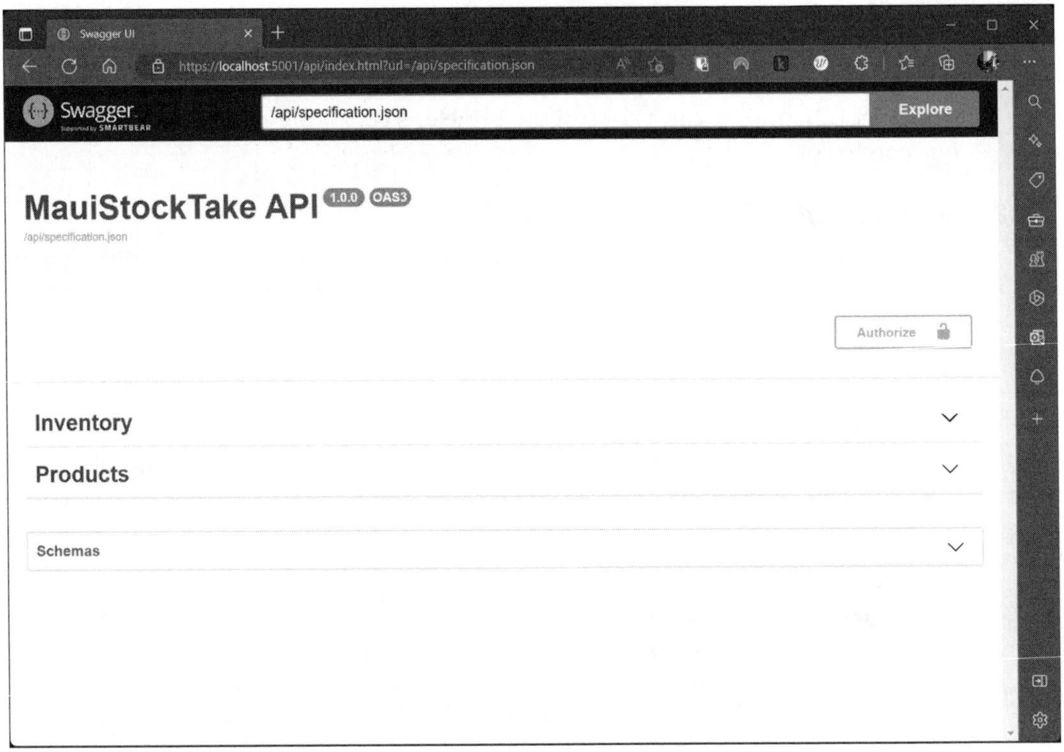

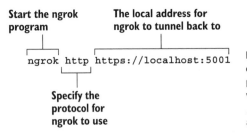

Figure A.3   The MauiStockTake API's Swagger page, running on localhost on port 5001

With your API running, you can open an ngrok tunnel by using the command shown in figure A.4.

Figure A.4   The ngrok command. The first part of the command (ngrok) invokes the ngrok program, and the next part (http) tells ngrok what protocol to use. The third part (https://localhost:5001) tells ngrok what local address to use.

TIP   ngrok is a standalone executable, so your command prompt must be at the path where the file is located. You can make life easier by copying the file to a sensible location (e.g., a folder in Program Files on Windows) add adding the path to your PATH environment variable (applicable on all platforms).

After you run the ngrok command, it will start the tunnel and show you the public URL it has generated that is tunneling back to your local machine. See figure A.5 for an example.

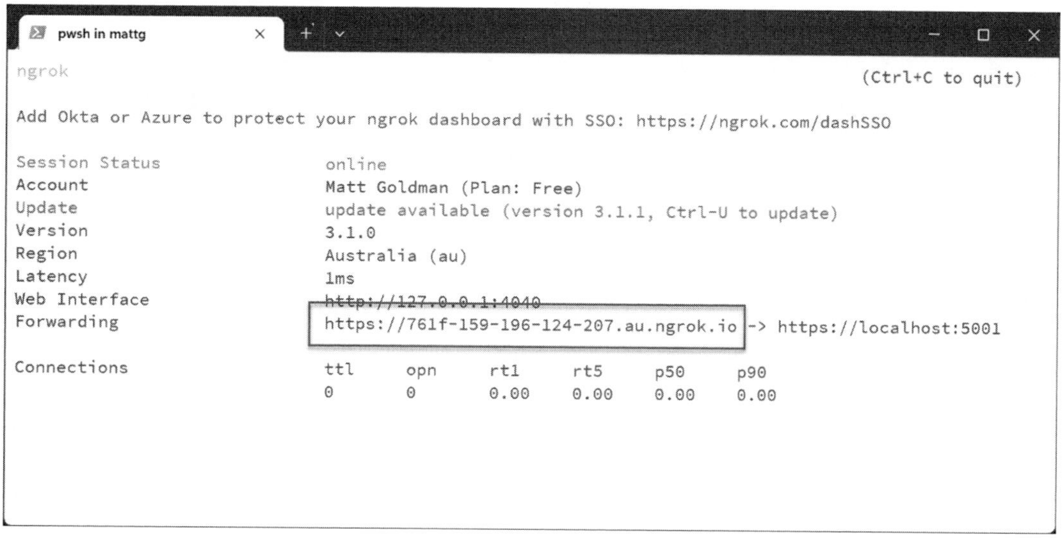

Figure A.5 When ngrok is running, it will show you the URL it has generated that tunnels back to your local machine.

With ngrok running, you can paste the URL it has generated into a web browser. Append /api on the end, and you should see exactly the same Swagger page you saw in figure A.3.

Now that ngrok is running, you can use the URL it has generated in your .NET MAUI app. You don't have to worry about SSL certificates, and the URL will work no matter what platform you're running on, whether on a physical device, an emulator, or a simulator.

appendix B
Upgrading
a Xamarin.Forms app
to .NET MAUI

Support for Xamarin.Forms ends on May 1, 2024, meaning after this date, there will be no fixes or updates shipped (and, of course, no new features either). If you maintain a Xamarin.Forms app, you'll need to upgrade to .NET MAUI before then to stay in support.

Depending on the nature and complexity of your app, you may be able to reuse nearly all of your code. In other cases, you may need an almost complete rewrite of the UI (or 100%, if you're switching to MAUI Blazor). .NET MAUI is an evolution of Xamarin.Forms and shares a lot of similarities, but it's also been rewritten from the ground up, which means upgrading is not as simple as updating some package references.

In this appendix, we'll take a high-level look at the process of upgrading an app from Xamarin.Forms to .NET MAUI based on a real-world case study. At SSW, we built the SSW Rewards app in Xamarin.Forms in 2019. It has now been updated to .NET MAUI (release pending at the time of this writing), and in this appendix we'll examine the process involved in the upgrade.

SSW Rewards is open source, so you can see the pull request where the .NET MAUI version was merged here: http://mng.bz/x4Yg. Additionally, the team is putting together a video documenting our learnings from this process. At the time of this writing, this video is not currently available; however, it will be published on SSW's YouTube channel, which you can find here: https://www.youtube.com/@sswtv.

This appendix contains notes and observations of the process of upgrading the app from Xamarin.Forms to .NET MAUI. While there was undoubtedly considerable work involved, a lot of the refactoring reduced complexity and left us with a much simpler, cleaner, and easier-to-maintain app.

B.1   The .NET Upgrade Assistant

The .NET Upgrade Assistant is a tool designed to simplify the process of updating legacy .NET code projects to modern versions. The following links provide information about the upgrade assistant, how to install it, and some .NET MAUI-specific notes:

- https://github.com/dotnet/upgrade-assistant
- https://github.com/dotnet/upgrade-assistant/blob/main/docs/maui_support.md
- https://github.com/dotnet/maui/wiki/Migrating-from-Xamarin.Forms-(Preview)

While the .NET Upgrade Assistant will run on your code and make changes to it, we didn't find that the end result was a usable codebase that we could work on. The .NET Upgrade Assistant updated namespaces and references and did the bulk of the work, but we found the process of switching from a three-project solution in Xamarin.Forms (the shared library and the iOS and Android projects) was easier to achieve manually.

We created a fresh .NET MAUI project and used it as the basis of our updated version; however, the code that had been updated by the .NET Upgrade Assistant was invaluable, and we copied and pasted almost everything from the code that was updated by the upgrade assistant into our new .NET MAUI project.

B.2   Importing code

Following the namespace and reference updates automatically completed by the .NET Upgrade Assistant, we copied nearly all of the code from the shared project into the new .NET MAUI project. At this stage, we just brought the files across without making any changes to them. We did this in reverse-dependency order:

1 Models
2 Services
3 ViewModels
4 Views

The Views didn't need any changes at this stage; while we did need to make several tweaks, these were visual bug fixes rather than build errors and came later in the process (see section B.6). The .NET Upgrade Assistant updated the C# and XAML namespace references, replacing Xamarin.Forms namespaces with .NET MAUI namespaces, which allowed us to import the code files without further effort.

B.3   *Updating to modern patterns*

.NET MAUI uses modern patterns not available in Xamarin.Forms—for example, the generic host builder pattern and built-in dependency injection. Because we didn't have these features in Xamarin.Forms, we had several workarounds in the legacy version of the app. For example, we used TinyIoC and a custom `Resolver` class. In the .NET MAUI app, we removed these and registered all dependencies with the built-in DI container. This required a fair bit of refactoring; many ViewModels and Views made calls to the `Resolver` class, and we updated these to constructor-inject dependencies instead.

.NET MAUI also simplifies management of resources and assets. Fonts and images are significantly easier to use in .NET MAUI. In the Xamarin.Forms app, we had multiple versions of many images (one for each resolution on each platform). With .NET MAUI, we were able to eliminate these (as this is managed automatically with Resizetizer) and use a single image asset instead. In the Xamarin.Forms app, fonts were registered as a static resource, whereas in .NET MAUI they are registered in `MauiProgram` and referred to by name. This necessitated some more refactoring as we had converters for displaying icon fonts, which would choose between Font Awesome for branded icons, such as the Angular icon, and Fluent Icons for nonbranded icons, like a search icon. Previously, these converters returned the font resource from the app's dictionary; in the updated .NET MAUI version, they simply returned a string with the name of the font.

In the Xamarin.Forms app, we had a base service that had a protected `HttpClient` that could be used by derived services. In the .NET MAUI app, we updated it to use the `IHttpClientFactory` pattern and registered the client in `MauiProgram`.

We also had to update the app icons and splash screen. Fortunately, this is much easier in .NET MAUI, and this was a quick update using existing assets.

B.4   *Updating dependencies*

Many of the packages we used in the Xamarin.Forms app don't work in .NET MAUI. For example, a core feature of the app is QR code scanning, and in the legacy app, we used `ZXing.Net.Mobile.Forms`. This package isn't available for .NET MAUI; however, a port of the underlying ZXing library is - `ZXing.Net.Maui`, created by Jonathan Dick on the .NET MAUI team; you can find out more about it here: https://github.com/Redth/ZXing.Net.Maui.

While we didn't use any UI component libraries, we did have three key UI dependencies. The first was SkiaSharp, which was used to create a custom circular progress bar control. Initially, we replaced this with a new control created using the `Microsoft.Maui.Graphics` library. However, there were some bugs, and while we were able to work around these, `Microsoft.Maui.Graphics` is still listed as "experimental." So, we decided not to introduce additional technical debt but instead revert to the SkiaSharp control with a note to replace it with `Microsoft.Maui.Graphics` once it's stable.

Microsoft.Maui.Graphics

`Microsoft.Maui.Graphics` is a new library for drawing and manipulating 2D graphics. It allows you to draw shapes and paths and render and manipulate graphics files and text. While it's included as part of .NET MAUI, it is independent and can be used in other .NET project types, too.

The original plan for this book included a chapter on creating controls with `Microsoft.Maui.Graphics`; however, as it is not yet stable at the time of this writing, the content included too many workarounds to be of sufficient value. If you are interested in seeing the code from that chapter, you can see the Maui Batmobile repo in GitHub here: https://github.com/matt-goldman/MauiBatmobile.

To find out more about the `Microsoft.Maui.Graphics` library and how you can use it in your .NET MAUI apps, check out the official website at https://maui.graphics.

The second UI dependency was on Lottie, a library for displaying Lottie animation files. Lottie files are JSON files describing vector frames of an animation and is an efficient way to include animations in mobile apps. Lottie is made by AriBnB, and the library used in the Xamarin.Forms app, `Com.Airbnb.Xamarin.Forms.Lottie`, has not been ported to .NET MAUI; however, Lottie animations are supported in the `SkiaSharp.Extended` package. We included this package in the .NET MAUI app and refactored our code for displaying Lottie animations to use this new library's syntax.

Using the built-in `DisplayAlert` API in .NET MAUI is good for simple messages or actions, but for windows or dialogs that retain in-app branding, you need something else. The third UI dependency was on a package called `Rg.Plugins.Popups`, which was used for displaying popup dialogs. When we first started working on the update, this package hadn't been ported to .NET MAUI, so we initially rewrote all our dialogs to use `Popup` from the .NET MAUI Community Toolkit. But before we finished, a new version of `Rg.Plugins.Popups` specifically built for .NET MAUI called `Mopups` was released, so we switched to this.

The last dependency update was to remove the `CrossMedia` plugin, which we used for custom avatars (users can take a photo or select one from their gallery). This plugin isn't compatible with .NET MAUI, and .NET MAUI has built-in support for the camera and gallery anyway.

B.5   *Platform specifics*

Updating the platform-specific elements of the app was the simplest part of the process. The platform specifics consisted of three things: app manifest (`AndroidManifext.xml` and `info.plist`), custom renderers, and a web callback activity for Android (to handle OAuth redirects back to the app).

Updating the manifests was simple; we just copied over what we had in the Xamarin projects. Updating the custom renderers to use the new handlers architecture was very straightforward too, and in fact, updating to .NET MAUI made this even easier.

In the Xamarin.Forms solution, we had a subclassed `Entry` control in the shared project and a custom renderer in each platform project. In the .NET MAUI app, we simply had the single subclassed control with the handler mappings in the same file.

The web callback activity was just copied from the Xamarin project to the `Platforms | Android` folder in the .NET MAUI project. The only change was to remove the reference to `Xamarin.Essentials` and convert to a file-scoped namespace.

B.6 *Fixing bugs*

At this stage, we had a technically working app. It would build and run, although it looked janky, and there were functional and visual bugs. Some of these had to do with slight differences between Xamarin.Forms and .NET MAUI. For example, thickness values are handled differently and had to be tweaked. In other cases, the logic of how .NET MAUI renders some things is different to how Xamarin.Forms worked.

One example is scrolling views nested inside a stack layout. In Xamarin.Forms, we had `CollectionView` inside `StackLayout`. In .NET MAUI, if you place a `CollectionView` (or any scrolling view) inside a `StackLayout`, `VerticalStackLayout`, or `Horizontal-StackLayout`, it doesn't scroll. This is a change in behavior from Xamarin.Forms; in .NET MAUI a stack layout can expand infinitely off-screen, so the child view doesn't detect that its height is constrained and therefore does not enable scrolling. We worked around this by updating all our scrolling views to be contained inside a `Grid` instead.

This is the final step of the update to .NET MAUI. We will continue to tweak the code and fix UI bugs as we discover them. But at this stage, even though there will always be more work to do, we consider the update complete.

index

RELATED MANNING TITLES

Building Web APIs with ASP.NET Core
by Valerio De Sanctis

ISBN 9781633439481
472 pages, $59.99
April 2023

Pro ASP.NET Core 7
by Adam Freeman

ISBN 9781633437821
1300 pages *(estimated)*, $69.99
Fall 2023 *(estimated)*

ASP.NET Core in Action, Third Edition
by Andrew Lock

ISBN 9781633438620
926 pages *(estimated)*, $69.99
Fall 2023 *(estimated)*

Practical Automation with PowerShell
by Matthew Dowst

ISBN 9781617299551
416 pages, $59.99
March 2023

For ordering information, go to www.manning.com

Hands-on projects for learning your way

liveProjects are an exciting way to develop your skills that's just like learning on-the-job.

In a Manning liveProject you tackle a real-world IT challenge and work out your own solutions. To make sure you succeed, you'll get 90 days full and unlimited access to a hand-picked list of Manning book and video resources.

Here's how liveProject works:

- **Achievable milestones.** Each project is broken down into steps and sections so you can keep track of your progress.

- **Collaboration and advice.** Work with other liveProject participants through chat, working groups, and peer project reviews.

- **Compare your results.** See how your work shapes up against an expert implementation by the liveProject's creator.

- **Everything you need to succeed.** Datasets and carefully selected learning resources come bundled with every liveProject.

- **Build your portfolio.** All liveProjects teach skills that are in-demand from industry. When you're finished, you'll have the satisfaction that comes with success and a real project to add to your portfolio.

Explore dozens of data, development, and cloud engineering liveProjects at www.manning.com!